Practical Oral Communications

Communication in Action: Getting a Job

Appendices

Communicating in Business

Communicating in Business

Norman B. Sigband,
University of Southern California

David N. Bateman,
Southern Illinois University

Scott, Foresman and Company
Glenview, Illinois
Dallas, Texas
Oakland, New Jersey
Palo Alto, California
Tucker, Georgia
London, England

To my wife, Joanie—N.B.S.

To my wife, Marianne—D.N.B.

Library of Congress Cataloging in Publication Data

Sigband, Norman B
    Communicating in business.

    Includes index.
    1. Communication in management.   I. Bateman,
David N.   joint author.   II.   Title.
HF5718.S53   1981   658.4'5   80-24509
ISBN 0-673-15175-1
    2   3   4   5 - VHJ - 85   84   83   82   81

Acknowledgments

"Proceed with Caution: Communication Barriers" by C. B. Stiegler. Appeared in *The Secretary,* February 1976. Reprinted by permission of the author.

"How to Improve Your Vocabulary" by Tony Randall. Adapted by permission of International Paper Company.

"10 Secrets of Better Sales Letters" by Sig Rosenblum. Reprinted by permission from *Sales & Marketing* magazine. Copyright 1977.

"Your Personal Listening Profile" by Dr. Lyman K. Steil, published in a Sperry booklet, n.d. Reprinted by permission of Sperry Corporation and the author.

Abridgement of "You and Your Telephone" reprinted by permission of New York Telephone.

"Selling Yourself in Interviews" as excerpted in MBA October/November 1978, from *Getting a Better Job* by David Gootnick. Copyright © 1978 David Gootnick. Reprinted by permission of McGraw-Hill Book Company.

"How to Be an Employee" by Peter F. Drucker from *Fortune,* May 1952. Reprinted by permission of the author and *Fortune Magazine.*

Preface

We live in a world of communications, which influence all our actions. How well we manage and how well we cope depend largely on how well we communicate. This book has been written to help students make the progress they desire and need in bettering their own ability to communicate. *Communicating in Business* differs from other business communication texts in that it not only covers the skills needed for everyday communication in a non-technical, non-theoretical way but also teaches written, oral, and listening skills within the context of acquiring and holding a job. The very latest practices in business communication are stressed and reinforced through extensive applications and illustrations.

Organization

Communicating in Business is structured to take the student logically and systematically through the communication process. Part I, "Principles of Effective Writing," presents business writing as a three-stage process of outlining, writing, and revising. Parts II and III, "Practical Business Letters" and "Practical Business Reports," cover the basics of letter and report writing, using extensive examples and illustrations and including whole chapters on such important topics as modern business communications systems and visual aids. Part IV, "Practical Oral Communications," covers a number of traditional and innovative oral communication topics, including speeches, interviews, listening techniques, and meetings. The final section of the skills of research, letter writing, and interviewing that the student has learned in earlier chapters can be applied to the task of finding a job. The text closes with two detailed appendices—one on grammar, and one on letter format/mechanics—and a sample long report.

Key Features

A number of special features make teaching and learning easier:

□ **Dilemma/Decision:** Each chapter begins with a "Dilemma," a practical business communication problem whose suggested solution is found in a "Decision" presented at the end of the chapter.

□ **Objectives Checklist:** The key concepts to be discussed are presented in checklist form at the beginning of each chapter, allowing students to check them off as they gain understanding.

□ **Marginal Notes:** Notes in blue summarize key points in the text. Notes in black refer students to information presented in appendices.

□ **Questions, Exercises, and Applications:** These items, presented at the end of nearly every chapter, reinforce the ideas of the chapter by allowing students to immediately apply their understanding.

□ **Readings:** Seven non-theoretical articles expand upon key topics presented in the text, including vocabulary building, use of the telephone, and employment interviews.

Supplementary Items

In addition to these key features presented within the body of the text, two supplementary items make *Communicating in Business* a truly revolutionary teaching package. For the instructor, *Teaching Business Communications Effectively* presents a variety of powerful teaching tools, including quizzes, examination questions, exercises, and a variety of other items. For the student, *Business Communication Applications and Exercises* provides immediate reinforcement and practical extensions of the materials presented in the text. Both supplements should prove invaluable to student and teacher in achieving the goal of effective communication.

Acknowledgments

As with any work of this type, the authors received a great deal of assistance not only from their own students but from other people as well. We would like to especially thank Lois J. Bachman of the Community College of Philadelphia, who reviewed the entire manuscript and also assisted in developing Appendix 1 and many of the end-of-chapter questions and exercises. Special thanks are also due James D. Bell of Central Michigan University and C. Douglas Spitler of the University of Nebraska-Lincoln, who reviewed the entire manuscript and made many excellent suggestions.

The encouragement of Dean Jack D. Steele of the University of Southern California and of Dean John R. Darling of Southern Illinois University has been invaluable.

The following instructors reviewed portions of the manuscript and contributed greatly to its final structure:

George Gebhardt, Essex Community College
Julie Hungar, Seattle Community College
Eva Kelly, Brevard Community College
Fern McCoard, El Camino College
Francis McCraig, Elgin Community College
Barbara Jewell, Fort Steilacoom Community College
Michael W. Bartos, William Rainey Harper College
Mary Williams, Clark County Community College
Natalie Seigle, Providence College

Finally we must thank the editorial staff of Scott Foresman: Jim Sitlington, who worked with us to develop the book concept and guided us for two years; Dane Tyson, who spent months revising, editing manuscript, and contributing ideas; Barbara Schneider, the designer; and Shirley Stone and Jeanne Schwaba.

And of course, the greatest acknowledgment must be made to our families for their patience, effort, and support—to our respective wives, Joan Sigband and Marianne Bateman, and the Sigband children, Robin and Glenn, Betsy and Roger, and Shelley.

Norman B. Sigband

David Bateman

MEMO

From: Norman B. Sigband
    David N. Bateman

To: Students

Communication is a powerful force; how we communicate affects every relationship. It may be the relationship you maintain with your employer, your parents, or your friends. Or it may be the communication between businesses and consumer, or between you and businesses as you seek a job. Or it may be the carefully designed discussions between nations. But in every case, the communication will influence the relationship.

At this phase of your life, you may be concerned with doing well in your classes, receiving a promotion on the job, improving the personal relationship you have with a member of the opposite sex, securing a new job . . . and all of these require effective communication.

Regardless of how skilled you may be as a secretary, an accountant, an engineer, a nurse, a mechanic, or a manager, your progress will be strongly influenced by your ability to communicate.

In the world of work, effective communication has become absolutely essential. Not only are there the familiar oral and written interactions—in meetings, telephone conversations, memos, letters, reports—but now we have a whole new world of communication through electronic and information-management systems.

Although this book has the major objective of making you a better communicator, it also has specific goals:

To help you understand the process of communication, the barriers that can be encountered, and the pathways available to assist you in achieving objectives

To improve your ability to think through problems, organize ideas, and plan a piece of communication

To write with force, clarity, and conciseness: memos, reports, proposals, resumés, letters, and briefs

To teach you to perform basic research, evaluate the information gathered, and present it in a well-substantiated and thoroughly justified report

To improve your ability to speak before groups in both short and long presentations

To help you conduct effective interviews and meetings

To encourage you to listen with sensitivity and discrimination

To help you plan and carry through a successful job search

The overall goal—to improve your ability to communicate—will help make your life more productive, enjoyable, and easier, on the job, at home, and at play.

Contents

Part I
Principles of Effective
Business Writing

Part II
Practical Business Letters

Part III
Practical Business Reports

Part IV
Practical Oral Communications

Part V
Communication in Action: Getting a Job

Appendices

Communicating in Business

Part I
Principles of
Effective Business Writing

Dilemma

This Dilemma poses a typical business problem. How would you solve it? Compare your analysis with the Decision on page 14.

Mark Bernardi had just sat down at his desk Monday morning when his boss, Evelyn Marshall, entered the office.

"Mark, have you finished that report I asked you for?"

"Report?"

"Yes, the short report on the Jefferson factory personnel problem. I assigned it to you last week."

"Oh, yeah, Ms. Marshall. I think I remember it."

"Think you remember it? I need it now!"

"Well, why didn't you tell me?"

"I told you I needed it *soon*."

"Well, how was I supposed to know that *soon* meant *now*?"

"Any moron could have understood what I meant."

"Well, when I was working under Mr. O'Shea, he always told me the exact date he wanted a report. *And* he never called me a moron."

With that remark, Ms. Marshall turned red and charged toward the door, pausing just long enough to say, "Well, you're not working for Jack O'Shea any longer, and don't you forget it."

No, Mark didn't quit his job after this little encounter, nor did he try to transfer back to Mr. O'Shea's department. What he *did* was try to analyze the situation. He took out a sheet of paper and listed on it what he felt were the major barriers to communication between himself and Ms. Marshall. He then listed the various steps each could take to help overcome their communication problems.

Communication and You

1

Here is a list of the objectives you should understand by the time you complete this chapter. Place a check mark in the box beside each as soon as you feel ready to apply your understanding in a practical situation.

☐ The meaning of the term *communication*

☐ The importance of communication in modern society

☐ The objectives of communication:
    To obtain understanding as the sender intends
    To elicit a favorable response
    To build good relations

☐ The basic reasons why communication sometimes breaks down:
    Distractions
    Lack of knowledge
    Emotions, biases, and attitudes
    Inadequate listening
    Difference in perceptions
    Language
    Competition for attention

☐ The importance of *feedback* in the communication process

We live in a world of communication: a world in which people react violently or peacefully to a statement, an action, or a concept. Pick up the newspaper, snap on the radio, or flip on the TV for proof. A world leader directs a statement of hostility to another (communication), and tanks begin to roll! A president or prime minister steps down (communication), and peace settles over a torn and battered nation. A representative speaks in the United Nations (communication), and fifteen minutes later, rioting and bloodshed take place six thousand miles away. Nations, companies, families, and individuals in today's world constantly act and react as a result of communication.

Communication has become so dominant in our lives that many of us vote for the best communicator rather than the best statesman. We buy the most heavily advertised breakfast cereal rather than the most nutritious. We vacation at the most attractively pictured resort rather than at the most comfortable recreation area.

Is this all bad?

Certainly not! It is simply the world we live in: a world of communication with almost instantaneous transmission and reception involving computers, satellites, high-speed presses, television, data phones, and other sophisticated devices. Such electronic message systems permit the paramedic to speak to the heart specialist thirty seconds after the former has knelt at the side of the coronary victim. And five seconds later the patient's heartbeat rhythm can be viewed on the monitor by the specialist. Millions of items of information can be stored and retrieved in seconds. Thousands of long-distance phone messages can be transmitted instantly with the help of satellites. Untold numbers of financial transactions can take place in minutes.

The point is simply this: communications intrinsically are neither good nor bad. However, the way communications are *used* can make the situations in which we live, work, and play either good, bad, or indifferent. One fact is certain: the way you communicate with others, and they with you, can make an important contribution to your life-style—making your activities, your relationships, your job, your life easy and enjoyable or difficult and upsetting.

And that is what this book is all about: *communication and you.* It affects you, your relationships, and your job. It also touches everyone else individually, too—your family, your friends, your fellow workers, and your classmates. Communication has a tremendous impact on all aspects of our lives.

A Personal Observation

Let's follow George Grange around town. We can look, listen, and note specifically how his friends use communication in their job activities and in their lives in general.

For example, there is Marty McFadden who is in sales. George had lunch with him last week and then, on Marty's invitation, attended the company's sales meeting. Marty is now a district sales manager and supervises twelve sales people. It really surprised George to see Marty in action. Marty had pre-

Communication plays a vital role in personal, national, and international relations.

Is it *patient's* or *patients'*? Why? (See Appendix 1.)

The way we use communications can make our daily activities easy and pleasant or difficult and unrewarding.

MOMMA by Mell Lazarus. Courtesy of Mell Lazarus and Field Newspaper Syndicate.

pared six carefully drawn and easily legible charts on which he based his talk, and before the meeting everyone present had received an agenda. Marty quickly covered sales, new products, a change in advertising allowances, and the increase in commissions. He then called on two of the sales people for reports, opened the session for discussion, and closed the meeting one minute ahead of the scheduled cut-off time of 3:00 P.M.

As the sales personnel filed out, George could hear and feel the optimism, the high level of excitement, the commitment, and the warm friendship which existed between Marty and his sales personnel. That Marty McFadden was some communicator!

At Bellville Memorial Hospital, George stopped in to see Maria Torres. She had attended junior college with George and had gone on to the university. She majored in biology and took nurse's training. As an R.N., she specialized in patient and family counselling at Bellville Memorial.

George could see Maria through the plate glass in her office door. She was in a small room with an elderly couple. George watched her speak and the couple nod. As Maria continued to talk, George saw the white-haired woman lean back and begin to relax. Maria picked up a book and explained a diagram to the couple. As they studied the diagram, Maria's arm circled the woman's shoulder. After a moment, the man looked up, said something, and smiled. Maria closed the book and they all stood and continued to talk. Maria took the elderly woman's hand and impulsively the woman embraced Maria. As the door opened, George could hear the elderly woman say, "Your optimism about our daughter's surgery tomorrow morning has meant so much to us."

When the couple walked by George, he heard the woman say to her hus-

A sales manager's career advances because he is a good communicator.

A nurse's career advances and her self-satisfaction increases because she is a good communicator.

Communication and You   **5**

band, "Oh, I feel so much better; it's as though a weight has been taken off my heart." Although George hadn't heard a word she said, he knew Maria was a great communicator.

However, George couldn't say the same thing for Bob Tomasino. Bob was an excellent mechanic but as a communicator . . . wow! George had been at the Chevrolet agency just yesterday; he had brought his car in for a badly needed tune-up. While there, he looked around the service area for Bob, an old high-school buddy. As he walked toward Bob, he heard the service manager say, "Bob, this is Dr. Kellstrom. We wondered if you could tell him about his car's transmission which you worked on."

Bob Tomasino replied, "Why? Don't you trust me, Doc?"

"It's not that at all, Mr. Tomasino," the doctor stated. "However, the car is relatively new, the job was expensive, and I wonder how well the transmission will function in the future."

A mechanic's career suffers because he is a poor communicator.

"Sorry, Doc," replied Bob, "but I can't give you a prognosis. All I can tell you is that your transmission is in good health now. A lot of you people are such hard drivers, it's a wonder the transmission lasts as long as it does!" The doctor's face flushed, but before he could reply, the service manager guided him toward the customers' lounge.

It's and *its;* do you know when to use one or the other? (See Appendix 1.)

Well, thought George to himself, perhaps it's Bob Tomasino's method and manner of communication that has kept him at the same job level today as when he started four years ago. Perhaps today wasn't the best day to talk with Bob; besides, it was getting pretty late. George Grange left the Chevy agency.

Then George remembered that he had to stop at the supermarket and do the shopping. This would give George an opportunity to see Michael Gross, another old buddy and the manager of the Super Value store on Jackson Street.

As George walked into the supermarket, he almost bumped into Betty Fallson. Betty had been elected class treasurer all four years in high school and had finished an accounting preparation program at Condor Junior College.

"How goes it, George?" was Betty's greeting.

"Great," said George Grange. "And what about you?"

"Well," responded Betty, "I have had better days. Today was a real loser."

"What happened?" queried George.

"Well, you remember that when we were in school, I wasn't the world's greatest speaker or conversationalist. Today, I really regretted that speaking was my weak area. You see, I had an important job interview with Carlson and Carlson, the CPA firm. I'd gotten as far as the senior partner today. I guess they were impressed with my straight-A accounting average in school, the academic awards I've received, and the scholarship which I was able to maintain. But in today's interview I really froze. My answers to questions were all *one-worders.* And when I was asked open-ended questions on accounting techniques and new developments, I found myself tongue-tied. And I knew I had to be articulate. I was told the position required meeting with clients to discuss the results of audits as well as to present ideas on new accounting

An accountant's career suffers because she is a poor communicator.

and management services the company could supply. Well, the long and short of it was simply that they told me my application would be kept in the open file."

George really couldn't think of much to say to reassure Betty Fallson except, "Don't let it get you down, Betty. You'll hit the jackpot one day 'cause you're a great accountant. But maybe you should take some kind of course in speaking, or interviewing, or something."

At that moment the store manager, Michael Gross, walked up and enthusiastically pumped George's hand. Michael had been in charge of this store for only five months and its sales were up 25 percent. As George walked to the manager's office, he noted that Michael called every clerk, department manager, and checker-cashier by name. They all responded with a smile. At one point, Michael stopped to introduce George to the winner of the Employee of the Month Award. Michael was careful to list all the young lady's accomplishments for George while she beamed with pleasure. Yes, Michael Gross was a great communicator. It was easy for George Grange to feel the high level of store employee morale and to understand why Michael's store was the chain's leader in percentage sales growth.

A retail store manager's career advances because he is a good communicator.

As George drove home after shopping, he thought about his friends. For the first time he looked at each one's communication patterns. It was interesting to note that sales manager Marty McFadden and nurse Maria Torres were not only very competent in their jobs but loved what they were doing. And both, George noted, were excellent communicators. Auto mechanic Bob Tomasino and accountant Betty Fallson were certainly knowledgeable in their respective fields, but both communicated poorly. Interestingly enough, they were not attaining their potential nor achieving personal job satisfaction. And both certainly rated a zero as communicators. On the other hand, Michael Gross, store manager for Super Value Store, was moving up the management ladder and he was a most effective communicator.

The meanings of *respectful* and *respective* differ in what way? (See Appendix 1.)

Was there some connection, George wondered, between job success and competence in communication? As George looked just at the people around him, he had to conclude yes. And he was correct. Research has shown that major corporations list *ability to communicate* as a vital factor in a person's promotability. That attribute is noted as being more important than such qualities as education, hard work, and appearance.

As George thought about the afternoon, he also recognized that communication was more than words. For example, he had only seen Maria's nonverbal communication; he hadn't heard a word she said! But he also remembered how Bob Tomasino's attitude as well as words had caused problems with the physician.

The more George thought, the more he recognized that communication was more than talking. In fact, if he were to define communication, he would have to conclude that it is:

The sending and receiving of information, attitudes, and emotions— verbal and nonverbal—that always produces a response.

A Rocket Scientist   A Hippie   A Frog

Words create symbols
(pictures) in people's minds.

But, George thought, we all communicate to achieve a purpose. If we achieve our goals, we probably can say we communicated successfully. But what are those objectives or goals?

First, people should understand our words as we intend to have the words understood. When we say *early* or *inexpensive,* the receiver should interpret those words as we do. If we say "pad," will the reader always have the same picture in mind that we do?

It's always nice to have people respond when we communicate with them. Of course the best response is a favorable one ("Okay, Betty Fallson; you've got the job!"). However, even an unfavorable response has value, for it tells us where we stand. And of course, no response is a type of response that tells us a great deal. Finally, because we live, work, and play with others, it's nice to maintain, retain, or build good relations.

As George approached his house, he took inventory of the objectives of communication as he saw them:

*Communication
objectives are:*
1. understanding;
2. response; and
3. good relationships.

1. To make sure the receiver understands the communication as the sender intended;
2. To obtain a response — hopefully favorable; and
3. To build good interpersonal relations.

In reviewing the day and his friends' communications, George was aware that some had achieved none of these three objectives, others had gained some of the three, and others had managed all of the three.

As he walked up the path to his home, George remembered the communication model which he had studied in school had looked like this:

Only a few friends were able to achieve that pattern. For others, the communication process looked more like this:

There were many explosions, breakdowns, barriers, and obstacles as the message went from Mr. A to Ms. B and back from Ms. B to Mr. A.

Let's analyze the situation and see if we can determine what some of those barriers are so that we can improve the *channels* of our own communication.

Communication barriers block the achievement of the three communication objectives.

Why Communication Breaks Down

Obviously it is difficult to enjoy consistently the pattern of communication that is reflected in the first of the two drawings. On the other hand, if we are aware of some of the barriers, obstacles, and roadblocks which we all encounter from time to time, we can make an effort to avoid them.

Distractions

Distractions caused by noise, appearance, smell, and other things can create communication barriers.

Ever present in our busy society are constant distractions. Certainly clattering typewriters, nearby conversations, blaring TV sets, and even the presence of other individuals can cause problems when we are attempting to carry on an important discussion with another person. The solution is usually simple: eliminate the distraction by closing the door, moving to a quieter office, turning off the TV set, providing adequate time for the interview or meeting, or taking other steps necessary to eliminate the distraction.

Distractions occur just as frequently in written communication as in oral. The page that is typed from top to bottom and from side to side with almost no margins and only two heavy block paragraphs on the page certainly creates a negative reaction in the reader. And that is a distraction. The page that has misspellings, strikeovers, or a chart that is too complex will prove distracting. And again the message is lost.

Distractions are created by the speaker whose voice is squeaky, who jingles coins, and who is unaware that his socks don't match. Here again appearance creates a distraction from the message. But all these can be corrected with a little effort.

Lack of Knowledge

Lack of knowledge on either or both the sender's or receiver's part can create a communication barrier.

Lack of knowledge of the subject matter on either the sender's or receiver's part can create barriers. This is often difficult to determine because many individuals will react positively when asked, "Do you understand how this works?" even when they *don't* understand. Their response involves emotions, face saving, and a dozen other reasons. The fact remains that the feedback is not accurate and communication breaks down. Constant monitoring of feedback, for example, by watching facial expressions or body language, helps eliminate this barrier. In addition, be careful not to talk or write over or under the heads of others.

Emotions, Biases, and Attitudes

Emotions, biases, and attitudes can create communication barriers

Barriers can be created by emotions, biases, and attitudes. They may arise suddenly (when a specific word is heard) or they may be long-term. Learn to recognize your own as well as the other person's distracting emotions and attitudes and take steps to eliminate or at least understand them. Of course, emotions, attitudes, and biases that are developed and reinforced over a period of years can't be eliminated easily. But if they are understood by one or both parties, communication may improve.

Inadequate Listening

A major cause of communication breakdown in our society is inadequate listening. The good listener hears not only the facts presented but also the feelings behind the stated facts. It is often much more important to respond to the unstated feelings ("I'm disappointed," "I'd like a compliment," "you're unreasonable," "do you love me?") than it is to respond to the spoken words. Effective listening to others is not easy. Our deep involvement with *our* problems, *our* goals, *our* feelings makes it difficult for us to hear what is really communicated. If we will listen carefully with understanding and concern for the speaker, however, the message may very well come through loud and clear.

Poor listening on either or both the sender's or receiver's part can create a communication barrier.

Differences in Perception

A major cause of communication breakdown is a difference in perception — due to position (boss/worker, parent/child); cultural values (Hispanic/Irish, white/black, European/Oriental, poor/rich); appreciation of time or space (American/Latin, Tahitian/Japanese). When two individuals perceive a situation differently, communication barriers may arise. The boss who sees the job as vital and the worker who perceives it as boring will find communication difficult. The seventeen-year-old son who sees a car as an absolute necessity and the father who sees such a purchase as a ridiculous expenditure will encounter problems in a discussion. The husband who perceives an after-work-stop for a drink as "necessary relaxation with the boys" and whose wife sees it as a drinking binge will have problems communicating.

In each instance, it is not vital that one agree with another to achieve good communication. However, if each will understand why the other party sees what he or she sees, will accept the other person's right to see things differently, and will verbalize that understanding, communication may improve.

Differences in perception on either or both the speaker's or listener's part can create communication barriers.

Language

Language itself can be a critical barrier. In fact, we have an entire field, semantics, devoted to understanding language in the communication process. Words make pictures in people's minds. How does a wealthy businessman interpret *inexpensive* as compared to an impoverished welfare recipient? What does an accountant visualize when he hears *pen* as compared to a hardened criminal? What does *pig* mean to a farmer, a city dweller, a street-

Language use, interpretation, or understanding can create communication barriers.

wise delinquent, or an iron worker? And how often do we choose certain words to paint the picture *we* want: *firm* instead of *stubborn; excitable* instead of *disturbed; relocation center* instead of *concentration camp; cute* instead of *beautiful;* and *thoughtful* instead of *inarticulate?*

If we remember that words have different meanings for different people and that denotations are different from connotations, we will find communication easier and more effective.

Competition for Attention

Competition for attention can create a communication barrier.

A significant barrier to effective communication often is created by competition for attention. We live in a society of information overload, and it is certainly difficult at times to *hear* the message that is important for us. Magazines, reports, books, newspapers, letters, and dozens of media for the printed word are directed at us. Speeches, discussions, radio stations, telephone calls, and TV programs surround us with sound. We often are buried in communication.

In order to protect ourselves, we often hear and do not listen, see and do not connect. Nevertheless, the communicator must find a solution. And it is really quite simple. Most of us really don't care if the other reports are not read as long as *ours is;* we aren't terribly concerned when the other speeches are not heard, so long as *ours is;* and we are not upset if the personnel director doesn't listen too carefully to our rival for the job opening, so long as she *hears me.*

The solution? It's to make our report better; our speech more interesting; our interview comments more attractive, so we can beat the competition. In other words, we have to manufacture a better product. And is that production of a superior report, an arresting speech, a successful interview easy? Certainly not! For most of us, hard work is required to create an excellent, concise, clear report; a persuasive, interesting speech; a well-balanced, complete interview. But difficult as it is, creating that superior communication is well worth the effort.

Feedback

Feedback is vital to effective communication.

One factor that acts as a constant barometer of communication effectiveness is feedback. The alert communicator will constantly tune in on feedback to determine how effectively the message has been or is being received and interpreted.

Feedback is not always easy to use as a guide. Often people will pretend that they do understand when they really do not. Of course, pride or emotions may be involved. At times the nonverbal glance at the watch tells us more accurately than his words ("Oh, take all the time you need") about his time commitment. And feedback may come too late to assist us. ("I had no idea you felt that way." "Well, I do, and I guess it's gone on for so long, there is nothing we can do about it now!")

There can be no doubt that our constant awareness and monitoring of verbal and nonverbal feedback in the communication process is vital. In summary we may say:

1. Feedback is necessary to give us some indication of the effectiveness of the communication taking place.
2. It is both verbal and nonverbal.
3. It often is not accurate ("Of course I understand").
4. It may be secured too late to correct or improve an earlier communication.

Bringing It All Together

If we ask George Grange to examine the partial list of barriers above and then think of his friends—Marty McFadden, Maria Torres, Bob Tomasino, Betty Fallson, and Michael Gross—he could probably carry through some perceptive matching of characteristics. Some of the barriers listed above obviously contributed to the communication breakdowns he witnessed. On the other hand, monitoring of feedback was instrumental in obtaining the understanding and effective relationships he did see.

As George thought about the communication process, he learned a good deal about his friends. But he probably learned more about himself.

MEMO

To: Students
From: The Authors
Subject: Communication and You

To succeed in your chosen career, you *have* to be a good communicator. Take a moment to look at your own communication. Are there barriers you should avoid? Are there new means you should select? Think about it, and about your communications with those individuals with whom you work, live, and play. You may find life easier.

Decision

1. BARRIERS ON MY PART
   a. *I don't listen attentively:* For example, I hardly remembered that report, though Ms. Marshall spent nearly a half hour last week explaining what she wanted.
   b. *I sometimes argue needlessly:* Instead of just getting to work when Ms. Marshall said she needed the report, I insisted on arguing over her instructions.
   c. *I sometimes let words slip out without thinking about them first:* My mention of Mr. O'Shea sounded more like a criticism than a suggestion.

2. BARRIERS ON MS. MARSHALL'S PART
   a. *She is not always careful to say exactly what she means:* The word *soon* meant one thing to her and another to me.
   b. *She sometimes chooses words carelessly, without thinking about their effects:* Using the word *moron* made us both angrier than was necessary.
   c. *She sometimes lets biases get in the way of her listening:* Because she has suffered discrimination in the past, she *interpreted* my mention of Jack O'Shea as a sexist slur of her capabilities.

3. POSSIBLE SOLUTIONS
   a. We both must learn to listen better, for facts as well as feelings.
   b. We both must learn to choose our words better so that our meanings are clear and we don't offend each other.
   c. We should both try to be more understanding of each other's point of view.

CHAPTER REVIEW

Questions

1. Choose one of George Grange's five friends whose communication skills are described in this chapter. Based on the information supplied in the text, indicate the following information about this friend:
   a. name and position;
   b. communication skills needed for his or her job;
   c. the friend's communication strengths on the job;
   d. the friend's communication weaknesses on the job;
   e. your overall evaluation of this person as a communicator.

2. It is said sometimes that we hear but do not listen; read but do not connect. Can such responses ever be worthwhile? Explain.

3. Why is feedback important as a communication device? Is it possible to have too much feedback? Explain.

4. Is it possible to receive verbal and nonverbal feedback simultaneously? If the messages conveyed disagree with each other, which one will the receiver rely on usually?

Exercises

1. Choose two excerpts from a speech or comments from a recent news magazine or newspaper. Explain how those statements made a favorable or unfavorable impact on national or international affairs.

2. Select an individual you know whom you would classify as a poor communicator. Analyze his or her communication patterns and list the barriers which you feel that person creates.

3. Find a newspaper article which discusses a problem that involves language as a contributory or primary factor. Present that article with some brief comments.

4. Select a national or international figure (Margaret Thatcher, Anwar Sadat, Jimmy Carter, etc.) and explain why you feel that person is a good or poor communicator. Be as specific as possible.

5. Select a friend, a family member, or a co-worker and explain why you feel he or she is a good or poor communicator. Be as specific as possible.

6. Pick three sets of closely related words and indicate how each creates different symbols (pictures) in the receiver's mind. Here is one set as an example:
   Firm: Fair and neutral. Someone who takes a position after careful thought.
   Single-minded: Biased. An individual who considers only his own point of view.
   Stubborn: An individual who develops a biased point of view and will not change regardless of logic or facts.

7. "Competence in communication is necessary for job success." Choose one of the following professions and discuss the oral and written communication necessary for success in that field:
   a. accounting;
   b. marketing;
   c. banking;
   d. insurance.

8. Select one college class that you attend which usually interests you and one class that you attend which rarely interests you. In these two classes, compare the existence of the following communication barriers:
   a. distractions;
   b. instructor's tone of voice and nonverbal mannerisms;
   c. your bias and attitude toward the course content;
   d. your inadequate listening habits.

Dilemma

*This Dilemma poses a typical business problem. How would you solve it?
Compare your analysis with the Decision on page 30.*

Shelley Wilkerson has worked as the administrative assistant for five years for Honey Bee Jams and Jellies. It is a relatively small firm and is located in Southern California.

In the past five years more and more distributors in the Midwest have requested Honey Bee products. As a result, the president of the firm, Roger Seamans, has thought about establishing a small plant in Wisconsin or Michigan.

Such a plant could easily supply the big markets of the Chicago-St. Louis area, cut enormous freight costs, be close to a source of fruit supply, and increase company profits enormously.

Of course there are problems: cost of construction or plant purchase, source and availability of labor, transportation, markets, local tax and health laws, and on and on.

What Mr. Seamans needs is a report that pulls together all the loose ends, comes to some conclusions, and offers some recommendations.

He asks Shelley to prepare such a report. It will be presented to the five directors (owners) of Honey Bee. The meeting is scheduled to take place in fourteen days.

Shelley decides to organize the report by following these preliminary steps:
1. Define the problem, purpose, and audience;
2. Select a logical order of development; and
3. Draw up a complete outline for the report.

Planning Your Communication

Here is a list of the objectives you should understand by the time you complete this chapter. Place a check mark in the box beside each as soon as you feel ready to apply your understanding in a practical situation.

☐ The importance of planning before communicating

☐ The five basic steps in planning any written communication:
    Defining the problem, purpose, and audience
    Deciding what to say
    Finding a logical order of development
    Making an outline
    Reviewing and revising your outline

☐ The major types of logical development:
    Deductive
    Inductive
    Chronological
    Geographical
    Spatial
    Functional
    Analytical
    Synthetic
    Simple to complex

☐ The advantages of outlining your communications

Almost any activity that has an objective—a 650-mile auto trip or the construction of a building—starts with a plan. When that plan is carefully arranged and the activity to reach the goal follows that plan, effective results are achieved. If we wish to reach San Francisco, 650 miles away, by tomorrow at 3:00 P.M., our plan should include the selection of the shortest route with the fastest highways. If the objective is to reach San Francisco two days later and explore the beautiful coastline along the way, our plan would include an entirely different route. The point is that a plan is necessary for both.

Similarly, if we are to construct a building, organize an office, set up a production line, arrange a meeting for all supervisors for next Wednesday morning, wire a piece of electronic equipment, or perform surgery, *a plan is vital.* That plan will permit us to move forward in a logical, precise method to achieve the designated objective. If it is a building, the blueprints (plans) tell us exactly what materials, in what sizes, are needed to be placed in which positions. Construction is not carried on in a haphazard fashion. Even in surgery, the patient's lab reports, blood tests, X rays, and medical history permit the doctor to design a plan. On the basis of it, the doctor knows what type of anesthetic to use and what type of surgery to perform.

All this is also true of communication. If we are to achieve our objective quickly, logically, and most efficiently, we need a plan. The organization for a simple five-minute oral presentation or a fifty-five-minute interview, for a sixteen-line memo or a sixteen-page report needs a plan. Without it, most of us omit key ideas, become repetitious, or communicate in circles. The logical plan permits us to go forward from one point to another until we reach our objective as we follow the quickest and most direct route.

Organizing the Plan

Arranging a logical, workable plan isn't hard if you follow five simple steps:

1. Define your problem, your purpose, and your audience;
2. Decide what you want to say;
3. Find a logical order of development;
4. Make an outline; and
5. Review and revise your outline.

The remainder of this chapter will look closely at each of these five steps.

Define Your Problem, Purpose, and Audience

Very often in writing a report, we will be asked to look at a problem. For example, why has production decreased? Is there a market in this area for our product? Why has employee theft increased? Should we enter the toy manufacturing business? Why is employee morale so low? What will the population trend be in this area in the period 1985–1995?

It is absolutely vital that the writer clearly recognize the problem and not confuse it with a symptom of the problem or a secondary issue. For example, the increase in employee theft may possibly be a symptom of the real problem—poor morale. Another example might be the decline in sales of a retail shop. Superficial examination may lead one to believe the problem arose because of lower prices offered by a competitor. A more thorough evaluation indicates the basic problem to be poor service offered by the store's clerks. Note, however, that in both of these cases, solutions can be implemented for the superficial problem, but the fundamental problem will still go unresolved. Frequently, working on one problem will cause the more basic one to surface. Let us look at an example or two to see how this would work in practice.

Determine the specific problem with which the communication will be concerned.

Situation one   Mr. Phillip Goulde, purchasing director of the Sherman Corporation, writes to ask if your company sells inexpensive cartons which can be used to store papers and documents. The *problem* is simple: a customer needs an inexpensive storage filing carton. We have such an item: the Protecto File Carton. Now let's move to our *purpose:* to persuade the Sherman Corporation to buy. Finally, our *identification of the reader* is simple: the letter is signed by Mr. Goulde, purchasing director. This means that our letter in response will have to contain specific prices, delivery information, descriptive data on the product, and other related facts.

Determine the purpose of the communication. Is it to sell? To inform?

Situation two   Now let us examine a situation a little more complex. The president of the Lyons Company asks our opinion, as head of planning and development, about the advisability of Lyons' moving into the packaging of our food products in institutional sizes (extra large) for sale to restaurants and hotels. We now serve the consumer market only, and package products in small-size containers.

"Let me have your report on this for the board of directors' meeting in three weeks," the president says. And he turns and walks away.

The *problem* in Situation Two is fairly straightforward: Can Lyons manufacture its food products in institutional-size containers and sell them at a profit? To arrive at the answer will require surveys, cost analysis, questionnaires, interviews, market analysis, production reviews, etc. Once that is completed, the report for the board of directors must be prepared for the *purpose* of informing the readers so they can make an intelligent decision. And because we know that the members of the board come from a variety of business organizations and represent a bank, an insurance company, a canner, a transportation firm, and other organizations, we have identified the readers as business people. However, we also recognize that these individuals will probably possess relatively little knowledge of the complex sales and manufacturing problems of the Lyons Company. We therefore have an indication of what approach to take.

Why is a colon used here and not a semicolon? (See Appendix 1.)

Determine who the reader is and what his or her bias is.

These steps, then, are the initial ones in preparing the communication: What is the *fundamental problem,* if any, we wish to work on? What is the communication's *purpose:* to inform, to analyze, to persuade, or to compare? And *who are the readers?* Are they company officers? Consumers? Stockholders? Prospective customers?

Decide What You Want to Say

Believe it or not, deciding what you want to say can often be the easiest part of writing an effective business communication. Many people believe this decision is harder than it really is because they confuse *what* they want to say with *how* they want to say it. Deciding *how* to say something—ordering your material properly and actually writing paragraphs and sentences effectively—*can* be a difficult task. But simply gathering together the points you want to make is not nearly so difficult.

In most situations, your analysis of the communication's *problem* and *purpose* will define what you want to say. For example, Mr. Goulde's letter tells us the points we'll want to make in reply. We can list these in whatever order they happen to come to mind.

Don't worry about the order now, just try to jot down everything you'll want to say.

1. We received Mr. Goulde's letter of November 5.
2. We do make a file cabinet like the one he requests: the Protecto.
3. The Protecto carries the Office Management Association Seal of Approval as a result of Baxter Labs' tests.
4. The Protecto is made of reinforced, fire-resistant fiberboard.
5. Many major organizations use the Protecto: General Motors, AT & T, the Department of Defense, Douglas Aircraft, etc.
6. The Protecto is available in 2- and 4-drawer models, and in brown, gray, or green.
7. Free drawer slides and file separators are included with the Protecto.
8. The Protecto is sold in quantities of 12 units, at prices of $18 per unit for the 2-drawer model and $28 per unit for the 4-drawer model.
9. Volume discounts are available.
10. One free cabinet will be given with each dozen ordered before December 1.

In other cases, the research we do into the problem will tell us *what* we want to say. What we want to say in our report on the Lyons food containers, for example, will come directly from the results of our various surveys and analyses. Again, we don't want to worry at this stage about the *order* in which we'll present these results. The important thing is to get the points we want to make down on paper in whatever order seems convenient.

Find a Logical Order of Development

Once we've got the points we want to make in our communication down on paper, our next step is to put them into an order that makes sense. Logic in the development of a message is absolutely vital if the reader is to be favorably impressed with the message. Most of us can overlook the fault of a misplaced comma or even an error in spelling, but if the entire message lacks logic in its development, we will usually put it aside, tune it out, or simply not buy the idea.

For example, the politician begins a speech by telling us of the community's great need for a bridge over the west fork of the Campbell River; then he reminds us of his outstanding voting record in the previous congress. He continues by noting the damage caused by the flood five years ago and then moves to how many bridges neighboring counties erected. He comes back to his unwavering stand on farm prices . . . and soon causes us to tune out because his argument was not logical. He went in circles, got off the track, and in general, did not build a convincing case for his idea.

Logic in communication demands that we follow a consistent pattern in developing ideas. The pattern we use can give unity and even beauty to the total communication. Here again we can turn to architecture for an example. If a brick wall for the face of a building follows a consistent pattern, it helps us appreciate the architectural theme. Let us say each tier of bricks is laid so that four are faced broadside and the fifth endwise; or three red bricks, one rust; or four tiers of four-inch bricks, two tiers of six-inch bricks. There is logic here and we can follow the order of architectural development.

Good logic makes communication easier.

However, if the face of the building reflects a hodgepodge of brick sizes, designs, and colors, it would only communicate to us the work of a confused individual. We would not accept it any more than we would accept a series of confused ideas.

Below are listed several different orders of development. In most cases a communication, whether it is written or oral, will follow a specific type. However, one can combine logically one or more types. Here again we can go back to the building. The tiers can alternate logically between six- and four-inch bricks and further on have four tiers of rust-color bricks and one tier of red. The total effect still will appear logical to the viewer. The same is true with the orders of development listed below. With care, two or more can be used to structure a logical presentation.

Remember that you can combine some of the basic orders of development for an effective communication.

Deductive development   You will recall our earlier example of the Lyons Company considering the packaging of its food products in large-size containers. The outline on page 26 shows we began with a general statement that there are several firms that manufacture our line of food products in large-size containers. We then attempted to discover what their specific products are and their level of sales. From this point we researched what potential we have in the field as well as the details of our labor supply, physical plant expansion, cost of marketing, and a dozen other details. Finally, we came to a conclusion and made a specific recommendation.

In this line of reasoning, we began with a general statement, gathered detail after detail, and finally deduced that packaging our food products in large-size containers was a good or a poor idea. This method of development, from general to specific, is referred to as *deductive.*

Inductive development   This order of development goes from the specific to the general. We may begin by stating that under the leadership of Tom Foster, his department enjoyed increased production; his subordinates' morale was high; loss and breakage in his department had dropped; expenses in his department had declined; and profits had increased. Thus, following inductive development from specific to general, we can conclude that Tom Foster is an outstanding department head.

Chronological development   In this order, we use time blocks as a logical pattern. We may begin with the founding of the firm in 1915 and move up to the present. Or we may begin with today and move backwards, or trace developments month by month. This order is used in writing about a situation and very frequently in visual aids. Most charts, tables, and graphs use a chronological pattern in presenting ideas.

Geographical development   This development follows a logical pattern from the point of view of space. We may comment first on our operations on the East Coast, move through the Midwest, and on to the West Coast.

Spatial development   Here the order follows a logical space designation. We may begin with the reception area, move to the office complex, go to the factory area, and on to shipping.

Functional development   Because functions in an organization frequently occupy their own space, this order may be similar to spatial. We could begin with the sales department, go to production, on to personnel, research and development, warehousing, accounting, shipping, and administration.

Development by analysis or synthesis   Before we write our communication, let's be sure we have recognized the elements involved. Employee morale is down: let's analyze. The work force has been cut, pay increases for this period have been dropped, Christmas bonuses have been eliminated, the employee recreation and education programs severely curtailed, etc. Thus, we began with a situation: low employee morale. We then analyzed to determine the contributing factors.

Or we may examine many diverse elements: can they be put together or synthesized to result in an overall theme? Our parking lot is crowded, the checkout lines are long, the clerks and cashiers are far from courteous, and our food displays are rather unattractive. Let's put all these together (synthesize) and determine if there is a common thread in an overall situation. What causes all this? With what results?

Simple to complex development   Readers whose knowledge in a specific area may be somewhat limited find this method of development very satisfactory. The writer will begin by explaining a relatively simple activity in, let us say, a manufacturing process and gradually take the reader from there to a complex procedure. Understanding is facilitated and the discussion appears logical.

Prepare an Outline

In order to prepare an outline, you must understand the problem, purpose, and audience of your communication, the basic points you want to make, and the logical order in which you'll make them. Then you are ready to prepare an outline which serves as your guide in writing your communication. It helps you to see the relationships between topics, and it reveals in advance whether your letter or report is logical.

Sometimes an outline can be quite simple. The outline you would use in responding to Mr. Goulde's request, for example, might look like this:

1. Acknowledge the Sherman letter;
2. Indicate that we can fill the request;
3. Sell the product (Protecto File Cabinet):
   a. Note quality;
   b. Describe its construction, appearance, and other attributes;
   c. Comment on product's usefulness;
   d. List prices for quantity sale;
4. Prove our points by citing names of satisfied users and the results of impartial tests;
5. Obtain action by asking for the order.

Your outline should cover all the points on your original list.

This outline could be written on a separate sheet of paper, at the bottom of Mr. Goulde's letter, or on the back of its envelope. But the plan should be somewhere so that it can be reviewed, revised, and corrected.

In the case of a longer communication, putting together an effective outline can be a bit more complicated. Although some authorities will spend many pages discussing the mechanics of making up such an outline, the only really important thing to remember is to organize items in such a way as to be able to recognize quickly the major and minor points. Figure 2–1 on page 24 shows a short outline for a report on the location of a new fast-food restaurant. Notice how the structure of the outline reveals the logical relationships between the topics discussed.

The logic of your communication is reflected in the outline.

Now let's review the Lyons Company case presented earlier in the chapter. The *problem* is whether to distribute our food products, now sold on the consumer market, to institutions in large-size cans, cartons, and jars. Obviously,

Figure 2–1
Outline for a Report

```
      I.    Population of Bellville Community (1st Main Heading)
            A.  By economic level (1st subtopic under Main Heading I)
                1.  Poor (1st subtopic under A)
                2.  Middle class (2nd subtopic under A)
                    a.  $6,000-$10,000 per year (1st subtopic under 2)
                    b.  $10,000-$25,000 per year (2nd subtopic under 2)
                3.  Wealthy (3rd subtopic under A)

            B.  By ethnic pattern (2nd subtopic under Main Heading I)
                1.  Black, 45% (1st subtopic under B)
                2.  Caucasian, 41% (2nd subtopic under B)
                3.  Other ethnic groups, 14% (3rd subtopic under B)
                    a.  Latino, 6% (1st subtopic under 3)
                    b.  Oriental, 5% (2nd subtopic under 3)
                    c.  Native American, 3% (3rd subtopic under 3)

      II.   Competitive History (2nd Main Heading)
            A.  Major competitors before 1970
                1.  Eat 'n' Pork
                2.  White Tower
                3.  Howard Johnson's
                4.  Other

            B.  Major competitors, 1970-present
                1.  MacDonald's
                2.  Kentucky Fried Chicken
                3.  Other

            C.  Future competition

      III.  Traffic Patterns (3rd Main Heading)
            A.  Auto
            B.  Pedestrian
```

such a move to penetrate a new market will be tremendously expensive. The *purpose* of the report is to provide decision-making information for the readers, the company's board of directors.

In a case like this, we might make *two* outlines. The first is a general outline which could be used, before we look into the problem, to provide us with some direction as we conduct our research. A second, more detailed outline would then be made, after the research is completed, to organize our findings before writing the report. Figure 2–2 on page 26 shows an example of the kind of outline we might put together before we begin to write in order to give us direction. Notice again how the organization of topics into main headings and subheadings makes the logic of the communication easy for the reader to see and understand.

For long reports, you may make an outline before *and* after your research.

Review Your Outline

In the Sherman Corporation situation previously discussed, we can see the immediate value of an outline. Let us assume we have made the following outline at the bottom of the inquiry letter from the Sherman Company:

1. Refer to Sherman letter of November 5;
2. Positive response: Protecto Files;
3. Describe product:
    a. 2-drawer and 4-drawer models available;
    b. Fiberboard construction;
    c. Fire resistant;
    d. Choice of three colors;
    e. Dimensions;
    f. Unit prices and quantity discount prices;
4. Note previous purchasers (GM, Western Electric, Shell Oil);
5. Call collect; we will ship within 24 hours;
6. Special offer: 1 free with each dozen files ordered—until Dec. 1 only.

A quick review of the outline reveals that a key selling point is omitted— tests on the Protecto by Baxter Labs—and that the special offer is not in the most logical order. A revision of the outline will look like this:

1. Refer to Sherman letter of November 5;
2. Positive response: Protecto Files;
3. Describe product:
    a. 2-drawer and 4-drawer models available;
    b. Fiberboard construction;
    c. Fire resistant;
    d. Choice of three colors;
    e. Dimensions;
    f. Unit price and quantity discount price;
4. Note previous purchasers (GM, Western Electric, Shell Oil);
5. Call collect: we will ship within 24 hours;
6. Special offer: 1 free with each dozen files ordered—until Dec. 1 only.

Also reports of tests on Protecto at Baxter Testing Labs.

Figure 2–2
Outline for Lyons
Company Report

```
I.    Companies Presently Marketing Products in Institutional-Sized
      Containers
      A.  The Supreme Company
          1.  Products
          2.  Estimated sales
          3.  Market penetration
      B.  Bailey and Saxon, Inc.
          1.  Products
          2.  Estimated sales
          3.  Market penetration

II.   Market Research for Lyons Penetration
      A.  Public agencies (hospitals, prisons, schools, offices)
          1.  Products
          2.  Potential sales
      B.  Private entrepreneurs (hotels, restaurants, bars)
          1.  Products
          2.  Potential sales
      C.  Private agencies (hospitals, nursing homes, convalescent
          homes, universities)
          1.  Products
          2.  Potential sales

III.  Physical Requirements for Product Production
      A.  Manufacturing area
      B.  Shipping feasibility
      C.  Storage and inventory areas

IV.   Financing and Cost for Product Production
      A.  New equipment required
      B.  Additional labor force
      C.  Cost of additional raw materials for product

V.    Conclusions

VI.   Recommendations
```

Quite obviously it took us just a minute to make the two changes in the outline noted above. However, if we had been required to retype the whole letter to make the changes, a needless expenditure of at least six dollars would have been made, and the message would have been delayed. Or, even worse, the letter might have gone out without noting the free offer, resulting in a lost sale or anger on the part of the customer that he had not been informed.[1] Figure 2–3 on page 28 shows the final letter written from the above outline.

Similarly, as we study our outline for the Lyons report, we may decide that it is more logical to treat "Financing and Cost for Product Sales and Distribution" (Main Heading V) before "Physical Requirements for Product Production" (Main Heading III). Likewise, since our readers, the board of directors, are very busy people, perhaps "Conclusions" (Main Heading VI) and "Recommendations" (Main Heading VII) should be put at the beginning of the report instead of at the end.

If these changes are logical and should be made, imagine how much easier they are to accomplish in an outline *before* the report is written rather than *after.* Attempting to move paragraphs and pages from one portion of a completely written report to another part can be terribly frustrating, difficult, time consuming, and expensive.

Review your outline carefully before you write. Make sure it's logical and that you haven't left out any important points.

Outlining saves time and money.

The Advantages of Planning and Outlining

Although the advantages of planning our communications are quite obvious, perhaps we should list a few specifically.

1. An outline that is logically developed will normally result in a logical communication.

2. Segments of an outline can be evaluated to determine if individual portions are being treated superficially or in too much depth. Here again, it is easier to make changes in the outline than in the finished report.

3. The order or method of development can be checked for consistency. If the writer wishes to develop the presentation on the basis of time, cause and effect, or space (geographical), such development may be evaluated in the outline.

4. An outline or plan is also valuable because the writer can check to determine if all the key and necessary points are included. Additions, deletions, or changes can be made much more easily to the outline than to the finished communication.

[1] In early 1980, the Dartnell Corporation estimated the cost of the average business letter to be well over $6.00.

Figure 2–3
Letter Written from an Outline

Farnsworth Corporation

Office and Stationery Supplies
2100 S. Hampton Drive
Chicago, Illinois   60024

November 10, 198-

Mr. Philip Goulde
Purchasing Agent
Sherman Metal Corp.
1425 S. Market Street
Oak Brook, Illinois 60025

Dear Mr. Goulde:

Thank you for your letter of November 5th concerning your interest in
the possible purchase of "storage type" filing cabinets.

We can fill your need with a quality product that has secured
excellent reception: The Protecto File Cabinet.

The Protecto is available in either a 2- or 4-drawer model and is
designed especially for storing materials that are vital but to which
daily access is not necessary.

The Protecto is constructed of fiberboard, with all stress points
reinforced with heavy-gauge metal. Nylon drawer slides and file
separators are provided. All materials have been treated for fire
resistance. Both models are available in a choice of three colors:
slate gray, rust brown, and hunter green. Please see the enclosed
pamphlet for specific dimensions and construction details.

The Protecto is sold in quantities of one dozen units at a cost of
$18.00 per 2-drawer and $28.00 per 4-drawer unit. When purchases of
more than 12 dozen are made, the cost drops to $16.00 and $24.00,
respectively. And for orders received prior to December 1st, we will
be happy to include one free file cabinet for each dozen ordered.

The Protecto has been purchased in quantity by many of America's
largest organizations: General Motors, AT&T, the Department of
Defense, Douglas Aircraft, among others. In addition, it has received
the Office Management Association Seal of Approval as a result of
extensive testing by Baxter Labs.

Please call me collect today at 346-8133, and your order for Protecto
File Cabinets will be on its way tomorrow.

Cordially yours,

Ken Tanaka

Ken Tanaka
Sales Manager

5. And of course the outline saves the communicator's time and money. How much easier it is to change an outline than to change the finished product.

It is also obvious that a relatively long outline for a report or a proposal will also serve as the document's table of contents. Of course some of the subpoints may be dropped, but the major headings and their immediate subtopics can be arranged in the table of contents. In addition, when underlined and printed in capital letters as topic headings in the report itself, these headings tell the reader the subjects of the paragraphs that follow and help to guide the reader through your presentation.

MEMO

To: Students
From: The Authors
Subject: Planning

To achieve any goal—reaching a distant city, writing an effective business letter or report, giving a speech, finding a good job—you have to begin with a workable plan. The purpose of the plan is to guide you; however, not to bind you unnecessarily. If circumstances change, you should always be ready to revise your plan. The ability to draw up a thorough yet flexible plan can be an important key to all your communications and to your future career success.

Decision

Here is the outline Shelley Wilkerson used to prepare her report.

The Problem: Should Honey Bee Jams and Jellies establish a manufacturing/distribution plant in the Midwest?

Purpose of Study: To determine if it is economically feasible to establish a plant in the Midwest.

Audience: Board of Directors (owners) of Honey Bee Jams and Jellies.

Order of Development: Functional

Outline of Report

    I. Financial aspects of plant construction
       A. Funds available in Honey Bee
       B. Financing balance
          1. Sources of funds
          2. Cost of borrowing
   II. Labor
       A. Availability
          1. Administrative personnel
          2. Manufacturing personnel
          3. Support personnel
       B. Cost of Labor
          1. Administrative
          2. Manufacturing
          3. Support
       C. Labor organizations in area
  III. Source of materials
       A. Product sources
       B. Supply sources
  IV. Market for products
       A. Midwest markets
       B. East Coast markets
   V. Transportation
       A. For products and supplies (incoming)
       B. For products (outgoing)
       C. Employee
  VI. Financial analysis
       A. Projected costs (five-year basis)
       B. Projected income (five-year base)
 VII. Conclusions
VIII. Recommendations to the Board of Directors

CHAPTER REVIEW

Questions

1. Why is it important to define the problem before communicating?

2. Why is it important to determine the purpose of the communication before communicating?

3. Why is it important to identify the reader or listener of the communication before communicating?

4. Why is it important to make a plan before proceeding with any activity?

5. How does an outline, made up prior to writing a report or a business letter or giving a speech, assist you in creating a better communication?

6. In reviewing the outline, before writing or speaking, what specific items should you check to be sure your communication will prove effective?

7. What is the difference between inductive and deductive reasoning? Choose one topic and explain how you can apply each method of reasoning to reach a conclusion about this topic.

Exercises

1. Refer to the letter in Figure 2–3 in this chapter. List all the strong points you can find in it that indicate that a logical outline was prepared before the letter was written.

2. Examine a corporate annual report. What is the purpose of attractive annual reports prepared by corporations?

3. Name the different groups of readers of corporations' annual reports. What information in the report is important to each group?

4. Compose an outline which could lead to an effective plan for you to obtain part-time employment relating to your college major. Be sure the outline follows the procedural steps you will take to secure the job.

5. Refer to your college's latest catalogue and study the curricula offerings. Prepare an outline you would follow if you were asked to discuss the various business programs available in your college.

6. Describe a task you completed in a part-time or full-time job that you have held. Start with the simplest factors and end with the most complex part of the task.

7. Give the task description listed in Exercise 6 orally. Then ask five members of your listening audience for feedback on the steps you described. If there is a discrepancy in what you said and what the audience understood, discuss some ways communication of this type could be improved.

8. One advantage of outlining is that the points in the outline later can serve as headings in a report. This suggests that we can uncover the outline used in preparing a report by looking at the headings used in the report. Try to uncover the outline used in preparing the financial report you examined in Exercise 2.

9. Just as letters and reports always should be logically outlined, so should chapters in a textbook. Looking at the various headings used in this chapter, see if you can reconstruct the outline used in preparing it. Is the order of development logical? Could you suggest any other ways the chapter might be logically organized? If so, prepare an alternative outline for the chapter.

Applications

1. John Washington received ten shares of Prince Electric Company stock for a high-school graduation gift. The quarterly dividends are being

reinvested and John usually receives statements of his up-to-date account four times a year—March, June, September, and December. When John checked his records, he realized that he had not received any mail from the company since June. The September and December mailings had never arrived. Write an outline for a letter John will send to the electric company searching for the missing dividend reinvestment information.

2. Assume you have just received the following business letter. You have the products in stock and you can manufacture the special display case requested. Furthermore, you have checked and found that Mr. Burke is quite correct: he does have a $39.50 credit due. Complete the outline which you will use to assist you in dictating your reply. All that is required is the outline. Mr. Burke may also be interested in one of the five new jewelry outdoor display signs which you now have available. You have a brochure describing them.

3. Outline the letter shown in Application 2. Using your outline as a guide, offer your criticism of how well planned Mr. Burke's letter was.

4. Sara Henderson, a busy administrative assistant, claims that outlining and planning business letters before dictating them wastes too much company time. Justify your agreement or disagreement with Sara's comment.

5. Make up an outline of the brief report below. After you have completed the outline, comment on whether or not the writer planned the report effectively.

March 4, 198-

Franklin Fixture Corp.
12000 South Ventura Ave.
Santa Barbara, CA 94545

Dear Sir:

Will you kindly ship us two of your new Model #120 Jewelry Display cases. We would like these in the blond finish described in your catalog for Spring 198-. We would also like to know if you can manufacture the same case but with a special modification?

We would like the case to be eight feet in length instead of six with the entire front made of glass instead of just the upper display area. Obviously we wish to use the upper and lower areas for display purposes (see rough sketch enclosed). Of course this case should also be in blond finish to match the Model #120s. This reminds me of another modification in the Model #120 which we desire. All doors and drawers must be fitted with locks. Naturally, on the special eight-foot case, we would like fluorescent lights in the lower area as well as in the upper.

Please note also that we never received a $39.50 credit on our account requested in my letter of January 5, 198-. Why not?

Please acknowledge above.

Sincerely,
Burke's Jewelry

Bernard Burke
Owner

This is to report on the three areas requested in our division for the first quarter of 198-.

In the area of human resources, we have had very little change in personnel. In section one we did add 28 salaried personnel while losing 12. In hourly, we maintained a total personnel count of 470-500. We did have one resignation of an administrative level individual.

In the aspect of training, we carried through programs for 20 salaried individuals in-house and 98 hourly in-house during the first quarter of the year.

In our second major category--production--we have registered a major increase over last year (same period) for both lines. In the case of Kent, we registered a 10 percent increase as compared with the same period last year for Models #101, #102, and #103. For our York Line, the advance for the same period was even better--14 percent--for Models #401, #402, and #403.

Finally, in the area of sales, we are fortunate that the sales of Kent, as compared to the first quarter last year, were 330 dozen for Model #101, 480 dozen for Model #102, and 410 dozen for Model #103. This compares with 290, 410, and 360 dozen for Models #101, #102, and #103 respectively. In the case of the York Line, sales were 320, 360, and 330 dozen for Models #401, #402, and #403 as compared with the same quarter last year of 290, 210, and 290 dozen for Models #401, #402, and #403 respectively.

As for sales personnel we have gone from 55 salespersons and 5 district managers last year in this quarter to 61 and 6 in the first quarter of this year.

On the basis of the above information and my reports #202 and #203 submitted ten days ago, I make the following recommendations:

   1) Use Arnett Placement Bureau for the acquisition of all new salaried personnel;

   2) Hire one additional training administrator for our Training Staff;

   3) Begin the use of the Beta Sales Test on July 1 for all sales personnel hired.

6. Donald Arnold is the sales manager for the Midwest Auto Supplies Company. His boss has asked him to write a short report on the feasibility of bringing out a new line of auto exhaust pipes to fit small foreign cars. After researching this question, Donald came up with the following points he wants to make in his report:

a. The total market for exhausts is 300,000 per year.

b. The largest manufacturer of exhausts designed specifically for foreign cars sells 33,000 per year.

c. It is also possible to adapt custom exhausts made for American cars to foreign specifications.

d. The largest manufacturer of adapted exhausts sells 21,000 per year.

e. The average price for a custom exhaust is $47.

f. The average price for an adapted exhaust is $38.

g. Midwest could adapt the exhausts it currently makes for American cars at a cost of $4. The cost of producing the American exhausts is $8 per unit.

h. Midwest could build an assembly line to produce custom exhausts at a cost of $500,000. Custom exhausts could then be produced at a cost of $12 per unit.

i. Custom exhausts are most popular on the West Coast. They are also very popular in the South.

j. The total market for exhausts can be divided as follows: 200,000 custom, 100,000 adapted.

k. By the end of three years, Midwest might reasonably expect to capture 10 percent of whichever market segment it chooses to enter.

l. Donald's neighbor Fred has a custom exhaust on his Honda Civic.

See if you can put the points Donald wishes to make in his report into a logical order using an outline. Are there any points that won't fit into a logical outline? If so, what would you suggest Arnold do with those points?

Dilemma

This Dilemma poses a typical business problem. How would you solve it? Compare your analysis with the Decision on page 49.

Becky Trujillo is the advertising assistant for Continental Store in Baton Rouge, Louisiana. A new three-story, modern store will have its grand opening in just twenty days.

This outlet will be the fifth store in the Continental chain and is located in a growing suburban center just outside of Baton Rouge. The other four stores are located in New Orleans and its suburbs.

Becky's task is to write a combination sales and goodwill letter to a select mailing list of prospective customers in the Baton Rouge area.

Prior to writing the letter, Becky noted a few facts concerning the new store:

1. Completely modern, air conditioned
2. Four full floors of merchandise
3. Products: appliances; furniture; men's, women's, and children's apparel; sports equipment; gourmet foods; radio, TV, and stereo equipment; auto service center
4. Charge accounts: available to qualified applicants
5. Opening day gifts and prizes: each customer will receive a gift of Modern Lady Cosmetics. In addition, three RCA color television sets, two stereo systems, and one full-length mink coat will be given to 6 lucky individuals who make purchases on the first day
6. Continental's well known "Satisfaction guaranteed or your money refunded" policy will be in effect
7. Free delivery service within 40 miles of the store

Becky's supervisor has requested that she write a sales-goodwill letter to be mailed to 15,000 prospects (all women) who live in the Baton Rouge area.

Putting Ideas into Words

3

Here is a list of the objectives you should understand by the time you complete this chapter. Place a check mark in the box beside each as soon as you feel ready to apply your understanding in a practical situation.

☐ The ten basic rules for effective writing:
  Keep sentences short, on the average
  Use the simple rather than the complex
  Select familiar words
  Avoid unnecessary words
  Use active, not passive, sentences
  Write as you would talk
  Use terms your reader can picture
  Relate your writing to your reader's experience
  Use variety in your writing
  Write to express, not impress

☐ The use of the Gunning Fog Index to check the readability of your writing

☐ The major keys to achieving an effective business writing style:
  Emphasis
  Unity and coherence
  Imagination
  The *You* attitude
  Courtesy and tact
  Positive and negative tone
  Correctness and precision

Because most of us are extremely busy, we often don't take the time to write properly. Or it may be that we don't always appreciate the need for time and the proper mental attitude necessary to write effectively. Too often an individual will spend two weeks evaluating a new site for one of the chain's new outlets. She will check the site, gather data on the demographics of the neighborhood through surveys and interviews, measure the traffic flow, examine long- and short-term growth patterns of the area, review the industrial expansion and the labor shifts . . . and a dozen other tasks. After spending many days or even weeks gathering this vital information, she will attempt to turn out a complete, logical report in two hours. That report then will serve as a basis for decision making that may well involve a half million dollars. Unless the writer is extremely adept, chances are good that the report produced in two hours, on a topic this complex, will probably be second rate.

What is the difference in meaning between *cite, site,* and *sight?* (See Appendix 1.)

What is the difference between *adapt, adept,* and *adopt?* (See Appendix 1.)

Good writing—whether a business letter, a short memo, or an extensive proposal—requires time, thought, concentration, and effort. Effective writing is not easy for most of us, but it need not be difficult if we understand the problem, know our purpose, identify our reader, and organize a suitable outline.

Effective writing also requires time, thought, and concentration.

Once this planning stage is completed, the next step is to get your ideas down on paper. The first writing effort should be done quickly and, if possible, without interruption. Your basic objective simply is to write out the ideas in the order reflected in your outline. Don't worry about a poor word choice, an awkward sentence, a misplaced comma. Those all can be corrected or refined in the rewriting or editing process. At this stage, your goal is simply to get your ideas on paper as quickly, logically, and completely as possible.

Your first draft should be written quickly. Get your ideas down, and edit for word choice, correctness, and punctuation later.

Ten Principles for Effective Writing

Some years ago, Robert Gunning suggested that effective writing can be quite easy if you follow ten simple principles.[1] You can use these ten principles when you're writing your first draft, or you can wait until the first draft is written and then apply the ten principles in revising it.

#1: Keep your sentences short on the average.

1. **Keep Sentences Short, on the Average.** Gunning does not object to sentences which are thirty or forty words in length so long as there are several that have five or eight words. On the average, sentences should be short. Obviously if all sentences are short, the result is a choppy cadence. Some long, some medium, some short. Keep sentences short, on the average.

Not this:
Working as an electrician, which, by the way, can be a difficult and exacting job, is a most satisfying career but it does require a good deal

---

[1]Robert Gunning, *New Guide to More Effective Writing in Business and Industry.* Copyright © 1963 by Gunning-Mueller Clear Writing Institute, Inc. Reprinted by permission.

*of study which after a hard day serving as an apprentice can be a
heavy strain on one's health and peace of mind.*

But this:
*Working as an electrician is a most satisfying career. It does require a
good deal of study.*

2. **Use the Simple Rather than the Complex.** There is little point in saying,
"He used a variety of circumlocutions in an effort to articulate his concep-
tualized references on societal values . . ." when we can say, "He talked in
circles in an effort to express his ideas on . . ."

#2: Express your ideas
as simply as you can.

The English writer George Orwell once translated a passage from the
Bible into complicated, modern English. Which version of Ecclesiastes do
you prefer?

*Objective consideration of contemporary phenomena compels the con-
clusion that success or failure in competitive activities exhibits no tendency to be commensurate with innate capacity, but that a considerable
element of the unpredictable must inevitably be taken into account.*

*I returned, and saw under the sun, that the race is not to the swift, nor
the battle to the strong, neither yet bread to the wise, nor yet riches to
men of understanding, nor yet favor to men of skill; but time and
chance happeneth to them all.*

3. **Select Familiar Words.** In this sense, Gunning means *familiar to your
reader.* In one case it may be a *sabulous consistency;* in another, *sandy.* Why
say, "The wound was exacerbated, which resulted in a major and dangerous
intumescence of . . ." rather than "The constant irritation of the cut resulted in a dangerous swelling . . .?" Which way to say it depends on who the
reader is.

#3: Use everyday words.

4. **Avoid Unnecessary Words.** So often writing is padded because some
individuals may feel that a twelve-page report is more impressive than a six-
page one; that a two-page memo is more effective than a half-page memo.
But that is nonsense. The best way to impress a reader is through the clarity
and conciseness of what has been written.

#4: Cut out extra words,
phrases, and sentences.

Why say, "May we take this opportunity to bring to your attention at this
time the fact that we will not in the future (as we have in the past) manufacture and distribute our Parkhurst line after November 15," when all that is
necessary is "The Parkhurst line will be discontinued after November 15?"

Not this:
*It is almost impossible, in this highly competitive world, much as we
would like to, to immediately step into well-paying jobs, which are few
and far between at best, right after leaving school.*

But this:
*It is almost impossible to step into a well-paying job right after leaving
school.*

In addition to cutting words, phrases, and clauses to achieve conciseness and greater clarity, it can be very effective to use tables, charts, and graphs for the same purpose. Note how much easier it is for the reader to understand the table below as compared to the text. And notice also how much easier it is to assimilate, compare, contrast, and retain the information in the table as compared to the paragraphs.

Not this:

On the whole, although our three lines of lamps—the Cape Cod, Capistrano, and Contemporary—have been moving well, there has been a steady and significant decline in one as the following figures indicate. (All figures rounded to nearest unit).

In the first quarter of the year, the Cape Cod sold 85 units (12 lamps per unit) as compared with 48 for the Capistrano and 95 for the Contemporary. Then the Cape Cod had a major year, going from 110 to 160 to 180 in the second, third, and fourth quarters respectively. The Contemporary stayed steady with 90 units in the second quarter while the Capistrano recorded 35. In the third and fourth quarters the Contemporary sold 92 and 98 units respectively. However, the Capistrano continued to slide by posting a 30 for the third quarter and 24 for the last segment of the year.

On the basis of these data, it is my recommendation that . . .

But this:

LAMP SALES

(In units—12 lamps per unit)

Lamp Style	1st qtr.	2nd qtr.	3rd qtr.	4th qtr.
Cape Cod	85*	110	160	180
Capistrano	48	35	30	24
Contemporary	95	90	92	98

*All figures rounded to nearest unit

Not only is the table a far superior piece of communication than the paragraphs—from the point of view of clarity, but it is also much more concise.

#5: Use the active voice.

5. **Use Active, Not Passive, Sentences.** The active voice usually gives our writing more interest and life.

Passive: A sales increase was noted.

Active: Sales rose sharply.

6. **Write as You Would Talk.** Our writing should *sound* like our speech. Use the reader's name; perhaps a colorful word in common use; an informal term now and then. Obviously we really don't want to duplicate our speaking as it is often repetitious and contains a fair number of *ers* and *ahs.* However, the personal tone achieved in speaking is something we should try to catch when we write.

#6: Try to make your writing sound like your speech.

Avoid	Say Instead
As in the above	*Above*
Advise	*Tell*
Attached please find	*Attached (or enclosed) is*
Esteemed order	*Your order*
Hereby acknowledge	*We received*
Permit me to say	*(Just say it!)*
In order to arrive at a decision as to whether or not	*To decide whether*

Perhaps a good rule of thumb to remember is: If you wouldn't say it that way, don't write it that way. Who would say, "I hand you herewith"? Probably no one. That's why it shouldn't be written, either.

7. **Use Terms Your Reader Can Picture.** Here again the reader will determine the word choice. "The law enforcement officer, because of the exigencies of the situation, moved with alacrity in an effort to terminate the advance of the . . ." is one way of saying it. A better picture might be secured through "Moving like lightning, the policeman tried to block the . . ."

#7: Use words that create pictures in your readers' minds.

8. **Relate Your Writing to the Reader's Experience.** To arouse interest in your writing, ideas should be presented from the readers' points of view; their values; their benefits. Note how the reader will profit; "Your firm will receive a clear 7 percent profit, rapid turnover of merchandise, and an excellent reputation." Not "Our excellent sales have resulted in our stock going up, the number of our employees increasing, and our company expanding."

#8: Show how the reader will benefit from what you present.

9. **Use Variety in Your Writing.** Insert short, sharp sentences among the longer ones. Use an attention-getting word or an alliterative series of words.

#9: Use attention-getting words and ideas to arouse interest in your writing.

Never before has man had such a capacity to control his own environment—to end thirst and hunger—to banish illiteracy and massive human misery. We have the power to make this the best generation of mankind . . . or to make it the last.[2]

Even an informal word or a colloquialism in the middle of a very formal statement will give spice to your writing.

[2]From the speech by President John F. Kennedy to the United Nations, September 20, 1963.

Effective writing is not easy for most of us.

#10: Write as concisely as possible. Your objective is to express yourself clearly, not to impress your reader with quantity.

10. **Write to Express and Not Impress.** Perhaps our educational system is somewhat to blame for individuals whose writings are padded, pompous, and wordy. In school we may have been told to produce a fifteen-page paper or a three-thousand-word essay. It might have been wiser to request a paper or an essay that is only as long as is necessary to cover the topic.

Eliminate the extra paragraphs, sentences, and words. Remember, the best way to impress your reader is with the clarity and conciseness of your message. To bury your ideas in a sea of words will reflect no credit on you.

Gunning's Fog Index

The Gunning Fog Index measures the readability of the writing.

One good way to check whether you have applied Gunning's ten principles effectively is to measure the readability of your writing by using Gunning's *Fog Index*.

1. *Find the average number of words per sentence. Use a sample at least 100 words long. Divide the total number of words by the number of sentences. This gives you the average sentence length.*

2. *Count the number of words of three syllables or more per 100 words. Don't count: a) words that are capitalized; b) combinations of short easy words like* bookkeeper, *c) verbs that make three syllables by adding* ed *or* es — like created *or* trespasses.

3. *Add the two factors above and multiply by 0.4. This will give you the Fog Index. It corresponds roughly with the number of years of schooling a person would require to read a passage with ease and understanding.*[3]

[3]Gunning, *New Guide*, pp. 9–11.

If the index is quite low (8–12), your writing will be read and comprehended easily, for it is at the eighth- to the twelfth-grade level. If the index is at about sixteen (senior college level), comprehension of it is more difficult. If the index is at—say 23—it is probably rather *misty* and at about 28, we might say "the fog is rolling in."

Writing that has a readability index of 8 to 12 is easy to comprehend; 20 to 25 is very difficult.

For example, the following memo on safety has a Fog Index of 16/17[4]:

SAFETY

Since general safety conditions are one of the responsibilities you have within your department, we would appreciate your disseminating the following information.

In a recent inspection of all areas the most obvious hazard detected was the manner in which office equipment is placed or used in relation to personnel movement or traffic. All personnel in your area should be made aware of possible Safety Hazards and take precautionary measures at all times so that a high "Safety Level" may be maintained.

1. *Electrical cords on equipment such as typewriters, adding machines, etc., should not be permitted to lie loose on the floor where the possibility of someone tripping over them exists.*

2. *When not in immediate use, desk and file drawers should be kept closed at all times.*

The safety measures described in the memo would have a better chance of being followed if the memo were rewritten with a Fog Index of 7/8:

SAFETY

Safety in your department is your responsibility. Please see that your people are made aware of hazards and that they take measures to prevent them.

A recent inspection revealed a chief hazard to be office equipment placed in the way of people moving about.

1. *Electrical cords of typewriters, adding machines, etc., should not lie loose on the floor. Someone may trip over them.*

2. *Keep desk and file drawers closed when not in use.*

[4]Ibid., pp. 9–11.

Most magazine, newspaper, and company publication editors check the readability index of their efforts.

Readability formulas by many authorities now are easily found and quickly applied. Almost every magazine editor attempts to determine the readability level of subscribers and then writes or edits all articles to meet that level. The same is true of editors and writers of newspapers, annual reports, textbooks, employee manuals, etc. If we know that our work force is made up of various ethnic groups with an average educational level of first-year high school, doesn't it make sense to write at that level? To write higher will only result in a low readership and comprehension.

It is necessary to understand that Gunning does not believe the formula is the only answer to getting your materials read. He feels strongly that we must have something to say! But if our important message is expressed in a way that makes comprehension difficult or impossible, then good ideas are lost forever. And that is a pity.

Keys to Style

In the preceding pages, we have emphasized the value of conciseness and logic in writing. But there are other qualities which are vital if the business letters, memos, proposals, and reports you write are to be effective.

Emphasis

There are several methods for obtaining emphasis in your writing.

At times it is desirable to emphasize key points in our writing. This may be for sales purposes or simply to turn the spotlight on a key idea. Emphasis can be obtained in a number of different ways. If we use *placement,* we will probably note the key idea in the beginning of our discussion, again in the body, and probably at the conclusion. Or we might use *proportion,* which is simply giving more space and words to the central idea, than to other concepts in the presentation.

Repetition is also useful in emphasis. The key idea is repeated several times in order to emphasize it. The simple use of *format* or *mechanics* in layout is still another way to highlight emphasis. Underscoring, use of colored inks, extremely generous use of white space, cartoons, sketches, photographs, capitalization, and boldface type are all mechanical methods of emphasizing a key idea.

Attention-getting words, phrases, or *alliterative statements* may gain emphasis also. However, the best way to emphasize a key idea is through excellent writing. The presentation of ideas should be so arresting and well done that the reader will focus on the idea presented. If the reader remembers a key concept because of the superior manner in which it is written, this is a far better method than using underlining or colored inks.

Unity and Coherence

Unity is simply the quality of *oneness.* A short paper or a segment in a larger one normally has one key topic or idea. The topic sentence leads us toward it; other sentences develop the idea; the paragraphs expand the idea and concepts further.

In essence, the sentences and paragraphs all move toward the basic idea. Phrases, sentences, or paragraphs which do not make a direct contribution to the development of the total idea must be eliminated. To permit them to remain can only lead to possible digressions and the introduction of extraneous ideas.

Unity is achieved when all ideas contribute to the central theme.

Coherence is simply the orderly connection of one idea with another so that each follows smoothly and logically toward a predetermined objective. Transitional words, phrases, sentences, and even paragraphs assist readers as they move through your paper. The ideas build on one another with persuasive coherence. The basic idea of transition (from the prefix *trans* or across) is to assist the readers or listeners in moving from one idea to the next.

Coherence is achieved when ideas interconnect and follow each other logically.

When the writer uses transitional devices with skill, ideas follow one another in a smooth and interesting manner.

Imagination

All too often the individual involved in business writing may feel that imagination is better left to the novelist, the TV writer, or the author of a movie script. Certainly imagination is needed in those instances, but it is just as important for the writer of reports, employee orientation manuals, and policy guides.

A word, an analogy, a figure of speech, or a reference with which the reader can easily identify may cause the idea to jump off the page. Business, with all its changes, is exciting. Why shouldn't the language used to describe business activities also be exciting?

Use your imagination to choose ideas and words that will arouse interest on the reader's part.

To achieve vibrancy in speaking and writing, we must avoid clichés and worn-out similes, drop hackneyed and stereotyped words and phrases, and eliminate pompous and boring statements.

Of course, good taste must be retained. Street jargon, extreme colloquial expressions, and unusual word choices may have no place in a report or a journal article. On the other hand, there is no law that states we must be as formal in our word choice as a turn-of-the-century board of directors' report.

Note the life and enthusiasm that seems to be a part of the following excerpts from recent reports and letters:

> *The results of our market test certainly indicate we are on the right track. Continued consumer acceptance of our product will give us a year-end profit in very solid black figures.*

*We can offer our customers a completely winning combina-
tion: quality products, guaranteed performance, same-day
delivery, competitive pricing, and forty years of customer
satisfaction.*

*We have been selling the same four lines out of the same four
buildings to essentially the same number of customers for
too many years.*

*This is the year to diversify and expand; next year will be too
little and surely too late.*

*If we are looking for reasons not to grow, there are plenty:
shortage of energy, high unemployment, rising inflation. But
no firm ever grew by listing reasons why it couldn't. I say let's
list the reasons why we can: a product whose time has come;
quality that is unquestioned; a market that is assured; and a
distribution system that has been proven.*

*My recommendation is "Full Speed Ahead for Progress and
Profits with our new Contemporary Winner Line."*

None of the above is meant to be as memorable as a quotation by John F.
Kennedy or a paragraph by Winston Churchill. But they are a departure from
much of the dry, hackneyed phrasing often found in today's reports and letters. When you have an idea, and the words—though informal—come from
your heart, state them. As long as they are in good taste and logically related
to the discussion, there is no reason why you should not use them.

The *You* Attitude

**Always try to present ideas
to show the reader how he or
she will gain, profit, enjoy,
and obtain value from your
suggestion or
recommendation.**

Whenever possible, try to involve the reader or listener in your presentation.
Too often business communication is formal, stiff, and impersonal. The result is frequently a message that sounds pompous and forbidding. Business
itself is exciting and interesting because people—with all their emotions,
feelings, biases, desires, and hopes—are involved. There is no reason why
business communication should not reflect some of that. Obviously such
reading is not designed for paperback books, TV stories, or movie scripts. On
the other hand, there is no reason why reports or letters should be dry, ster-
ile, and unfeeling.

Perhaps the best way to keep your readers involved is to take a *you* attitude
in your writing. Simply stated, the *you* attitude is writing or talking from the
readers' or listeners' point of view. It is projecting the benefits the product or
service will bring to the readers—not the writer. It is showing and telling
the readers how they will benefit; it is communicating from the readers'/
listeners' viewpoint.

Not this:

We have found that our sales have increased significantly during our last fiscal year as the result of producing quality products. These products, which you and 1300 other Made-Well dealers distribute, have become the American farmer's first choice in fencing materials. As a matter of fact, our employees have increased by 22 percent in this last year and our sales have almost doubled.

But this:

We are delighted that Made-Well Products have proved valuable for our dealers. In this past year, you and our other customers have found our 500 – 5 Policy valuable – Orders over $500 earn a 5 percent discount. We wish to continue that policy and add a new one that should increase your sales and profit margin.

Beginning October 1, we will provide you with a monthly advertising kit that should increase your sales and profit margin. There is no cost to you provided your monthly purchases exceed $800. The kit consists of . . . and here is how you can use it for your benefit:

Note in the second example that the emphasis is placed on the readers, *not* the writer. An effort is made to explain how the readers profit, benefit, enjoy, and are involved. And what reader doesn't appreciate that type of approach? All this requires is writing with the *you* in mind, rather than the *I* or *we*.

I or *We* Attitude	*You* Attitude
Our company has expanded and our profits increased as a result of our products	*You will find that our product will sell rapidly and afford you a profit margin . . . .*
We are in need of funds and that is why your overdue bill must be	*To maintain your excellent credit reputation, please remit . . . .*
The recognition accorded our efforts is well deserved and assures our customers that	*Our customers find that Excello Products sell quickly at a full 20 percent profit . . . .*
We are concerned, for the product you returned can't be returned to stock and sold	*Because we want you to be completely satisfied, we are sending you a new . . . .*

Courtesy and Tact

Courtesy is vital to the business transaction to make it flow more smoothly. Busy as we are, we should remember how important those few extra words are. But they must always be conveyed sincerely and honestly. If the comment is injected to "sound like a nice guy," it will have the *sound* but not the sincerity.

Courtesy is the act of closing a letter with a "thank you," "we appreciate," "it was nice of you to remember." Courtesy is remembering to acknowledge a statement made in the letter you received. It is the extra sentence you insert which comments favorably on a sale, a reward, or a goal accomplished.

Perhaps a good definition of tact is: saying what needs to be said—in a rather difficult situation—and not antagonizing or irritating the reader or listener. Being tactful only requires choosing the correct words. It does not mean *avoiding* what needs to be said but simply saying it correctly.

Tactless	Tactful
We received your letter in which you claim we did not ship	*Your letter of December 3 indicated we did not ship . . . .*
You failed to list the model number	*Please list the model number desired . . . .*
I was surprised to learn that	*I learned from your letter . . . .*
You obviously lost the data we sent	*We are sending a duplicate of the data . . . .*

Positive and Negative Tone

Often we notice a letter's positive tone or approach, or a speaker's positive, not negative, comments. What is meant by positive and negative tone? Stated simply, a *positive tone* is one that gives us a favorable, enjoyable, even desirable association with a product or service. And a *negative tone* plants a seed of doubt or conveys an image that is unfavorable, undesirable, unattractive, or even frightening.

Negative	Positive
Complaint Department	*Adjustment Department Customer Service*
We hope you won't find our product unsatisfactory.	*We are sure you will find our product satisfactory and profitable.*

If you decide to buy our product	*When you buy our product . . . .*
You won't have difficulty operating our new mower if	*Our new mower will operate efficiently and easily when . . . .*
We hope you won't feel this is an imposition on your time	*We are sure you will agree this is time well spent when . . . .*

Under usual circumstances, your statements should carry a positive tone. However, it is possible to be *too* positive. When that happens, we often accuse the writer of being hard sell or pushy.

There are also some situations when the writer *desires* to arouse an unfavorable tone, fear, or a negative reaction. That may be done to focus on a problem or a potential problem. However, that should be quickly followed by a positive solution.

Negative Situation	Positive Solution
Are you adequately protected from the financial loss of a devastating fire?	*Our fire insurance provides peace of mind, financial protection, and . . . .*
Are you certain your breath doesn't offend?	*Being popular in a crowd is assured when you use . . . .*
Advancing years spent in near poverty	*Financial security and comfortable post-retirement years are yours when . . . .*

Correctness and Precision

For some peculiar reason, we all pay special attention when we see an error in writing or hear one when an individual speaks. It's difficult to understand why we do this. Perhaps it makes us feel superior to the writer or speaker. Whatever the reason, when we see or hear an error, we usually focus on it and, as a result, often lose the remainder of the message.

An individual who spoke for one hour and twenty minutes was asked by several people in the audience, "In your introduction, didn't you mean 'Western Electric' and not 'General Electric'?" Here is a case where the listener heard the error in the first few minutes of the speech and probably tuned out for the rest of the presentation. Because we are human, we can't hope to eliminate all errors, but we should be aware of how damaging they may be to our communication efforts. Because of that, we must take the time to be as correct and precise as possible in our writing and speaking.

Provide time for review and revision. Carefully check all items about which you may have some doubt. Be precise: Do you mean *disorganized* or *unorganized?* Should the word be *uninterested* or *disinterested?* Is the correct choice *farther* or *further?* It is often wise to obtain the help of another person who can read your report or paper with a more critical eye and greater objectivity than you.

Concluding Comments on Writing

The business world, it is often said, runs on paper wheels. Many of those wheels are the reports, letters, and proposals which you and your fellow employees complete. Although the task of writing may not be simple for you, it can be rewarding and challenging—when you do it well. And you *can* do it well when you practice and follow the suggestions made in the previous pages.

There is a further consideration that is important. Many of you will be employees in a large organization. Quite typically, the spotlight does not seek out individuals quickly in big organizations. Of course, hardworking people with ability will be recognized and promoted.

However, the alert employee also knows that reports, proposals, and letters are read by top management. Therefore, you may wish to seize every opportunity to write, and to write so well that the reader will say, "This is a great report: clear, complete, concise, and well-substantiated. Its conclusions are logical and its recommendations are valid. Making a decision based on this presentation is not at all difficult. Who wrote this excellent analysis?"

And the spotlight is on you.

MEMO

To: Students
From: The Authors
Subject: Effective writing

Effective writing is not a simple task. As a matter of fact, it is usually hard work that requires, as one famous writer has said, "the application of the seat of the pants to the seat of the chair for an unlimited amount of time." But do take the time to write as well as you can. You will be rewarded for your efforts.

Decision

Here is the sales letter Becky Trujillo prepared for prospective customers of the new Continental Store.

Continental Store

606 Jefferson Street
New Orleans, Louisiana 70140

June 12, 198-

Ms. Wilma Kaper
300 North Main Street
Port Allen, Louisiana 70143

Dear Ms. Kaper:

You're Invited!

Yes, you're invited to a party for the opening of Continental's new store in Port Allen. And just to turn the tables, we're giving gifts to the guests! Please come to the festivities, so we may present you with a gift of Modern Lady Cosmetics.

In addition, six lucky guests who make purchases on the opening day, June 27, will be eligible for one of the special gifts: one full-length mink coat, three RCA Color TV sets, and two Fisher stereo systems.

You will find the new Continental store in Port Allen to be absolutely outstanding with its four full floors of merchandise. Shopping here will save you time because of convenience; save you money because of our discount prices; and save you effort because of services. On the four floors you will find appliances, furniture, men's, women's, and children's apparel, sports equipment, gourmet foods, an auto service center, and dozens of other departments which you have come to expect at Continental.

In addition, Continental in Port Allen is pleased to offer you:
Free delivery service of merchandise (within 40 miles);
Charge accounts to qualified applicants;
Satisfaction guaranteed or your money refunded;
Three restaurants in the building for your dining pleasure.

So, Ms. Kaper, please come to our party on June 27, browse through the store, and please pick up your gift from The Customer Service desk on the first floor. We look forward to seeing you.

Sincerely yours,

Becky Trujillo

Becky Trujillo
Advertising Assistant

CHAPTER REVIEW

Questions

1. Why do you feel effective writing requires time, thought, and concentration?

2. What is the advantage of getting your ideas down on paper as rapidly as possible instead of stopping frequently to check a spelling, find a better word or revise a phrase or sentence to improve clarity?

3. Why is it important for editors of magazines, newspapers, and employee publications to maintain their material at a specific readability level?

4. Of Gunning's ten suggestions for effective writing, which two do you personally seem to violate most frequently? Can you explain why?

5. Of Gunning's ten suggestions for effective writing, which two do you feel people most frequently violate?

6. Is it possible to have a piece of writing that has a low readability index but would still have little or no value? Explain.

7. Define the following terms from the point of view of effective communication:
   Emphasis
   Clarity
   Correctness and precision
   Unity
   Coherence
   Imagination
   Reader-oriented

8. Why can an error (lack of correctness) be so damaging in business writing? What relationship, if any, is there between errors and the reader's image of the organization?

9. Under what instances would the business writer want to inject a negative tone in his message?

Exercises

1. Determine the Gunning Fog Index for the readings below. Rewrite each to reduce the Fog Index; show the use of the index and your final figure.
   a. In the disturbing and turbulent period in which we presently live, it is understandable that many individuals entertain anxieties and insecurities that result from uncertain economic situations, disturbing political factors, upsetting crime conditions, and frightening international incidents that produce a mental and psychological set that leads, on the part of many people, to serious questioning of their own values, directions, and goals. Because we have little control over these many outside forces, we would be wise to attempt to ignore them and thereby avoid the impact they have on us. However, that is impossible unless we divorce ourselves from daily living. Perhaps a better solution is for us to learn how to most effectively cope with conflict-producing situations.
   b. There is much to be said for channeling our vocational preferences away from the highly skilled areas such as medicine, law, engineering, etc., because of the long period of time required for the education, the cost of securing the training, the over-supply of professional personnel which presently exists, and the steadily decreasing economic return. On the other hand, there is much to recommend the selection of a trade or an entrepreneurial venture for a vocation because of the high economic return which is presently possible, the heavy demand for such personnel which exists, the shortage of individuals in these areas, and personal satisfaction achieved from constructing a home, building a cabinet, wiring a system, installing an air conditioning unit, etc.

2. Present a piece of writing from a newspaper, book, or magazine that reflects some of the qualities listed in Question 7. Mark specific passages as being *reader-oriented, imaginative,* etc.

3. Using your business communications textbook or any other business textbook, apply the Gunning Fog Index to check the readability level of the contents of your book. In writing, describe your application of the Index and present your conclusions.

4. Interview a person familiar with his or her organization's written business communications. Give this person a typewritten list of Gunning's ten suggestions for effective writing. Ask the interviewee to do the following with this list:
   a. Rank the items according to their importance for effective writing.
   b. Rank the items according to the number of violations he or she observes in the company's outgoing written communications. The suggestion with the most violations will be first in the ranking; the suggestion with the least violations will be tenth in the ranking.

5. Why is it more effective to use concrete words that your reader can picture rather than abstract terms? Support your answer by doing the following:
   a. Choose a topic and select concrete vocabulary to express your thoughts about the topic
   b. Using the same topic, select abstract words to express your thoughts about the subject.

c. Compare the effectiveness of the two methods of communicating ideas.

6. Choose one of the magazines you read for enjoyment or entertainment. Apply the Gunning Fog Index to check the readability level of the articles published in the magazine. Compare your findings with those of your peers in class.

7. Select a favorite item of clothing from your wardrobe. In writing, attempt to sell the item to the reader. Use the four methods of emphasis mentioned in this chapter. In one paragraph emphasize the style of the item of clothing over all its other virtues. In a second paragraph emphasize its comfort and ease of care rather than its style.

8. Ruth Landings, an accounting certificate student, had been assigned a five-page research paper by her business communications instructor. Her class was told that both content and mechanical precision (correct spelling, grammar, punctuation, etc.) would count toward the report grade because the project represented a form of business communication. Ruth devoted much time to researching the contents, but since she wasn't going to "wind up as a secretary," she didn't bother to check the mechanical precision of her report when she handed it in. Upon earning a D grade, Ruth told her instructor that she did not deserve a penalty for the misspellings and grammar errors because the only important part of the report was the content Discuss your opinion in this matter either orally or in writing, as instructed by your professor.

Dilemma

In her position as administrative assistant for Continental Stores, Becky Trujillo reviews all quarterly reports submitted by division managers. She has just received the following report, which she feels is long, poorly organized, and difficult to read. Becky has decided to rewrite this report.

Continental Store

To: President, Continental Stores
From: Tom Franklin, Manager, Furniture and Appliance Dept.
Date: February 1, 198-
Subject: Second Quarterly Report

This is to report on sales of furniture, small and large appliances, and sales personnel for Department Four for the second quarter of this year.

Sales of furniture for this quarter were $960,000. This was a $310,000 jump over the previous quarter which is quite significant considering that we only increased sales personnel, for the entire department, by two full-time personnel from the previous quarter. As for small appliances, sales went from $140,000 to $160,000. One of the interesting factors here is the break-down in sales of the individual items, (see attached listing of sales figures of individual products for Department Four.)

For some unexplained reason, sales of the Kitchen Perfect Food Processor really went off the sales chart and although we did not advertise the item, we just could not keep them in stock. Of course, it is a good product, and at a consumer price of $49.00 each, it can't be beat--but of course, that is another story.

Now when we get to large appliances, we must divide those sales into three categories. In Category A, sales were $335,000; in Category B, they were $295,000; and in Category C, they went up to $630,000. These figures were a real surprise because for last quarter, Category A only hit $210,000 while in B, they were $260,000. But all things considered, we did well because our sales personnel per sales dollar were less for this quarter than last: 8 full-time and 4 part-time for this quarter as compared to 6 full-time and 4 part-time for last quarter.

Decision, see page 70

Revising and Rewriting

Here is a list of the objectives you should understand by the time you complete this chapter. Place a check mark in the box beside each as soon as you feel ready to apply your understanding in a practical situation.

☐ The two basic steps in the revising process:
   Reading and analyzing
   Editing

☐ The major kinds of editing necessary in a business communication:
   Edit for clarity
   Edit for conciseness
   Edit for format
   Edit for organization and proportion
   Edit for completeness
   Edit for style

☐ The importance of the revising process in writing effective business communications

One of the attributes that every competent writer possesses is the ability to revise. This is the art of reviewing and editing material you have written to improve its basic quality.

Revising consists of two steps.

The process of revising usually involves two distinct steps: 1) reading and critical analysis; and 2) editing for logic and thought, organization and proportion, clarity, conciseness, format and appearance.

Of these two steps, the first is probably the most important. If it is not done, or is accomplished superficially, you may jump into the second step and begin to cut and slash with abandon and often with poor results.

Read and Analyze

Before reading and analyzing your material, ask yourself to define the problem, specify the purpose, and identify the reader of your message.

Once you have completed the first draft of your writing—whether it is a fifteen-line memo or a fifteen-page report—put it aside. After twenty-four hours or so have passed, pick it up but don't read it. Just think. Ask yourself all or some of the following questions:

What was the precise problem I wanted to deal with?

What was the primary purpose of the message?

Who is the reader?

How busy is the reader? How much time does the reader have?

Ask yourself also if you have used the correct approach and if you have supplied the reader with adequate data and recommendations.

Does the reader want information, conclusions and recommendations? Or just the information?

Have substantiating statistics been included?

Is the total message sufficiently persuasive? Objective? Diplomatic?

As you read the first draft, you should ask yourself if the answers to these questions are easily and quickly apparent. This initial step in the editing process basically involves an analysis of your ideas and thought. For example, in this analysis, if you now feel more substantiating statistics are needed, then those should be obtained. If it is determined that the paper is not sufficiently persuasive or diplomatic or effectively organized, any or all of these changes can be made. However, it is the careful thought in the first step that determines the actual changes which will be made in the second.

Major Goals of Editing

Once you have analyzed your first draft and have decided what needs to be changed, you can begin editing to improve your writing. There are six major goals you should work toward as you review your communication.

Edit for Clarity

As you read through a draft of the paper, you should be constantly alert to clarity. If any phrase, clause, or sentence is the least bit unclear, it should be immediately revised. If there is any possibility that a reader may misinterpret, misconstrue, or misunderstand any statement, it should be revised. The final written product should be crystal clear: every phrase, every sentence, every paragraph, every section!

Quite often, clarity will be achieved by the simple technique of 1) putting related words together, or 2) converting one long sentence into two or more short ones.

1. Martin threw, at great risk to himself, for had it exploded, he would have been severely injured, the sputtering hand grenade.

    Edited:
    At great risk to himself, Martin threw the sputtering hand grenade. Had it exploded, he would have been severely injured.

2. Sabrina, who had been playing tennis all morning and was breathing very heavily by midday, stopped.

    Edited:
    Sabrina stopped playing tennis; she had been at it all morning and was breathing very heavily by midday.

3. Outstanding college students, for highest grades, easier goal attainment, and greatest personal satisfaction, should work to their full potential.

    Edited:
    Outstanding college students should work to their full potential for highest grades, easier goal attainment, and greatest personal satisfaction.

4. When one paints, it is wise to make adequate preparation for if this isn't done and one finds he is short an item such as masking tape or a special type of brush, or patching plaster, then it is difficult to suddenly stop and get involved in shopping for the item or items that would have been secured had proper preparation been made before the task was begun.

    Edited:
    When one paints, it is wise to make proper preparation before beginning the task. Once one has begun to paint, it is most inconvenient to stop and go shopping for missing items.

Although we have all probably heard the well-known quotation concerning clarity, it may be worthwhile to cite it again:

When editing for clarity, strive to make every phrase, every sentence, every word crystal clear.

We must write not only so clearly that we will be understood but so clearly that we can't possibly be misunderstood.

Edit for Conciseness

In editing for conciseness, eliminate every extra word, phrase, and sentence.

In many of Gunning's recommendations on improved writing, the emphasis is on achieving conciseness. Gunning suggests reviewing what one has written so that words and phrases which are not needed may be eliminated. Perhaps the most important argument for conciseness is the correlation between it and clarity. Almost invariably when a verbose statement is made concise, clarity increases.

1. We have noted, that by and large, many of our customers (and we have about 900 now) prefer to make their purchases from our company by telephone and they usually call in before noon.

   Edited:
   We have noted, that by and large, many of our customers (and we have about 900 now) prefer to make their purchases by phoning in their orders from our company by telephone, and they usually call in before noon.

   Final:
   Many of our customers prefer to make their purchases by phoning in their orders before noon.

2. One of the most important activities carried through today, simply because it hasn't been done before for many reasons such as lack of sophistication, funds, the know-how and not to even mention training personnel is the training of middle managers in the food industry so they may move up to the upper management positions which are becoming available.

   Edited:
   One of the most important activities carried through today, in the food industry simply because it hasn't been done before for many reasons such as lack of sophistication, funds, and know-how and not to even mention training personnel, is the training of middle managers in the food industry so they may move up to the upper management positions which are becoming available.

   Final:
   One of the most important activities carried through today in the food industry is the training of middle managers so they move to upper management positions which are becoming available.

Editing for conciseness can make a big difference in the *appearance* and the

Figure 4–1
Editing for Conciseness
a. Unedited Memo

emco

EMCO OIL COMPANY

```
To:       All Division Personnel
From:     Louisa Sanchez, Division Manager
Date:     January 4, 198-
Subject:  Change in work hours for all personnel

May I call to your attention, beginning February 1st, all personnel of
this division will conform to the new work schedule, which is
recognized to be a major departure from our previous one, which is
noted for your perusal below.

        Monday through Friday:  9:00-5:00 p.m.
        Saturday:               8:00-12:00 noon

It is hoped that all personnel will note the above and follow said
schedule without deviation therefrom whatsoever.
```

emco

EMCO OIL COMPANY

```
To:       All Division Personnel
From:     Louisa Sanchez, Division Manager
Date:     January 4, 198-
Subject:  Change in work hours

Beginning February 1 all personnel will conform to the new work
schedule:

        Monday-Friday:  9:00-5:00 p.m.
        Saturday:       8:00-noon
```

effect of a business communication. Notice, for example, how the memo in Figure 4–1a becomes more powerful in Figure 4–1b, after it has been revised. Likewise, readers are a lot less likely to understand the message in Figure 4–2a than they are the same message in the revised Figure 4–2b.

Figure 4–2
Editing for Conciseness
a. Unedited Memo

California Foods Company

```
To:      M. T. Head, Executive Vice-President
From:    R. T. Kamaguchi, Personnel Director
Date:    January 20, 198-
Subject: 4th Quarter Report
```

Our new hires in three categories for the fourth quarter were 85 part-time, 112 hourly, and 14 administrative. This compares with 10 administrators hired in the 3rd quarter and 62 part-time and 80 hourly for the same period. The increase in the 4th quarter is due to the Christmas demand.

Training in the 4th quarter consisted of 8 checker classes, 4 for box boys, 3 in sanitation, 3 in managing front-end operations, and 3 two-hour programs in Shoplifting Detection. The front-end classes are 6 hours each, sanitation is 3 hours and the box boy and checker classes always run 4 hours each. I should also point out that in our hiring of personnel, we secured eight in the professional category: 3 CPAs, 2 engineers, 2 RNs and 1 nutritional biologist were hired in the last quarter as compared with the 3 in the third period.

Safety worked out quite well for us for we only had 12 reportable-type accidents among employees in the 4th quarter in our stores, 2 in the warehouse, and 3 elsewhere (in transit, on trucks, etc.). This compares favorably with the 3rd quarter's record of 8, 2, and 2 in the same categories. As for training in the 3rd quarter, there was none because of vacation periods when training is halted.

However, it should be noted that we had a total of 20 customers reporting accidents on our property. This number is up from 14 in the 3rd quarter. All these are handled by our insurer: California Insurance Co.

One thing I want to suggest again, as I have in the past, is that we establish a relationship with Bellville Community College so we may recruit personnel actively there and that we consider hiring a training director on a half-time basis for the chain. And we still need safety reminder signs in all backrooms where most of our employee accidents take place.

Figure 4–2
Editing for Conciseness
b. Final Memo

California Foods Company

To: M. T. Head, Executive Vice-President
From: R. T. Kamaguchi, Personnel Director
Date: January 20, 198-
Subject: 4th Quarter Report

INTRODUCTION

The information below covers the activities of the Personnel Division,
4th Quarter, 198-

NEW PERSONNEL
Acquisition of   Training

Job Category	4th qtr.	3rd qtr.	Class	No. of Hours per Class	No. of Classes 4th qtr.	3rd qtr.
Part-time	85	62	Checkers	4	8	N
Hourly	112	80	Box Boys	4	4	O
Administrative	14	10	Sanitation	3	3	N
Professional			Front-End Op.	6	3	E
CPAs	3		Shoplift. Det.	2	3	*
Engineers	2	3				
RNs	2		*Vacation period: no classes			
Nutr. Bio.	1					

SAFETY
Reportable Accidents

Category	4th qtr.	3rd qtr.
Employees		
Stores	12	8
Warehouse	2	2
Elsewhere	3	2
Customers	20*	14

*Handled by California Insurance Company

RECOMMENDATIONS

1. Recruit personnel from Bellville Community College
2. Hire a half-time Training Director
3. Post safety reminder signs in all stores' back rooms

Figure 4–3
Editing for Conciseness
a. Unedited Memo

CHATEAU BABY TOYS, INC.

Palos, New Mexico 88032

```
TO:       S. Sherman, Executive Vice-President
FROM:     K. Bradford, Production Superintendent
DATE:     September 12, 198-
SUBJECT:  Production Report, Third Quarter, 198-
```

Our third quarter has proved to be rather erratic in the production of
our three major lines (which this report covers) and in our two
different plants: Cargill and Fremont. One factor that was apparent
was the need for new presses at Cargill and the need for action on
employee turnover at Fremont. I would surely recommend the Sharp
Presses over the King Presses if we decide to go that route at
Cargill.

Production of the AM, RM, and SM lines at Cargill were slightly up
over the previous quarter: AM--62,000 units; RM--19,000 units; and
SM--29,000 units for this quarter. Previous quarter production was
AM--66,000; RM--21,000; and SM--34,000. Although this quarter's
increase is not world shaking it is certainly far ahead of third
quarter production last year which was: AM--49,000; RM--12,100; and
SM--19,000.

Also, the presses need to be examined at Cargill. Downtime for this
quarter has increased substantially. On the 101 Presses we had 32
hours of downtime as compared to 20 hours last quarter and 12 for the
same quarter last year. Our 202 Presses, downtime went from 40 hours
for this quarter last year to 55 hours 2nd quarter last and a whopping 82
hours this quarter. So you can see why I'm recommending a good hard
look at the new Century models of Sharp Presses.

Now when we come to production at Fremont, we have a different story
from Cargill. Of course, Fremont is about half the size of Cargill.
For the three lines at Fremont, we ran AM--24,000 units; RM--8,000
units; and SM--20,000 units for this quarter. The previous quarter
for Fremont showed AM--22,000; RM--6,000; and SM--18,000. However
last year for this quarter at Fremont, production for AM was 19--000;
RM--7,500; and SM--20,000. Perhaps these figures can be explained by
an employee turnover of 3% for this quarter at Fremont, as compared
with 3.5 for the previous quarter and 1.5 percent last year, third
quarter. Also at Fremont, we had much better luck with downtime on
presses than we had at Cargill. for example the 101 Presses numbered
4 hours downtime for this quarter, 6 for the last quarter and only 2
for last year's third quarter. The 202 presses did equally well: 12
hours downtime for this quarter; 10 hours last quarter, and only 8
down hours for third quarter last year.

Figure 4–3
Editing for Conciseness
b. Final Memo

🐻 CHATEAU BABY TOYS, INC.

Palos, New Mexico   88032

```
To:       S. Sherman, Executive Vice-President
From:     K. Bradford, Production Superintendent
Date:     September 12, 198-
Subject:  Production Report, Third Quarter, 198-
```

Production

Production of our three major lines has increased substantially at both plants for this quarter.

PRODUCTION

Line (in thousands of units)	Cargill			Fremont		
	3rd qtr. 198-	2nd qtr. 198-	3rd qtr. Last yr.	3rd qtr. 198-	2nd qtr. 198-	3rd qtr. Last yr.
AM	62	66	49	24	22	19
RM	19	21	12	8	6	7.5
SM	29	34	19	20	18	20

Press Downtime

As noted from the figures cited, the downtime on Cargill presses has cut substantially into our production figures and into our return on investment.

DOWNTIME
(in hours)

Plant	3rd qtr. 198-	2nd qtr. 198-	3rd qtr. Last yr.
Cargill			
#101 Presses	32	20	12
#202 Presses	82	55	40
Fremont			
#101 Presses	4	6	2
#202 Presses	12	10	8

Recommendations
1. Replaces all presses (both #101 and #202 models) at Cargill during the last quarter of this year.
2. Consider the Century Models #221 and #222 as replacements for those presently at Cargill.

Statistical data in tables are much easier to use as compared with the same data presented in sentences within paragraphs.

Figure 4–4
Editing for Format
a. Unedited Letter

 Culver Copier Corporation, 412 Raleigh Road, Louisville, Kentucky   40238

August 3, 198-

Mr. Earl Forum
Forum Electric Corp.
421 North Wales Drive
Atlanta, Georgia 30342

Dear Mr. Forum:

Thank you for spending time with me last week as we reviewed the
Culver Copier 101. I imagine you are as impressed with its
performance as are many other business executives. You will recall
that the Culver can produce almost 200 copies per minute, is available
on a lease or buy basis, free service for five years, and no charge
for replacement parts for the first three years. And all this at
highly competitive prices whether you buy or lease.

This unit is now in operation at over half of America's leading 500
companies and is the unit that is used exclusively by the U.S.
Department of Defense.

In addition, the Culver Copier produces excellent copies on all types
of office stationery; no need to purchase special paper. Call us
today, Mr. Forum, and we can have a Culver Copier working for you
within a week.

Sincerely yours,

William T. Stonier
William T. Stonier
Sales Manager

Figure 4—4
Editing for Format
b. Final Letter

Culver Copier Corporation, 412 Raleigh Road, Louisville, Kentucky   40238

August 3, 198-

Mr. Earl Forum
Forum Electric Corp.
421 North Wales Drive
Atlanta, Georgia 30342

Dear Mr. Forum:

Thank you for spending time with me last week as we reviewed the
Culver Copier 101. I imagine you are as impressed with its
performance as are many other business executives.

Some of the outstanding features of the Culver Copier are:

        200 copies per minute;
        Copies on ALL types of stationery;
        Free service for 5 years;
        Free replacement parts for the first 3 years;
        Available on a buy or lease basis;
        Competitively priced.

This unit is now in operation at over half of America's leading 500
companies and is the unit that is used exclusively by the U.S.
Department of Defense.

Call us today, Mr. Forum, at 213/505-0001, and we can have a Culver
Copier working for you within a week.

Sincerely,

William T. Stonier
Sales Manager

Editing for conciseness can be fun as well as extremely satisfying. That satisfaction is derived from noting how clarity has been improved by cutting the length of a communication.

Edit for Format

There is probably nothing that will cause a busy executive to throw aside a report or a proposal more quickly than to open it and find page after page of heavy block paragraphs typed from top to bottom, side to side, with no headings, titles, or variety in appearance. Just a glance at such a format tells the reader he is faced with a time-consuming and formidable task—a task that he will gladly skip or put aside. An analogy can be drawn in public speaking. The speaker who drones on and on, with no variety or attention-getting statements, is sure to bore the listener as are the *heavy* pages guaranteed to frighten away the reader.

The dictionary defines format as the "shape, size, and general makeup of a publication." When we edit for format, we obviously do so for the same reason we edit for organization, conciseness, or clarity—to improve readability. In figures 4–2a and 4–2b, the changes which have been made in editing for conciseness have also resulted in editing for format. As the number of words decreased, the format changed. The result was an improvement in readability.

Some of the methods that can be used to improve the format of a piece of writing are:

- short paragraphs;
- wide margins;
- topic headings and subheadings;
- listings or enumerations;
- indentation;
- underlining;
- change and variety in typeface;
- use of boldface;
- separations; and
- tables, charts, graphs, and other visual aids where appropriate.

For example, in Figure 4–3b on page 62 see how the topic headings and tables have improved format, as compared to Figure 4–3a, and how they have made reading and assimilation of information easier. The same situation exists with letters. Compare Figures 4–4a and 4–4b.

Edit for Organization and Proportion

In Figure 4–5, it is obvious that the organization of the letter to Mr. Fryer would be improved if the descriptive items of the Continental File Cabinets were all in one paragraph. Rereading and editing makes that simple to do. The letter is then improved *before* it is mailed.

Figure 4–5
Editing for Organization

WILSHIRE OFFICE PRODUCTS
388 Marine Drive
Los Angeles, California   90099

September 10, 198-

Mr. Carl Fryer, Manager
Parker's Stationery Center
1400 Constance Street
Kansas City, Missouri 64141

Dear Mr. Fryer:

Consistently satisfied customers and a 100 percent margin of profit
for you!

Yes, Mr. Fryer, we know the above statement sounds almost
unbelievable, but it is true--provided you place your order within
thirty days.

It is our Continental File Cabinet that is on sale. These five items
come equipped with sliding drawers, all-nylon bushings, and a generous
supply of file separators for each drawer. And in addition, each
cabinet is constructed of 100 percent Fairbanks steel.

The Continental line carries the Seal of Acceptance of the American
Stationer's Association and has been purchased by such firms as
General Electric, the California Company, and Santa Fe Railroad.

And another important factor to add to the qualities listed above, the
Continental line comes in your choice of six different decorator
colors as well as a choice of drawer locks or not.

See the enclosed descriptive folder for full details and call us
collect at 555/443-2011 so your order may be shipped immediately.

Sincerely,

Manuel Ortego

Manuel Ortego
Sales Manager

Encl.

Be sure also that your communication is effectively organized, complete, and stylistically sound.

The same would be true of *proportion.* If the writer reread the letter to Mr. Fryer and found that 80 percent of it was devoted to description of the product, he could quickly make the necessary change. That revision would involve eliminating a segment to improve the proportion of one topic to another in the body of the letter.

Edit for Completeness

Your communication won't achieve its purpose if you haven't given your reader all necessary or requested facts. Figure 4–6a, for example, makes a strong recommendation to the reader but provides no facts to support that decision. The revised version (4–6b) *proves* that sales have been declining by reproducing the year's sales figures.

Edit for Style

Sometimes in the hurry to get a communication written down on paper, we forget to pay attention to matters of style—courtesy and tact, the *you* attitude, and the other topics we discussed in Chapter 3. Be sure to edit for style, so that tactless communications like the memo in Figure 4–7a won't cause explosions among customers or fellow workers. Figure 4–7b shows a more courteous version of the same basic message.

Figure 4–6
Editing for Completeness
a. Unedited Memo

```
To:       S. Siegel, Executive Vice-President
From:     L. T. Farmer, Sales Manager
Date:     February 5, 198-
Subject:  Termination of Operations, Unit #52

Because of the declining sales of Unit #52, I recommend that the
operations of this store be terminated with the close of business and
leave obligations of August 31.
```

Figure 4—6
Editing for Completeness
b. Final Memo

```
To:       S. Siegel, Executive Vice-President
From:     L. T. Farmer, Sales Manager
Date:     February 5, 198-
Subject:  Termination of Operations, Unit #52
```

As you will recall from my Special Report of November 27, 198-, we
have attempted a variety of activities (advertising, change in store
manager, special sales, etc.) in an effort to improve the sales record
of Unit #52. However, the overall drastic change in demographics in
the area of the store's location has been such that sales have
declined steadily.

SALES RECORD*

Month	Sales	Month	Sales
Jan.	$34,500	July	$25,215
Feb.	32,350	Aug.	24,100
March	28,380	Sept.	19,480
April	27,650	Oct.	18,670
May	27,705	Nov.	16,820
June	25,655	Dec.	15,110
		Jan.	13,005

*See special report for statistical data on income, expenses, and
overall return on investment.

Recommendation

The operations of this store be terminated with the close of business
and lease obligations on August 31, 198-.

Figure 4–7
Editing for Courtesy
and Tact
a. Unedited Memo

GEM FOODS

```
To:       B. L. Carey, Manager, Store #144
From:     M. L. Kelly, Manager, Personnel Division
Date:     August 31, 198-
Subject:  Completion of Forms 205


I received your memo of July 23, in which you claim this office did
not send out Form 205 for each of your store's full and part-time
personnel.

This statement is wrong on your part; I'm sure that if you review your
incoming paper file, you will find copies of Form 205 for each of your
assigned personnel.
```

b. Final Memo

Change organization: add to
product description section.

GEM FOODS

```
To:       B. L. Carey, Manager, Store #144
From:     M. L. Kelly, Manager, Personnel Division
Date:     August 3, 198-
Subject:  Completion of Form 205


Thank you for your memo of July 23, in which you indicated your office
did not receive Form 205 for each of your store's personnel.  Our
records indicate these were forwarded on July 17.

Perhaps, however, they went astray.  In any event, I have enclosed
duplicate copies.  Please complete these and return them as soon as
possible.
```

Concluding Comments

Carry through your revising in the two-step process suggested. First read and critically analyze. Make certain your paper answers the critical questions: Has the problem been dealt with? The purpose defined? The reader identified? The recommendations made?

Once this is done, move to the second step of editing:

edit for clarity;
edit for conciseness;
edit for format;
edit for organization and proportion;
edit for completeness;
edit for style.

And finally, read the finished paper with care. Gremlins have a way of getting into the typewriter and changing the spelling of words, transposing letters, and even omitting complete phrases and sentences.

Never, never submit a paper which you feel doesn't reflect your best effort. At times we are pressured to "get this in by 2:00 this afternoon." However, if you know you can't do a good job by 2:00, you are probably wise to submit nothing and request more time. You can try to explain inaccurate figures, incomplete data, inadequate research, and sloppy writing by stating, "But there wasn't time . . . and you wanted it by 2:00!" But no one will hear you. Instead, they will remember your inaccurate figures, incomplete data, inadequate research, and poor writing.

If you can't communicate at your best level, you're wiser not to communicate at all!

MEMO

To: Students

From: The Authors

Subject: Revising for Effective Writing

Very few writers are able to sit down at a typewriter and hammer out a perfect piece of writing. Ernest Hemingway revised and rewrote some sentences in his novels as many as fifty times! Thus you shouldn't be angry or embarrassed if your own writing isn't perfect the first time through. Instead, take the time to read and analyze your writing carefully and to edit and re-edit as necessary until you're convinced it is the best job you can do.

Decision

Here is the report that Becky Trujillo edited and rewrote.

Continental Store

```
To:        Jonathan MacIntosh, President, Continental Stores
From:      Tom Franklin, Manager, Furniture and Appliance Department
Date:      February 1, 198-
Subject:   Sales Report, Furniture and Appliance Department,
           Second Quarter, 198-
```

Sales, Furniture and Appliance Department
Second Quarter, 198-

	Second Quarter 198-	First Quarter 198-	Percentage Change
Furniture	$960,000	$650,000	+48%
Small Appliances*	160,000	140,000	+14%
Large Appliances			
Category A	335,000	210,000	+60%
Category B	295,000	260,000	+13%
Category C	630,000	560,000	+13%

* See attached listing of sales for individual items.

Please note that although sales for the second quarter for this department
were significantly higher than sales in the previous quarter, the personnel
in this department were increased by only two full-time employees.

CHAPTER REVIEW

Exercises

1. Rewrite the following sentences. Attempt to improve clarity, conciseness, and unity.
   a. It is important for executives in all fields of endeavor, regardless of what their past habits have been, to be adept at analysis and decision making.
   b. Please send us information on your rust-resistant paint, in the colors of white and black with special emphasis on price for twelve-gallon lots, in one-gallon containers, for our use on the various equipment which we have that requires paint of this type, such as tractors and snowplows.
   c. We have forty-eight available for immediate shipment to you of our Number #24 lamp bases.
   d. Please send samples to Mr. Bosch, Mr. Green, Ms. Kelly and in addition, if it is possible, you might want to send me the set of samples also.
   e. The forty-four cartons which you wanted will be shipped to you, and in addition, forty will go to Farmers Corporation, and finally, we will also ship, as per request, 50 cartons to Konig Company.

2. Choose a feature article from a newspaper or magazine and indicate how you would edit it for logic in thought, organization, and proportion. Staple the article on the left side of an $8\frac{1}{2} \times 11$ sheet of paper and note your comments on the right.

3. Do the same exercise as Exercise 2 above; however, this time, title the assignment, "Editing for Conciseness," and rewrite it, striving for improved clarity and conciseness.

4. Obtain a business letter (individually typed or mass produced). Comment on the format of the item, noting especially balance, attractiveness, type styles, use of wide margin, color, appropriateness, etc.

5. Edit the following items for logic, clarity, and conciseness.
   a. Although Mr. Ling frequently called on a variety of assistants to assist him in his many functions (some of which we were not aware), the help provided by the assistants was not always satisfactory and he often had to do the job or jobs (as the case may be) over again.
   b. In 1980 we were able to almost double the sales we had compared to the previous year. That is, we went from 2150 units to 4100 units which is just about what happened in 1977 and 1978 in Kansas when we also installed an M−20 Cutter there as we did here. Interestingly enough, when we installed the M−20 Cutter here, our production personnel dropped from 680 to 510. In Kansas, the production personnel dropped 180 people in one year from 850.
   c. We were able to secure the 10 Keystone Carriers which we had ordered originally on Invoice 650 in just 10 days after our request which was quite unusual for in the past when we ordered Keystone Carriers (and other items also) we not infrequently had to wait for up to 30 days
   d. If you find that it is in your best interest, as well as that of your company, your suppliers, employees, customers, government agencies, and other publics with whom you are in contact, then you should maintain sales hours on Saturdays.
   e. This is to report on sales activities for April in the usual areas of personnel, sales volume, sales advertising. In addition I want to comment on sales training which I have not covered in previous reports this year.
   And as a matter of fact, I want to begin with that area: training. As you may recall, all Sales Personnel, Class I, attended the Carpenter Sales Program from January through March (10 sessions) at a cost of $10,000. This involved 12 personnel.
   Now, comparing, our sales volume in April with the previous month we grossed

$950,500 in April as compared to $890,000. Of course, as the weather gets warmer, our sales increase. This figure of $890,000 was accounted for by A21 at $150,000, A22 at $210,000, A23 at $315,000, B60 at $100,000 and B70 at $115,000. The $950,000 sales volume for April broke down to A21 at $170,000, A22 at $210,000, A23 at $310,000, B60 at $115,000, and B70 at $145,000. Also on training, you will recall that our Class II Sales Personnel (6 people) took the Sales Management Program of Carpenter (at a cost of $8500) from January through February (8 sessions).

In the area of personnel we had a total of 12 Class I personnel in April as compared to 10 in March and 6 Class II Personnel for both months. Sales support personnel went from 7 in March to 9 in April.

Sales advertising, as usual went over budget. In April we placed $28,000; $14,000; and $4,000 in ads in newspapers, magazines and trade journals. This is slightly up from March when we had a total of $42,000 divided among $26,000 for newspapers, $10,000 for magazines and the balance for trade journals.

Also under training I should mention that I attended the University of Michigan Executive Marketing Manager four-week program. I found it very valuable except for some repetition with the program I took last year at Columbia. This Michigan deal cost $2600 (includes tuition, housing, meals).

6. The following sentences reflect a negative connotation. Rewrite each sentence in a more positive way.
   a. The box is half empty.
   b. Bertha James, a senior at the local college, missed being on the Dean's List only once in her first three years at college.
   c. You will not be sorry when you purchase our new fall shoes and handbags.
   d. You will receive the merchandise without any more delay.

7. Gunning wrote, "Use active—not passive—sentences." Revise the following passive sentences to make your writing more alive.

a. The exciting article was written by Mary Blake.
b. The Best Suggestion Award was given by the company to the recently hired junior accountant, William Flanagan.
c. The important procedures to be followed by the computer operators were discussed by the three managers of computer services.
d. The meeting was chaired by dynamic, entertaining Mina Pastuchiv, the vice-president of Delta Pi Epsilon.

8. Revise the following (where you feel revision is necessary) to insure conciseness and clarity and improve tone.
   a. Now that your car's transmission has been repaired, I do hope you don't continue to have trouble with it.
   b. When I complete my presentation, I don't believe you will feel it was an imposition on your time.
   c. I hope you won't be dissatisfied with the purchase you made from our organization.
   d. Enclosed please find, as per your instructions, your check for $68.50.
   e. Hoping to hear from you, in regard to possible association, we remain . . .
   f. It was unfortunate that your initial order from us arrived three days late, four items short, and an error in billing.
   g. The analysis report on the X100 motor has been completed and we will forward it to you immediately.
   h. Please send me details on your new rust-resistant paint which you advertised in a recent issue of Industrial Plant because of our interest in possibly purchasing your product for possible application to several of our products (railings, gutters, drain guards, and gate posts) in our plant in this state as well as for use in our other twelve facilities in the United States.
   i. We don't feel any difficulties will be encountered if you will follow the suggestions made by our engineers in the application of our product.
   j. I would like to have a job with your firm that will lead to rapid advancement and an impressive salary.

Applications

1. Gene Adams received a letter from a customer complaining that the payment reminder sent to her was unfair as she had sent in her $7 check to cover the exterminator's monthly service in her home. Gene quickly checked the customer's account and saw no record of her payment. He wrote the following letter:

Dear Mrs. Greenwood:

We cannot understand why you are so annoyed. As far as we can see, you did not pay for last month's service. If you wrote the check, then maybe you forgot to mail it. After all, we all make mistakes once in a while.

Obviously, we cannot give you credit for your payment just because you said you mailed it to us. The best thing for you to do is stop payment on the check you claim you sent us, and mail us another one to cover the past due amount.

Yours very truly,

Gene Adams
Customer Service

If mailed, this discourteous letter would surely antagonize Mrs. Greenwood. Rewrite the letter using a more courteous tone and the *you* attitude.

2. Wilbur Taylor, a senior partner in a well-known accounting firm, has been dictating business letters for more years than he wished to remember. He asked Janet Grace, a part-time typist and full-time college student, to type this letter.

My dear Mr. Evans:

At this time, due to the fact that my partner is ailing, I wish to inform you that we cannot meet as previously planned. In the event that George Pierce returns to the office next week, in accordance with our discussion of last month, we will set a new time and date for the meeting.

Kindly remember me to your esteemed colleagues.

Cordially yours,

Wilbur Taylor

Janet Grace had just completed a course in business communications and mentioned to Mr. Taylor that his letter would be improved by substituting modern expressions for the older ones. Janet was given the opportunity to revise the letter and eliminate the hackneyed phrasing. Rewrite the letter for Janet.

3. Jennifer Kane, a unit manager, dictated the following letter for her new secretary to type and mail. Fortunately, Jennifer looked over the typed letter before it was mailed because this is what she discovered:

May 3rd, 198-

Ms. Phyliss Brown
632 S. 63rd St.
Phila., PA 19001

Dear Ms. Phyllis Brown

We have reveiwed your request of June 3 and have made some difinite decisions relating too it.

As you mentioned the cost of service and supervicion would bring the total of the expansion to more then $16500. In veiw of this we has come to the conclusion that we will not at this time able to expand are program.

Please remine me next year at this time so we can reconsider the change once again.

Sincerly yours,

Jennifer Kane

The new secretary had omitted all internal punctuation and had misspelled several words. There was a grammatical error that was not dictated, and the date and inside address also had errors. Rewrite this letter making all the needed corrections.

Readings in Communication

PROCEED WITH CAUTION: COMMUNICATION BARRIERS

C. B. Stiegler, Ed.D.

The very heart of a business is the profitable return on its investment in people, systems, machines, and furnishings. This profitable return is obtained through the efficient and effective sharing of information, which is the very heart of communication.

In today's business environment, complexities of business organizations, the knowledge and paperwork explosions, technological advances, and governmental controls have increased the pressures upon personnel at all levels to effectively use their knowledges and skills to produce quality products and services in less time and at less cost. These same pressures, however, make it difficult for business people to avoid the violations of fundamental concepts for effective communication. As a result, companies are not able to maximize employee potential, and employees are not getting maximum rewards from their work with and through other people in the organization.

Today's professional secretary is an executive assistant who integrates administrative and technical knowledges and skills to accomplish the goals of the organization. To withstand the pressures in today's business environment, the efficient secretary puts forth every effort to develop, refine, and update specialized knowledges and skills. This same effort must also be applied to the development and refinement of communication knowledges and skills—knowledges and skills which serve as a catalyst for the secretary's work with and through other people.

Because of the pressures in the business environment, the time limitation of only 24 hours in a day, and the fact that most of us have been speaking, gesturing, reading, writing, and listening for many years, it is all too easy for the professional person to become lazy in his or her concentration upon the refinement of communication knowledges and skills.

Effective communication techniques are the tools by which one builds good human relations and accomplishes the objectives of the organization. Therefore, it is important that effective professional secretaries be constantly alert to any sloppy habits, poor attitudes, or ineffective techniques that might prevent them from "getting across" to other people.

When you discuss the effective utilization of reading, writing, listening, speaking, and nonverbal skills in the business environment, particularly as utilized by the professional secretary, you could spend many hours discussing do's and don'ts; however, there are some basic concepts which are fundamental to, and which serve as a foundation for, all effective communication techniques. These concepts stress the importance of providing positive reinforcement in every communication situation.

Positive reinforcement involves "putting people at ease" in the communication process. Whether you are speaking with, writing to, or listening to another person or persons, your positive reinforcement *facilitates* open communication (people do not feel threatened), *promotes* responsive listening habits, *reflects* the "you" attitude, *minimizes* business pressures, *facilitates* the flow of information—vertically and horizontally, and *increases* efficiency.

The professional secretary can provide positive reinforcement in day-to-day communication activities by following guidelines such as these:

Participate 100 percent in every communication situation.

Jim Stiene, sales manager of a corrugated carton firm, went to his secretary's desk to explain some procedures for the preparation of a series of reports. Hazel, a very efficient secretary, acknowledged Jim's presence. While Hazel listened to Jim, she stacked a couple of papers on her desk, moved an object, and noticed one or two people moving around the office. When Jim finished his comments, he asked Hazel if she had any questions; Jim was a little uneasy for fear some of the points in his directions had been missed.

Even though Hazel may have heard every word Jim said, her poor listening techniques made him feel uneasy. When you are talking with or listening to another person, it is imperative that you concentrate (with mind and body) 100 percent on what is being said. Your listening techniques not only serve to give you information, but they also serve to reinforce and to give feedback to the person with whom you are communicating.

Because of her inattention, Jim is not sure that Hazel heard everything he said. His question may have put Hazel on the defensive; if she did have a question, it would or could emphasize the fact that she was not listening as carefully as she should have been. In this situation, to put Hazel at ease and at the same time ascertain the effectiveness of her listening techniques, Jim could ask this question: "Hazel, to be sure that I have not omitted any important details, would you mind repeating the instructions." This review makes it possible for Hazel to clarify or obtain any points that she may have misunderstood or missed without any negative connotations.

Always use a positive approach.

Suppose that a person whom you supervise had been sitting there for 15 or 20 minutes frowning at some pages of material. You decide something is wrong; the person probably needs some assistance. You go over and say, "Do you have a problem, Dick?"

The wording of the question to Dick may imply to him that you think he is not capable of handling the situation. That may be true; however, since both you and Dick probably know the "score," it is not necessary for you to reinforce the negative aspects of the situation. The negative approach might cause Dick to be ill at ease, say no, and start working. It takes positive reinforcement to serve as the key to open communication. A statement to the effect that you have the time to be of assistance to Dick is a signal that you are ready to help him if he needs you. There are no unhappy implications; and under these circumstances, he is more likely to say yes and explain the problem.

Make feedback a natural occurrence.

Cheryl Reams was talking with her employer about equal employment opportunities in the company. The employer prefaced the explanatory comments with this sentence: "As you know, we have a firm policy here to promote every qualified woman."

Maybe so; maybe not. But, by putting it that way, the employer has made it difficult for Cheryl to take issue with the statement. Words and phrases such as *naturally, I am sure, as you know, honestly,* or *obviously* are, perhaps unconsciously, a disarming introduction that will cause the listener or reader to be ill at ease in asking questions or disputing statements.

Feedback in a communication situation enables you to determine the effectiveness of your communication efforts. Positive words, statements and questions by you that encourage interaction in the communication process, appropriate pauses in the communication process, and observance of nonverbal facets of communication are techniques which increase your chances of communicating effectively.

Use courtesy as the "cushion" in your communication processes.

To get a report reproduced and circulated, Michael Grimes left this note attached to the report: "Make five copies. Send one to each of the five people listed below."

On most days, this note would not generate any negative reactions; on a hectic day, however, it may carry authoritative overtones. On pressure-piled days, it is all too easy to fall into the trap of giving commands, issuing orders, skipping over the small courtesies that make life pleasanter and easier for everyone.

Beginning notes, memos, verbal requests, etc., with phrases like *when you have time, please, I need some help, would you please* and including *thank you* will get the message across far more effectively and achieve better results.

Praise often — and be specific.

Harold Robbins, an administrative secretary for the railways, received final copy approval on a report which he researched and compiled for his employer, Rogers Gerhardt. Rogers, when he returned the report to Harold for final preparation and circulation, attached this note to the report: "A great job! Prepare six copies. . . ."
Rogers' note to Harold was accepted as a compliment, but Harold felt no real elation.

Rogers did not realize that it is not enough to say to Harold that his work was "great." Praise is a many-faceted communication device. And, statements of praise are qualitatively different one from another.

Statements of praise should be specific. If you use general comments like *great, good, excellent,* etc., you will find that they often have a supportive effect initially but soon ring hollow.

Rogers should have been specific in his comments to Harold about the fine work that he did on the report. He should have taken the time to indicate that Harold's meticulous research efforts and his planning and organization of the report would contribute a great deal of information to the regional managers. Rogers should have stressed the point that this type of work saves the company a great deal of time and money because it serves as a solid foundation for decision making.

If comments concerning performance are negative, a sufficient measure of time should be taken to talk with the appropriate person to provide constructive criticism. The point is that it is all too easy to (1) overlook the need for praise, (2) provide only general or shallow comments, (3) use praise indiscriminately, and (4) overlook the need to develop effective techniques for communicating praise.

Provide objective, impersonal criticism.

A report comes to Janice Blake; it is typed incorrectly. She takes it to the typist and begins with this comment: "Clare, you have several mistakes in this report."

The responsibility for the correctness of the typed report is already known to both Janice and Clare. If copy needs to be checked and/or retyped, the responsibility clearly lies with Clare; however, the point can be made so that Clare is at ease, gets the job done, and gives her support and cooperation willingly. Impersonal and objective feedback shifts criticism from the person to the work — "There are some figures in this report that don't look quite right to me. Would you please check them for typographical errors."

Frequently use personal names in spoken and written communication.

Jean Locklear supervised a receptionist, two typists, and a clerk in a southern firm. Jean frequently disseminated verbal information, asked and answered questions; however, she infrequently used the names of the personnel when she directed and/or interacted with them.

The recognition of a person or persons in the communication process calls them to attention, gives them a feeling of individuality, contributes to their enhancement of self image, and initiates their receptivity to your thoughts and actions.

Identify your purpose for communicating.

Sandy Simpson telephoned the correspondence secretary, Peggy Johnson, to see if Peggy had a few minutes in which to talk to Sandy. Peggy said yes and wondered about the purpose of the meeting. For no particular reason, Peggy felt a little uneasy.

When a person with whom you are going to talk or to whom you are writing knows the purpose of the communication activity, he or she has an opportunity to formulate thoughts pertaining to your purpose. The person feels at ease because he or she is entering a situation which has been identified. Uncertainty is unsettling; most people are uneasy with the possibilities of the unknown.

It is not a simple process to provide positive reinforcement in the day-to-day communication situations. Language barriers, interpersonal barriers, situational-timing barriers, and organizational structure and procedural barriers are factors which hinder effective communication. However, the effective communicator—the professional secretary—realizes that open communication is possible when positive reinforcement is used as the catalyst in the foundation of effective techniques in reading, writing, listening, speaking, and nonverbal skills.

HOW TO IMPROVE YOUR VOCABULARY

Tony Randall

Recently the International Paper Company sponsored a series of advertisements on the "Power of the Printed Word." The advertisements emphasized the need for all of us to "read better, write better, and communicate better." As part of its series, International Paper asked Tony Randall—who is on the American Heritage Dictionary Usage Panel and loves words almost as much as acting—to tell how he has acquired his enormous vocabulary.

Words can make us laugh, cry, go to war, fall in love.

Rudyard Kipling called words the most powerful drug of mankind. If they are, I'm a hopeless addict—and I hope to get you hooked, too!

Whether you're still in school or you head up a corporation, the better command you have of words, the better chance you have of saying exactly what you mean, of understanding what others mean—and of getting what you want in the world.

English is the richest language—with the

largest vocabulary on earth. Over 1,000,000 words!

You can express shades of meaning that aren't even *possible* in other languages. (For example, you can differentiate between "sky" and "heaven." The French, Italians and Spanish cannot.)

Yet, the average adult has a vocabulary of only 30,000 to 60,000 words. Imagine what we're missing!

Here are five pointers that help me learn — and remember — whole *families* of words at a time.

They may not *look* easy — and won't be at first. But if you stick with them you'll find they *work!*

What's the first thing to do when you see a word you don't know?

1. Try to guess the meaning of the word from the way it's used.

You can often get at least *part* of a word's meaning — just from how it's used in a sentence.

That's why it's so important to read as much as you can — different *kinds* of things: magazines, books, newspapers you don't normally read. The more you *expose* yourself to new words, the more words you'll pick up *just by seeing how they're used.*

For instance, say you run across the word "manacle":

The manacles had been on John's wrists for 30 years. Only one person had a key — his wife.

You have a good *idea* of what "manacles" are — just from the context of the sentence.

But let's find out *exactly* what the word means and where it comes from. The only way to do this, and to build an extensive vocabulary *fast,* is to go to the dictionary. (How lucky, you *can* — Shakespeare *couldn't.* There *wasn't* an English dictionary in his day!)

So you go to the dictionary. (NOTE: Don't let dictionary abbreviations put you off. The front tells you what they mean, and even has a guide to pronunciation.)

2. Look it up.

Here's the definition for "manacle" in *The American Heritage Dictionary of the English Language.*

man-a-cle (mǎn′ i kl) *n.* Usually plural.
1. A device for confining the hands, usually consisting of two metal rings that are fastened about the wrists and joined by a metal chain; a handcuff. **2.** Anything that confines or restrains. — *tr. v.* **manacled, -cling, -cles.**
1. To restrain with manacles. **2.** To confine or restrain as if with manacles; shackle; fetter. [Middle English *manicle,* from Old French, from Latin *manicula,* little hand, handle, diminutive of *manus,* hand. See **man-²** in Appendix.*]

The first definition fits here: A device for confining the hands, usually consisting of two metal rings that are fastened about the wrists and joined by a metal chain; a handcuff.

Well, that's what you *thought* it meant. But what's the idea *behind* the word? What are its *roots?* To really understand a word, you need to know.

Here's where the detective work — and the *fun* — begins.

3. Dig the meaning out by the roots.

The root is the basic part of the word — its heritage, its origin. (Most of our roots come from Latin and Greek words at least 2,000 years old — which come from even earlier Indo-European tongues!)

Learning the roots: 1) Helps us *remember* words. 2) Gives us a deeper understanding of the words we *already* know. And 3) allows us to pick up whole families of *new* words at a time. That's why learning the root is the *most important part of going to the dictionary.*

Notice the root of "manacle" is *manus* (Latin) meaning "hand."

Well, that makes sense. Now, other words with this root, <u>man</u>, start to make sense, too.

Take manual—something done "by hand" (manual labor) or a "handbook." And manage—to "handle" something (as a manager). When you emancipate someone, you're taking him "from the hands of" someone else.

When you manufacture something, you "make it by hand" (in its original meaning).

And when you finish your first novel, your publisher will see your—originally "handwritten"—manuscript.

Imagine! A whole new world of words opens up—just from one simple root!

The root gives the *basic* clue to the meaning of a word. But there's another important clue that runs a close second—the *prefix*.

4. Get the powerful prefixes under your belt.

A prefix is the part that's sometimes attached to the front of a word. Like—well, *prefix*! There aren't many—less than 100 major prefixes—and you'll learn them in no time at all just by becoming more aware of the meanings of words you already know. Below are a few. (Some of the "How-to" vocabulary-building books will give you the others.)

Now, see how the *prefix* (along with the context) helps you get the meaning of the italicized words:

● "If you're going to be my witness, your story must *corroborate* my story." (The literal meaning of *corroborate* is "strength together.")

● "You told me one thing—now you tell me another. Don't *contradict* yourself." (The literal meaning of *contradict* is "say against.")

● "Oh, that snake's not poisonous. It's a completely *innocuous* little garden snake." (The literal meaning of *innocuous* is "not harmful.")

Now, you've got some new words. What are you going to do with them?

5. Put your new words to work at once.

Use them several times the first day you learn them. Say them out loud! Write them in sentences.

Should you "use" them on *friends?* Careful—you don't want them to think you're a stuffed shirt. (It depends on the situation. You *know* when a word sounds natural—and when it sounds stuffy.)

How about your *enemies?* You have my blessing. Ask one of them if he's read that article on pneumonoultramicroscopicsilicovolcanoconiosis. (You really can find it in the dictionary.) Now, you're one up on him.

So what do you do to improve your vocabulary?

Remember: 1) Try to guess the meaning of the word from the way it's used. 2) Look it up. 3) Dig the meaning out by the roots. 4) Get the powerful prefixes under your belt. 5) Put your new words to work at once.

That's all there is to it—you're off on your treasure hunt.

Now, do you see why I love words so much?

Aristophanes said, "By words, the mind is excited and the spirit elated." It's as true today as it was when he said it in Athens—*2,400 years ago!*

I hope you're now like me—hooked on words forever.

	PREFIX	MEANING	EXAMPLES	
(Lat.)	(Gk.)			(Literal sense)
com, con, co, col, cor	sym, syn, syl	with, very, together	conform sympathy	(form with) (feeling with)
in, im, il, ir	a, an	not, without	innocent amorphous	(not wicked) (without form)
contra, counter	anti, ant	against, opposite	contravene antidote	(come against) (give against)

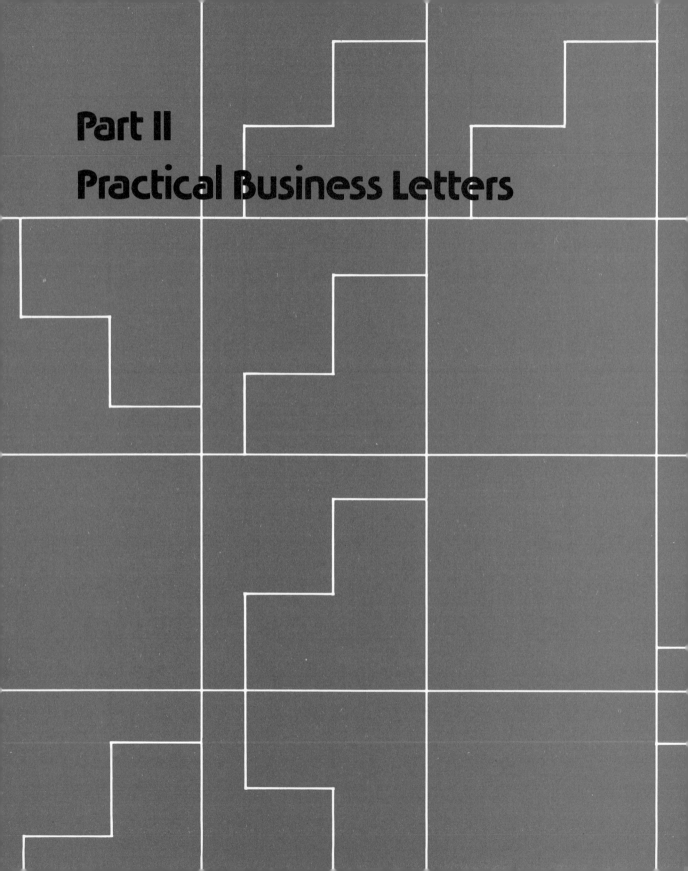

Part II
Practical Business Letters

Dilemma

Robert Hayakawa lives in San Francisco and attends Bay Area Community College. In June, just two months away, he will complete his course of studies and receive his Associate in Arts degree in computer programming.

He is aware that IBM will open a new sales facility in Sacramento, California at about the same time he will finish school. Because he has family in the Sacramento area and thinks highly of IBM, he wants to explore job possibilities with the firm. However, Robert already has an offer to begin work in June as a computer programmer with Barber and Barber in San Francisco.

In any event, he has decided to write an inquiry letter to IBM prior to submitting his resumé. He wants to know if IBM will be hiring personnel for the Sacramento facility, if they will need programmers, whether such assignments will be long term, if travel will be required, whether his very limited experience will be a factor in the firm's decision, and whether IBM is in a position to accept resumés from job applicants. It is now early April; he has committed himself to giving Barber and Barber a definite answer by mid-May.

Decision, see page 94

Letters of Inquiry 5

Here is a list of the objectives you should understand by the time you complete this chapter. Place a check mark in the box beside each as soon as you feel ready to apply your understanding in a practical situation.

☐ The importance of letters in the modern organization

☐ The five Cs of inquiry letters:
    Courtesy
    Clarity
    Completeness
    Conciseness
    Correctness

☐ The basic format to use in writing routine inquiry letters:
    Setting
    Problem
    Urgency
    Confidentiality

☐ The main points to include in a non-routine inquiry letter:
    Purpose
    Specific questions or requests for action
    Due date for reply
    Confidentiality
    Friendly close

☐ The difference between a request and an inquiry

Thousands of organizations—public, private, and government—generate millions of letters each year. Most of these carry the lifeblood of the firms that originate or receive them. The messages assist the organization in accomplishing its objectives: hiring personnel, obtaining raw materials, selling products, collecting funds, making adjustments, generating sales, initiating contracts, answering inquiries, and many other activities that move the organization forward. As can be seen, there is some measure of truth in the statement that "business runs on paper wheels." And many of those wheels are designated business letters.

The accuracy of this statement can be appreciated if you visualize a large insurance firm with headquarters in a major urban center. The company issues life, medical, casualty, fire, auto, disability, and a variety of other types of coverage. Hundreds of company agents are involved; they operate out of dozens of offices in the United States. And the company serves some three million policy owners either as individuals or as members of group plans.

In all of these, there are dozens of different situations involved: inquiries, claims, information, sales, adjustments, credit, collections, goodwill, and on and on. Although some of these areas can be handled by form letters, prewritten letters, and even computer printouts, a very large segment of the situations must be carried through by individually written or dictated business letters.

An organization's letters can tell the public a great deal about the organization itself.

Therefore, to the thousands of individuals who receive letters from this insurance company each day, that letter *becomes* the firm. If the letter is clear, the company is well organized; if the letter is courteous, the firm is concerned; if the letter is reader-oriented, the company is caring. On the other hand, the letter that is curt, hackneyed, confused, or incomplete reflects to the reader similar qualities of the company. The letter, in essence, *is* the organization to the reader.

The Five Cs of Inquiry Letters

Probably the most frequently written letter in an organization is the letter of inquiry. Whether that organization is a large corporation, a small company, a school, a garage, a supermarket, or a baseball team, it has questions, from time to time, which need to be answered.

What do the dots indicate at the end of each unfinished phrase? (See Appendix 1.)

What does the machine cost?
Where does one order . . . ?
How do you get . . . ?
Can you meet with us . . . ?
What colors are available in your . . . ?
Can you send me . . . ?
How did you . . . ?
What are the dimensions of . . . ?
Will you consider speaking?

It is absolutely imperative that inquiries be made clearly and specifically so that precise answers to questions may be received. It is those answers which are vital in making decisions involving the purchase of a million-dollar piece of electronic equipment, or a TV set for the home or employee lounge.

If the individual responding needs to ask you more questions or if he or she does not really answer the questions you asked, the chances are *you* wrote a poor letter of inquiry. In that situation, you not only have the time, effort, and cost of writing another letter—you also do not have the information you need. Audits of company correspondence show this to be one of the primary problems in business communication: incomplete inquiries.

Well-written inquiry letters can make an important contribution to the success of a firm.

One way to make sure that your inquiry letters are effective and get you the information you need is to remember a set of basic letter-writing principles known as the *five Cs:*

Remember the five Cs.

C–1: Courtesy

You are asking for information; certainly the more courteous request will receive the better response. Do not be abrupt and do not demand information. Ask politely. It makes little difference whether the reader will profit from your inquiry or not. For example, you want information on the possible purchase of an air-conditioning system as compared to a request for information on how the receiver handles delinquent accounts of overseas customers. In every case, the letter of inquiry should be tactful and courteous.

C–2: Clarity

If we send an inquiry like this, how can the receiver reply?

If the fan on the #18 Norco Exhaust System is satisfactory, send it out by Service Freight.

"Send *it*"? Send what? The fan or the #18 Norco Exhaust System?

Why is "Send it" enclosed in quotation marks? (See Appendix 1.)

Do you carry the Carper File Cabinets and the Carper #21 End Tables? If so, do they come in Burnt Orange and Slate Gray?

How to answer this? Did the writer want both items in both colors? Or each in *a* color? Or one in the first color and the other in the second color?

At times, the careful rereading of the inquiry against our own checklist will tell us quite accurately how clearly we have written.

C–3: Completeness

Without boring the receiver, provide all the necessary information so your questions can be answered completely. Give the reader enough background so the receiver can tune in to your specific problem. If our inquiry neglects to

note whether the air-conditioning system we need is five tons or ten tons, obviously the respondent can't quote prices, cite brands available, installation dates, or other vital information.

Many companies state that the most common fault in the inquiry letters they receive is that "something important has been omitted and therefore we can't send back an intelligent answer."

C–4: Conciseness

The concise letter requesting information stands the best chance of being answered. The longer the letter you write the more burdensome the answering is going to appear to the receiver. A helpful method for keeping your inquiry concise is to organize carefully, then indent and *list* your series of questions.

C–5: Correctness

Double-check your letter to insure that the data included are correct. Correct answers cannot be given when incorrect information is provided by the inquirer. Much time, effort, and money can be saved by making sure that your question is stated clearly and that any supporting information is properly indicated.

The Routine Inquiries

The routine inquiries involve those situations that are common to the writer and will most likely be very routine to the receiver. Such routine inquiries usually are answered by a descriptive flyer or brochure, a catalogue, or a price list.

Since the routine inquiry letter is written frequently, it is important for you to evolve a routine style and format. This will enable you to prepare such letters rapidly. The following steps may be helpful:

1. *Setting.* Briefly, in one or two sentences, state why you are making the inquiry. For routine situations that is all the space or history that is needed. Remember, the problem is probably common to the receiver, and it is not necessary to provide a detailed, historical analysis.

2. *Problem.* Clearly and precisely state the problem that needs answering. The clearer your statement of the problem, the better your chances are of obtaining an accurate answer. Sometimes it is necessary and helpful to outline the problem and/or list the data you need.

Remember these keys to effective routine inquiries.

3. *Urgency.* You are making a request and cannot expect an immediate turnaround. However, if you provide the receiver with a time constraint, "please reply by January 15," the respondent will usually comply.

**Figure 5–1
Routine Inquiry
Letter**

ARCHITECTS

424 Cadiz Drive
Phoenix, Arizona   80551

May 4, 198-

Conover Specialty Fabricators
1420 West Canfield Avenue
Conover, Iowa 52031

Dear Sir or Madam:

We have just completed the ordering of new furniture for the
Vacationland Motel which we are constructing in Miami, Florida.

Each of the 225 guest rooms will have a wall unit that is designed to
serve as a combination dresser-desk unit. The top right side has an
enclosure into which the color TV sets will be placed (see drawing and
dimensions attached).

Does your firm manufacture a base on which the sets can be mounted
that: 1) swivels approximately 30 degrees left and right from center,
and 2) is equipped with a locking device that can be fixed to the
dresser-desk top?

Because we wish to make a decision regarding purchase within 15 days,
we need your reply concerning the above, plus prices, prior to May 20.

Thank you very much.

Sincerely yours,

Shelley Wilkey
Purchasing Manager

Encl.: 2

4. *Confidentiality*. Although few routine inquiries ask for confidential information, state your willingness to observe privacy if the situation warrants it.

The nature of your letter is most dependent upon the setting in which it is written and your knowledge of the receiver. Therefore, quickly assess the situation. Sometimes you may be writing to a *title* and not a person you know; that is, "Personnel Director, Forum Electrical Corporation" versus your acquaintance, "Janet Jackson, Personnel Director, Forum Electrical Corporation." Your familiarity with the receiver will influence the nature of the questions you ask and the amount of background information you must include. If you are writing Ms. Jackson, who you know is familiar with your problem, there is probably no need for background history. If you are writing an unknown personnel director, you will probably need to establish the history in more detail.

What is the difference between *personal* and *personnel*? (See Appendix 1.)

Figure 5–1 shows an example of an effective routine inquiry. Notice how this letter carries out each of the five basic steps for writing routine inquiry letters.

Using forms for routine inquiries can cut costs.

In some organizations there are routine kinds of information needed on an ongoing basis. For example, many small independent merchants who cannot stock complete lines of their suppliers' products will keep on file the suppliers' catalogues. In order to keep these reference guides up to date, such merchants will often develop a standard form letter requesting the latest catalogue or change sheet. Figure 5–2 shows an example of a form letter used for such routine requests and inquiries.

Non-Routine Inquiries and Requests

Whereas the routine inquiry letter is frequently used, the non-routine inquiry letter is not. The kind of problem addressed in the non-routine letter is unusual. It is unusual to the writer and most likely also to the receiver. The "unusualness" makes the non-routine inquiry letter different.

First of all, you obviously will not have a duplicated form for the non-routine letter and you probably will not have a clear form established in your mind. Each situation and each letter is so different that a form approach would be impossible. However, just because the non-routine letter is unique does not mean that the basic steps for letters of inquiry and the five Cs are not applicable.

The five Cs are as important to non-routine inquiries as to routine inquiries.

In actuality, the basic steps and the five Cs come into full play in the non-routine letter. Because your request is unusual, it will be necessary for you to provide more background or history. You may have to justify the need for the information. Also, one factor that may make the letter unusual is the need for confidential information. The point is, all of the steps noted earlier play a vital role in the non-routine letter. The writer needs to carefully implement the five Cs in this letter.

It is very likely that the request you make will never be made by another individual. It will probably take the receiver some extra time and effort to re-

ARCHITECTS
424 Cadiz Drive
Phoenix, Arizona 80551

February 2, 198-

Herman Household Fixtures
2100 East Lansing Street
Lansing, Michigan 43611

Dear Sir or Madam:

Because this division of Haskel and Haskel Architects selects all
lighting fixtures for the commercial buildings we design, may we have
a copy of your (Spring 198- catalogue) and (current price list).

Thank you very much.

Sincerely yours,

Shelley Wilkey

Shelley Wilkey
Purchasing Manager

Figure 5–2
Form Letter for Routine
Inquiries and Requests

Figure 5-3
Non-Routine
Inquiry Letter

Gallery West Imports

1411 W. Olympic Avenue
Hollywood, California 90071

June 1, 198-

Mr. Sam Tumkosit
Sales Manager
Thaisilk International
439 Baugh Lane
Poplar Bluff, Mo. 63901

Dear Mr. Tumkosit:

You may recall our meeting at the May Giftware Conference in Chicago and our brief discussion of sales with Latin American firms. Because we have been thinking of moving into that market, I was pleased to learn of your experience. I now would like to take advantage of your offer of assistance based on your Latin American sales in the last few years.

1. What percentage of your sales dollar can be allocated to paper work?

2. How do you handle returned merchandise?

3. Do your sales personnel call on accounts or do you use sales representatives?

4. What percentage of your accounts become delinquent and what dollar volume does that represent?

5. How cooperative are Latin American nations in working with your firm?

6. Is the percentage of merchandise lost in shipping higher or lower than in national shipping? If so, how much?

I realize that these questions are broad, but if you can answer them from your point of view, and add related information, I would be appreciative. Because we are now planning policies for our next fiscal year, your reply by June 15 would be most desirable. Of course, any information which you cite as confidential will be retained as such.

Thank you very much.

Sincerely,

Alice Mark Minton

Alice Mark Minton
Vice President, Sales

AMM/gm

Figure 5–4
Non-Routine
Inquiry Letter

Printing Company
20 Big Roack Road
Fairfield, Iowa   52556

February 13, 198-

Mr. Raymond C. Andrews
Owner
R.C.A. Printing, Inc.
Newton, Iowa 50208

Dear Mr. Andrews:

About two years ago you held a unique open house for members of your
community. As I recall, during your town's annual Downtown Summer
Festival and Fair, it was possible for townspeople to visit your print
shop and to learn about printing generally and your various services
specifically.

Our community is going to have a summer festival and I am considering
holding an open house similar to the fine one you provided for the
people of Newton. Your thoughts on the open house will be most
helpful to me.

Could you please provide me with the following information:

1. What kinds of materials did you distribute to the people who
    came to see your operation? Would you please enclose some
    examples?

2. What kind of turnover did you have? Did adults come
    primarily to see your facilities? Did children come--are
    there any special problems in permitting children to see your
    operation?

3. What changes would you make if you were to sponsor a similar
    open house in the future?

4. Did you feel that you performed a worthwhile public service
    in sponsoring the open house? Did you secure any new
    business that can be related to the open house?

The planning committee for our community's festival needs to know by
April 15 if I will sponsor an open house at our plant. Therefore, if
you could send me the requested material and information by April 1,
it will be most helpful. Of course, any material or information you
prefer to be held in confidence will be. Also, if it is inconvenient
for you to write a response, perhaps you could call me collect.

Thank you very much for any help you can give us and for your
cooperation.

Sincerely,

Nathan B. Cox, Owner

Figure 5—5
Letter of Request

Kalamazoo Plastics
Industrial Park, No. 10
Kalamazoo, Michigan 49001

February 19, 198-

Mrs. Mary Beth Duncan
Exciting Travel, Inc.
504 Europe Street
Kalamazoo, MI 49003

Dear Mary Beth:

Because you are one of the few successful businesswomen in our
community, Mrs. Allison Jennings (owner, The Drug Store), Mrs. Maria
Boaz (manager, Titan Auto Supply), and I would like you to join us in
a presentation. Professor Olga Mayor of the business department at
Central Community College is teaching a special seminar on Women in
Business this semester. The twenty students in the class are reading
much of the current literature, but Professor Mayor would like the
students to be able to ask businesswomen some direct questions.

Allison, Maria, and I think the opportunity to interact with the
students will be challenging personally and also beneficial for the
students. The format for the seminar is not formal. Professor Mayor
thought it would be good if we could each:

1. briefly explain our businesses and our duties (in five minutes
    or less);

2. note two or three of the advantages and disadvantages facing
    us in business today;

3. respond to the questions from the students.

The seminar meets every Tuesday and Thursday from 1:30 p.m. to 3:30
p.m. in the Atworth Building, Room 117. It would be convenient for
Allison, Maria, and me to meet with the students on March 7, 9, or 14.

Could you join us? Which date is most convenient for you? Could you
please let me know by February 26 if you will be able to join us?

I sincerely hope you can participate with us; if you have any
questions or concerns, please call me immediately at 459-7374.

Cordially,

Barbara C. Henry

Barbara C. Henry
President

P.S.   Allison just phoned me and thought it would be nice if we could
       have lunch prior to the seminar with Professor Mayor, who is
       available on each of the three days. So, we all hope that you
       can participate in the seminar and also join us at 11:45 A.M.
       for lunch at the Radclif, 1700 W. Elm. The lunch will provide
       us an opportunity to check notes and to get to know Professor
       Mayor.

spond to your request. Therefore, attempt to make your request as simple and as easy as possible to respond to. The points included in most non-routine inquiries are basically the same as for the routine inquiry:

1. Purpose of the inquiry;
2. Specific list of questions or specific request for action;
3. Due date for reply;
4. Assurance of confidence, if applicable;
5. Friendly close.

Before you sign that letter, ask yourself if it contains all the points listed above which are necessary (assurance of confidence may not be found in every letter of this type). Then review it to make sure that it reflects the qualities of the five Cs. Figures 5–3 and 5–4 show examples of non-routine inquiry letters.

A specific kind of non-routine inquiry letter is the letter of request. Such a letter asks the receiver to take some kind of action beyond just answering. Such requests might include: writing your state representative to explain why you are not in favor of the increased workmen's compensation tax, and requesting that he or she vote *no* when the bill is brought before the legislative body; asking a prominent businessman to talk to your monthly management luncheon meeting on June 15 concerning your firm's successful program for reducing absenteeism; or requesting that a female executive join several other businesswomen in presenting a round-table discussion to female business students at the community college on February 17.

A request demands more than just a response from the reader.

These requests call for more than a return letter. They ask the receiver to take some overt action. Therefore, these letters often need to provide a strong justification for taking the desired action. Often it is not enough to just ask "Can you give a presentation?" or "Can you serve?" It will be necessary for you to explain the benefits involved. Figure 5–5 is an example of a letter of request.

What is the difference in meaning between *overt* and *covert*? (See Appendix 1.)

MEMO

To: Students
From: The authors
Subject: Inquiry letters

In organizations today, the old saying that "time is money" increasingly holds true. Inquiry letters which don't get the results you need are a waste of both time *and* money. Your ability to write inquiry letters that will get the job done effectively and efficiently will make you an asset to your organization.

Decision

Here is the letter of inquiry Robert Hayakawa wrote to IBM seeking information on possible job placement.

1421 Cable Car Street
San Francisco, California 94113
April 2, 198-

Mr. Robert Kelly, Director
Personnel Department, Western Region
International Business Machine Corp.
1518 Wilshire Boulevard
Los Angeles, California 90009

Dear Mr. Kelly:

It is my understanding that IBM will open its new Sacramento, California, facility in June of this year.

Because I will be finishing my course of studies in Computer Programming at Bay Area Community College at the same time, I am interested in discussing job possibilities.

I would like to submit a formal resume to you if your firm will be hiring programmers for your Sacramento facility. I would also appreciate learning from you:
1. If assignments will be relatively long term;
2. If travel will be required; and
3. If my limited job experience will prove to be a major factor in my application.

Like everyone in this field, I am tremendously impressed with IBM and would like to make a contribution to the firm's progress.

Because of other possible commitments which I have, Mr. Kelly, may I ask for your reply prior to May 15.

Cordially yours,

Robert Hayakawa

Robert Hayakawa

CHAPTER REVIEW

Questions

1. With regard to inquiry letters (routine and non-routine), indicate very briefly the importance of:
   a. Courtesy;
   b. Clarity;
   c. Completeness;
   d. Conciseness; and
   e. Correctness.

2. Why is it economical for some firms to prepare *form* letters of routine inquiry?

3. From the point of view of the reply, how do the routine and non-routine letters of inquiry differ?

4. Why is it almost vital to include a due date for reply in non-routine letters of inquiry?

5. Is it always necessary to have an assurance of confidence in every non-routine letter of inquiry? Explain.

6. Is it important to emphasize the *you* attitude in the following letters of inquiry? Explain your answer!
   a. You ask another college's newspaper editor to suggest helpful procedures to you, the newly appointed editor of your school's paper.
   b. You send out an inquiry letter to a customer who had sent a check for six men's dress shirts but did not specify the sleeve length.

7. When writing a letter of inquiry, why is it good to number and list your questions rather than present them in paragraph form?

8. When writing a letter of inquiry, it is good practice to make it easy for the reader to comply with any request or answer any questions you may ask. List at least five ways you can make it easier for the recipient to do what you ask.

Exercises

1. Choose an industry that has career possibilities for you when you graduate from college. Think about writing to five companies or institutions that may have opportunities in your chosen career, inquiring about the many facets of a job in the career path. Write an outline for a letter of inquiry that you would want to mail to these five organizations.

2. Refer to Exercise 1. After writing the outline for the letter of inquiry, select five names and addresses of companies or institutions that you can ask for information on your chosen career. Write a rough draft of the letter of inquiry, which will include five questions that you wish the recipient to answer about the organization.

3. Refer to Exercises 1 and 2. If you were to follow through and mail the letter of inquiry assigned in these questions, you would want to further check the effectiveness of your letter. You should do this by exchanging it with another classmate's letter. In class, the peer editing can be done singly or in teams at your instructor's request and with your instructor's guidance.

4. Select one of these five organizations with which you are most familiar:
   a. a savings and loan bank;
   b. a tool manufacturing company;
   c. a life insurance company;
   d. a small accounting firm; or
   e. a women's boutique.

   Suggest the types of routine inquiry letters sent out by the business you selected and specify in each case whether a form letter or individually written letter would be more effective.

Applications

1. Write a letter of request to satisfy any one of the following situations:

   a. You had to miss the local Chamber of Commerce special meeting on Safety Regulations for the Small Business. Reading the local Chamber's monthly newsletter you discover that Mr. Rex Norton of the State's Safety Commission gave a speech that evidently contained much information that would be helpful to you and your firm, Jack's Cafe. Write Mr. Norton requesting that he send you a copy of his speech.

   b. You will complete the two-year program at Bellville Community College this coming June. Ask for information from Ohio State University and Illinois Institute of Technology regarding their electrical engineering programs. The former school is a public state institution; the latter a private university.

2. The following inquiry letters are both so broad and general that neither would serve a useful purpose for the writer. Revise one or both.

Mrs. Roberta Gomez
Quick Stop Printing
121 South Lake Street
Chicago, Illinois 60025

Dear Ms. Gomez:

My brother-in-law, who lives in Chicago, tells me that you do a good deal of printing for his business and that apparently your operation is successful.

I am interested in securing a Quick Stop Printing franchise for myself here in San Diego, much like the one you have in Chicago.

Because you have had yours for three years, according to my brother-in-law, I would appreciate receiving information from you before I make an investment.

Please let me know the advantages and disadvantages of owning a Quick Stop Printing franchise based on your experience.

Thank you very much.

Sincerely yours,

George Watson

Mr. John Karr, President
Columbus Lions Club
c/o First National Bank of Columbus
600 Jefferson Street
Columbus, Ohio 43215

Dear Mr. Karr:

One of the members of the Studio City Lions Club was recently in Columbus on a Sunday when your organization sponsored a brunch for three different community centers.

It was his feeling that all three were very successful and resulted in a very handsome financial return for your organization.

We would like to do the same thing and derive a profit for use in our various charitable endeavors.

Will you kindly send me all the details on your brunch so we may profit from your efforts.

Thank you for any help you can give us.

Sincerely,

Marion Kribbitz
Program Chairperson

---

3. Lisa Garden, a paralegal secretary, was asked to follow through on a new file involving some accident claims by a client. The total money involved in the entire claim was less than $200, and Lisa was impatient as the client had not yet answered two letters of inquiry asking for some important facts. Lisa wrote this letter to Mr. Gordon, the client.

Dear Mr. Gordon:

On January 3 and again on February 3, we wrote to you asking for the names and addresses of your doctor and your insurance agent. You failed to answer us.

How do you expect us to proceed with your claim if you do not give us this important information? If we do not hear from you by the end of this month, we will have to put your file aside.

Yours truly,

Lisa Garden

This letter lacks tact and empathy. It also discourages future business. Improve this letter by revising it and supplying any details that would make it effective.

Dilemma

George Lincoln and his father operate a relatively small firm that supplies
notebooks and folders to companies, associations, and colleges for
conferences, management development programs, and training sessions.
Almost invariably the orders they receive require printing the title of the
conference, the name of the sponsoring organization, the date, and the
organization's symbol, or logo, on the cover. Printing is also often carried
through on the back cover (usually just the symbol) and on the spines of
the notebooks.

George has sold Columbia Air Conditioning Company between 350–450
notebooks for its Spring and Fall sales conferences each year since 1975.
Columbia has always ordered from George's most expensive line and has
paid promptly. In a word, Columbia is an excellent customer.

Mr. Lewanthal, president of Columbia, just called. He was more than a little
upset because he has just learned of a major printing error on the
notebooks' covers. The word *Air* was omitted and all titles read *Columbia
Conditioning Company.* In addition, the error was discovered *after* three
secretaries spent almost an entire day inserting all the printed material
into the notebooks!

George assured Mr. Lewanthal that his request for immediate replacement
of all notebooks would be taken care of. He further promised Mr.
Lewanthal that the corrected notebooks would be delivered within forty-
eight hours and a complete adjustment would be outlined in a letter.

As an adjustment, George and his father will replace all notebooks without
charge and compensate Columbia for an estimated sum based on sixteen
hours of work for each of the three secretaries. Now George must write
the letter to Columbia outlining this adjustment.

Decision, see page 120

Letters That Say Yes

6

Here is a list of the objectives you should understand by the time you complete this chapter. Place a check mark in the box beside each as soon as you feel ready to apply your understanding in a practical situation.

☐ The importance of building sales and goodwill when you write a yes response

☐ The three-step process for assuring your responses are complete:
    Check off points requiring comment
    Make an outline from those points
    Write or dictate from that outline

☐ The use of guide letters to answer routine inquiries

☐ The basic steps in answering non-routine inquiries:
    Acknowledge the inquiry
    Say yes
    Provide information needed
    Make constructive suggestions where possible
    Add a sales appeal
    Close the letter in a friendly manner

☐ The techniques of responding favorably in various claims situations
    Buyer at fault
    Seller at fault
    Third party at fault
    Fault undetermined

☐ The ways to build goodwill in responding favorably to orders

Because of the multitude of operations in which most organizations are involved, a great many inquiries are received. Within the company, employees may inquire about pension programs, specific employee benefits, purchase plans, transfer and promotion opportunities, etc. From outside the company, a variety of inquiries, orders, requests, and claims arrive daily.

For some of these requests, orders, and claims, your response must be no. Saying no without losing a potential customer can be difficult, and we'll look closely at how it can be done effectively in the next chapter. When a favorable yes reply can be given to such messages, the writer has an excellent opportunity to build sales and goodwill. To respond favorably and not build on the situation is simply not good business. For that reason, as much care should be taken in saying yes as we almost automatically exercise when the reply must be no.

Say yes as carefully as you would say no.

The most important thing to remember about any response is that it must be complete. Certainly if Mr. Bailey of Ekko Electric sends a letter to Vermont Office Supply Company and inquires about Model #14 desks, Style #23 chairs, and Foreman Filing Cabinets, he expects to receive information on all three. If the respondent should somehow forget to include in the reply letter the data on the filing cabinets, Mr. Bailey will probably assume they are not available. He may decide, "If I can't get the cabinets, I won't order the desks or chairs from Vermont either." And a very profitable sale goes to a competitor because the reply letter was incomplete.

It is really quite simple to make sure that your response is complete when you follow three easy steps. First, go through the message and place check marks next to each point that requires a comment in your response. Second, turn those check marks into a topic outline. This can be done in the margin of the letter you are answering, at the bottom of the page, or on a separate sheet of paper. Finally, use that outline as a guide to write or dictate your response. Notice how this simple three-step process is used in Figure 6–1(a–c). It goes without saying that carefully rereading the final copy is still another way to make sure that you have covered all bases.

Remember these three steps for complete responses.

Responses to Routine Inquiries

Responses to routine inquiries usually can be handled by a flyer, a price list, or a form letter.

Most routine inquiries can be handled in one of two ways: 1) those which can be answered by a price list, bulletin, pamphlet, brochure, or computer printout; and 2) those which can be answered with a form letter or a *guide letter* individually typed or prepared on an automatic typewriter. These guide letters can then be personalized by inserting the name, inside address, and salutation using the inquirer's name and address. These are replies to routine inquiries. The inquiry should be handled as carefully as an order, for each has the *potential* for generating sales—in one way or another—in the future. Note the difference in Figures 6–2a and 6–2b. They both say yes but the tone of the two is very different. And interestingly enough, because they are both form letters, the cost of 6–2a is almost equal to 6–2b.

Figure 6–1
Preparing a Response
a. Inquiry Received

STEP #1

EKKO
Electric Company

404 N. Fourth Street
Bellville, California 91602

February 10, 198–

Mr. R. T. Johnson
Vermont Office Supply Co.
114 N. Vermont Avenue
San Diego, California 80061

Dear Mr. Johnson:

As you may recall, we purchased a quantity of Vermont desk lamps #441
earlier this year which proved very satisfactory.

I have just examined your fall catalog for this year and I have
questions on several items.

1. Is it possible to obtain your Model #14 desk with four drawers
   on both the right and left sides instead of three? If so,
   what would the total charge be for each desk if we purchase
   twelve?

2. Your Style #23 chairs come in a choice of three colors: blue,
   black, or brown. Is it possible to obtain twelve of these
   chairs upholstered in orange? (See color swatch enclosed.)

3. Can your Foreman Filing Cabinet be made with locks (quantity:
   24)? If so, what would the cost be for each?

Because we have expanded our office area, we will require additional
equipment as soon as possible. For that reason, your reply is needed
prior to March 3.

Sincerely yours,

EKKO ELECTRIC CO.

P. T. Bailey

P. T. Bailey
Office Manager

Figure 6-1
Preparing a Response
b. Outline of Response

STEP #2

```
Outline For Ekko Electric Letter

    1.  Acknowledge inquiry of February 10, 198-

    2.  Comment and thank for past business

    3.  OK on desk Model #14--4 drawers OK; $185 each; 4 weeks
        delivery

    4.  OK on orange upholstery--no extra charge; 3 weeks delivery

    5.  OK on Foreman with locks, $92 each; immediate delivery

    6.  Suggest a.  Central Supply units
                 b.  matching desk sets for #14

    7.  Close (call collect)
```

Figure 6–1
Preparing a Response
c. Letter of Response

VERMONT
OFFICE SUPPLY
COMPANY

114 N. Vermont Avenue
San Diego, California 80061

February 15, 1981

Mr. P. T. Bailey
Office Manager
Ekko Electric Co.
404 N. Fourth Street
Bellville, California 91602

Dear Mr. Bailey:

Thank you for your letter of February 10. It is always a pleasure to hear from customers that we have had the pleasure of serving.

I am happy to tell you we can complete all your requests at highly competitive prices:

1. Yes, we can supply our Model #14 desk with four drawers on each side. Cost in lots of twelve: $185 each. Delivery: four weeks.

2. Our #23 chairs can be made up in orange upholstery. Cost: no extra charge. Delivery: three weeks.

3. Foreman Filing Cabinets are available with locks. Cost: $92 each. Delivery: immediate.

You also may be interested in several of our new Central Supply Units. They match the style of the Model #14 desk, are ideal for storing office supplies, and form a most attractive base for a decorative lamp or plant. In addition, matching desk sets are available for the Model #14 desk: waste basket, pencil holder, letter opener, etc. See enclosed brochures for full description and prices.

You may be sure that we will be delighted to process your order immediately for all the items. Just call me collect, Mr. Bailey, and we will go to work.

Cordially yours,

VERMONT OFFICE SUPPLY CO.

R. T. Johnson

R. T. Johnson
Sales Manager

Encl: Sales Fliers

HOWARD INDUSTRIES, INC.

82 FRONTAGE ROAD   FAIRFIELD, CONNECTICUT   06437

_____

_____
_____
_____

Dear Sir or Madam:

Received your inquiry of recent date.

Enclosed please find our 19____ catalog. Information on your inquiry
may be found on page _____ .

Hoping to hear from you in near future, we remain

Sincerely yours,

Customer Relations

HOWARD INDUSTRIES, INC.

82 FRONTAGE ROAD   FAIRFIELD, CONNECTICUT   06437

_____

_____
_____
_____

Dear _____:

Thank you very much for your recent inquiry concerning our products.

Because most of the items we sell are not only described but also
pictured in our latest catalog, I have enclosed a copy for your
reference. Information on the specific product about which you
inquired may be found on page _____ .

As you know, Bailey's policy of guaranteed satisfaction assures you of
obtaining exactly what you want. This factor, plus low prices, high
quality, and fast service, has permitted us to serve you and thousands
of other customers since 1900.

We have also enclosed our Specials of the Month flyer. Please list
your specific needs on the order blank, plus any of our Specials and
mail it today. All merchandise will be shipped within twenty-four
hours after we receive your request. We look forward to serving you.

Sincerely,

Dola Davis
Customer Relations

Note that in letter 6–2b a strong effort is made to understand the buyer's point of view and to make him feel welcome and appreciated. When compared to the cold, impersonal tone of 6–2a, the contrast is striking. Even when brochures, price lists, or specification sheets are sent, there is always room for a courteous and friendly cover letter. Such a letter literally *covers* the other material. The enclosures provide the requested information and the cover letter is a *plus* that can build goodwill through a response emphasizing the five Cs.

A cover letter literally covers the materials requested and allows the writer to relate additional information in a friendly tone.

Responses to Non-Routine Inquiries and Requests

Although most of the inquiries and requests can be answered by a form, price list, or a pre-prepared letter, there will be others which cannot. Such inquiries must be answered by an individually dictated or written response. For example, special measurements are needed, unusual materials must be obtained, additional data are required, specific billing information must be conveyed, or other out-of-the-ordinary conditions must be communicated. All these situations require a personally written letter which not only says "yes, we can do it" but also adds vital information.

In all such situations, it is beneficial to follow this method of response:

Remember these key features in your responses to non-routine inquiries.

1. acknowledge the inquiry;
2. say yes or make the grant;
3. provide the information requested or refer the reader to a source where it may be obtained;
4. if appropriate, add a constructive suggestion;
5. include a sales appeal for a product or service, and build goodwill; and
6. close with a friendly statement.

Note how the organizational plan suggested above is followed in Figures 6–3 and 6–4.

As is obvious, these letters were written to answer specific inquiries and requests. Unlike the routine inquiries, it would be most difficult to prepare form responses for such situations.

Responses to Claims

The entire process of transferring merchandise from seller to receiver is, on the whole, more complex today than ever before. More firms are using sales representatives rather than their own sales personnel, commercial freight forwarders instead of their own trucks, and computers and computing companies rather than the company accountant. The old, relatively simple, buyer-seller relationship is disappearing. More middlemen are involved as well

Figure 6-3
Response to Non-
Routine Inquiry

BAIN & KELLY REAL ESTATE

219 W. 35th Street
New York, New York   10052

October 15, 198-

Mr. Arnold Kaper
421 Custer Avenue
Evanston, IL 60202

Dear Mr. Kaper:

Your interest in the Midvale Building is appreciated. We are happy to
supply the data which you requested in your inquiry of October 10.

The building contains four 3-bedroom apartments. Each of the
apartments has approximately 1400 square feet of living area. The
enclosed floor plan applies roughly to all four units. You will note
the attractive layout, the two full baths, and a separate dining room
area in each apartment.

Each unit is also allotted two parking spaces in the ground-level
garage which is, like the building itself, under full security. You
will find the rents listed on the enclosed data sheet.

You indicated a number of the Kellogg Company executives were to be
transferred here from the firm's Chicago headquarters in March. That
date should coincide almost perfectly with the availability of the
apartments, which will be ready for occupancy in 60 days.

Please call me today so we may make arrangements for you to examine
and tour the Midvale Building. It will be apparent to you, as you
observe the design, heating, cooling, and plumbing systems, the
construction materials used, and the built-in quality, why we have
been Long Island Builder of the Year for the last five years.

Please call me, Mr. Kaper, 201/556-1234 so we may arrange a time for
your visit that is convenient for you.

Sincerely,

Edna Duncan

Edna Duncan, Manager

Encl.

Figure 6–4
Response to Non-
Routine Request

WILSHIRE OFFICE PRODUCTS
388 Marine Drive
Los Angeles, California 90099

14 June 198-

Mr. David Barlin
Chicago Home Products, Inc.
Merchandise Mart
Chicago, IL 60601

Dear Mr. Barlin:

Yes, we can fill your request!

Our Model #415 display cases can be modified to your specifications.
And, as you requested, we can have them ready for delivery to your
various store locations by August 3.

Enclosed is a specification sheet and price list. The former reflects
the changes in Model #415 which you desire. Please check the
specification sheet, initial it, and return immediately. The
quotation sheet enclosed lists the price per display case, plus the
added charges for specific modifications.

As with all our products, the finest stainless steel is used on all
exposed surfaces, natural rubber provides air-tight seals, and the
contemporary styling assures you of high consumer response to products
displayed.

Please call me collect at 213/654-0000 and work will begin on your
order immediately.

Sincerely,

Manuel Ortego

Manuel Ortego
Sales Manager

Encl.: 2

as others, such as union representatives, sales representatives, government regulatory personnel, and special interest groups. All this leads to more communications, more problems, and at times, additional opportunities.

Although claims always have been part of business, the increasing complexity of business has resulted in a growth of the number of problems which arise. For that reason the handling of claims has become a procedure by which both buyer and seller operate in an atmosphere which recognizes that errors do occur and that mistakes can happen occasionally.

Competent managers frequently look upon claims as being helpful, for they point to areas of company activity that need strengthening or revising. It really matters little whether the claim is on the retail or wholesale level. When a number of claims are received involving a specific area, attention is usually needed to that aspect of business.

Responding to a claim should be seen as an opportunity, not a problem.

Because lines of business are different (perishable products such as fruit compared to non-perishables such as furniture), it is often necessary for firms to establish adjustment policies for claims. On the whole, these usually are generous, giving the customer the benefit of the doubt. Obviously future business with and profits from that customer are involved. In those instances in which claims are entered that are not legitimate, they may be granted for goodwill purposes. But sooner or later, adjustments are halted.

Frequently an industry will have an adjustment policy that is widely followed among most companies. Such a consensus makes the handling of claims in that field easier because of the standard policy among *all* firms.

Buyer at Fault

The key to building goodwill in a claim situation is the manner in which an adjustment is handled. If the adjustment is made *or* refused graciously, goodwill usually can be retained. However, if the claimant is questioned at length and badgered, and *then* the adjustment is made, ill will results. In fact, most of us would prefer a refusal of a claim that has been courteously explained than a grant that has been grudgingly and reluctantly made.

The tone of your letter is vital in building goodwill.

The *tone* of the grant is vital if the buyer is not to become irritated and angry:

> *Poor:* Although your firm is obviously at fault, we are making the adjustment.

> *Revised:* We have credited your account under these circumstances.

> *Poor:* Had you read the pamphlet enclosed with the appliance, your claim would not have come up. Nevertheless, we are sending you the check you requested.

Your choice of words will determine the tone of your letter.

Revised: Your check has been forwarded. However, for your
future satisfaction, it is suggested that the pamphlet of directions for all Ace products be read
and followed.

Poor: As you can see, your claim is thoroughly without
merit. However, we have credited . . .

Revised: Your account has been credited; we recognize that
from time to time a situation such as you
described will occur. In the future, however . . .

Figure 6–5 is an excellent example of a letter that is almost sure to lose a
good customer. Compare it with the letter in Figure 6–6 addressed to Ms.
Johnson, a case where the buyer is also at fault.

In letter 6–5, the grant is made *after* the explanation of how the buyer is at
fault. If the grant is made first, the reader has the favorable answer and may
not continue to read. Or if the reader does continue, the impact of the explanation may be lost.

Remember this *organization*
in responding to *buyer at
fault* claims.

Thus, the organization of the letter, *buyer at fault—favorable reply* is:

1. a statement referring to the specific transaction;
2. a tactful explanation of how and why the buyer is at fault. Care must
   be taken to avoid embarrassing the buyer or causing him or her to
   lose face;
3. a gracious grant of claim;
4. a sales appeal if appropriate; and
5. a friendly statement to close.

Following this organizational pattern is important when the buyer is at fault
and the claim is granted. Equally important is the tone in which the grant is
made. If the yes isn't communicated graciously, it probably should not be
communicated at all. This also assumes, however, that the explanation of
how the buyer is at fault is made clearly and tactfully.

Seller at Fault

In situations in which the buyer is at fault, the seller has the options of 1)
granting, 2) refusing, or 3) compromising in the adjustment. However, if the
seller is at fault, these choices do not exist. Ethically, the seller should grant
the claim.

When your company is at
fault, explain *after* the claim
is granted.

This letter is never an easy one to write. How do you explain your error (as
the seller) and still retain the buyer's confidence? After all, the buyer is primarily interested in whether she will receive the $72 adjustment from you and
not in a detailed explanation of how her shipment was misdirected. If the error is not explained, she may feel that the seller often confuses orders. If

DONOVAN ELECTRIC
303 TRINITY ROAD
BOSTON, MASSACHUSETTS 02174

Figure 6–5
Poor Example of a
Favorable Response to
a Claim: Buyer at Fault

March 10, 198-

Mr. Edward Kelly, President
MAP Consultants, Inc.
2442 Fifth Avenue
New York, NY 10025

Dear Mr. Kelly:

We received the carton containing the six #402 desk lamps which we
shipped to your firm over 90 days ago. In your cover letter you
suggested we make an adjustment and credit your account.

It is true, they are not the color you requested, but it is also true
that our policy is that all claims must be entered within 30 days. We
now have six lamps on hand that are last year's model. Furthermore, I
noted that two of the cartons have been opened and the lamps
apparently used.

Nevertheless, you have been a customer of our firm for several years
and the adjustment which you requested ($210.00) has been made. We
have, however, charged your account $18.50 for the original shipping
charges on these desk lamps.

We hope this arrangement will meet with your approval.

Sincerely,

Maureen Kearney

Maureen Kearney
Credit Manager

Figure 6–6
Good Example of a
Favorable Response
to a Claim:
Buyer at Fault

WILSHIRE OFFICE PRODUCTS
388 Marine Drive
Los Angeles, California   90099

July 3, 198–

Ms. Louisa Johnson, President
Johnson Furniture Mart
4502 Clark Street
Tulsa, Oklahoma 50492

Dear Ms. Johnson:

We received your letter of June 27 in which you inquired about
discounts on your invoices issued in March and April of this year.

You are certainly correct. All customers are entitled to a reduction
of 2% when payment is made within 10 days of receipt of merchandise.
However, in the case of the three invoices in question, checks were
received well past the 10-day period.

This policy of payment discount is standard in the furniture industry.
Nevertheless, we are well aware that your organization opened for
business just a few months ago and you must have encountered all the
problems that go with such an activity. For that reason, we have
followed your request and credited your account, in this particular
case, for $51.80.

I have enclosed a flyer describing our July special for preferred
accounts. We are sure you will find this Brite Glos line of lamps an
excellent seller. Please call us collect at 892-3400 and place your
order for these fast-moving items today.

Sincerely yours,

Bob Philips

Bob Philips
Customer Service

Encl.

there is too much explanation, the buyer may not read it at all or become aware suddenly that your system is really faulty.

When the seller is at fault, there is a dilemma. An explanation of how the error occurred is necessary. However, if such an explanation is too detailed, it can compound the situation. If none is made at all, the buyer may simply accept the adjustment and take her business elsewhere.

But mistakes *do* happen. The best answer is to open your message with a frank and direct statement that you have made an error, that the adjustment is being made, and that you will attempt to do a better job in the future.

The following organizational pattern makes sense when the seller is at fault:

Remember this *organization* for *seller at fault* responses to claims.

1. an opening which gets in step with the reader and implies the grant will be made;
2. an explanation if a reasonable one can be made. If the explanation will only emphasize the error, it should be omitted;
3. the grant and an attempt to regain the customer's confidence;
4. a sales appeal (if appropriate); and
5. a friendly close.

Notice how this pattern is followed in Figure 6–7.

At times, the seller may even determine an error has been made before a claim is made. This might happen if the seller discovers that a bad lot of merchandise has been shipped and it is on the road or is already in the buyer's warehouse. Or the seller may hear from some of his buyers, but not all, about an unsatisfactory lot of merchandise. In such cases, or any others, the seller should make adjustments before he receives claims. Such action builds goodwill and improves the firm's reputation.

A good explanation can help build goodwill.

Third Party at Fault or Fault not Determined

In many transactions between buyer and seller, a third party is involved. This may be a broker, a shipper, a distributor, or another. It is not unusual that the loss or damage involved in the claim took place while the merchandise was in the third party's warehouse, on his truck, or in his possession.

In such cases, if the seller receives a claim, a courteous reply should explain the third-party involvement. In some instances the seller may wish to offer assistance in processing the claim. And if the claim comes from a small retail merchant, the seller may even offer to initiate the claim with the third party on behalf of the buyer. Many sellers prefer not to get involved in a claim situation where they have no legal responsibility. However, others feel the goodwill gained makes the situation worthwhile, as in Figure 6–8.

You can build goodwill by helping the buyer even when your company is not at fault.

There are other claim situations which do arise. At times both parties may be at fault, or the responsibility for the fault cannot be determined. Each of these cases must be handled individually, with the primary objectives of retaining the customer and building goodwill.

Figure 6–7
Favorable Response to
a Claim: Seller at Fault

 Karpet Kleen Kompany

646 Woodley Road
Virginia Beach, Virginia   23419

June 15, 198-

Mrs. Ruth Okada
1220 Fairlane Avenue
Virginia Beach, Virginia 23419

Dear Mrs. Okada,

We can appreciate how irritated you must have been when you returned
home to find that our cleaning crew had worked only on your downstairs
carpeting. We were well aware that your request was for <u>all</u> carpeting
to be thoroughly cleaned. However, that request was not made on the
work order which the crew had.

Although the graduation party you held has now come and gone, we hope
you will permit us to schedule a time to correct the error and clean
the carpeting on the second floor of your home. As you know, the
charge for that was to be $54.00. We would like to adjust it down to
$30.00 to cover the cost of labor only.

Please call me at 791-6000 so we may schedule a time to suit your
convenience.

Sincerely,

Al Johnson
Manager

 **Electronics, Inc.**

751 MacLean Avenue
Dallas, Texas 75223

November 22, 198-

Ms. Patricia Fairbanks
Purchasing Manager
Ekko Electric Company
404 N. Fourth Street
Bellville, CA 91602

Dear Ms. Fairbanks:

We were sorry to hear that three of the ZRM TV sets, shipped in our
order #21632, arrived at your firm's warehouse with the cabinets
slightly damaged.

As you recall, our arrangement with your firm is that all merchandise
will be picked up at our distribution center by the carrier with whom
you make a contract. When Taylor Trucking Company received order
#21632 at our center, all items were inspected by their driver.

Enclosed is a copy of Taylor's inspection receipt indicating all items
were in excellent condition.

In the event you do not have copies of Federal Transportation
Commission form #365, I have enclosed several. When completed, these
are to be filed with the carrier--Taylor Trucking Company--and the
Commission.

If we can assist you in any other way in processing your claim with
Taylor Trucking, please call us at 403/221-8793.

Sincerely,

Lamar Jefferson

Lamar Jefferson
Shipping Director

Figure 6–8
Response to a Claim:
Third Party at Fault

Responses to Orders

Thousands of orders are processed each day. In many cases an acknowledgement form or letter is not used; the order is received on Tuesday and shipped on Thursday. If the order cannot be filled completely, the missing items are shipped a few days later.

This holds true for most routine orders. However, when special merchandise is requested, or when items have to be manufactured to precise specifications for a special situation, or when the order or service involves a large sum of money, most firms feel an acknowledgement of the order is wise.

If, for example, a firm orders a Kellogg Double-Run Cutter, model #300 for $12,850, the manufacturer is wise to acknowledge that order. If the buyer receives an acknowledgement for a Kellogg Single-Run Cutter, model #200, also at $12,850, he can call or wire the correction. In this way, both buyer and seller save time and money and avoid problems. Most such acknowledgements are handled by sending a duplicate of the order or the invoice to the buyer immediately after the order is received and prior to its processing. In many instances, a copy of the computer printout serves the necessary purpose. In other situations, a form or guide letter or even a post card completes the communication loop. All these carry essentially the same message:

Why is this quotation indented? (See Appendix 1.)

Thanks for your order of September _____. It is being processed and will be shipped October _____ via Fast Freight Forwarders.

You can build goodwill through your acknowledgements of orders from both new and steady customers.

However, there are a few instances where an individual letter should be used to acknowledge an order that is being filled. When a customer places an order with a firm for the first time, the customer may be told the company has been happy to add his or her name to the list. This also gives the firm opportunity to state very clearly the terms of sale, payment requirements, what the adjustment policy is, and other vital factors that may well serve to avoid future problems.

This type of letter can be prepared in advance and the names filled in. Very often a form acknowledgement (a duplicate of the invoice) can be sent with the letter. Figure 6–9 shows an example of a good response to a first-time order.

In addition to sending a letter of acknowledgement in a situation such as the above, it is also wise to send a letter to steady customers from time to time. The purpose, of course, is to simply say, "We appreciate your on-going business and want to take a minute to say, thank you." Figure 6–10 is an example of a response to an order from a steady customer. It is an example of one that doesn't have to be written . . . but is. This type of letter will often build goodwill and enhance customer relations.

Thus, in the many situations which arise where we can respond favorably, we should not only say yes but also seize the opportunity to build goodwill

HILOUGH DRUGS

220 Valley Road
Memphis, Tennessee 38131

Figure 6—9
Favorable Response
to an Order:
New Customer

December 6, 198-

Mr. Malcom Nader
President, Nader Drug Store
4545 W. Adams
Evansville, Tennessee 38123

Dear Mr. Nader:

Your order of December 3 is now being processed. We hope this will be
the first of many we will have the pleasure of shipping to you.

This merchandise will be forwarded on December 8 via Fern Freight
Lines under the terms agreed upon.

Your credit line has now been established, and it affords you a 2%
discount when bills are paid within 10 days of receipt of merchandise.
This savings can add a significant amount to your profit margin in a
year's time. You may, however, elect to pay all invoices net within
30 days of delivery.

We are pleased to offer our steady accounts various free services.
One of these is our monthly bulletin, <u>Health Care</u>. If you desire, we
will send you 1000 of these every month free of charge. These may be
distributed to your retail accounts or enclosed with each prescription
you fill. We have found that consumers appreciate receiving these.
In addition, your company's name is imprinted on each copy; that
assists in building goodwill for your firm.

You also will find that our advertising department is available for
counsel and suggestions to assist you.

These are just a few of the services we offer for your use. We hope
this will prove to be a long and satisfactory relationship.

Sincerely,

Elizabeth Petrocelli

Elizabeth Petrocelli
Sales Manager

Figure 6–10
Favorable Response
to an Order:
Steady Customer

**KELLY'S
PRINTS AND PHOTOS**

4183 Stearn Avenue
Salt Lake City, Utah 84139

March 20, 198-

Ms. Donna Gramper, Manager
Hainsville Hardware
820 Davis Street
Hainesville, Utah 84141

Dear Ms. Gramper:

Your order of March 15 is being processed and will be shipped
according to your usual instructions.

We did want to take this opportunity to tell you that your business is
appreciated. As in the past, we will make every effort to supply you
with quality merchandise at very competitive prices.

We appreciate your confidence in Kelly's and you may be sure we will
do everything possible to continue to merit your patronage.

Sincerely,

John Gabriel
Office Manager

and sales. When we respond positively to someone who desires information, an adjustment, or a favor, we also can build customer relations in that same message. In so doing, we also build for the future.

MEMO

To: Students
From: The authors
Subject: Favorable responses

To say yes to an inquiry, a request, a claim, or an order is easy—almost anyone can do it. But to use that opportunity to its best advantage—to help the organization build goodwill and future sales—requires practice and skill. Don't be satisfied with just saying yes.

Decision

Here is the letter outlining the adjustments which George Lincoln wrote to Mr. Lewanthal.

Printing Company
20 Big Roack Road
Fairfield, Iowa   52556

April 25, 198-

Mr. Carl Lewanthal, President
Continental Air Conditioning Company
400 East Lansing Drive
Chicago, Illinois 60026

Dear Mr. Lewanthal:

We "goofed" and we're sorry.

As we promised, the corrected notebooks were delivered to your headquarters office by special messenger service within forty-eight hours of your call. In addition, your account has been credited for $288 to cover the forty-eight hours of secretarial work involved in processing the content of the Spring Conference Notebooks.

We really are not sure how the error in printing your firm's notebooks occurred. However, we are well aware that the problem caused you inconvenience and frustration.

In any event, Mr. Lewanthal, we want you to accept our apologies. We look forward to a continuation of our relationship and your autumn conference notebook request.

Cordially yours,

George Lincoln

George Lincoln
Manager

CHAPTER REVIEW

Questions

1. How can sales be generated when responding to inquiry letters?

2. What three methods may be used for responding to routine inquiries?

3. What has *tone* to do with building goodwill in a favorable response to a claim?

4. With the increase in computer billing, do you feel the potential for an increase in the number of claims has taken place? Explain.

5. What specific organizational pattern should be followed in sending a favorable response to a claim when the seller is at fault? Why is there disagreement on the order?

6. Should a favorable response ever be sent to a buyer when the fault has not been determined to be the buyer's or the seller's? Explain.

7. What is the value of acknowledging an order with a specific listing of all items, prior to the order's shipment?

8. What is the value of acknowledging orders from:
   a. new customers?
   b. steady customers?

9. When writing a letter that is transmitting good news, would it ever be beneficial to give the good news at the end of the letter rather than near the beginning? Explain your answer.

Exercises

1. Select a local company that sends and receives a large quantity of business letters. Interview one of the company's administrators who is very familiar with the firm's correspondence. Inquire about the following:
   a. the method of dictating or transmitting letters to typists;
   b. the company policy on letter format and content for letters giving a favorable response; and
   c. the use of form letters, word processing equipment, and computerized mailings.
   Write your findings in a short report.

2. Most often a form letter, a duplicate of the order form, or a note will be sufficient when you are acknowledging a customer's order. List at least five situations that would call for an individually written letter of acknowledgement rather than a form similar to the one printed on page 105 in this chapter.

3. Refer to Figure 6–5 in this chapter. The message lacks tact and is antagonistic. Study the contents and revise the letter so that it retains goodwill and satisfies the customer.

4. Jacqueline Jupiter bought a dining room table and chairs from a local furniture store. When she complained that the table was slightly scratched, the store sent a furniture repairman to her home to refinish the table's surface. Jacqueline is still not satisfied, even though it is difficult to see anything wrong with the table, and she wants the company to replace the table with a new one. Is she more likely to buy furniture from this company in the future in situation *a* or *b* below. Explain.
   a. the company gives into her claim but very grudgingly and reluctantly.
   b. the company does not give into her claim but very courteously explains why.

Applications

1. The following responses may very well build ill will even though they are favorable. Revise and rewrite any or all of them and submit those requested to your instructor.

Dear Mr. Mesa:

We received your recent request to credit your account for $172.00 on the basis of the return of three sets of Nordic Stainless Steel #130.

If you will check our Wholesale Catalog #51, you will note these items were offered to our dealers on a "Special Clearance; No Return" basis. This was clearly printed in several different places in the catalog.

However, we do recognize that you have been a good customer for over ten years and on that basis, we have approved your request and are mailing you a check for the $172.00.

In the future, please read all sale conditions carefully. We are happy to cooperate in this instance and look forward to our continued association.

Sincerely yours,

Dear Mr. Boon:

I received your letter in which you asked that I address your student organization on "Careers and Opportunities in the Health Care Field."

First, I must commend you on your leadership of this student organization. On the other hand, you must recognize that to a busy physician, two weeks' notice for a talk is hardly adequate. Nevertheless, I have been able to re-arrange my schedule so that I will be with you at 2:00 p.m. on August 3. However, my time is limited and I must insist on getting away no later than 3:30 p.m.

I look forward to being with you and trust that you will have the usual items available, such as a flip chart, microphone, rostrum, etc.

Sincerely,

Dear Ms. Perilli:

We received the two Nordic blouses which you returned with a request for credit to your account.

Unfortunately, <u>both</u> had been completely unwrapped and tried on. Naturally these items cannot be returned to stock without their original packaging. We aren't quite sure what we can do with them. However, we have credited your account for the purchase price ($36.00) of both.

In the future, please follow our adjustment policy which is outlined in the enclosed booklet, a copy of which is sent to each charge customer annually.

Sincerely,

---

2. You are the customer relations manager for a discount linen supply company. You recently received this letter:

January 25, 198-

326 South 13 Street
Philadelphia, PA 19105

Ladies and Gentlemen:

I have recently moved into an old but large house that has three bathrooms and one powder room. After spending much money on updating the plumbing and tilework in these rooms, I am now ready to buy a quantity of towels, washcloths, and bathroom accessories.

Your company has been recommended to me as a favorable one to do business with. Do you think you can be of service to me?

Sincerely yours,

Mrs. Rose Covington

Answer Mrs. Covington's letter supplying any additional information needed to add her to your list of satisfied customers.

3. You work for a wholesale stationery company. Recently an employee in your shipping department sent a gross of old marking pens to a customer. He knew they were old, but he assumed they had not dried up. The customer complained to you as soon as he realized the pens were useless. Knowing that it was your company's fault you are prepared to make a full adjustment, but you are wondering what explanation you should give your customer. Should you mention your employee and the old supplies? Indicate in writing the best way to explain the defective shipment.

4. You are a personnel manager for a wholesale dry goods company. You placed a help wanted ad in Sunday's newspaper for a new college graduate interested in a position as your assistant. Many impressive resumés were sent in, and you are now interested in mailing letters to five applicants asking them to come in for an interview. You would like them to fly to Akron at company expense during the last half of July, and you want them to call you collect to say if they are interested. Write a letter appropriate for all the applicants.

5. Refer to Application 4. Karen Brooks, an applicant for the job of personnel assistant, was the individual chosen to fill the opening. She has returned to her home in Columbus and is awaiting word of her acceptance or rejection. Write a letter to Ms. Brooks offering her the position. You may also wish to remind her of the following items discussed at the interview:
   a. salary is $13,000 per year plus an excellent fringe benefit package; and
   b. starting date is August 25.
   Be careful not to be presumptuous by taking for granted she will definitely accept the offer.

6. This June, Martin Welsh will graduate from the local community college with a two-year degree in drafting. The program interested Martin so much that he has decided to enroll in a four-year college to earn a bachelor's degree in engineering technology. He applied to five nearby universities and was pleased to receive catalogues and letters of interest from all of them. What did not please Martin was that all the letters were form letters and all of them said just about the same thing in the same way. His name and address and the name of his program were the only individually typed items on the letters. Put yourself in Martin's place. Would these form letters annoy you? Do you have any suggestions that would be beneficial to both the institutions and their applicants in this situation? Give your answer orally in the class.

Dilemma

Frank Faxon has been employed by Ekko Electric Company. Frank's firm handles a full line of shop equipment representing a dozen manufacturers: motors, shop tools of all types, lifting, cutting, and welding equipment, hand tools, and so on.

Frank has just received a letter from Barton's Buick Agency. It is signed by James Lee Jones, Service Manager. Mr. Jones indicates that both of the 2-horsepower motors purchased from Ekko "burned out after minimal use because they were obviously faulty to begin with and we therefore want them replaced at no charge or a total credit issued to our account.for $280.00." Interestingly enough, Barton's did not even bother to return the two motors and when Frank called, Mr. Jones said they had discarded the motors because "they were no good anyway."

Frank checks Ekko's files and finds that Barton's Agency *did* purchase two GE 2-horsepower motors almost two months ago. Although Barton's Agency has been a good customer, Frank decides to refuse the claim for several reasons. All of Ekko's catalogues and invoices clearly state that "claims must be entered within 10 days of receipt of merchandise and faulty items returned for inspection." Furthermore, Frank knows that General Electric products are carefully manufactured and will not burn out unless they are misused or used beyond their stated capacity. And, incidentally, Barton has had a disproportionate number of claims as compared to Ekko's other accounts. Ekko has, however, approved all of them in the past.

Frank has decided to write Barton's Buick Agency an adjustment letter in which he refuses to grant this claim. He has determined carefully which reasons he will use to justify his position. He keeps in mind, of course, that Barton's Agency has been a good customer for many years and he wants to continue that relationship.

Decision, see page 137

Letters That Say No

7

Here is a list of the objectives you should understand by the time you complete this chapter. Place a check mark in the box beside each as soon as you feel ready to apply your understanding in a practical situation.

☐ The basic psychology of saying no

☐ The importance of explaining before you refuse

☐ The basic organizational pattern for a no letter:
Introductory acknowledgement
Explanation of situation
Refusal (often implied)
Constructive alternative suggestion
Sales appeal
Friendly close

☐ The kinds of situations in which firms must sometimes say no:
Requests
Claims
Orders

In our personal and business lives, we often are required to say no to others. In most cases, the individual probably feels that the request is reasonable and acceptable. Therefore, when we say no, that reply certainly has the potential for arousing a negative reaction or even antagonism.

When we say no to an individual, we must do so tactfully to avoid arousing ill will.

The response to the refusal will largely be governed by the manner in which we make that refusal. If the rejection is conveyed in a tactless, poorly organized manner, it is almost sure to arouse opposition. On the other hand, if we transmit the message courteously and tactfully, it may be accepted and respected. It is all in how we present the *no*.

The Psychology of Saying No

Let us assume that a college instructor feels it is a good idea to bring his computer programming class to a firm's computer installation for a practical on-site visit. If we visualize *his* point of view, he probably sees himself as a very dedicated teacher who is going far beyond the call of duty in making the appointment, arranging busses, and taking care of the dozen details involved in transporting thirty-five students from the college to the company's offices. He feels his request is reasonable and desirable for all parties concerned.

What is the difference in meaning between *irritate* and *aggravate*? (See Appendix I.)

If our reply should open with a "No; sorry we can't accommodate you," it is easy to understand his irritation and even anger. If, on the other hand, we *explain* the situation, and permit him to conclude that the answer must be no, we may retain his friendship and goodwill.

What is the difference in meaning between *whether* and *weather*? (See Appendix 1.)

The key concept to keep in mind in all refusals, whether they are oral or written, whether they are made to your employee, a customer, your parent, spouse, child, or friend is: Explain *before* you refuse.

In all refusals, oral or written, explain the reason for refusal *before* you refuse.

In almost every situation in which a refusal or unfavorable answer must be given, there is usually a reason. If that reason for refusal is tactfully, sincerely, and courteously presented, most readers or listeners will say, "I can understand; I can appreciate the situation." This does not mean the individual will be happy. All we are trying to do is explain in such a way that we will retain goodwill and *not* arouse antagonism as a result of our no.

Follow this organizational pattern for refusal.

In almost all situations, written or oral, in which a no or unfavorable response is called for, you should remember to follow this organizational pattern:

1. An introductory statement which acknowledges the request or inquiry. If possible, the writer should try to get in step with the reader;
2. An explanation of the situation that makes the refusal necessary;
3. The refusal. This may be implied; in other cases, it should be expressed directly to avoid any possible legal complications;
4. A constructive suggestion or alternate plan;
5. A sales appeal (for a product or goodwill); and
6. A friendly close.

Note how these six steps are carried out in Figures 7–1 and 7–2.

Figure 7–1
Saying No to a
Request

SYSTEMS PLANNING CORPORATION

11394 N.W. 23rd Street
Washington, D.C. 20071

March 29, 198-

Professor Edward Numbers
Department of Mathematics
Gittburg Community College
Gittburg, Maryland 20304

Dear Professor Numbers:

You are correct, Professor Numbers, it would be excellent for your
students to have the chance to spend some time with us. The
experience could add to the students' educational growth.

As you may recall, our facilities are restricted somewhat and I doubt
whether the 35 young men and women really would be able to observe
very much over one another's shoulders. More important, however, is
our contract with the Department of Defense. We now are running data
that are classified. Only those few employees who have received
government security clearance are permitted to carry through
operations. This situation should continue; our government contract
has 24 months to run.

On the other hand, we do have an excellent movie on computer
programming which was filmed here at our facilities. We will be
delighted to have your students view it in your classroom or in our
company auditorium. If you like, I can be present to answer
questions.

Please call me, Professor Numbers, at 348-4800, to let me know how we
can assist you in your educational program.

Sincerely,

Anita Juarez

Anita Juarez
Director of Programming Services

The writer opens with a
friendly acknowledgement of
request.

Here is the explanation for
the refusal.

The refusal is implied.

A suggestion of an
alternative permits the letter
to conclude on a positive
note.

**Figure 7–2
Saying No to a
Request**

**Bakers
Fashions
Inc.**

102 Main Street
Racine, Wisconsin   53467

February 19, 198-

Ms. Greta Church, President
Ladies' Union for a Free America
429 Chapel Road
Racine, Wisconsin 53467

Dear Ms. Church:

Thank you for your recent letter requesting that Bakers again present
a Spring Fashion Show as part of the fund-raising effort of your
group. We certainly commend you and your organization for the
generous community service which all of you contribute.

As you know, we always enjoy working with groups such as yours.
However, in the three years previous to this one, we received so many
worthwhile requests, we encountered a problem. Because we had only
one fashion team and the number of requests increased tremendously, it
became necessary to accept some invitations and not others. Certainly
we were placed in an undesirable position with many of our friends.
You therefore can appreciate why we elected to seek an alternate
method of cooperation in place of the fashion shows.

We have enclosed five Bakers gift certificates, each valued at $20.00.
We do hope you will use these in your fund-raising efforts with our
good wishes.

Bakers is always eager to assist you and our other good friends in
Duluth.

Sincerely,

Katherina Anderson

Katherina Anderson
Public Relations

Encl.

The writer gets in step and
commends the reader.

Here is the explanation for
the refusal.

The refusal is implied; it is
not necessary to refuse
directly.

An attempt is made to build
goodwill through a positive
close.

"If you've come to borrow, Mr. Sanders, I'm afraid you've come to the wrong place."

Another factor that is important, in addition to the organization of a refusal letter, is the promptness of a reply. Of course, *all* letters should be replied to quickly. However, that factor is especially important in an inquiry about a product, a claim, or an order.

When you must say no, reply promptly.

If the reply can be a yes, the situation is satisfactory for both parties. However, if we must say no, we should do so quickly so the individual may make alternate arrangements. If we delay our reply and then send a no, it may be too late for the individual to select a different course of action. Obviously, the receiver has every right to be irritated in such a case. The proper course of action is always to reply promptly, especially in the case of a refusal letter.

These, then, are the principles of refusal. This chapter presents various situations in business and other organizations where the "no" statement must be made.

Refusing Claims

Most companies find that each day's mail brings in a certain number of requests for adjustments. In many cases where the review determines that the fault is not the firm's but is the buyer's, the company will want to refuse. In addition, there are those instances in which refusal must be made because of

When it is necessary to refuse a buyer who is at fault, the same letter organization is followed.

"Reply in the negative with a cleverly worded affirmative answer."

local or national statutes. This might be the case in which medical prescriptions, once received by the buyer, may not be returned to the place of purchase for credit. In many states, undergarments or other personal items may not be returned once they have left the store.

In Figures 7-3 and 7-4, notice how the closing paragraph or paragraphs are positive and make a strong effort to lessen the impact of the refusal. Also, in both cases, the tone is friendly and businesslike. In addition, the explanation of how the buyer is at fault—always made *before* the refusal—is conveyed tactfully.

Refusing Orders

Remember: In all refusal situations, explain *before* you refuse.

At first glance, it may seem impossible to you that there would be orders which must be refused. But that situation does arise from time to time. For example, we cannot fill an order which arrives with incomplete information; at other times, the buyer's credit is not in good standing; or perhaps we are out of stock, or simply do not handle the merchandise requested.

Here are some of the situations which may arise in which an order is received but the sale declined:

APEX
MOTORS

240 Burr Street
Barnesville, Iowa   50011

April 10, 198-

Mr. George Brown, Division Manager
Wilcox Tool and Die Company
Wilcox, Nevada 89900

Dear Mr. Brown:

As you can appreciate, we were very concerned when we received your
recent letter telling us the six #304 Apex Motors which we shipped to
you on March 8 did not prove satisfactory.

Because these are excellent motors, which we have supplied to our
customers for fifteen years, we immediately sent, with your
permission, two of our Quality Control personnel to your plant.

They reviewed the situation with your Mr. Carmen. In every instance,
the equipment called for 20- to 24-horsepower motors. This
requirement was noted on the metal plates attached to your four
Costello Mixers and two Costello Shredders. However, the Apex Motors
which you requested and received from us were all 12-16 horsepower.

I think you will agree that in this instance the motors were
underpowered for the job. It is no wonder their performances were not
satisfactory. On the other hand, you can appreciate our position in
not being able to honor your request.

Our stock of motors is one of the most complete on the West Coast,
ranging from a fraction of a horsepower up to 200 horsepower. In many
cases, the equipment or machinery carries a specification tag which
indicates the type and power motor needed for maximum efficiency. If
you will let us know what your future needs are, we can have the motor
power source delivered within twenty-four hours of your request. Or.
if you prefer, we can have one of our engineers check your equipment
for the motor needed, prior to your placement of an order.

Sincerely yours,

Terry Newman

Terry Newman
Manager

Figure 7–3
Saying No to Claims

Friendly opening

Explanation of situation

Implied refusal

Constructive suggestion

Sales appeal (goodwill)

Figure 7–4
Saying No to Claims

HILOUGH DRUGS
220 Valley Road
Memphis, Tennessee 38131

September 23, 198-

Ms. Joan Hasagawa, Director
Young Folks Play-Time Camp
Ice Water Road
Franklin, Tennessee 38142

Dear Ms. Hasagawa:

Friendly opening

We were as delighted as you that the Young Folks Play-Time Camp had so
little need for first-aid and pharmaceutical supplies this past
summer. The fact that you have most of the supplies left, which you
received in Order #204 of June 2, certainly speaks well of the health
care which the children received.

Explanation of the situation

One of the statutes of this state concerning drugs indicates that when
materials are accepted by the buyer, they may not be returned to the
seller for resale. This legislation is designed to protect all users
and insure that drugs and drug supplies are fresh, untouched, and
fully effective. We know that the materials you received from us,

Implied refusal

which you wish to return, are unopened. Yet, we are faced with
obeying the law and are sure you will understand our position.

**Constructive suggestion and
sales appeal of goodwill**

One item which we have just received is available: the Young
Americans First-Aid Program. This twenty-page booklet can be supplied
to you, free of charge, in quantity. If you will let us know how many
you can use, we shall reserve that number for delivery to you early
next June. We will also include the Instructor's Guide, posters, and
sample first-aid materials. Call today at 213-1119 to make your
reservation.

Sincerely yours,

Elizabeth Petrocelli

Elizabeth Petrocelli
Sales Manager

1. The buyer is a poor credit risk;

2. The buyer has exceeded his or her credit limit;

3. Company, local, or federal regulations involving sales, franchising, or distributorship might be violated;

4. Merchandise requested is not handled or stocked by seller;

5. Filling the order would prove unprofitable because of the limited quantity ordered, distance to be shipped, or modifications requested.

Figures 7–5, 7–6, and 7–7 are examples of letters which must refuse a potential buyer's order. Note that in every case, a brief and courteous explanation is made *before* the refusal. And the refusal itself is handled in a courteous and tactful manner. In addition, the tone is positive and the sales appeal quite strong. The letters seem to say, "This is the situation; it isn't good, but we feel you will understand. Now let's continue on a businesslike basis in the future."

Concluding Comments

As was stated in the introductory portion of this chapter, saying no is never easy. Yet we are required in life to make such a statement to someone almost daily. We recognize that such a communication situation rarely can result in everyone being delighted. However, if we remember the principle of explaining before we refuse, the message will probably be accepted by the receiver as the sender intended, and the relationship has a better chance of continuing on a satisfactory basis.

MEMO

To: Students

From: The Authors

Subject: Unfavorable responses

Saying no is never easy, and it is particularly difficult when you have to refuse a customer whose future business you don't want to lose. The key to saying no without losing goodwill is to first explain why you must refuse and only then make your refusal. The reader of your communication will rarely be happy to be refused, but if you do your job well, at least that reader may not be angry or offended.

Figure 7–5
Saying No to an Order

Imperial Electronics, Inc.　　826 Oak Street　　Portland, Oregon 97253

August 14, 198-

Ms. Alice Willey, Manager
Johnstown Office Supplies
4207 Stone Avenue
Des Moines, Iowa 53201

Dear Ms. Willey:

Friendly opening

We received your order #511 in today's mail along with your completed application for a line of credit with our firm.

We evaluated very carefully the financial data you submitted and were happy to receive positive comments from the references you listed.

However, we are all aware that our industry--at both the wholesale and retail levels--is not enjoying the healthy state of three years ago.

Explanation of situation

In your particular case, it is our feeling that your present asset/liability ratio is not as well balanced as it should be. Of course, that is due to the fact that your firm is relatively young, and your area recently encountered major labor problems which negatively affected your sales.

Constructive suggestion

We suggest, Ms. Willey, you continue your purchases on a cash basis. This will result in immediate 2 percent discounts and no end-of-month bills to bother you.

Friendly, positive close

Your order is now being processed. Please call us collect, at 002/113-7564, so we may determine on what date it may be shipped to arrive on a C.O.D. basis.

Sincerely,

Peter Jonas

Peter Jonas
Credit Representative

Figure 7–6
Saying No to an Order

mpi **MARTIN PRODUCTS, INC.**
1114 Wentworth Avenue
Ogden, North Dakota 58621

May 4, 198-

Mr. Alfred Seamans
206 Bums Avenue
Jackson, Mississippi 39288

Dear Mr. Seamans:

We were pleased to receive your recent order for Martin Products. I
need not tell you how happy you made us with your kind comments
concerning our line of Martin Fast-Gro Pesticides.

For most of the states of our nation, we are permitted to ship
directly to customers. However, on January 1 of this year, your
state's Department of Environmental Protection put into operation a
regulation which restricts out-of-state direct shipment of pesticides
to users. (You probably overlooked a statement of that fact which
appears on page 45 of our winter-spring catalog.) However, it is
possible for us to deal directly with state-approved pesticide
distributors.

I have enclosed a list of certified dealers in your area. If you will
let us know which source you prefer, Mr. Seamans, we will call and ask
that distributor to accept delivery of the items you requested. In
that way, you should have your merchandise with a minimum of delay.

Thanks again for your interest in Martin's Products.

Sincerely yours,

Annette Sorrano

Annette Sorrano
Customer Service Representative

Encl.

Friendly opening

Explanation of situation

Constructive suggestion

Positive close

Figure 7–7
Saying No with Goodwill

Western Home Products

878 Sheridan Road
Miami, Florida 33541

April 2, 198-

Mr. John Cates
1371 Phelps Luck Drive
Columbia, MD 21046

Dear Mr. Cates:

Friendly opening

We received your order #5112 requesting our introductory line of home repair products. We certainly appreciate this first request from you.

Explanation of situation

For some years, we have attempted to work with our customers to assure them of the highest profit margin possible. One way we do this is to cut delivery costs by shipping orders that call for a minimum of $200 worth of merchandise. You undoubtedly were not aware of this policy of ours.

Constructive suggestion

In any event, may we suggest you call us collect to increase the size of your order #5112 from $130 to something over our minimum. I have enclosed our Summer Specials Catalog. You may be especially interested in the reduced prices on our Easy-Operate line of hand tools (pages 21-26). These items have all been reduced 25 percent.

Friendly close

If you will call us today, Mr. Cates, at 999/898-0003 your order will be shipped tomorrow.

Sincerely yours,

Thom Kurowski

Thom Kurowski
Customer Service Representative

Encl.

Decision

Here is the letter of refusal Frank Faxon wrote to Mr. Jones.

EKKO
Electric Company

404 N. Fourth Street
Bellville, California 91602

December 3, 198-

Mr. James Lee Jones, Service Manager
Barton's Buick Agency
8100 South Jackson Street
Cleveland, Ohio 44324

Dear Mr. Jones:

Your letter arrived today concerning the two GE 2-horsepower motors,
Series 21, which you purchased from us on October 20.

As you would guess, we were quite concerned to learn that you did not
find them satisfactory. Because these are GE's heavy-duty motors,
which are all pretested, we are concerned.

As you may have noted, all our catalogs, invoices, and individual
items are tagged or printed with the notation: "Claims must be
entered within 10 days of receipt of merchandise and faulty items
returned for inspection." This policy is standard throughout the
industry and is designed to give you and other service agencies
excellent products and services.

Because of this policy, and in fairness to all other accounts, you can
appreciate why we cannot approve your request for a $280 credit.

We have instructed our Mr. Mardian, a senior engineer who is familiar
with your operations, to call on you next week at your convenience.
He would like to check the motors and your application of them for the
purpose of suggesting the most efficient use of similar units. We
want to do everything possible, Mr. Kelly, to assure you of securing
top-level satisfaction with our products.

I have also enclosed a flyer on the new Double-Duty Hanover Power
Drill. Usually offered at $99.00, it is being sold to our preferred
customers until December 15 for $59.00. Please call today and your
request will be filled and shipped tomorrow.

Sincerely yours,

Frank Faxon

Frank Faxon
Vice-President

Encl.

Questions

1. What is psychologically wrong with refusing a request *before* explaining the reason for refusal?

2. Why is it important to reply promptly to a request that cannot be granted?

3. Why is it especially important to be tactful in a claim-refusal situation in which the buyer is at fault?

4. List at least five situations in business in which it might be necessary for a seller who has the merchandise to refuse to sell to a buyer.

5. Figure 7–2 is well written and positive in tone. In fact, the first paragraph seems so positive that the reader may expect good news rather than bad news. Study Figure 7–2 and answer the following questions.
   a. Does paragraph one suggest that a yes answer will follow? Explain your answer.
   b. Should the company be apologetic when it is offering $100 in gift certificates?
   c. Could this letter be written in such a way that it would follow the good-news format in Chapter 6 rather than the format in this chapter? Explain.

Exercises

1. Visit the credit office of a local department store. Interview the credit manager or one of the credit assistants. Request any form letters that are mailed to customers refusing them credit cards. Bring the letters to class and evaluate their effectiveness in maintaining goodwill.

2. Compare the organization of a letter that says yes with the organization of a letter that says no by giving the outline you would write for each of these situations.
   a. A recent high-school graduate has applied to your college for acceptance in the nursing program. You can accept the graduate.
   b. The same situation as above except the class list is already filled and you cannot accept the graduate.

3. If you must reject a qualified applicant for a manager-trainee opening because another candidate was better qualified, what alternatives can you suggest to the rejected applicant so he or she will not feel very antagonistic toward your firm? List four or five alternatives that could be helpful.

4. Visit your college admissions office. Ask for the form letters sent to applicants that:
   a. accept a student as an applicant; and
   b. reject a student as an applicant.
   Compare the organization and contents of these two letters and write your comparison in paragraph form.

Applications

1. The government Nuclear Regulatory Commission does not permit any firm to sell or lease items in the health-care field that are radioactive without a permit issued by that agency. You have just received an order for several items from the Government Medical Center of a newly created third world nation.

   Reply and refuse to fill the request. Explain the situation and offer a solution.

2. For the past two years Franklin Furniture in Kansas City has had obvious difficulty with declining sales, cash flow, heavy competition, etc. You have worked with Mr. Franklin in every way possible and three months ago you even raised his credit limit to $2500. This morning you received a request from him for merchandise in the amount of $840. You check and find his account now stands at $2750 outstanding to you.

   Write Mr. Franklin and refuse to fill this $840 order on credit. Offer an alternate suggestion. Remember, Franklin Furniture has been a customer for many years.

3. You work for the Entertainment Book-of-the-Month Club. For the last three months a subscriber, Mr. Warren Blenders, has not only failed to return his notification card but has sent back the three monthly selections mailed to him. The three selections showed evidence that they had been handled and had smudges and folds on the pages. Mr. Blenders claims he didn't order the books and doesn't want to be charged for them. You believe the books were read and then returned, but you lack 100 percent proof. Write to Mr. Blenders handling the situation in the most advantageous way for your company.

4. Both of the refusal letters below are handled poorly. Revise one or both and submit them to your instructor.

Dear Madame:

We received your order of September 8 for housewares in the amount of $170. We agree that all these items, noted in our Autumn Festival Catalog are well worthwhile. However, we regret to tell you that it is impossible to fill your request. A check of your account indicates a delinquency position that is now over two months old.

If you will clear your past-due position, we will be able to consider filling on credit the $170 order you submitted.

Dear Mr. Hernandez:

Your request for one of our new "Back to School" signs for use in your store display was received today.

Unfortunately, we must refuse your request because the size of the order that accompanied the request was far below the $800 minimum required.

Our fall catalog indicated the terms by which it was possible to obtain the sign. Perhaps you missed the explanation. However, they (the signs) are very costly to us, and we just can't give them out to everybody

If you would like, we can send you our fall poster collection, which you can use to advertise twelve different sale items. Or if you can call in an increase in your last order and bring it from $350 to $800, we can make arrangements.

Please let us know.

---

5. You are the assistant buyer for junior women's sportswear in a branch store of a well-known company. In January, many blouses and skirts were offered at a 50-percent price reduction and the sale was designated "as is" because too much handling had caused snags and minor tears in some of the items. Ms. Barg, a customer, had purchased a lined woolen skirt; when she discovered the lining was torn and there were two pulls on the side of the skirt, she wanted her money back. She had paid $25 for a $50 skirt. "As is" sales stipulate no returns for any reason. Write to Ms. Barg refusing her request but maintaining goodwill and a chance for future business.

6. William Powell, a recent college graduate, has opened a small retail stationery store in an office building. He has the promise of several of the companies in the building that they will patronize him. Mr. Powell has asked you, a stationery supply distributor, to extend him $2500 in credit. You have checked his assets and since he has no credit record and few assets you must, at this time, offer him C.O.D. terms only. As an incentive, you can extend him a 5 percent discount on all C.O.D. purchases. Write to Mr. Powell giving him this information.

7. As personnel manager for a large bank in Memphis, you receive many letters from college students each April requesting summer jobs. Frequently, you have openings for summer workers to fill in for vacationing full-timers. This year, however, no summer employees will be hired, but that may not be the situation next summer. Write a letter that you can send to all of the applicants for summer employment which will leave the door open for possible summer employment in the future.

Dilemma

Although Harry Kellian's service station is only a half mile from the Conover Community College campus, he numbers few faculty members among his customers. Therefore, he has decided to send a sales letter to all 300 faculty (full- and part-time) who are listed in the Conover Community College Bulletin. Harry is after much more than gasoline and oil sales, for it is in repairs, tune-ups, and related work that his profit margin is significant. Harry feels that a motorist who consistently buys gasoline at a particular station will also use the other services.

Harry has decided to offer a free Merriam-Webster Collegiate Dictionary to any faculty member who purchases a total of 100 gallons of gasoline. He will attach a card to each letter in which credit is already given (punched out) for ten gallons of gas. Total purchases must be made within the next ninety days. The bookstore value of the dictionary (latest edition, hardbound cover, over one thousand pages) is $12.50. Now Harry must write the sales letter and design the card enclosure.

Decision, see page 153

Effective Sales Letters

8

Here is a list of the objectives you should understand by the time you complete this chapter. Place a check mark in the box beside each as soon as you feel ready to apply your understanding in a practical situation.

☐ The four fundamental sales principles:
  Know your product or service
  Know your market
  Know your customer
  Know your competition

☐ The functions and uses of sales letters

☐ The four basic steps in developing an effective sales letter:
  Gaining the reader's attention
  Describing the product or service
  Proving the claims
  Convincing the reader to act

☐ The effective use of promotional material

☐ The basic sources for developing a useful mailing list

Almost every memo, report, or letter you write has a sales orientation. Ask yourself if there is a bit of sales in the internal office memo you write to a fellow worker concerning the current project you are conducting. Is there a sales thrust to the report you prepare for your boss? Are there sales aspects in the letter of application you prepare for a potential employer? The answers are probably yes.

Most business letters have some sales appeal.

Obviously the letter that has the sole purpose of generating interest or sales for a product will be clearly sales oriented. The sales approach of the other letters, reports, or memos may have a selling appeal that is not quite as obvious. However, they may still try to sell your idea, concept, or plan.

Basic Principles of Selling

The written approach to sales has a very definite relationship to the sales approach you may have studied in a basic marketing course. Before attempting to write a sales message (or have a professional firm write it for you) it is necessary to make sure you have satisfied the four basic sales principles:

Why is this phrase enclosed in parentheses? (See Appendix 1.)

Before writing a sales letter, you must know thoroughly the four basic sales principles.

1. **Know your product or service.** It is vital that the communicator know the item to be sold. This means knowing its strong and weak points. What are its major advantages? How is it superior to competitive products? What possible questions about the product or service may the buyer raise?

2. **Know your market.** Know the general market conditions for the product or service. What market segment will find the product or service attractive? What will the market pay for the product? In what geographical area may the major portion of the market be found?

3. **Know your customer.** In sales it is important to know as much as possible about the customer in the market. Be able to identify the customer's specific needs and know how your product or service satisfies those needs. For example, the market for a new refrigerator may be the American family. However, the upper-economic-level customer in that market may look for new, modern features in the refrigerator, while the low-income customer may find capacity or price more attractive in the same refrigerator.

4. **Know your competition.** In most instances the customer will be well aware of the competitive product or service. Therefore, it is necessary for the communicator to know the competition in order to anticipate questions or objections and also to be able to point out how his or her product is superior to the competitor's.

A sales letter should contain a specific appeal for a particular audience.

Once you know the product or service, the potential customer, and the market, you can select the specific appeal which the buyer will probably find attractive. The appeal must be identified and then aimed at the audience in a specific manner. It is possible that the same product can have different appeals to different people. For example, the very small automobile appeals to the upper-income person because it is "sporty"; it appeals to the middle-income individual because it is "efficient"; and it appeals to the lower-income population because it is "economical." Knowing your audience, the product or service, and the competition, you should be able to clearly determine how it appeals to the various audiences which make up your market.

A Case Study in Selling

For our purposes let's work through a sales approach for Hank's Hardware in West Point, Virginia. West Point is a wealthy suburb of a metropolitan area. Most families are headed by a male who is a white-collar manager or executive; the male executive tends to work long hours and may be forced to be away from home for extended periods of time. Also, many of the women in West Point hold professional positions. The end result is that neither the husband nor wife is available to handle the many routine chores of maintaining a house.

Why is *nor* used here instead of *or*? (See Appendix 1.)

The Problem

In his store Hank offers a variety of materials for general household needs: light fixtures, storage cabinets, small plumbing fixtures, small electrical items, standard doors, shutters, and other goods. About 75 percent of his floor space is devoted to these items. He sees that because of his clientele's income, position, and time commitments, his sales of general household materials are declining.

Evidently the home owners are going to independent carpenters and lumber stores to hire people to help them out with their small projects around the house. Overall, Hank's sales of general maintenance items are dropping. Does this mean that the 75 percent of the store space allocated to maintenance items is to be discontinued? Should something else be stocked?

A Solution

Hank feels he can increase sales by offering a new service. To introduce the new service, it will be advantageous for Hank to gain the attention and interest of potential customers. Hank's idea, based on his knowledge of his customers and their activities, is to offer them a home maintenance program.

Instead of the homeowners having to hunt for an electrician, a carpenter, or a general laborer when they need a new light fixture hung, a new cabinet installed, or the plumbing repaired, Hank will offer a service to take care of these light chores. It will only be necessary for the customer to call Hank. He then will contact the appropriate worker from his pool who, in turn, will call the customer to make final arrangements. Hank's financial gain is that whatever is used in the project will come from his store. Hank also feels that the homeowners who call his store for service will remember the help he has provided and goodwill will be increased.

What is the difference in meaning between *continually* and *continuously*? (See Appendix 1.)

If successful, Hank will not have to alter his store's orientation and he probably will gain additional traffic because he will be continually in the mind of the customer. It may be a good idea—but how can Hank sell the idea to the people of West Point?

1. Not all West Point people frequent his store.
2. Not all West Point people know of his store.
3. Some customers have left because they do not have a need for his maintenance materials; they hire independent workers.

Hank is convinced that his service will be convenient, less expensive and more reliable for the busy families of West Point. Analyzing his situation and his market, Hank can make three basic appeals: convenience, lower cost, and reliability.

Now, with the major appeals in hand, how can the sales principles be applied and Hank's service sold? Should he try to sell his service on a door-to-door basis? Obviously he can't be away from his store to do that. Should he go on radio or TV? The answer to that is, no; those media are too costly. How about billboards or newspapers? Again the cost is high.

What's the solution for Hank? The best answer is to use sales letters. Now that Hank has made the choice, let's watch him move forward.

Developing the Sales Letter

There are four basic parts of the sales letter—*interest, description, proof*, and *action*. Using Hank's situation and the complete sales letter presented in Figure 8–1 as a guide, these four parts can be examined.

Grab Your Reader's Interest

Convince your reader to open and read your letter.

We all receive large numbers of letters—much of it mass mailings that sometimes are referred to as *junk mail*. It makes no difference how worthy your cause or how good your proposal, if you cannot gain the immediate interest of the recipients to open your letter and read it, your message is wasted.

Getting the letter opened   Since Hank's mailing will go only to the 1500 households in West Point, he can afford to have the envelopes look as if they have been individually typed versus a worn address label placed on the envelope. Furthermore, he can take the time to have a new colorful postage stamp actually placed on the envelope instead of having the letters stamped by an

Figure 8–1
Sales Letter

Hank's Hardware
300 Main Street, West Point, Virginia 23181

April 20, 198-

Dear Neighbor:

Nuts to you and more at Hank's!

It is most inconvenient when the new light fixture must be wired, a
sink drain cleared, or an extra cabinet installed. . . and there is no
one at home who has the time available. In the past you have been
forced to leaf through the Yellow Pages and/or seek assistance from a
neighbor to solve the problem. The reliability of the resulting
service was marginal.

Responding to your needs and to your situation, we are instituting the
"Call Hank" Service.

For any type of minor, routine house repair we will take the guessing
out of the process. The area's top independent plumbers, electri-
cians, and craftsmen have been assembled by Hank. When you have a
household maintenance problem, call Hank. We immediately will have
the appropriate skilled individual contact you.

No more hours of telephoning to locate who you need--just one call to
Hank will solve the problem. And, besides being assured of top labor,
you will be getting top materials; all materials used by these people
will come directly from Hank's Hardware. All materials from Hank's
are guaranteed against any flaw in workmanship; if any item from
Hank's fails, it will be replaced at no charge.

Hank's will maintain a roster of 500 households who can take advantage
of this free service.

You will want to take immediate advantage of this offer by completing
and mailing the enrollment card today. To join the initial roster of
"Call Hank" satisfied customers you must enroll by May 15.

We look forward to serving you and your neighbors with this additional
service.

Cordially,

Henry Henniger

Henry Henniger, Owner

Encl.: Enrollment Card

electronic posting machine. These are ways he can attempt to gain interest and get the letter opened. He may desire to have just his address or P.O. box noted as the return; the receiver will be curious as to who has sent the personal letter. Hank may even consider using a brightly colored envelope. These are some techniques to motivate the receiver to open the envelope.

Getting the letter read   Once opened, the letter must now be read. There are a number of techniques that might be used to attract interest in an offer.

You can arouse the reader's interest in a variety of ways.

1. A sample of the product can be included if it is feasible to provide a sample; sometimes we receive samples of toothpaste, perfume, or soap in the mail.

2. Photos or sketches of the product can be sent to the potential customer if the item is tangible and can be represented graphically.

3. Gadgets and gimmicks such as providing a pencil to mark a response on an enclosed return card can gain attention; include a stamp for mailing the response; provide a paper mock-up of the product; insert an item that will draw attention to the letter, the product or service.

4. An unusual opening sentence to the letter can be used that will make the reader want to read more. This might be a story, an interesting quote, a startling statement, reference to the recipient's problem, etc.

What is the difference in meaning between *proceed* and *precede*? (See Appendix 1.)

Once the customer has opened the letter, Hank may proceed in one of the following ways. He can glue a small nut to the top of the page and start out:

We now offer more than nuts at Hank's . . .

Or without any attachment, he can begin:

Tired of the hassle of finding the electrician, the plumber, or the carpenter when you have a small job to be done around the house?

Or another approach could be:

You have much in common with Arthur and Sarah Kennedy who live in West Point. Arthur works sixty hours a week and his wife Sarah is active with her career as an engineer; they both enjoy spending as much time as possible with their children. It is a problem to keep the house running smoothly. No one has time to locate the plumber, the electrician or the carpenter to do all those little jobs that plague households like yours.

Note how the opening of the letter can start to appeal to the specific clientele.

In gaining the readers' interest there are two very definite items that must be accomplished—get the envelope opened and get the letter read. If the mailing is going to a diverse group of people, it will be necessary to take special care so that your approach does not insult or anger a segment of the group receiving the letter.

In Hank's situation, he is promoting an intangible *service* and therefore his situation is a bit more difficult than if he were attempting to sell a *product* such as a new style of microwave oven, a new lawn sweeper, or a new handy set of screw drivers. But it is still very possible for Hank to gain the readers' interest.

Describe Your Product or Service

Once the interest of the receiver is captured, it is necessary to describe the product or service. You generally will have the reader's attention for only a relatively short time. Therefore, it is imperative to describe the item in concise terms. Yet, it may be advantageous to insert some favorable adjectives.

The sales letter can refer the reader to additional items, such as an enclosure, to obtain detailed information. In the letter, attempt to create a verbal picture in the readers' minds of the item or service available to them. Design your description in terms of how it will solve the readers' problem. How will it aid them? Naturally, the readers are going to be looking at the letter with a selfish outlook—what is in it for them. Your description, then, must address the particular wants of the readers and offer ways to fulfill those needs.

A sales letter should create a verbal picture.

In the case of Hank's Hardware, the reader will be the husband or wife in a situation where it is assumed that both the wife and/or husband are busy. Many of the routine household maintenance jobs are left for the individual who may be at home for a day that week.

Building the appeal—convenience, economy, and reliability, in this case—into the description is important. The letter must gain the reader's interest quickly. Hank is promoting an intangible service. It is sometimes more difficult to discover the correct words to describe an intangible service than it is a tangible product. However, that picture must be built.

There are alternative ways to prepare the description. You may prefer first to point to the service and then explain its benefits to the customer, or reverse the order and note benefits before explaining the service. In every case, it is important to explain the advantages to the reader in understandable terms and from his or her point of view.

Prove Your Point

The American buyer wants proof that the product or service you are trying to sell is worth the money. In selecting that support or proof, you must consider the audience. What approach will appeal to your customer? For instance, if you are selling children's toys, the child audience will be won over by fun and pleasure; the parent audience will be won over by challenge and learning value. It is frequently the case that you support sales for one audience with

Offer proof of your claims to your audience.

one kind of proof and another kind of proof for another audience. Various forms of support can be used in the sales letter to indicate to the receiver that the ideas presented in the letter are valid.

Samples are often enclosed with sales letters; generally shirt sales letters include a swatch of cloth. Words can only go so far — *soft, fine texture, beautiful.* If it is possible to enclose a sample, this provides a means of going beyond the words. The sample can be seen and touched. The words can only attempt to elicit a favorable picture; the sample can prove it.

What is the difference in meaning between *imply* and *infer*? (See Appendix 1.)

Guarantees are a way of proving the product or service is reliable. When you state the proof as a guarantee, you are implying that the item is of such high quality, the firm stands behind it. A guarantee to return the buyer's money if the product isn't satisfactory — a "money back guarantee" — can also be effective.

Trial offers not only get the product in the house but they permit the potential buyers to sell themselves. Try the laundry detergent. If it does not clean your clothes better, return the unused portion. Use the water softener for one month — if your skin does not feet better, we will remove the equipment.

Testimonials by well-known personalities (a movie star, an astronaut) or by noted rating groups (Good Housekeeping, university testing services) are ways to add credibility to a product or service. Testimonials can be most helpful when attempting to prove that an intangible service is good. A respected person saying "I tried it and I liked it" will be appealing to many.

Statistics derived from polls or other sources may sway some people. How many times have you heard "Eight out of ten dentists surveyed said. . . ."

Hank cannot enclose a sample of the service. But he can support that it is a good idea. For instance:

> *Millie Miner, president of the West Point Garden Club and wife of industrialist Herbert Miner, reports that the "Call Hank" service has saved her many hours of work and is the greatest convenience since the automatic dishwasher.*

> *Any product used by the expert worker from Hank's is guaranteed to perform to your satisfaction. If it does not, it will be replaced at no charge to the customer.*

There are various ways, even with an intangible service like Hank's, that proof can be used. These clearly relate that it is not only Hank — but others — who feel the reader should consider the service.

Convince Your Reader to Act

Action is vital to making a sale.

If the sales letter concerns insurance, ties, shirts, etc., the action request is to return the enclosed order form immediately. The writer attempts to move the receiver to immediate response. At other times, the next step is not to buy the product or service, but to inquire further — request a brochure, ask a salesperson to call, or accept a demonstration.

If some immediate action is needed, it can be encouraged in one of the following ways:

Special low price until June 30, 198-.

Also, the receiver can be told explicitly what to do:

Sign the enclosed card and mail it now.

Cut out the coupon and return it today.

Your signature and 25¢ will get you the brochure by return mail.

What is the difference in meaning between *explicit* and *implicit*? (See Appendix 1.)

In Hank's case, he needs to plant the seed and make his point so well that the readers of his letter will call when they need the service. If all is under control on the home front, there is no need to call Hank. But when there is a need for the service, Hank will want the reader to remember him. There are options available:

There are many methods to motivate the reader to act.

1. Enclose a sticker for a phone: "Call Hank: Phone 472 – 1300"

2. Enclose a note pad for placement near the phone which says on each sheet "Call Hank: Phone 472 – 1300"

Or, if he desires to get a more immediate response he could limit the service to 500 households.

If you desire to be a member of Hank's select service group, return the enclosed card today.

The appeal for action must be clear and explicit. Obviously, if the writer cannot stir the recipient to action, there will be no positive result to the sales letter.

Using Promotional Material

At times, the sales letter does not provide sufficient space to adequately describe a complex service or expensive or involved product. It is necessary to provide an enclosure that includes a detailed description, explanation, photos and/or drawings.

What to Enclose

The enclosure to the sales letter or promotion piece can take several forms:

A promotional piece can highlight or add information to your sales letter.

1. Product/service descriptions printed on 8½-by-11-inch paper.

2. A simple black-and-white folded insert with offset printing and pictures.

3. A full-color brochure, perhaps several pages in length.

If it is necessary to provide an enclosure, it probably will be beneficial to receive some professional assistance from a printing house or an organization specializing in such mailings. There are a number of factors that must be considered in determining how to approach the promotion piece:

1. The number of promotion pieces needed will influence the cost of the piece. For 500 copies, it probably would be prohibitive to produce a color brochure.
2. The nature and cost of the product or service being promoted. If the product sells for $2.00, one cannot spend 50¢ to produce a promotion piece.
3. The class of mailing. A first-class, letter is expensive enough; if a three-ounce brochure is included, the mailing cost soars.

All of these factors must be weighed against the result — what will stimulate the receiver to take action.

The Cover Sales Letter

If it is determined that some type of promotion piece is to be enclosed, the writer needs to write a cover sales letter rather than a sales letter.

If an enclosure clearly explains the product or service, carries clear descriptions of the item, and has a strong sales orientation, the cover sales letter may be designed to arouse sufficient interest to motivate the reader to examine the enclosure or promotion piece. In other words, a long letter is not necessary or advantageous in this situation.

In some cover sales letters, the sales principles of interest, description, proof, and action may still be followed, but they are made very concise.

If, for instance, Hank was running a special sale on Amana microwave ovens and the Amana company provided Hank with 1500 beautiful four-color brochures of the various styles and models, Hank could send the elaborate brochures with a brief cover letter such as the one in Figure 8–2. The letter outlines the advantages and directs a specific action for the reader.

A cover letter should be more concise than a sales letter.

Reaching Your Customer

The good message that is not received is wasted. Therefore, it is vital that the sales letter reach the prospect. A major concern in direct-mail sales letter operations is to make sure that the letters are sent to the desired audience and that the correct names and addresses are used.

There are a variety of places from which a mailing list can be secured. First, there are self-derived lists. *One's own customers* are a possible source. If individuals have done business with you they may be most receptive to hearing from you. *Public lists* that anyone may obtain can be used in building a mailing list; these include such sources as: city directories, voting lists, tax lists, and auto registrations. A useful source to consider in developing one's own list is the *Guide to American Directories for Compiling Mailing Lists.*

Remember, however, that obtaining the raw list is just the first step. One may feel that it is cheap to use the city directory for the list. But somehow all those names and addresses have to be removed from the book and placed

There are many sources of good mailing lists.

Figure 8—2
Cover Sales Letter

Hank's Hardware
300 Main Street, West Point, Virginia   23181

June 15, 198-

Dear Customer:

Modern Americans are now saving time and effort by preparing meals the
new way. . .the micro-wave way. No longer does an individual or
family need to wait a long period of time for food to be prepared.
Micro-wave cooking is efficient, quick, clean, inexpensive, and
permits you to serve mouth-watering meals in no time at all.

Read the enclosed brochure and learn why modern Americans like you are
switching to micro-wave.

During the month of July we can offer the Amway micro-wave oven to you
at a 15 percent savings off the regular low price. Come by and see
us. We will be pleased to answer any questions you have and
demonstrate the micro-wave to you.

See you in July!

Henry Henniger

Henry Henniger, Owner

Attachment

individually on each letter. That can be a very time-consuming activity. Also, if the list is transferred in such a way that it cannot be duplicated for future use, the process is very expensive.

Then there are purchased lists. This may be the most expedient way to secure a mailing list. There are a variety of places to secure, for a fee, a mailing list. *Other companies* may have customer lists they will sell you. *Associations* (for example, sales and trade groups) often will sell their mailing list to responsible organizations.

Mailing list firms that specialize in selling lists also can be helpful. Some of these firms can offer a very narrow list of prospects. If you desire to send a mailing to widows over the age of 65, with an annual income in excess of $20,000, who reside in a particular geographical area, such a list often can be provided. If you want lists of electrical engineers, nurses, or auto mechanics, such lists can be purchased. Whatever the manner of obtaining the list — doing it internally or going outside the organization — reliability and usability are important.

These are the features of a good, useful mailing list.

1. *Reliability:* Correct addresses (20 percent of the population moves annually), correct spelling of names, and appropriateness (is the person really a prospect for your product or service?) are important factors.

2. *Usability:* How is the list organized — has it been divided into some kind of logical categories, according to economic levels, ethnic characteristics, sex, age? Is it divided by zip code to meet current postal regulations? Is it prepared in a way that is easy to use and reuse?

All of these factors are important. It becomes obvious that the actual preparation for and mailing of the sales letter can be a sizable job in itself. Many businesses are not organized to handle mass mailings. Therefore, it may be wise to obtain the services of a specialized company that will print the letter, stuff, stamp, mail the envelope, and just send you a bill.

MEMO

To: **Students**

From: **The Authors**

Subject: **Sales letters**

Nearly every business communication you write in a modern organization will have a sales *slant.* The internal report will try to sell your ideas to the organization. Inquiries try to sell the reader on the idea that your letter should be answered. Responses sell the idea that yours is a smoothly run organization. The application letter that accompanies your resumé sells the talents and abilities you have to offer a firm. Although you may never have the opportunity to write a real sales letter in the course of your career, a great many of the communications you will write will benefit if you know the basic principles presented in this chapter.

Decision

Here is the sales letter Harry Kellian wrote to prospective customers of his service station.

CONOVER SERVICE STATION

600 Main Street, Conover, Ohio 23546

Dear Faculty Member:

It has <u>your</u> name on the cover . . . and it's free!

The "it" is the new edition of the Merriam-Webster Collegiate Dictionary . . . a $12.50 bookstore value. It's yours free of charge with your purchase of just 100 gallons of gasoline at our College Service Station.

It's our way of saying "Thank You" to our present and new customers who are satisfied with nothing less than excellent service. Here is what we can offer you:

Products: Gas, oil, tires, batteries, and a hundred other auto needs at the most competitive prices.

Car Care: A team of expert mechanics to tune, repair, and work on any aspect of your car's mechanical needs at prices far below what an auto-dealer charges.

Convenience: We will pick up and deliver your car to the Conover College faculty parking lot. All adjustments and repairs are completed while you're at work. And excellent "loaner" cars are available to faculty when necessary.

Guarantees: Every task, job, or service we perform is guaranteed to meet your full satisfaction or your money is refunded.

To prove all this to you, we just ask that you stop in for gasoline for the next few weeks. In no time at all, you will have purchased the required 100 gallons of gas (at the lowest price possible) and we will give you your Merriam-Webster Collegiate Dictionary. And while you are at our station, please note our Certificate of Recognition from the American Car Association and our Membership Plaque from the Conover College Alumni Association.

Please stop by tomorrow and bring the enclosed "Dictionary Card" with you. You will be happy you did.

We want to serve you!

Harry Kellian

Harry Kellian, Manager
Conover Service Station

Encl.

Questions

1. What is a *specific* or *central* sales appeal and why is it necessary to have one for most products and services?

2. What role does interest play in 1) getting the envelope opened, and 2) getting the letter read?

3. Under what conditions would one product have more than one central appeal? Explain.

4. What is meant by *description* in a sales letter? Why is word choice so important in developing an effective description section?

5. List several different methods for offering proof in the sales letter.

6. Would it be logical to use two different types of proof for one product? Explain.

7. Would a "testimonial from a movie star" type of proof be more effective for a purchasing agent of a large corporation than a "guaranteed-trial period"? Why?

8. Why is it sometimes necessary to prepare a promotion piece to accompany a sales letter?

9. What difference(s) exists in the sales letter between a cover sales letter with promotion piece and just a sales letter?

10. Why is direct mail looked upon today as a significant factor in many firms' sales approach?

Exercises

1. Discuss the value of including the following items in a letter attempting to sell tennis racquets to: 1) college students, and 2) members of a tennis club.
   a. respected opinion;
   b. use of the racket by a movie star; or
   c. verifiable facts and statistics.

2. What basic needs of the reader would you appeal to when you attempt to sell each of these products? Match the need with each product.
   a. the new dictionary for college students.
   b. window and door locks for homeowners;
   c. a Florida vacation in the winter for business persons; and
   d. a leather reclining chair for stockbrokers.

3. Carefully observe five different television commercials for different brands of the same product. Make a note of the product or service, sales appeal used, and your opinion of the effectiveness of the commercial. Compare the five sales appeals and rank the commercials with No. 1 representing your top choice for effectiveness. Write your findings in letter format to your instructor.

4. Refer to Exercise 3. Repeat the exercise but substitute five full-page magazine advertisements for the five television commercials. The advertisements should have both pictures and words.

5. When writing a sales letter, you can use an unconventional format in order to capture the reader's attention. Provide an unusual and appealing letter opening to sell the following products or services:
   a. a new trash truck for private trash collectors;
   b. a multivitamin with double doses of Vitamins C and E;
   c. an indoor hot tub; and
   d. a backyard playgym.

6. Collect three sales letters with their accompanying promotion pieces. Analyze each sales packet, looking for the sales letter components suggested in this chapter. Choose the one most effective packet and the one least effective packet. Orally compare the strengths and weaknesses of your selections.

7. Visit the public relations department of your college. Inquire about the methods used to promote your institution and request copies of advertisements and promotional material. Evaluate the appearance and content of promotional materials and the methods used by the college's public relations department to sell your college to the public. Submit your evaluation in writing to your instructor.

Applications

1. Select a product that is of interest to you, such as, an attaché case; an alarm-calendar quartz wrist watch; or a remote-control color television set. Any other comparable product can be selected. You have been asked to prepare a sales letter that will be sent to prospective buyers. Before writing this letter, jot down the answers to the following questions pertaining to your selected product:
   a. What tangible description and facts can you provide about your product?
   b. Is there a desire and potential market for your product? What type of customer may be interested in your selection?
   c. What competition would you have in the market you would select?

2. Refer to Application 1. Using the same product and the answers you provided to the questions, write an outline for the sales letter that would include all the sales letter components mentioned in this chapter. Exchange your outline with a classmate and participate in peer evaluation and critiquing.

3. Refer to Applications 1 and 2. Use the outline for the sales letter and write the complete sales letter for your selected product. Be certain it covers the following components:
   a. attention-catching opening;
   b. description of product;

c. proof sections; and
d. an action closing.

4. You are the manager of direct mail sales for the International Luggage Company. One of your finest items is the International Attaché Case, which has the following key features:

   Finest vinyl with the look of leather
   One brass combination lock
   Expands to 5 inches
   Contains 2 separators
   Comes with 3 brass initials of purchaser
   2-year guarantee on materials and workmanship
   Price: $59.95

   a. List what you feel would be the most effective central selling appeal for the above product for each of the following groups of potential customers:
      1. college students
      2. college professors
      3. male executives
      4. managers
      5. physicians
      6. women executives
      7. a government purchasing agency
      8. college bookstore purchasing directors
   b. List what you feel would be the most effective type of proof to offer each of the eight groups listed in Part a.
   c. Choose any two of the groups listed in Part a and prepare an effective sales letter for each.
   d. Choose two others of the groups listed in Part a and prepare a cover letter that might accompany a promotional piece on the International Attaché Case. Do not prepare the promotional piece unless your instructor requests it.

Dilemma

For several years, Nancy Montellani has worked for the Wilmette Department Store in Wilmette, Arkansas. The city has been growing rapidly and now has a population of almost 500,000.

Wilmette Department Store started a small consumer credit department three years ago. Last month, it was decided to build this area and actively encourage consumers to apply for credit (through the store's weekly newspaper sales advertisements).

The marketing director, Gilda Karu, now feels the store needs an excellent guide letter to be used when applications are accepted. Of course, the proper name, address, and date will be individually typed. She has requested that Nancy write this guide letter. Ms. Karu also suggests that a sales appeal be made to sell the Wilmette living and dining room line to those who are granted credit.

Decision, see page 197

Credit and Collection Communications

9

Here is a list of the objectives you should understand by the time you complete this chapter. Place a check mark in the box beside each as soon as you feel ready to apply your understanding in a practical situation.

☐ The importance of credit to modern organizations.

☐ The six basic kinds of credit communication:
    Encouraging customers to apply for credit
    Acknowledging receipt of credit applications
    Requesting credit information on applicants
    Responding favorably or unfavorably to applicants
    Communicating with former credit customers
    Seeking credit for your organization

☐ The dos and don'ts of collection communications

☐ The basic collection series:
    Simple reminders
    Oral statements
    Letters

☐ The main appeals you can use to convince a customer to pay a bill:
    Fair play
    Credit reputation
    Pride
    Fear
    Self-interest
    Collection agency
    Legal action

Almost all individuals and virtually all businesses today are involved in some form of credit operation. Credit is so widespread in the United States that if everyone suddenly had to pay his or her credit accounts with cash, there would not be enough currency available to accomplish the task.

Basic Credit Communications

Credit allows the user to carry on business when cash is not readily available.

Credit is beneficial both to consumers and to sellers. Using credit, consumers readily can obtain goods and services when needed; they need not wait until payday to make a purchase. The concept of providing credit to customers also is beneficial for retailers who desire to have a steady flow of customers—not just customers on payday. And credit is not limited to consumers: much of what retailers stock in their stores has been purchased on credit. This permits retailers to carry a larger inventory of stock than their cash position would permit them to purchase.

Many cash-and-carry retailers accept standard bank credit cards as cash. This is possible because the retailer will receive payment from the bank or firm sponsoring the credit on a regular basis; it is not contingent upon when the customer pays the card company.

There are three basic kinds of credit offered to consumers:

Consumers may use various types of credit arrangements.

1. the firm's own credit system, which permits the customer to pay the retailer directly within a specified time—generally thirty days. Often these accounts are *revolving*. The customer receives a bill once a month, pays it, and continues to make charge purchases;

Why is *between* and not *among* correct in this sentence? (See Appendix 1.)

2. an arrangement between the retailer and a financing company that permits the customer to purchase an item on an installment basis over a long period. This generally would be for a major purchase (television, dishwasher, clothesdryer, and other items) on which the payments will be made for eighteen or twenty-four months.

3. an agreement between the firm and a bank or national credit card company to honor the credit card.

Whatever the type of credit available to customers, it is going to involve some communication in order to attract and inform customers and to monitor the systems.

Seeking New Credit Customers

Credit customers usually do business with companies which have given them credit.

One of the challenges facing many businesses is how to obtain new credit customers. If customers have credit with a firm, they usually will be more likely to make purchases from that organization. Therefore, individuals who do not have a credit account with the company are to be identified and contacted.

The communication to a prospective customer often follows a five-point organization:

1. describes the available services and invites the recipient to use them;
2. attempts to get the prospective credit customer to contact the company;
3. establishes the company as polite and helpful;
4. indicates willingness to do something for the customer;
5. provides the customer an easy way to apply for a credit account.

The letter is an offer, not a promise of credit.

In some small retail operations, the methods of communication may not be very sophisticated; some will not use written communications. Instead, the store owner will offer credit and collect payments in person. This method may work for some very small retailers. However, for anything beyond the smallest operation, it may not be efficient. Instead, a friendly, personalized invitation to apply for credit will be more effective in reaching customers (see Figure 9–1).

The approach used by larger retailers (such as a major department store in a metropolitan area) or wholesalers (such as a box manufacturer who provides cartons to a canning company) will be less personal than the approach used by the neighborhood store. The larger operation will have a credit manager responsible for making the formal contact via mail. However, as Figure 9–2 illustrates, there are ways to personalize the appeal. Note that the logic and strategy are the same as in the letter written by the small retailer, but the tone of the letter is different.

Responding to Credit Applications

If you are successful in convincing potential customers to apply for credit with your organization, you should make an initial response as soon as the application reaches you. This response to the credit applicant can serve a variety of purposes, such as:

1. acknowledging receipt of the application;
2. indicating appreciation and thanking the individual for applying;
3. maintaining contact with a potential customer;
4. reminding the recipient of available products or services;
5. promoting current sales or featured products;
6. relating satisfaction with the response, but not committing the firm to a course of action regarding the extension of credit; and
7. revealing an operation that is courteous and efficient.

Application for credit should be acknowledged immediately.

The neighborhood store probably will encourage the potential credit customer to bring the completed application to the store by offering a gift if the customer visits the store and brings in the form. If the small retailer suggests

Figure 9–1
Seeking Credit
Accounts: Small
Retailer

Hank's Hardware
300 Main Street, West Point, Virginia   23181

June 3, 198-

Mr. and Mrs. Edmond T. Simmons, Jr.
2005 West Evergreen Avenue
West Point, VA 23181

Dear Mr. and Mrs. Simmons,

Start with a friendly opening.

WELCOME to the neighborhood! We have been part of this lovely area
for over fifteen years; it has been a pleasure to serve the basic
hardware and general household maintenance needs of your neighbors.
We take pride in this beautiful part of the city and we are pleased to
have you join us.

Most of our business is conducted with people like you who live within
a two-mile radius of our store. We enjoy knowing our customers and we
continually strive to serve them better with so many of the items
necessary for the home.

Besides having a complete hardware department, we also have a large
cooking section, housewares area, and a new greeting card section.
Our hours are designed for the life-styles of our clientele and we
know you will find them convenient.

**Note the advantages of
having a credit account.**

Knowing our neighbors--our customers--it is possible for us to offer
convenient credit to you. Not only would we enjoy serving you, but we
also would like to offer you our personal credit. This is our own
Hank's Charge--our credit arrangement is not connected with any bank
or huge corporation. In getting settled in your home you may find our
credit arrangements very handy.

**Make an effort to build
goodwill.**

Please accept the enclosed telephone emergency chart with our
compliments. It attaches easily to your phone and lists the numbers
for the local fire, police, and ambulance services. Also, in order
for us to get to know you better, if you complete the enclosed
application form for credit and bring it to our store, we will give
your family a Safety Flashlight--complete with light and batteries--
plus a special gift for each of your children.

**Suggest some action to
complete the offer.**

Why not join the rest of your neighbors as happy Hank's customers and
take advantage of the free gifts by applying for our personalized
charge?

Close in a friendly manner.

We look forward to meeting you soon and serving you for many years in
the future.

Sincerely,

Henry Henniger

Henry Henniger, Owner

Encls.: Emergency Telephone Chart
         Credit Application

Convenient Hours for Our Neighbors:
    Monday through Friday--10:00 a.m. to 6:00 p.m.
    Saturday--8:00 a.m. to 6:00 p.m.

Figure 9-2
Seeking Credit
Accounts: Large
Retailer

Continental Store
606 Jefferson Street
New Orleans, Louisiana 70140

May 3, 198-

Mrs. Norma Jenkins
1705 Pathway Drive
New Orleans, LA 70140

Dear Mrs. Jenkins:

Mr. Nathan Daniels in our Appliance Department indicates that you recently made a major purchase in his department; it was a pleasure for Mr. Daniels to serve you and we hope you are pleased with the item you purchased. We also encourage you to visit our eighteen other departments to become familiar with the various ways in which we can serve you.

Our aim is always to provide you with the best products and the most efficient service. One way we can serve you more efficiently is to have you open a VIP credit account with us.

VIPs are assured of quick service when making purchases, are provided a detailed record of all purchases, and receive other benefits such as our seasonal brochures and notices of special "after hours" sales. These sales are open only to our VIPs.

You are a Very Important Person to us, and we would like to serve you in some very special ways. Won't you complete the enclosed application so that we may consider you for membership in our VIP club?

Thank you for shopping Continental. We want to continue to serve you well.

Sincerely,

Alice K. Maloney

Alice K. Maloney
VIP Coordinator

Encl.: VIP Application

cc: Mr. Nathan Daniels

that the application be mailed, the proprietor may respond to the application with a simple pre-printed post card.

Larger retailers obviously will receive more applications and will respond in a more mechanical manner. These firms often use a completely pre-printed letter or an automatically typed letter that inserts the receiver's name in the appropriate places. (See Chapter 11 on automated letters.) The purpose of the letter is to let the person know the application was received, to maintain contact, and to provide a time frame as to when the customer can expect to learn about the status of the request. In this type of letter, you want to maintain a very positive attitude but not give the impression that credit will automatically be given (see Figure 9–3).

Wholesalers generally will take a somewhat different approach. Establishing credit for organizations is often more complex and time consuming than for retail customers, because the dollar commitment most likely will be much greater. Because of the time needed for credit evaluation, it is important to respond to the applicant with a letter indicating the application has been received. At the same time, it is possible to get the process moving toward establishment of a working relationship with the potential credit customer. Thus, the letter of response to the firm should be a sales-oriented letter, introducing the sales representative and providing additional information on products or services (see Figure 9–4).

Making the Credit Decision

It is necessary to check credit references.

Up to this point, the procedures relating to credit have been very routine and mechanical. No decisions have been necessary—mechanical steps have been followed in establishing contact with potential credit customers. However, a decision eventually must be made: Will you or will you not grant the applicant credit? In order to make that decision, you will need to obtain information from sources *other than* the applicant.

In theory, the decision maker is concerned with the applicant's capital, character, conditions, and capacity. But more realistically, what are the specific data needed and how can those data be obtained?

Credit information can be obtained from a credit association or credit references.

There are two basic methods that can be used in attempting to gather data so you can make the decision. The first, and perhaps the most predominant method today, is to retain a credit association or bureau. The association investigates credit applicants and provides you with information to aid in making a decision. Because of the volume of credit applications and the constantly changing legal factors concerning credit, many organizations find it best to rely upon a reputable credit bureau.

A second way is for an organization to engage in its own credit search. In this case it will be necessary to contact various references that the applicant has supplied. These requests are designed to make a response easy by clearly naming the individual requesting credit and by using the commonly ac-

Figure 9–3
Indicating Application
Received: Large
Retailer

Continental Store
~~~
606 Jefferson Street
New Orleans, Louisiana 70140

June 9, 198-

Mrs. Norma Jenkins
1705 Pathway Drive
New Orleans, LA 70140

Dear Mrs. Jenkins:

Your application for a credit account with Continental has been
received and currently is being processed. Thank you for your
application; we look forward to many years of serving you.

We hope you will be visiting our store soon and often. Each week we
have a number of sales in each of our nineteen departments plus a
variety of seasonal specials. Enclosed are a few brochures concerning
some of our current and future specials. Do try to take advantage of
them.

We will let you know about the credit arrangements within three weeks.

Cordially,

Alice K. Maloney

Alice K. Maloney
Credit Coordinator

Enclosures

Start with a friendly opening.

Promote current sales and
specials.

Close in a friendly manner.

**Figure 9–4
Indicating Application
Received: Wholesaler/
Manufacturer**

fashion frames
Elite Avenue
Evanston, IL 60201

July 29, 198-

Dr. Rodger Jinks, O.D.
707 Boeing Lane
DeKalb, IL 60115

Dear Dr. Jinks:

Your request for a credit account with Fashion Frames has been
received and is now being processed. You should hear from us
concerning the status of your credit within thirty days. We
appreciate your consideration and look forward to a professional
relationship with you.

As you know, we specialize in fashion frames. Today most eyeglass
wearers are becoming fashion conscious about their eye wear.
Therefore, our line of fashion frames will serve your discerning
clientele very well.

Enclosed is a brochure showing the brand-new Champs Elysees line of
frames that is available in this region only from us. We anticipate
that this European-type frame will be most popular among middle-aged
women in the coming months.

Our complete 395-page catalogue and sales and ordering kit will be
delivered personally to you. Ms. Dorien Oliver will be contacting you
within the week to meet with you, answer your questions, and provide
you with the extensive catalog of our current inventory.

Thank you for completing the credit application.

Sincerely,

Omar K. Abrahms

Omar K. Abrahms,
Manager

Encl.

cepted terminology of credit managers. These requests assure confidentiality; they are courteous and offer similar services to the recipient.

Both the large and small retailer will use very similar procedures in attempting to efficiently gather the applicant's credit record. A printed form (which is often part of the letter) will be used, on which the respective names can be inserted. Since the retailer will contact from three to six references for each applicant, there is a need for a quick and efficient procedure.

Efficient procedures are vital in obtaining credit information.

The contents of the letter and form are controlled by what the retailer feels is important in making the credit decision. Usually the current amount of credit outstanding, the highest amount of credit outstanding, the promptness in paying bills, the limits of credit and the length of the relationship are important factors in making the credit decision. Information in these areas frequently will be requested in the standard form sent to references (see Figure 9–5).

Why is *are* and not *is* used in this sentence? (See Appendix 1.)

You may be able to gain a faster response by noting the date you sent the letter and the date you need the data returned to you. As you recall, you want to get back in contact with the applicant within three weeks. That means you need a rapid turnaround from the references.

Again, the approach used by wholesalers will be a bit different. The primary differences between obtaining data on an individual retail customer and on a business are the amount of detailed information required and the greater hesitancy on the part of one firm to actively criticize another firm. Generally the organization requesting data will want some credit history on the applicant and information on the manner of its payments (see Figures 9–6a and 9–6b).

It is possible to create the form so that the name of the firm being investigated is not shown. Because of the nature of the request, the firm requesting data probably will receive a better response if the cover letter is individually typed and individually signed by the credit manager. Except for the greater sensitivity to privacy and the greater detail of information sought, the correspondence regarding a firm and an individual is similar.

Responding Favorably or Unfavorably to Applications

After the credit references of the potential credit customer are checked, a decision must be made and communicated to the applicant. It is nice to say yes, but sometimes it is necessary to say no. Basically, you want to report the good news and establish an ongoing credit relationship with the client. The letter generally will explain the credit terms and encourage the client to use your services and their credit.

When it is necessary to deny a person or a firm credit you still want to retain their goodwill and, if possible, their cash business. The element of tact is important, but at the same time you need to make it perfectly clear that credit is not being offered. It is possible to say no and still secure the individual or firm as a customer—a cash customer.

The letter granting or refusing credit should be extremely tactful.

Figure 9–5
Retailer's Request for
Credit Information

Hank's Hardware
300 Main Street, West Point, Virginia   23181

To: ACME Appliances
        803 West Avenue
        West Point, VA 23081

From: Hank's Hardware
        300 Main Street
        West Point, VA 23081

Date: June 17, 198-

Re: M/M Edmond T. Simmons, Jr.
        2005 W. Evergreen Avenue
        West Point, VA 23181

                                        Response Requested By: June 24, 198-

The above-named person(s) has listed you as a credit reference in
making application for credit.

Will you please provide us with information concerning his/her/their
payment record with you. This will aid us substantially in making our
decision; of course, the data you supply will be kept confidential. A
postage-paid envelope is enclosed for your convenience.

_ _

Current credit balance $ _____ .
The highest amount of credit outstanding was $ _____ on _____ .
Payments made: Promptly   Slowly   Begrudgingly
Credit limit with you: $ _____ .
Applicant opened account with you on _____ .

Additional comments:

Thank you for your consideration in providing these data; if we might
reciprocate for you--please contact us.

Encl.

A cover letter for a credit
information form is often
used.

Elite Avenue
Evanston, IL 60201

```
To:      Credit Manager
         Scientific Optical Supply
         3303 North Michigan Avenue
         Chicago, IL 60606

From:    Omar K. Abrahms, Manager
         Fashion Frames
         Elite Avenue
         Evanston, IL 60201

Date:    August 1, 198-

Re:      Dr. Rodger Jinks, O.D.
         707 Boeing
         DeKalb, IL 60115

File #:  1073

Dr. Jinks has requested a credit account with us and has listed your
firm as a reference.  It would be very helpful to us if you could
provide some basic information about your business relationship with
Dr. Jinks.

Will you please complete the enclosed form and return it to us by
August 12, 198-?  Of course, the information you supply will be kept
confidential.  If we might be of similar service to you in the future,
please contact us.

A pre-paid return envelope is provided.


Enclosures:
Credit form
Pre-paid envelope
```

**Figure 9–6a
Wholesaler's/
Manufacturer's
Request for Credit
Information:
The Letter**

Using a fill-in form helps to
obtain a quick response.

Elite Avenue
Evanston, IL 60201

File #1073

ACCOUNT HISTORY

Client established account with you on _____ .

Approximate $ _____ business transacted with client.

Highest credit outstanding $ _____ on _____ .

Highest amount due O/A $ _____ on _____ .

PAYMENT HISTORY

_____ Discounts

_____ Pays C.O.D., customer's request

_____ Pays C.O.D., your request

Pays: rapidly   slowly   very slowly

Has it been necessary to: (check)

_____ write collection letters?

_____ place account for collection?

_____ collect by attorney?

Comments:

Signature: _____

Title: _____

Date: _____

Communicating with Former Credit Customers

Sometimes customers will stray away from your firm. This can be due to a number of reasons—your sales representative has been lackadaisical, the customer has forgotten you, or another firm has attracted your customer. Whatever the reason, a segment of the market has been lost. Instead of forsaking these potential customers, this group of former credit customers should be contacted.

Whether you operate with a series of file cards or with a sophisticated computer system, it is relatively easy to identify credit customers who are not making use of their credit. If your clientele are retail consumers, it is good to follow up on these individuals. It makes no sense to keep accounts on individuals who are no longer active. The communication to former customers generally indicates an interest in them and seeks to discover why they have not been using their charge accounts. Such a letter promotes you as a considerate and efficient organization, while it announces any new services or products available now that were not available in the past.

As part of file maintenance, it is a good procedure to make contact with former customers once a year. Because about 20 percent of the population move each year, it is wise to use first-class postage and print *Address Correction Requested* on the envelope. These measures guarantee you will receive a notice from the Post Office if the individual has moved from the address you have posted in your files.

An effort should be made to reactivate former credit accounts.

Seeking Credit for Your Organization

In any organization, there will be times when it will be beneficial to make a purchase or a series of purchases on credit. This can be accomplished through a letter that is basically a letter of request—you are asking the recipient to take the action of granting you credit. The letter requesting credit should be like other letters of request—polite, precise on what you want, and should provide enough information so that the receiver can make an intelli-

A request for credit from an organization should include supporting financial data and an indication of future business.

gent decision. The request for credit generally has three parts: 1) a statement of request; 2) proof of financial stability; and 3) an indication of future orders.

It is advantageous to include some financial data (larger companies may enclose a financial statement) or indicate an easy way for the potential creditor to obtain credit references. This information aids in processing your order. Otherwise, the recipient will just send you a credit application blank and ask you to start at first base. It generally is considered tactless to ask for credit on a one-time purchase. If you expect the receiver to respond favorably, it will be to your advantage to indicate the probability of future orders (see Figure 9–7).

Because credit is an important part of doing business, it is necessary for the manager not only to know the financial aspects of credit, but also to understand how to communicate about credit effectively. Probably the easiest activity is to offer credit to a customer.

However, obtaining credit information and reporting that you will not offer credit is certainly not a simple (or enjoyable) communication task in credit operations. But because credit is vital in our society, the better you can communicate on this important matter the more business you will do.

Collection Communications

Collection communications must be carefully planned.

A risk of conducting business and extending credit is that some people can be very, very slow in paying their bills or may not wish to pay at all. Delinquent or unpaid bills are costly to the creditor. Therefore, something has to be done to gain payment. Just as communications must be planned for attracting credit customers, communications also must be designed to obtain payments from those customers who are negligent in paying their bills as scheduled.

There are four basic purposes to any collection communication:

1. obtain the payment;
2. maintain goodwill;
3. attempt to retain the customer; and
4. leave no doubt that you mean business.

The methods you use to achieve these four purposes will depend very much on the specific situation.

Dos and *Don'ts* of Collection Communications

Remember these dos and don'ts in collection letters.

Some definite guidelines can be followed to implement the objectives. There are some things you should do and there are some things you should definitely not do.

Hank's Hardware
300 Main Street, West Point, Virginia 23181

March 14, 198-

Hard Hammer Company
Box 735
Birmingham, AL 35201

Dear Sirs:

Will you please ship us the following order of hammers on credit so we
may stock your product immediately?

    24 #10s
    12 #15s
    12 #20s
    12 #22s
    24 #25s

We have been established in West Point for fifteen years and enjoy a
successful business. If you desire information concerning our
financial status you may contact:

    Mr. William T. Bently
    Vice-President
    First National Bank
    100 Main Street
    West Point, VA 23181   phone 804/549-3000

or Mrs. Howard T. Wentworth, Jr.
    President
    West Point Federal Savings
    10 West Point Avenue
    West Point, VA 23181   phone 804/549-8686

We are a member in good standing of the West Point Chamber of Commerce
(Mr. Ted Savanda, Executive Director, P.O. Box #1, West Point, VA
23181) and of the National Hardware Merchants Association.

Your product should be perfect for our clientele and we think we
should be able to place an order similar to this one six times each
year.

           Sincerely,

           Henry Henniger

           Henry Henniger, Owner

Figure 9–7
Seeking Credit for
Your Organization

Make the credit request.

Supply credit references.

Indicate possibility of future
business.

1. The **Dos** of Collection:
   a. Be courteous;
   b. Be specific in reporting the date when payment was due and when further action will be taken;
   c. Indicate the exact amount due;
   d. Incorporate a strong *you* approach.
2. The **Don'ts** of Collection:
   a. Do not apologize for asking what is owed you;
   b. Do not engage in a shouting contest and make idle threats; do not make physical or mental threats;
   c. Do not harass the individual;
   d. Do not lecture or sermonize.

In clear language, the creditor wants to call attention to a problem and get it resolved immediately. You must be careful how you word the statement asking for payment. Even though there is no doubt that the receiver owes you money, the courts have ruled that you cannot threaten, pester, or slander an individual in asking for payment. The *Dos* are important, but they cannot be presented in such a manner that the receiver might decide you are soft. On the other hand, you are not to come across as Attila the Hun.

The Collection Series

A series of collection messages is efficient and economical.

Generally the creditor will have a planned sequence of reminders and letters that can be sent to delinquent accounts. It is a fairly mechanical system, but it takes some careful organization and implementation. The series is not so foolproof that it will run itself, and certain changes are necessary according to the classification of the account: is the firm a good, fair, or poor risk? The collection series may consist of the following broad steps.

A simple reminder   Most of the time, the first contact with a delinquent account is a very routine reminder. This can take one of the following forms. A stamp or sticker is placed on the previous bill that may state—*Past Due, Please Remit Today,* or *Just a Reminder.* As an alternative, a preprinted note can be attached to the previous bill or sent in a separate envelope. (Beware of using post cards to call bad habits to a person's attention.) There are a variety of humorous reminders that can be purchased or that you can have designed individually. Many of these approaches are catchy or clever and gain attention.

An oral statement   If the simple reminder has not brought results, it may be a good idea, especially in smaller operations, to make a quick telephone call to the individual. A two-minute phone call could resolve the problem and be less embarrassing to you. There are logical reasons why a good risk has not responded—the address changed and you were not informed; the customer or a member of the customer's family died; the family has been away on vacation, or one of a multitude of reasonable explanations.

Letters   If payment has not been received after implementation of the simple methods just discussed, the next procedure is to start a series of letters. That is, you send one letter and follow it with others if you are not having success in getting the payment.

In attempting to convince the customer to pay, these letters use a variety of appeals.

1. *Fair Play.* This approach is based on the idea that you played fair and provided credit; the receiver should play fair and pay (see Figure 9–8).

2. *Customer's Credit Reputation.* The thrust of the message is that if payment is not received, the individual's credit rating may suffer (see Figure 9–9a).

3. *Pride.* As a well-meaning person of integrity, the customer is certainly ashamed not to meet the commitment.

4. *Fear.* You cannot threaten to put the recipient in debtor's prison, but fear may be instilled through the suggestion of courses of legal action available to the creditor.

5. *Self-Interest.* Although the payment is important to the firm, it is vital to the customer's self-interest. This argument appeals to the integrity of the *self* (see Figure 9–9b).

6. *Collection Agency.* Rightly or wrongly, agencies that collect bills have a reputation for accomplishing their goal—getting the payment. An appeal to not force the company to take this very unpleasant action may be effective (see Figure 9–10).

7. *Legal Action.* A simple statement that this is the *last call* may gain action. "If the payment is not received in _____ days, the next person you will hear from will be the firm's attorney" (see Figure 9–11). If this decision is made and communicated, the next institution the debtor hears from should not be the creditor. It is important, from a strategical and psychological point of view, not to pull back after communicating the action to be taken.

Billing Mistakes

As hard as an organization tries, it will periodically make mistakes. But if the organization can program communications to inform customers they are in error—i. e., behind in making a payment—the organization can also build an

Figure 9–8
Collection Letter:
Appeal to Fair Play

5430 Plainfield Street
Pittsburgh, PA   15217

Dear_____ :

It has now been _____ days since your account for $ _____ has
been listed PAST DUE. We are concerned as to why the payment has not
been made.

We have responded to your wants and provided what you ordered on
credit; certainly turn about is fair play. Therefore, won't you play
by the rules?

May we expect your payment by return mail?

Sincerely,

Anthony B. Just
Credit Manager

Figure 9—9a
Collection Letter:
Appeal to Credit
Reputation

Memorial Stationery Company

1535 Algonquin Road
Jackson, Mississippi   39263

_____

_____
_____
_____

Dear_____ :

Your account is delinquent and the head of our accounting department
has made a special effort to call this to my attention.

You must understand that I was surprised; in fact I had the accounting
department double check the account because your credit history is
good.

Obviously something must be wrong and there must be some good reason
for the non-payment. Won't you note on the opposite side of this
letter what the problem is? I would like to help you at this end.

You have been one of our good customers with an excellent credit
reputation. We both want that reputation maintained. Therefore, send
me either your check for $ _____ or a clear explanation for the
non-payment no later than _____.

Sincerely,

Marvin D. Kleinow
Director
Credit Relations

Figure 9–9b
Collection Letter:
Appeal to Self-Interest

Hank's Hardware
300 Main Street, West Point, Virginia   23181

_____

_____
_____
_____

Dear_____ :

Your account for $ _____ still has not been paid. I simply do
not understand your negligence. We must insist on payment when due.
It obviously will be in your best interest to clear this matter
immediately. If we do not receive payment in _____ days it will be
necessary for us to take action which will be harmful to your
interests.

Send us your check today in the enclosed envelope.

Mildred Anderson
Credit Department

Figure 9-10
Collection Notice

CROSS TIMING DEVICES

1225 Lehigh Avenue   Boulder, Colorado 80396

To: Ms. Kathy Nadden

From: Lawrence T. Stephens, Head
       Credit Department

Date: Wednesday, August 10, 198-

Because your account has been delinquent for _____ days, we will be
taking the following action one week from the above date:

> Your account will be submitted to our collection agency for
> immediate settlement. The agency, besides securing the
> payment from you, will also notify over 275 businesses in
> this area that you are a poor credit risk.

Won't you help yourself and help us by clearing this matter
immediately--send us a check for $ _____ today!

Figure 9–11
Collection Notice:
Announcement of
Legal Action

Hank's Hardware
300 Main Street, West Point, Virginia   23181

To:

From:

Date:

You are hereby informed that because we have not received satisfactory
settlement of your past-due account in the amount of $ _____,
your account is being referred to our legal firm.

After _____ 198-, your account will be in the hands of Byler,
Tyler, and Tims, 212 West Elm, Suite 222, Rockford, IL 60001 (phone
815/779-2332). If we have not received payment by the stated date,
all further communications should be made to Byler, Tyler, and Tims
who will be in charge of taking the court action against you.

cc: Byler, Tyler, and Tims

apology communication into the system. Perhaps customers will be less angered and feel that someone really does care if they receive a letter from a high official in the organization apologizing for the miscalculation. The letter can indicate that the firm truly regrets the error and the Vice-President for Customer Relations or President insists on knowing of these mistakes. The letter may suggest that further steps are being taken to correct the system and that the customer's understanding is appreciated (see Figure 9–12).

Concluding Comments

The responsibilities and rigors of credit and collection are present in most organizations today. Credit policies will change with the economy. The laws and regulations concerning credit seem to be in a constant state of flux as interest rates change. But credit communications continue. The communicator has a responsibility to keep up to date on the changes and to accurately reflect policy and regulations in clearly written statements. Just as the organization may take an aggressive attitude in attempting to attract credit customers, it can be necessary to take a most aggressive approach in attracting the credit payments. Communication is the vehicle.

Today it is possible, especially in larger firms, to go through the entire gamut of credit and collection communications without ever coming face-to-face with the customer. This lack of visual contact means that the notices an organization prepares must be excellent. Therein rests the challenge of credit and collection communications.

It sometimes is said that communication is an activity that defies measurement. Your credit and collection communications and their results can be measured—how many new credit customers do you attract, how many former customers return, and how many delinquent customers pay.

MEMO

To: Students
From: The Authors
Subject: Credit and Collection Communications

Every year, the importance of credit in our society grows. Some economists now predict that someday we may live in a cashless society. Knowledge of the basic types and techniques of credit and collections communications discussed in this chapter will be of increasing help to you in your career during the decades ahead.

Figure 9–12
Billing Mistake:
Letter of Apology

Continental Store
~~~
606 Jefferson Street
New Orleans, Louisiana 70140

May 28, 198-

Mrs. Maxine Robinson
1412 South Stormfern Avenue
Columbus, Ohio 43215

Dear Mrs. Robinson:

You are certainly correct . . . we did goof! And we want to tell you
how sorry we are for the inconvenience you encountered.

Your $75.00 payment for March was received and recorded by our
accounts receivable department. However, the recording was done on
our computer records where your designation is AB 432012.
Unfortunately our recording clerk transposed the last two digits in
your number and one of our other customers was credited with your
payment.

In any event, Mrs. Robinson, our "goof" has been corrected. We do
hope you will accept our apologies and a complimentary copy of Chef
Robaire's new book, French Country Cooking. This illustrated volume
is being mailed to you today with our compliments.

Sincerely yours,

Robert T. Farrell

Robert T. Farrell
Manager, Credit Department

Decision

Here is the guide letter Nancy Montellani prepared for the acceptance of credit applications.

Wilmette Department Store

1900 E. Lake Avenue   Wilmette, Arkansas 72203

_____

_____
_____
_____

Dear_____ :

We are delighted to enclose your Wilmette Department Store Credit Card.

This card may be used to make purchases in any of our branches or at our headquarters store. All you need do is present it to one of our clerks and it will be honored immediately. In addition, as one of our Preferred Customers, you will receive:

1. Advance mailings on all our sales;
2. Free delivery service of any item purchased;
3. Notice of Special Events open only to our Preferred Customers: Fashion Shows, Cooking Demonstrations, Financial Lectures, etc;
4. And a dozen other services; and
5. A free Maurice Fragon tote bag for shopping.

We also want to call your attention to a special offering we are having on our living and dining room furniture line. Please visit our display in the furniture suites. Until June 1, your Wilmette Credit Card will assure you of an immediate 15 percent discount off the listed prices.

These two furniture lines have received the Good Housekeeping Award for Creative Design as well as the Contemporary Furniture Award. We know you will agree that these items are outstanding and at prices thàt will never be better.

This is just representative of the hundreds of other items you will find at Wilmette Department Store at highly competitive prices. So come in tomorrow, _____ , and please bring your new Credit Card to the customer Service Desk on the fourth floor. We would like to present you with a free Wilmette leatherette shopping tote designed by Maurice Fragon.

Cordially yours,

Nancy Montellani
Credit Department

CHAPTER REVIEW

Questions

1. Some companies routinely send out six reminders or letters to delinquent charge customers before they turn the unpaid account over to an attorney or collection agency. Other companies may use a collection series of only three or four messages before they threaten action. What factors dictate the number of letters a company sends out to its delinquent customers before turning the account over for legal action?

2. In a typical collection series, what factors concerning the delinquent account determine the number of form letters and reminders versus the number of individually dictated letters? Describe the primary emphasis of each form letter and individual letter mailed out.

3. Would it be good business practice to send a duplicate invoice stamped "Please remit— This account is overdue" as part of a collection series? If so, where would it fit chronologically with the usual reminders and letters?

4. Some companies resort to sending out humorous past-due reminders with clever poems and cartoon characters to catch the reader's attention. Do you believe that a reminder such as this has a valuable role in a collection series? Explain your answer fully.

5. Is it wise to offer a delinquent customer an alternate way to pay his bill even though your company policy stresses "payment in full in thirty days"? If your answer is yes, where in the collection series would you suggest an alternate way to pay a past-due account?

6. Compare the advantages and disadvantages of collecting past-due accounts using the following three methods:
   a. dunning over the telephone by the store credit manager;
   b. sending a five-element collection series taking a total of three months; and
   c. mailing out one collection letter and then turning the account over to a collection attorney not affiliated with your company.

Exercises

1. Visit the credit department of the main office of a bank. Request copies of routine reminders that the bank sends to customers who are delinquent in paying their loans. Compare the contents and appearance of your reminders with those brought to class by your peers.

2. Interview either an employee at a collection agency or an attorney specializing in collections. Ask the interviewee questions pertaining to the follow-up procedures used to collect past-due accounts. In paragraph form, give the details communicated in the interview.

Applications

1. You are the credit manager for the Knoxville Department Store. It is located in Knoxville, a town of 750,000 people.
   a. Prepare a form letter that can be used to invite credit applications from all new individuals that take up residence in Knoxville.
   b. Prepare a letter acknowledging the receipt of a Request for Credit Account from those Knoxville individuals who responded to your invitation.
   c. Prepare a favorable response to be sent to Knoxville individuals who qualify for a credit account (maximum credit: $500).
   d. Prepare an unfavorable response to be sent to Knoxville individuals who do not qualify for credit. Remember, they may prove to be excellent cash customers.
   e. Prepare a collection series to be sent to Knoxville credit accounts who become delinquent in payment. Include the following: a reminder, two letters (identify the type of appeal used in each), and a final letter threatening legal action.

2. You are a credit assistant for Jack's Furniture Shoppe, and you have been assigned to work on the following past-due file.

Name of customer: Mr. James Hamill
365 Point Breeze Avenue
Miami, Florida 33109
Date of purchase: March 16, 198-

Items purchased: 1 bedroom suite	$1200
1 dining room set	$2000
	$3200
plus tax (5%)	+160
	3360
minus deposit	−500
owed on account	$2860

Balance due—April 30, 198-

Mr. Hamill has not communicated with your store, and the balance is past due. Write the appropriate reminders and letters to be sent to Mr. Hamill in the following situations:

a. Send the first past-due reminder to the customer with a friendly and courteous message.

b. Assume that three weeks have passed since you sent the first letter, and now you must write an individually dictated collection letter that is empathetic and courteous but firm.

c. Mr. Hamill has received a total of five letters from you but has not answered any of them. Write the final letter in your series expressing hope but also threatening legal action.

3. Martin Johnstone Catalogue Company sent out five collection reminders and letters over a three-and-one-half month period to Mrs. Agnes Parker. Mrs. Parker purchased $300 worth of school clothing for her five children and had not paid her bill. She did finally send in the money one day before the account was going to be given to a collection agency. One month later, Mrs. Parker received advertisements and a letter from the catalogue company enticing her to use her credit card again with a $300 limit. What is the rationale of the company encouraging a previously delinquent customer such as Mrs. Parker to resume credit purchases? How would you handle this situation if she were your customer?

4. Each year, you, as the credit manager of a women's dress manufacturing firm, select cash customers who have done business with your firm during the preceding year. You then send each a letter suggesting they apply for a credit account. Write the letter which will be sent to those dealers.

Dilemma

Margo Torres has just secured her first full-time job after completing her course of studies at Conover Community College. Her title is Accounting Assistant at Conover Freight and Transportation Company.

Margo feels that much of her recent good fortune is due to Mr. Albert Fine, an Associate Professor of Accounting at the College. She not only had two excellent courses under his direction, but he also wrote a very strong letter of recommendation in her behalf.

Margo has decided to write a thank-you letter to Mr. Fine.

Decision, see page 197

Letters for Special Situations

Here is a list of the objectives you should understand by the time you complete this chapter. Place a check mark in the box beside each as soon as you feel ready to apply your understanding in a practical situation.

☐ The reasons for writing letters of consideration

☐ The differences among the types of letters of consideration:
  Letter of appreciation
  Thank-you letter
  Congratulatory message
  Message of sympathy

☐ The various situations which might demand a letter of consideration

☐ The importance of goodwill to the organization

☐ The use of letters in building goodwill for your organization

What is the difference in meaning between *receipt* and *recipe*? (See Appendix 1.)

Many types of communication must be sent because of some pressing matter: calling attention to an overdue bill, placing an urgent order, indicating receipt of a credit application, attempting to promote a sale, and many, many instances. These letters become part of the everyday activity in any organization.

The messages studied in this chapter are less routine. They provide an opportunity to express your feelings about personal matters, comment on the accomplishments of another person, or simply build goodwill.

Today there are numerous alternatives available to replace or substitute for the written message of consideration and goodwill, such as clever printed messages. However, those messages were written by someone you do not know, and the messages were printed thousands of times on *thank-you* and *congratulations* cards. Isn't it better to receive a thought the sender created just for you and personally wrote to you? The message may thank the corporate officer for the time spent on the job interview with the writer; it may express appreciation for special assistance received or a dinner attended; or it may congratulate an individual on a promotion or new job.

What other mark of punctuation besides the semicolon could be used in this long sentence? (See Appendix 1.)

There are many types of situations calling for messages of goodwill and consideration. Some are very individual, written to one person for a specific reason. We will refer to these as *letters of consideration*. Others are more mass-oriented, in which the message relates to a class of individuals such as good customers, incomplete customers, or absent customers. We will refer to these as *goodwill letters*.

Letters of Consideration

Sometimes it may appear in these very busy times that courtesy, style, and consideration are not practiced as much as they should be. We all like to be treated in a respectful manner. By writing letters of consideration, you can project your respect for others as well as your feelings of appreciation. There are a variety of situations that call for letters of consideration.

What is the difference in meaning between *respectful* and *respective*? (See Appendix 1.)

These letters are all people-oriented communications. If business is, as one chief executive has stated, "90 percent people and 10 percent money," the importance of these people-oriented letters of consideration becomes obvious. The basic kinds of consideration letters include letters of appreciation, thank-you letters, congratulatory messages, and communications of condolence.

Letters of Appreciation

If an individual or a group of people in an organization go out of the way for you—certainly you can take a few moments to go out of your way. Specifically, you can write the individual or group to express your appreciation. The

situations that call for a letter of appreciation are almost innumerable:

Letters of appreciation thank the receiver for the time and/or effort expended.

1. A client rearranges her schedule so you can see her at your convenience;
2. A sales representative puts forth considerable extra effort to move an order rapidly through channels for you;
3. A person you know only because he is listed in your professional association directory agrees to meet you for lunch when you are in a strange city;
4. The president of a neighborhood political action group invites you to speak to the group on the need for additional commercial zoning in the area of your small business.

Someone has treated you in a special way; the person did not have to do it. For you to justify in your own mind that "words cannot express your appreciation . . ." is a cop-out. Words *can* express an explicit message, but silence on your part may reflect inconsideration toward a person who was thoughtful to you.

The letter of appreciation goes beyond simply thanking the receiver for being kind; it notes the consideration, the extra effort, and kindness extended. Figure 10–1 shows a good example of an effective letter of appreciation.

Thank-You Letters

The thank-you letter is similar to the appreciation letter. The basic difference is that the thank-you letter is related to a more typical situation for the individual being thanked. Some of these situations might include an evening of entertainment or conversation; a meeting or job interview arranged at your request (see Figure 10–2); or a reference letter written on your behalf (see Figure 10–3).

A thank-you letter is appropriate when you are invited to someone's home for a dinner, buffet, or other special event. If a person can go to the extra work and effort to bring you into his or her home, you surely can put forth the effort to thank that person in writing. This holds true whether you are entertained individually or with others. Such a thank-you letter can be written

A thank-you letter is a sign of courtesy and respect.

Figure 10–1
Letter of Appreciation

Hank's Hardware
300 Main Street, West Point, Virginia   23181

October 10, 198-

Mr. Raymond J. Bates, Sr.
President
East Bluff Homeowners Assoc.
212 East Thrush Ave.
West Point, VA 23181

Dear Mr. Bates:

All of us on the Bluff agree that the integrity of our neighborhood
must be maintained. The need for business to expand and our desire to
keep a vibrant residential section on the Bluff have similar
objectives.

It was kind of you to permit me to discuss the need for additional
commercial zoning on the Bluff at the Association meeting last
evening. I especially appreciated the opportunity to answer questions
from the membership and to discuss informally the proposed zoning at
the coffee session following the meeting.

If you or other Association members have additional questions, please
call me. I shall be happy to cooperate in any way possible.

Sincerely,

Henry Henniger
Henry Henniger

Figure 10–2
Thank-You Letter to
Interviewer

1414 S. Oak Drive
Chicago, IL 60025
May 25, 198–

Mr. Melvin Martin
Personnel Director
Jackson Corporation
1111 W. Soto Street
Chicago, IL 60010

Dear Mr. Martin:

This is just a brief word to thank you most sincerely for the time you
spent interviewing me on Tuesday.

What you had to tell me about the firm was exciting and challenging.
Since I've talked to you and learned more about your firm, I am
strongly convinced that I can make a significant contribution.

You will recall I have almost three years of data-processing
experience and a bachelor's degree in management-information systems.

Please call (767-0386) if you have questions, and again, my
appreciation for your interest and courtesy in meeting with me.

Sincerely,

Sandra Colfax

Figure 10–3
Thank-You Letter to
Reference Writer

```
                                              1414 S. Oak Drive
                                              Chicago, IL 60025
                                              May 25, 198-


        Prof. Robert M. Cates
        Dept. of Accounting
        Illinois State University
        Chicago, IL 60019

        Dear Dr. Cates:

        Thank you very much for taking the time to write a letter of reference
        for me to the Jackson Corporation.  Mr. Martin, who interviewed me
        there, told me how thorough and helpful your letter proved to be.

        I want you to know how much I appreciate your effort.  Your time is
        extremely valuable and I'm sure it is not easy for you to interrupt
        your busy schedule.  However, what you did for me was very important.

        Thank you very much, Dr. Cates.

                                         Sincerely yours,

                                         Ann Safier
```

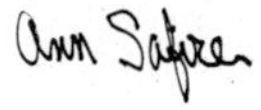

either on your business stationery or on your personal stationery. Your own good judgment must be the guide. Figure 10–4 shows an example of an effective thank-you letter for a pleasant evening at someone's home.

The attributes of both the letter of appreciation and the thank-you letter are similar. The point is that it is always in good taste to place your appreciation and thanks in writing.

Congratulatory Messages

People in the professions generally are active in various business, professional, governmental, religious, political, and/or civic groups. It is not uncommon that an acquaintance, customer, or friend will assume or be elected to a position of importance. The individual has worked hard to achieve the recognition. It only takes a moment to write a deserved letter to the person. If you operate a small business, think of how delighted one of your customers would be to receive a congratulatory letter from you.

In the small business situation, there is another alternative that may work well when you wish to send your congratulations. Have some folded cards printed. On the outside, have a message such as "read about your accomplishment," "saw your name in the news," or "you are in print." Insert the news clipping and write a brief message of congratulations. This is appropriate if you are going to try to keep up with many customers and want to add a personal touch to the procedure. It reveals that you recognize your customers and note their accomplishments.

A written message on a card may be used also as a congratulatory note.

This procedure is informal, but it can be appropriate for recognizing the accomplishments of associates when they are elected to an office in their fraternal association, celebrate their fiftieth wedding anniversary, or are written up in the press for some noteworthy activity. Figure 10–5 shows a sample of a congratulatory letter.

Messages of Sympathy

If a professional associate dies, you are in a position to write the family. To do nothing and to communicate nothing would be unkind. If the situation involves a person with whom you have worked closely and whom you have known for many years beyond just the organizational activities of work, a personally written message is desirable.

After expressing your sorrow, you can point to the person's accomplishments and contributions to the organization and society. If a member of an associate's immediate family dies and you know the associate well, you should express your sadness and extend your support to him or her during the period of bereavement. Figure 10–6 shows a sample letter of condolence. Certainly, these messages are not easy to write. But they are communications that will have a supportive effect on the recipient.

A letter of condolence should be written under the proper circumstances.

What is the difference in meaning among *write, rite,* and *right?* (See Appendix 1.)

Figure 10—4
Thank-You Letter

Continental Store
606 Jefferson Street
New Orleans, Louisiana 70140

September 22, 198-

Mrs. Timothy J. Norton
2 Northridge Lane
Newhampton, PA 10144

Dear Mrs. Norton:

After I had spent most of last Tuesday in meetings with your husband
and other officers in his firm, it was delightful to have an
opportunity to relax that evening in your beautiful home.

Your table was extremely attractive, the dinner was delicious, and the
company excellent.

Thank you for your kindness; you made a typical business trip an
unusual pleasure for me.

Sincerely,

Lora J. Dadson

Lora J. Dadson
Manager
Credit Services

**Figure 10–5
Letter of
Congratulations**

Elite Avenue
Evanston, IL 60201

March 10, 198-

Dr. Rodger Jinks, O.D.
707 Boeing Road
DeKalb, IL 60115

Dear Dr. Jinks:

Congratulations on your recent election to the presidency of the
Northern Illinois Optometric Association. I know you were
instrumental in the formation of the Association several years ago,
and I am pleased that you are continuing to provide leadership to the
group.

As you and your wife come to Chicago frequently, would you please
phone me before you come to the city the next time? Mrs. Abrahms and
I would enjoy taking you and your wife to lunch or dinner--whichever
is more convenient for you.

Sincerely,

Omar K. Abrahms
Manager

**Congratulatory letters are
usually brief.**

Figure 10–6
Letter of Condolence

1101 S. Temple Drive
San Diego, CA 90038
June 21, 198-

Mr. Robert Carlton
1515 West Ocean Drive
San Diego, CA 90044

Dear Bob:

I have just learned of the severe and tragic loss you suffered. I
want to tell you how sincerely sorry I am.

Although I only had the good fortune of spending a few hours with your
father, it was clear to me how much he loved you and how much pride he
had in your accomplishments. Of course, I feel I know him well, for
you frequently have discussed with me his many outstanding attributes.

I am sure you see many of his qualities in your children as well as
clear evidence of how much he contributed to his field and to his
professional associates.

Please accept my sincere sympathies, Bob, on your loss, and extend
them also to your family.

Cordially yours,

Leslie Anderson

Letters of consideration are explicit expressions of your thoughtfulness to another individual or group. The letter is written because of the consideration someone has shown you, or in the case of letters of congratulations or sympathy, your expression of consideration to others. It may appear to you that the letters discussed above are written rarely. That may be true but they—like courtesy and consideration—are always in style. It may be a simple thank you, a letter of appreciation, congratulations, or condolences. Individuals appreciate receiving them and you're a better person for writing them.

In all cases, the letter of consideration must be sincere.

Why is the apostrophe used in the word *you're*? (See Appendix 1.)

Customer Goodwill Communications

Goodwill letters may be sent to a variety of customers or clients—loyal customers, new clients, or absent customers (see Chapter 11). While letters of consideration are individually written for a specific situation, the customer-related goodwill letters usually are sent to a class of people, such as good customers (see Figure 10-7). The identical goodwill letter may be sent to hundreds of individuals. (See Chapter 12 concerning techniques of preparing mass-mail letters individually.) However, you want to create a special identification with the recipient.

Many organizations send messages of goodwill to customers at holiday time in December. These cards and letters are one way to express goodwill toward a customer or client. There are, however, other ways that may appear less mass-oriented and may not get lost in the rush of December mail. A greeting to customers at Thanksgiving or a letter of appreciation and goodwill near the Fourth of July may be appropriate.

It is important that your goodwill letters be sincere in approach and tone. But remember, too, that the purpose of the goodwill communication is not only to express a sincere idea but also to keep your organization's name in front of the individual.

MEMO

To: Students

From: The Authors

Subject: Letters of Consideration and goodwill

The letters discussed in this chapter are not the sort you will write everyday. Still, you should have an opportunity to write many of these letters in the course of your career. Knowing how to write them when the need arises can give you and your organization a special kind of aura in the eyes of those who receive such communications.

Figure 10–7
Letter of Goodwill

Continental Store

606 Jefferson Street
New Orleans, Louisiana 70140

November 15, 198-

Mrs. Elvira Jones
1335 Kalya Lane
New Orleans, LA 70143

Dear Mrs. Jones:

At this time of Thanksgiving, when we reflect on the greatness of our
country and its people, we at Continental wanted to take a moment to
thank you. We want you to know that we appreciate your continued
business; we hope we have earned your support for the future.

The weeks between Thanksgiving and Christmas are often hectic ones.
If there is any way we can help you with your shopping activities in
the coming weeks, please call on us. Next week you will receive our
Special Holiday Guide. I know you will find it beneficial in aiding
you in your shopping in these coming weeks.

All of us at Continental wish you and your family a most pleasant
holiday season.

Sincerely,

J. Jeffrey Swanson
President

**Holidays are appropriate
times for goodwill letters
to be sent.**

Decision

Here is the thank-you letter Margo Torres wrote her professor.

1433 South Fallow Avenue
Conover, Ohio 45222
April 23, 198-

Professor Albert Fine
Department of Accounting
Conover Community College
College Circle
Conover, Ohio 45235

Dear Professor Fine:

This is just a brief note to thank you most sincerely for your many contributions to my good fortune.

The two courses in accounting which I had under your direction gave me a thorough and solid foundation for my work at Conover Freight and Transportation Company. Not only did you share your knowledge with me, but you also motivated me to enjoy the field of accounting tremendously. And you did this in every session with good humor and sensitive concern for each student.

As for the detailed letter of recommendation which you wrote on my behalf, I have been informed by my personnel director that it played a significant role in my selection.

So, Professor Fine, my sincere thanks for all you have done for me. I feel fortunate to have studied with you in the past and to have you for a friend now and in the future.

With very warm regards,

Margo Torres

Margo Torres

CHAPTER REVIEW

Questions

1. What is the distinction, as noted in this chapter, between letters of consideration and goodwill letters?

2. Why is an individual letter of consideration usually superior in the response it receives than the readily available thank-you, "Congratulations," or condolence cards that can be purchased.

3. List several professional situations for the preparation of goodwill letters.

4. What advantage and disadvantage exist in sending out goodwill letters to coincide with a holiday or holiday season?

5. An owner of a business may find many occasions to send goodwill messages to three different groups of people with whom he or she does business. Name these three groups of people and list at least five specific business reasons to send goodwill letters to each one of them.

Applications

1. Assume you have requested one of your instructors to write a letter of reference for you. He has done that and apparently has done a very good job: your interviewer even commented on how complete it was. Write that instructor and thank him for his effort.

2. Assume you completed an interview this morning with the personnel director of a local firm. You are really excited by the job that is available. Of course, you are aware that she is interviewing a number of applicants for the position.
   Write a follow-up letter. Thank the director for her time and the information she shared with you. In a very discreet way, you may also wish to tell her how much you would like to have the job.

3. Jane Kendrick, the owner of a women's boutique, is trying to cut down on business expenses. She knows that the primary purpose of a goodwill message is to enhance warm feelings between the writer and the reader and that the profit motive is secondary. To save money, Jane has decided to stop sending all messages of congratulations and condolences to her steady customers. Do you think that Jane is being a wise businessperson taking this action? Explain your answer in detail.

4. Carlota Cortez graduated from the local community college with her friend, James Smith, ten years ago and has frequently thought of James' success in school despite his early years in an orphan home. Last week, Carlota read this announcement in the local paper:
   "James Smith, instructor of economics at Blair Community College, earned his Ph.D. degree on June 2 at Jamestown University."
   Carlota was so pleased to read about her old classmate's accomplishment that she decided to send him a letter. Write the letter for Carlota.

5. You are a computer programmer for a utility company and for the last six months you have worked overtime Sunday mornings to work on a special project. Last month, your family had two very special occasions necessitating being out-of-town two Sundays to help celebrate. At great hardship to her, another programmer, Elisa Dawson, left her family and filled in for you on the two Sundays. You did thank her orally but you now wish to put the thank-you in writing and send a copy of it to the vice-president so he will be aware of her commendable company spirit. Write this memo.

6. You are the proprietor of a small, discount hardware store in a newly developed community. You have decided to send a letter of welcome to the new home buyers and to enclose a free certificate for a duplicate house or car key with the letter. Although you would like to encourage future business, your primary purpose in sending the letter and certificate is to welcome a new neighbor. Write a goodwill letter that would be appropriate to send to the new home buyers.

7. The cost of dictating and transcribing business letters has increased considerably in the last few years. Budget-minded George Meers decided to cut down on expenses by composing form letters for messages of sympathy, congratulations, and welcome to be sent out when the need arose. Blanks were left on the form letters to fill in the name and address of the recipient and the type of occasion. The duplicated form letters required only a few minutes to complete and prepare for mailing. George was pleased with his money-saving method of sending goodwill letters. Would you be as pleased as George if you were a recipient of one of these letters? In writing, discuss your opinion of George's use of form letters for goodwill messages.

8. You are the buyer of women's hosiery at a department store in Washington, D.C. You have worked in this store for ten years and worked your way up from a sales clerk to an assistant buyer to your present position. One reason for your success was the constant help of Mr. Gerard Green, now retired, who was the hosiery buyer when you started your employment. You just learned that Mr. Green's wife of forty years has died recently. Write an appropriate letter of condolence to Mr. Green.

9. You are the vice-principal of a high school in Philadelphia, Pennsylvania. You have recently learned that Barry DeLia, a bookkeeping teacher, has won first place as captain of his string band in the New Year's Mummers Parade this year. You have heard many people congratulate him for this enviable accomplishment, but you have decided to write a short note of congratulations to him and place it in his faculty box at school.

10. The owner of a children's clothing store decided to send the following goodwill message to her charge account customers who paid their bills on time:

Dear Customer:

This is to acknowledge our appreciation for your prompt payment of our bills. Customers like you help us stay in business. Visit us again soon.

Cordially yours,

What, if anything, is wrong with this goodwill letter? If you see a need for improvement, revise the letter.

Dilemma

For the last six months, Roosevelt Jackson has worked as an office assistant at Oakville Community College's office of admissions. His supervisor there is Dr. Kathryn Cutler, the director of admissions.

In corresponding with applicants, the office uses a number of standard form letters. One of the most important of these is used when an applicant has submitted an incomplete package in which one or more of the required items has not been included. Every applicant for admission is requested to submit 1) a transcript from high school and all previous colleges; 2) a completed application form; and 3) a $25.00 application fee.

Recently, several applicants have submitted incomplete packages even *after* this form letter was sent to them, and Ms. Cutler believes that there may be a problem in the form letter. Therefore, she has asked Roosevelt to prepare a new form letter for this situation.

Decision, see page 217

Business Letters: Present and Future Systems

Here is a list of the objectives you should understand by the time you complete this chapter. Place a check mark in the box beside each as soon as you feel ready to apply your understanding in a practical situation.

☐ The three elements of the word-processing triangle:
   Equipment
   Procedures
   People

☐ The various electronic means of transmitting messages:
   Mailgram
   Facsimile
   TWX
   Telex
   Typewriter network

☐ The uses of form letters, guide letters, and computer-assisted letters

☐ The basic procedures for effective dictation

The slowest part in the process of writing may be getting the words out of the communicator's mind and onto paper. However, once the words *are* out, mechanical processing can speed it along. The current generation of typing equipment does much more than just type. It erases automatically, it has a memory, and it can automatically type your envelope after typing your letter. Perhaps your writing skills are not accelerating as rapidly as are changes in mechanical equipment, but once you have the idea, technology can provide ways to reproduce and transmit it very quickly.

The use of mechanical processing can speed and improve your communications.

The Typewriter

It is estimated that the new memory-capable typewriters will make the common electric typewriter obsolete. Before long, the standard electric machines will be as rare in the American office as the manual typewriter is now.

The cost of producing an individually written letter in 1980 was approximately $6.20 and the costs have been increasing approximately 10 percent annually. The best way to reduce that cost is to develop equipment and systems that will put the words on paper faster. If over a period of time you look at the *net* words per minute on paper among three different kinds of typing technologies, the results are startling. Of course, there are related dollar savings:

The cost of producing a business letter now is well over $6.00.

Type of Machine	Net Words per Minute
Conventional typing	10
Magnetic media equipment	30
Computer-assisted text processing	2000

It is estimated that U.S. businesses and the government mail about 60 billion first-class letters each year. If costs are reduced on those letters, enormous savings can be recovered. The technology of placing words on paper is changing rapidly to aid the organization in achieving these savings. But putting the words on paper is only one part of the problem—people and procedures are also involved.

Word Processing

The typewriter by itself can be a most effective tool. However, place it in an efficient system and its capabilities can multiply. An entire industry has been formed around *word processing.* Word processing can be seen as an equilateral triangle consisting of equipment, procedures, and people[1] (see Figure 11–1).

Word processing is now a vital and important industry in transmitting information.

[1]From "Word Processing Is . . . ," Lutheran Mutual Life Insurance Company, Waverly, Iowa.

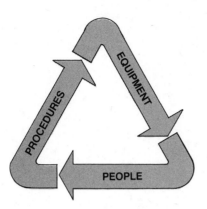

Figure 11–1.
Word Processing Seen as an Equilateral Triangle.

Reprinted courtesy of Lutheran Mutual Life Insurance Company, Waverly, Iowa

Equipment

The most sophisticated word-processing setup consists of the basic input units (dictation equipment) and output facilities (automatic equipment) plus individuals such as proofreaders, editors, and supervisors to monitor the process.[2] As represented in Figure 11–2, the word-processing system surrounds and supports the principal who is the initiator of the communication.

Often the initiator, using the telephone or dictating machine, dictates the message into a centralized unit where the message is stored until transcribed by a secretary working in a processing center. Such centers enable organizations to produce paperwork rapidly, efficiently, economically, and in a uniform professional manner. The manufacturers of output equipment emphasize the equipment side of the word-processing triangle, but the people and procedure sides are very important. Figure 11–3 shows how the communicator, equipment, and procedures are linked in the word-processing concept.[3]

What is the difference in meaning between *principal* and *principle*? (See Appendix 1.)

An efficient word-processing center operates on a systems approach involving input and output functions.

Procedures

As organizations create word-processing centers, complementary procedures are necessary in order to maximize word production. The procedures can include such factors as:

What is the difference in meaning between *complimentary* and *complementary*? (See Appendix 1.)

[2]Leonard B. Kruk, "Word Processing and Its Implications for Business Communication Courses," *Journal of Business Communication* 15(3), (Spring 1978):11.

[3]Ibid.

Figure 11–2.
The Word-Processing/
Administrative Support
System.

Figures 11–2 and 11–3 from
"Word Processing and Its
Implications for Business
Communications Courses" by
Leonard Kruk, *Journal of
Business Communication*
15 (Spring 1978):11. Copyright
© 1978 *Journal of Business
Communication.* Reprinted by
permission of Leonard Kruk.

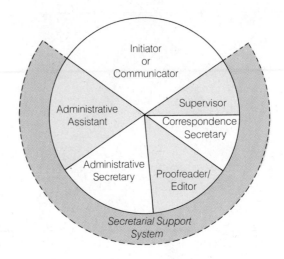

1. how to dictate;
2. what items have priority in transcription;
3. when to use form and guide letters;
4. what is acceptable input;
5. what is acceptable output; and
6. how to anticipate turn-around times.

Having excellent equipment is just the first step; the procedures guide the users and operators in the efficient use of the word-processing center.

People

What is the difference in meaning between *personnel* and *personal*? (See Appendix 1.)

The factor that makes the system work is the personnel involved. If one side of an equilateral triangle can be more important than another, people are the primary element. The personnel often can complicate the process, and that side of the triangle is the most difficult to control.

It is often hard for people to adjust to new systems and procedures. If managers are accustomed to carefully writing out their letters in longhand or dictating to a personal secretary, the adjustment to the more efficient but more impersonal word-processing center or dictation equipment may not be smooth. The word-processing center assumes dictation abilities which often are not present.

Figure 11–3.
From Idea to Print by
Word Processing

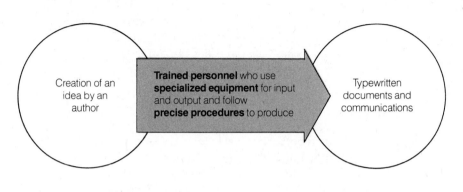

Creation of an idea by an author

Trained personnel who use **specialized equipment** for input and output and follow **precise procedures** to produce

Typewritten documents and communications

Electronic Communications

Organizations that have word-processing centers are in a position to accomplish other communication efficiencies. So far, we have traced the message out of the initiator's head, passed it on to a secretary in a processing center, and eventually into its final form. The next major hurdle is actually transmitting the message.

Traditionally, individuals and organizations have used the U.S. mails to transmit messages. Unfortunately, the mail service has grown in expense and simultaneously in problems. Therefore, organizations which send large volumes of messages have sought alternative transmission systems.

Electronics plays a major role in improving the transmission of information.

Mailgram

The Mailgram is sent using a cooperative system between Western Union and the U.S. Postal Service. The system permits the initiator to send the message via Western Union to a receiving station near the post office of the receiver. There the message is typed on paper, stuffed into an envelope, and delivered to the local post office. If the message is sent before 7 P.M., it should be received in the following day's mail.

The Mailgram is useful for various form letters, and the communication process has the advantage of providing a written message at a relatively low cost. This process cuts the delays associated with normal postal deliveries and is available to anyone with a telephone.

Facsimile

Using the telephone lines, *fax* communication permits the transmission of words and pictures. In organizations that need to quickly exchange detailed charts, graphs, and sketches, the fax process can be helpful. In order to use fax, both the initiator and receiver of the communication need a fax adapter for the telephone. The system legally sidesteps the entire U.S. postal service.

TWX and Telex

For organizations with geographically dispersed divisions that must communicate quickly, Western Union provides teletypewriter and teleprinter exchange services. The initiator and receiver both need a teletype machine in order to exchange information. These systems permit direct two-way communication and provide a written record of the conversation. It also is possible to communicate with other organizations that have the telecommunication equipment. These systems are vast networks with over 225,000 installations in North America.

Organizations find this mode of communication vital when it is necessary to simultaneously and quickly share important information with far-flung divisions and offices. Examples of this might be providing major statements by company officers, company stock reports, earnings data, basic news, or new procedures to meet a government regulation.

Typewriter Network

Using the lines of AT&T and linking typewriters, it is possible for organizations to create *original copy* material. The typewriters are linked in a network and can communicate with one another. By adding computers and satellites to the system, it is possible to produce even faster and clearer copy.

The era of electronic mail is present and is expanding. The various electronic delivery systems, when used in conjunction with word-processing centers, provide organizations with enormous opportunities to initiate, send, and receive *the written word* in seconds across thousands of miles. Also, when integrated with new computer filing systems, the need, expense, and length of time for handling paper can be reduced. The computer can store the message and reproduce it for you in writing or on a video screen.

Figure 11–4 is more than a futuristic picture; it is the way organizations are going to send written and pictorial data faster. From the input to the output and delivery, automation is speeding the communication process. The slowest element in the total process is the individual human.

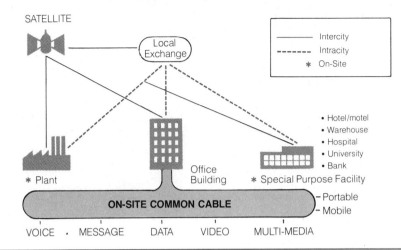

FUTURE INFORMATION NETWORKS

SATELLITE

Local Exchange

——————	Intercity
- - - - - -	Intracity
*	On-Site

* Plant

Office Building

* Special Purpose Facility

• Hotel/motel
• Warehouse
• Hospital
• University
• Bank

ON-SITE COMMON CABLE

– Portable
– Mobile

VOICE · MESSAGE   DATA   VIDEO   MULTI-MEDIA

**Figure 11–4
Electronic
Communications of
the Future**

Form and Guide Letters

Many communications are used again and again in business organizations. If it is possible to mechanize entire letters that are mailed frequently, and parts of standard letters that are repeated often, efficiency and expertise will be gained. Form and guide letters enable organizations to give standard responses to routine inquiries, sales situations, and claims. The forms and guides permit the organization to select the one best way to respond. This saves the manager's time and permits every letter to be carefully thought through and consistent in its tone and policy.

Form and guide letters permit organizations to make standard responses to large numbers of people at low costs.

Guide Letters

There are numerous internal and external memos and letters that are standard. Only selected parts need be inserted by the sender. Instead of having many managers each writing dozens of original letters, guides can be provided. These guide letters are distributed to all personnel who may have use for them, such as managers, secretaries, and word-processing personnel.

Each guide letter can then be appropriately titled and numbered. Also, each paragraph in the letter can be either numbered or lettered (see Figure 11–5a). Where a word-processing center is available, the initiator of the communication would mark the message by number and title (for example, #17—*Credit Card Request for Second Member of Household*). The initiator

Figure 11–5a
Favorable Response to
Credit Card Request
for Second Member
of Household:
Guide Letter

Continental Store
~~~
606 Jefferson Street
New Orleans, Louisiana 70140

_____

_____
_____ _____

Dear _____ :

**A**

Thank you for taking the time to write us concerning the availability
of credit extension to your (son, daughter, wife, husband, mother,
father) who resides with you.  Under Continental's liberal credit
policies for our fine customers, we will be pleased to extend a credit
card in your name to your _____ .  Simply complete the
enclosed form and return it to us.

**B**

As I am sure you can understand, there are some limitations on this
line of credit and of course you are responsible for any charges
incurred on this account.

**C**

You have been one of our customers for over _____ years and we hope
that by providing this additional service to you and your family, you
will be one of our happy families for many years to come.

**D**

If you or your _____ have any questions concerning this
credit arrangement or any of our other fine services, please call us.

**E**

(Best wishes for a pleasant holiday.)
(Best wishes for a delightful summer.)
(Best wishes.)

                                        Sincerely,

                                        *James J. Johnson*

                                        James J. Johnson
                                        Credit Manager


Enclosure:  Credit Agreement

also would provide relevant information including the full name and address of the recipient. If part of the guide letter is not exactly appropriate, the writer can dictate a substitute paragraph (see Figure 11 – 5b).

As the name suggests, the guide letter is a basic map. For a number of reasons, the initiator may need to take some detours—insert a special sentence or paragraph. But the approach, tone, and format which the organization has found to be successful is presented to all concerned individuals in the firm as a model.

### Form Letters

Whereas the guide letter is intended to point the writer in the correct direction, the form letter is more absolute. It is used as a standard response to a recurring situation or in a mass-mailing effort.

With modern techniques, it is possible to produce final-copy form letters that appear to be individually typed or almost as if the letter were created just for the receiver. With today's sophisticated recipients, it may be best not to attempt to create the illusion of individuality or to go to excessive expense to make the obviously mass-produced letter look as if it were created especially for one of the ten thousand recipients.

Also, there are times when the obvious form response is the most efficient mode of communication and will be appreciated by the receiver—a notice that the article ordered has arrived at the store, a reservation is confirmed at a hotel, or an appointment should be scheduled with the dentist.

The form letter is set up in a uniform way and is not to be changed. The only difference between the same form letter sent to Mr. Smith and Ms. Jones is that the appropriate name, address, and other brief items are inserted.

### Computer-Assisted Letters

Some of the modern automatic typing equipment have miniature computer memories that make it possible to connect the computer system with the communication process. There are situations where you may desire to send

Figure 11—5b
Favorable Response to
Credit Card Request
for Second Member
of Household:
Completed Guide Letter

*Continental Store*
~~~
606 Jefferson Street
New Orleans, Louisiana 70140

November 28, 198-

Mr. Raymond B. Dayton
1703 Drury Lane
New Orleans, LA 70147

Dear Mr. Dayton:

Thank you for taking the time to write us concerning the availability
of credit extension to your son, who resides with you. Under
Continental's liberal credit policies for our fine customers, we will
be pleased to extend a credit card in your name to your son. Simply
complete the enclosed form and return it to us.

As I am sure you can understand, there are some limitations on this
line of credit and of course you are responsible for any charges
incurred on this account.

In reviewing your request, Mr. Dayton, I noted that your family has
been doing business with us for over 60 years! We are pleased to have
been able to serve your family for several generations. I hope we at
Continental will continue to win your trust and shopping confidence.

If you or your son have any questions concerning this credit
arrangement or any of our other services, please call us.

Best wishes for a pleasant holiday.

Sincerely,

James J. Johnson

James J. Johnson
Credit Manager

Enclosure: Credit Agreement

form letters to individuals, but you also want to insert a variety of personal or individual data. Computer-assisted correspondence makes this possible.

For example, you want to gain additional sales from all your department store customers who made major kitchen appliance purchases during the past eighteen months. The store is opening a new *Kitchen Korner* department that will specialize in various kitchen aids. You feel that these recent customers will be likely prospects to use this new department. You can easily program your computer to select only those customers who made a purchase during the past 18 months; identify those who purchased a major kitchen appliance; and identify the appliance they purchased. You want to select customers who purchased one or more of the following: refrigerator, oven, or range.

Computer-assisted communication systems can save time and money by computer selection of information and/or prospects.

The basic form letter is prepared and space is left in appropriate places to insert the individual information (see Figure 11–6a). The newest generation of computer-assisted equipment automatically will merge the needed data and justify the right margin so that odd spaces are not left in the final copy.

For the purchasers of refrigerators, you may want to suggest they buy dishes that can go directly from refrigerator to stove or oven; for the purchasers of ovens, you may want to recommend they buy cookie sheets, baking sets, and casserole dishes; for the individual who purchased a range, you may recommend various kinds of cooking utensils and sets of skillets, pots and pans. Programmed correctly, the computer will match each individual purchaser with the appropriate listing of goods you are offering (see Figure 11–6b).

The computer-assisted letter is obviously not individual. But it is a valuable piece of correspondence, and it generally gets the receiver's attention. One important advantage of the letter is its ability to insert the recipient's name in the body of the letter, and most people like to see their names in print.

Dictation

As the previous sections of this chapter have indicated, communication can be made more efficient and less costly with the assistance of modern equipment. However, regardless of how much modern equipment is available, an *individual* has to start the communication process. If that person is not efficient in initiating the communication, the steps which follow suffer.

Competent people are absolutely necessary if modern communication equipment is to prove successful.

The word-processing center is based upon the *assumption* that an individual has oral input that is clear, well-organized, and concise. That is, the system starts with instant oral dictation. Unfortunately, the assumption that everyone can dictate efficiently and competently often is not valid. A recent study revealed that about 75 percent of the input into word-processing systems was in some form other than dictation.[4] That is a pity because dictation

Dictation is a key factor in making a communication system efficient and practical.

[4]Ibid., p. 13.

**Figure 11—6a
Computer-Assisted
Letter: The Basic Form**

Continental Store
606 Jefferson Street
New Orleans, Louisiana 70140

July 10, 198-

_____
_____
_____ _____

Dear _____ :

With people like you in mind, _____ , Continental has
created a new department. On Monday, July 15th, we are opening our
new KITCHEN KORNER. _____ , you especially are
invited to visit the department during our first week of service and
receive a free gift and special services. Conveniently located on the
third floor, the KITCHEN KORNER will provide you with the latest in
kitchen aids and small appliances.

For instance, _____ , to complement your new
_____ the KITCHEN KORNER will carry _____

_____ , you know that kitchen-related service and
advice is often difficult to obtain. Therefore, to complement our
KITCHEN KORNER, we will have a full-service repair unit for small
appliances as part of our department. Also, we always will have a
certified home economist on duty. The home economist will be able to
assist you in selecting the right appliances and cooking utensils;
this person also is available to answer your questions concerning
cookery.

_____ , just bring this letter with you when you visit
the KITCHEN KORNER between July 15 and July 20 and you will be able to
select a free gift from among twenty different items.

We look forward to seeing you soon and serving you in the future.

Sincerely,

Betty Bently

Betty Bently, Head
KITCHEN KORNER
CONTINENTAL STORE

**Figure 11—6b
Computer-Assisted
Letter: Completed**

Continental Store
~~~
606 Jefferson Street
New Orleans, Louisiana 70140

July 10, 198-

Mrs. James Dalton
202 Forest Avenue
New Orleans, LA 70144

Dear Mrs. Dalton:

With people like you in mind, Mrs. Dalton, Continental has created a
new department. On Monday, July 15th, we are opening our new KITCHEN
KORNER. Mrs. Dalton, you especially are invited to visit the
department during our first week of service and receive a free gift
and special services. Conveniently located on the third floor, the
KITCHEN KORNER will provide you with the latest in kitchen aids and
small appliances.

For instance, Mrs. Dalton, to complement your new range, the KITCHEN
KORNER will carry three separate full lines of skillets, pots, and
pans, plus numerous cooking utensils.

Mrs. Dalton, you know that kitchen-related service and advice is often
difficult to obtain. Therefore, to complement our KITCHEN KORNER we
will have a full-service repair unit for small appliances as part of
our department. Also, we always will have a certified home economist
on duty. The home economist will be able to assist you in selecting
the right appliances and cooking utensils; this person also is
available to answer your questions concerning cookery.

Mrs. Dalton, just bring this letter with you when you visit the
KITCHEN KORNER between July 15 and July 20 and you will be able to
select a free gift from among twenty different items.

We look forward to seeing you soon and serving you in the future.

Sincerely,

Betty Bently

Betty Bently, Head
KITCHEN KORNER
CONTINENTAL STORE

is really quite a simple process once a technique has been developed. And it does make a significant contribution to the efficiency and low cost of the entire communication system.

Why Dictation?

Most communicators start the process by writing the message out in longhand or by typing a draft. These procedures are all much slower than dictation. Most people can write about 10–20 words per minute and some managers can type a rough draft a bit faster, but they can speak 80–140 words per minute. Obviously, with non-oral input, the word-processing system often gets off to a very slow start.

Why don't more people use dictation? For some individuals, the process of dictation is frightening. Usually, it is due merely to lack of practice. After all, when you write, you can easily rework a paragraph three or four times. But think of the time wasted. In dictation, you need only pick up the microphone or telephone in a word-processing hook-up and speak!

Managers who do not dictate should learn to do so. Just as the quill pen and electric typewriter are not in harmony, so too the manager who writes in longhand and the word-processing center are also on different wave lengths.

Dictation Procedures

Remember these key points in dictating.

In some ways the process of preparing for dictation is similar to the steps in making an oral presentation:

1. identify the reader;
2. determine the purpose of the communication;
3. organize the ideas to be presented; and
4. outline the major and minor points to be covered in the dictation process.

Of course, before you move forward with any of these four points, you should know how to use the equipment—how to stop, erase, pause, and play back. But with that knowledge in mind, you can begin the dictation process.

Normally you will be initiating a letter or report or replying to the piece of correspondence just received. In any case, the reader must be identified: Is the recipient a customer? dealer? prospect? employee? government official?

Why is it acceptable to use a question mark after these single-word statements? (See Appendix 1.)

Next, what is your purpose? To complete a sale? make an adjustment? enter a claim? refuse a request? Knowing the purpose is important for it is the purpose that often determines the organization of the communication.

Everyone has a slightly different way of organizing or outlining the message to be dictated. Some individuals prefer to enter the outline in the margin or at the bottom of the letter being answered. Others find it easier to use a separate sheet of paper, and some people are comfortable making up the outline in their heads. Regardless of the method, an outline is vital. When it has been completed, review it for:

1. logical sequence of ideas (obviously it is easier to move ideas around in the outline than it is in the finished letter or report);

2. possible omission of ideas; and

3. possible duplication or addition of unnecessary topics.

Now, just one more point before dictating: Do you have the correct spelling of the recipient's name? the address? model numbers and specification data?

You will find that a little practice will help you become adept as a dictator. And you will save a great deal of time in the bargain. The key is the outline. If it is logical, sufficiently detailed, and carefully edited, dictating from it will prove to be very easy indeed.

The dictator should establish a reasonable speed of dictation; if you know the transcriber you can agree upon the speed. If you are dictating in a word-processing center, the organization will have established norms for dictating speeds.

Be sure to be very clear in dictating. Pronounce words distinctly and spell any unusual words or names. Also, provide the transcriber with oral clues as to where you want certain kinds of punctuation. Remember that the transcriber may be very unfamiliar with the situation which you know well; thus it will be up to you to dictate in a manner that will enable the transcriber to produce perfect copy.

Concluding Comments

Automation is coming to communication in the offices across the country. However, the weak link in the chain is the manager-communicator who often has not kept pace with advancing technologies. The equipment enables managers to communicate more efficiently, but the manager must improve his or her personal communication skills and procedures in order to take advantage of the modern automated communication systems.

By permission of Johnny Hart and Field Enterprises, Inc.

MEMO

To: Students

From: The Authors

Subject: Business communications today and tomorrow

The means by which people are able to communicate with each other are changing more rapidly today than at any other time in history. Knowing and understanding this new technology will help to make your work and your life easier in the years ahead.

Decision

Here is the new form letter Roosevelt Jackson prepared for applicants to Oakville Community College.

Oakville Community College
Office of Admissions and Records,
Oakville, Alabama, 35486

_____

_____
_____

Dear_____ :

Thank you very much for applying for admission to Oakville Community
College.

Processing has begun on your application. However, one or more of the items
checked below was not included in the material you sent to us.

    Certified transcript of secondary and/or previous college credits
    Completed application for admission form
    $25.00 application fee

As soon as the item(s) checked above is received, we will continue the
processing of your request. A reminder: All application materials must be
received no later than _____ .

We look forward to hearing from you as soon as possible.

Cordially yours,

Kathryn Cutler
Director of Admissions

Questions

1. Why has the cost of individual letters risen so dramatically in recent years?

2. Why are people so important in making a word-processing center efficient? Be specific. Group people into two categories—those inputing to the Center and those who work in the Center.

3. List several different types of electronic procedures. Select one used by your school or an organization (business, industry, or government) and briefly describe specifically how the system is utilized.

4. Name five specific situations in which a major direct mail company, handling children's toys, can use guide letters for its customers and prospects.

5. In business communications, is there a difference between a guide letter and a form letter? Compare the two from the points of view of cost and efficiency, and give an example for the use of each in an insurance company.

6. Define the following word-processing terms and words:
   a. basic input units;
   b. principal;
   c. output facilities;
   d. proofreaders;
   e. supervisor of word processing center;
   f. centralized unit.

7. Answer the following questions pertaining to business communications discussed in this chapter.
   a. Why is word processing considered impersonal?
   b. What problems arise for an executive adjusting to word processing after she has had her own private secretary?
   c. How does the Mailgram cut the delays of normal mail delivery?
   d. In what kind of business situations would the TWX and telex be most beneficial?

Exercises

1. Think of several specific methods you could use to keep the cost of business communications down. Discuss these methods in a memo written to your instructor.

2. Obtain descriptive information from one manufacturer of word-processing equipment. Write a short report on how such equipment can be used by a real-estate firm that maintains one headquarters and four branch offices in one large city.

3. Visit a local firm that has had a word-processing center for at least a year or more. Interview the supervisor of the word-processing center and learn about the various functions the center performs in the company and the advantages and/or disadvantages of the center to the organization. Write your findings in paragraph form; list where needed.

Applications

1. Prepare a guide letter to be used by all sales associates in the Knoxville Realty Company. This guide letter is to be sent to executives who are being transferred by their companies to their firm's offices in Knoxville.

2. List five specific situations for form letters to be used by sales associates who work for Knoxville Realty Company.

3. Prepare a form letter, to be individually typed, which will be sent to all clients of Knoxville Realty Company who have purchased a home through that firm.

4. Norman Obeta works for a collection agency and dictates many letters into a machine daily. The typists in the secretarial pool try to avoid Norman's dictation as his tapes are al-

most impossible to decipher with any speed or accuracy. When the typists complained to Norman, he claimed that anyone can dictate and that there are no special procedures to follow for good dictating skills. Help alleviate this problem by listing as many helpful guidelines as you can that will serve as dos and don'ts for dictators.

5. You are responsible for setting up a word-processing center for a pharmaceutical office. The center is just in the planning stage, and you are thinking about the components of the word-processing triangle. Using the triangle model, give a general description of the quantity and types of a) staff; b) procedures; and c) equipment you may want to consider for the center. (You may want to do some research or visit a word-processing equipment company before completing this assignment.)

6. A word-processing center can eliminate the job of the private secretary. Joel Finesteder, recently promoted to vice-president of sales, has always wanted the status of having his very own secretary. Now that his company has instituted a word-processing center, Joel will be denied this status symbol and he has denounced the efficiency of the center even before he has used it. Prepare a list of advantages of a word-processing center for Joel so he can see how he and the company will benefit from it. Include this list in a memo format. Remember to be tactful.

7. Dictate to a class member a thank-you letter to a businessman who, on your invitation, addressed your business communication class on "New Opportunities in the Job Market." His presentation was valuable and very well received.

Readings in Communication

TEN SECRETS OF BETTER SALES LETTERS

Sig Rosenblum

The sales letter may well be the most demanding test of communication there is. For in the purest form, its words *alone* must do the job. Without the help of color, illustration, or other frills, the writer must take the reader down the path to a sale.

In other words, you want to get someone you may never have seen to write that check, drop it into the mail, and actually feel good about it. That's communication! If you get to know the simple skills—the 10 secrets—of the successful sales letter, then your selling, both on paper and in person, will click more often.

Secret no. 1: select selling ideas

Good writing, as such, has little to do with the successful sales letter—the one that jolts the reader out of his indifference. You may fashion the fancy phrase, but people may still turn from it with a yawn. Without selling ideas, your letter will not work. It may impress. It may even entertain. But it will not sell.

Nothing could be more obvious. Nothing is more often forgotten. So pack your letter with powerful sales arguments. Grammar, style, vocabulary take a back seat. The reader wants reasons to buy.

One helpful way to get a handle on these reasons is to draw a line down the middle of a sheet of paper. Head one side *Benefits* and the other, *Objections*. In this way, you separate on paper and in your mind the reasons people will buy and the reasons they will not.

If your newly developed marine product is

waxed nylon line rather than raw rope, what does that mean to those using it? It means— we'll assume—that your line will not burn their hands as raw rope will when they tie up at the dock. It will not mar finely finished wood surfaces. It won't scratch painstakingly polished brass. It costs less per foot.

Spell out those benefits in terms your reader understands. In terms of what he actually does, feels, wants, dislikes. Make sure you have authentic appeals. And lots of them. However well you handle words, you can't write a sales letter unless you select selling ideas.

Secret no. 2: hop the fence

Use a you-oriented approach. But don't just stuff the word *you* into your letter. This recalls a joke: "Well, that's enough about me. How did you like my last book?" Using *you* won't do it. Your letter should be built around the needs, fears, desires, profit, and happiness of the reader. It should proceed from his side of the fence. And that's where you should be when you write it. What do you think of this?

We have just built a new factory, a massive edifice of brick and steel that reflects the progress we have made in over five decades of activity.

Does this writer have an edifice complex? No, he was sitting on his side of the fence when he should have looked at the factory from his customer's backyard. If he had, he would have asked, What does the new factory *mean* to the customer? It means better delivery. He'll like that. He'll get his goods faster.

Almost anything can be turned around and expressed from the viewpoint of the reader:

Our new finger-molded handle . . . .
Better: It won't slip from your grip.

Our prices are right.
Better: You'd gladly pay twice the price.

Slant the language and the thought toward the reader. He is interested in himself, his problems, his opportunities, his comfort. He is not interested primarily in you and your product. The only reason the customer buys *anything* is to help *himself*. Be on his side. Hop the fence.

Secret no. 3: don't waste words

This doesn't mean to use terse, clipped, stingy writing without the transitions that give grace and style. But use your blue pencil on sentences filled with fat and bloated with bombast:

No doubt there are sufficient and ample reasons unknown to us why you have been tardy with your last payment—now so long overdue.
Better: I'm sure there's a good reason your payment is late.

There is a saying among writers: "Cut it 'til it bleeds." Keep removing the flab until the substance of the thought is in danger. Why should you strive for lean writing? Not just because it is muscular and attractive. But because lean writing moves people to action.

Secret no. 4: be specific

If your new screwdriver works faster, tell the fellow at the other end of the mail route *how much* faster. Tell him the number of additional screws he can drive. What will he save in dollars and cents? Or time? If you use flabby, fuzzy claims such as "very fast" and "improved performance," a snicker of skepticism will cross the reader's mind. Don't shirk the essential drudgery. If time and motion studies are needed, make them. Get the facts. And get them to the reader:

Our much-improved Twisty screwdriver . . . .
Better: Here's how to drive 1,500 more screws in an eight-hour shift. . . .

Our poly bags hold a lot more than ordinary bags.
Better: That means you get 20 more peanuts, two more doughnuts, or one more apple in this bag.

Secret no. 5: be believable

It is not enough for your sales story to be true. It must *sound* true, too. What do you do when there is an embarrassment of riches—when the plain facts seem exaggerated? Here's what the author did for GAF's Ozalid line:

Each sales letter in the series featured a photo of a skeptical executive at the top of the page. His expression conveyed extreme challenge and suspicion. In one letter, the headline had him saying: "These figures phony?" The letter itself answered:

Happily, no.

Spectacular, perhaps. You can control 80% of your copying costs at once. And, in all likelihood, reduce your costs 75%! That's what we hear from firms much like your own. They save thousands of dollars every year.

If the letter had blandly stated that the reader could reduce his costs 75%, there would have been a lot of raised eyebrows out there.

There are many ways to gain believability.

Use testimonials that ring true. Develop solid facts and figures that build your case point by point.

Secret no. 6: watch your windups

Most sales letters are improved by deleting the first sentence. We call this sentence a windup because it lets the writer "get into" his subject. But if you don't immediately arrest the reader's interest, *he* will not get into the subject, and into the wastebasket go you and your message. That is why your very first word—your "opening"—must be compelling.

Powerful openings grab the reader in an iron grip. Here are some of my own favorites:

No matter how hot or cold your salesmen are now, this plan will make them sell better.

Be skeptical, sir. I'm going to prove it to you.

A fellow salesman is going to help you slash your tax payments this year.

These letters don't pussyfoot around. They sell—from the opening bell.

Secret no. 7: write in three phases

It's a common misconception that "real" writers do it all effortlessly, without fumbling.

Writing is tentative—a little here, a little there, rather than a master stroke, complete in an instant. More like sculpting than taking a snapshot. Your first attempts will *never* be more than an approximation of what you want. They must be incomplete and clumsy to *some* degree. It isn't easy to accept that. But try.

How does writing "happen" anyway? Those who have studied the creative process seem to agree that it is broken into three distinct phases. In the first phase, you round up facts, absorb ideas, explore approaches. This is a period of *taking in*. In the second phase, you put down ideas, make notes, outlines, doodles. *You try to get things out.* The direction of the first phase is opposite that of the second phase. But both

are characterized by extreme *openness*. Many observers have compared these phases to play. They are random, unstructured—anything goes.

But there is a third phase: the editorial, critical phase. Here you kill inappropriate words and ideas. Just as the first two phases were marked by openness, this phase is highly discriminating and selective. Here you filter, prohibit, weigh and balance subtleties.

When the writer tries to be *open to new ideas* and at the same time exercise his critical judgment and *filter ideas,* he gets into trouble. You cannot do both at the same time.

But if you keep these phases more or less separated, you will produce better ideas much faster than you ever thought possible. Yet, some of your brainchildren *will* prove unusable—even just plain dumb. And you'll use a lot of paper. So what? It's the ideas you get that count, not the ideas you throw away.

Secret no. 8: put in people

You'd never guess from most sales letters— indeed most business writing—that there are *people* on this planet:

A payment is due in the amount of . . . .
Past experience strongly suggests . . . .
The matter under review . . . .
The fulfillment of this obligation . . . .

Is anybody living and breathing out there? Or hoping, fearing, planning? You'd never think so from a peek at the files. But they are. So the vigorous writer brings people—himself and the reader—into the action. Let's put some life into the examples above:

Yes, Mr. Kelley, you do owe us $18.36.
For five years, Jack and his people have . . . .
I'm thinking about what you told me last week . . . .
If you can do what you say . . . .

When you introduce people into your writing, you help create a word picture of someone doing something. And a *word picture* is a lot easier to grasp than an *abstract concept*, which must then be translated into specifics in the reader's mind.

Secret no. 9: mimic the movies

Good film makers keep their cameras moving. If we are watching a cowboy ride across the prairie, the camera might start with a long shot, zoom in slowly, circle the man, shoot up from ground level, with the sun silhouetting the lonely rider, then rise and shoot down from a boom or helicopter. Just a man and his horse plodding across an open plain. But the agile camera works its alchemy—and light, shadow, angles, and accents cast their spell.

There's a lesson here for the writer: if you vary the pace, tempo, shading, and beat of your prose, the reader will find it far more interesting. An example here will help us:

This cleaner is guaranteed to please you and no matter why you are dissatisfied you can return it and your money will be refunded cheerfully without delay of any kind or argument about the merit of your complaint. That is our promise.

What is wrong here? For one thing—to use film language—this sentence is shot in one focus, from one angle, in one mood. It is too static. Suppose we do what the camera does and add sparkle and movement:

What if you're not satisfied with this cleaner? Perfectly O.K.—whatever your reasons. Just send it back. And quick as a flash, you'll have your refund. No quibble. No question. Could anything be fairer than that?

This version moves. Statements are made into questions. A boring cadence is broken into uneven accents. Quite apart from the substance of the paragraph, the form contains *surprise*. This works in the movies—and on the printed page, as well.

Secret no. 10: keep it active

Perhaps you've noticed a certain overlapping: if you select selling ideas, you are inclined to be specific. Something specific is likely to be from the reader's side of the fence, hence believable. And so it goes: one rule helps another. And if you cast your ideas in *active* rather than passive form, your sentences tend to be shorter. They tend to *move*:

The present situation is viewed by all involved with a great deal of concern.
Better: *We're concerned about this.*

The certainty can be said to exist . . . .
Better: *I'm certain . . . .*

There they are: 10 simple secrets—just waiting to be used. By men and women who want to sell themselves and their ideas more vigorously and have the courage to do so.

Part III
Practical Business Reports

Dilemma

For several years, Quality Auto-Parts Company has had a successful operation on the East Coast. However, more and more of their products are being shipped to the Midwest in response to orders. Freight costs are high and service to dealers often is delayed.

Geraldine Lipkowitz, regional manager of the east coast facility, frequently has suggested that Quality Auto-Parts open a midwest distribution center. This idea was discussed at length at the last company monthly meeting. The president of the company made it an *action item* and requested that Geraldine prepare a report. On the basis of her findings (to be presented in the report), the directors of the firm will vote on whether Quality Auto-Parts should move ahead with a midwest distribution center.

Geraldine's initial assignment is clear: choose a midwest city, determine what items to investigate, and decide what research methods should be used in the investigation.

Decision, see page 245

Keys to Effective Reports

Here is a list of the objectives you should understand by the time you complete this chapter. Place a check mark in the box beside each as soon as you feel ready to apply your understanding in a practical situation.

☐ The role of the written report in modern organizations

☐ The eight basic steps in planning a report:
    Define the problem
    Identify the reader
    State a purpose
    Define terms
    Establish procedures
    Consider scope and limitations
    Evaluate time and money constraints
    Make an outline

☐ The chief sources of secondary information that can be used in preparing a report:
    Books
    Periodicals
    Newspapers
    Reports, bulletins, and brochures
    Government documents

☐ The basic methods of primary research that can be used in preparing a report:
    Questionnaires
    Interviews
    Observation
    Experiment

Although managers sometimes complain about writing a report, it has a vital role in the organization today. The report, in a very real sense, is the vehicle which enables the organization to gather data in a single, coherent document, build understanding, solve problems, and make decisions. With personnel changing positions, government agencies desiring information on how decisions were made, and top management wanting situations summarized for review, the written report is a basic responsibility of managers.

Reports may have different purposes: to inform; to recommend; to analyze; and to compare.

Reports in the organization are generally problem- or opportunity-oriented. Sometimes the report is written in order to identify and explain a problem facing the organization (information). At other times, it is prepared to present possible solutions to problems (recommendations). Or the report may be used to analyze a situation or describe how a unit or department is attempting to overcome previous or present problems (analysis).

In business and other types of organizations, the report also is an action-oriented document. It is not a theoretical paper on an abstract and inconsequential question. The report puts a fence around a problem, presents an analysis of a situation, offers justified conclusions, and finally, makes carefully substantiated recommendations.

Reports can play an important role in decision making.

It is through the report-writing process that managers can present a rationale, build a case, and reach a decision. All the steps in the process — identifying the problem, purpose, and audience, collecting and analyzing the data, and assembling the report itself — are carried through for one purpose. That purpose is for the reader to make an effective decision.

Preparing to Write

In Chapter 1, we discussed the importance of planning before writing any business communication. In the case of a report, an effective plan is especially important. "Time is money" is an old saying, and a report that rambles, a report that leaves out significant information, a report that doesn't achieve its purpose — that report is a waste of time *and* money.

Follow these eight steps in preparing a report.

Designing an effective plan is not difficult if you make sure to follow eight basic steps:

1. define the problem;
2. identify your reader;
3. state your purpose;
4. define your terms;
5. establish your procedures;
6. consider your scope and limitations;
7. evaluate time and money constraints; and
8. make an outline.

Let's look at each of these steps a bit more closely to see how they can help you construct your plan.

Define the Problem

The first task of the decision maker/report writer is to identify the problem and state it accurately, objectively, and clearly. This step often can be the toughest in the entire report-writing process. Your boss says, "The problem is ineffective personnel." That may be his conclusion after he has reviewed the situation. However, the problem really may be poor supervision, inefficient equipment, labor troubles, or a dozen other factors which contribute to the boss's view of "ineffective personnel."

Step One: Define the problem clearly and accurately.

Your statement of the problem puts a verbal fence around the situation and insures, to some degree, that the planning, research, conclusions, recommendations, and decisions will remain within the fenced area. In many situations, the problem can be stated in a paragraph or two. However, when investigating more complex problems or when reporting on problems with which the reader of the report is unfamiliar, it may be necessary to provide more information in stating the problem.

Identify the Reader

Before attempting to solve a problem, you must know who desires to have the problem solved. Who is going to be the primary reader of the report? Will there be secondary readers and is there a potential of wider circulation of the report? Who reads the report can influence what goes into the report.

Step Two: Identify who will read the report.

If you are to prepare the report for someone very familiar with the situation, many items can be left out of the report or mentioned in a superficial manner. On the other hand, if you are writing the report for an individual who is unfamiliar with the situation, you will need to go into much additional detail and you probably will need to provide historical background.

The reader also will influence your research method, your writing syle, your word choice, the complexity or simplicity of your graphic aids, how forcefully you state recommendations, and to some degree, what material you emphasize and de-emphasize. In short, as with any other written or oral message, knowing your audience is a key to effective communication.

State a Specific Purpose

Whereas the statement of the problem may be somewhat general, the statement of the purpose is very specific. The purpose statement does not have to be a complete sentence; it can be a single simple statement. The purpose statement is exact, precise, and narrow. Some representative purpose statements could be:

Step Three: State your purpose narrowly and realistically.

to determine why the Northeast Missouri Lab has increased its efficiency;

to investigate if the amount of employee pilferage varies significantly among our six retail outlets;

to analyze the morale of selected Quality Auto-Parts laborers;

to determine if Continental should implement a flex-time system;

to determine how to reduce absenteeism on the second shift.

In longer reports and in more complex situations, it is possible to have multiple-purpose statements. But again, each should be stated individually in the simplest manner.

Define the Terms

Step Four: Define key terms to avoid confusion between writer and reader.

It is your responsibility to gain agreement on what is really being investigated. Clearly stated problem and purpose statements aid in clarifying the situation. Defining terms adds greater specificity.

What do you mean with such terms as *absenteeism, flex-time,* or *employee pilferage?* You may mean one thing and the reader may interpret another. Therefore, to eliminate problems on the front end, before you start your investigation and research, you must make sure all concerned are on the same wave length.

Working definitions do not always match dictionary definitions.

In defining terms, you use working definitions that may not be identical with dictionary or common usage definitions. You are defining the terms in the context of the particular investigation. For example, a personnel text might define *absenteeism* as "the failure of employees to report to work when they are scheduled to work." However, your organization is plagued with some employees who, during one year, accumulate over seven absent days. Therefore, you might want to define absenteeism as "any situation where an employee accumulates seven or more unexcused days off during a calendar year."

Establish the Procedures

Step Five: Establish procedures to get the information you need.

How are you going to collect the data you need to analyze the situation and solve the problem? As a researcher/decision maker you must identify what kind of information you are going to need, where it is, and how you can gain successful and reliable access to it. The following section of this chapter, dealing with primary and secondary sources of information, details sources where you may obtain information. Some of the procedures that one conceivably might use to gather data include:

a mail questionnaire;
a standardized test;
library research;

an experiment;
interviews; or
personal observation.

Organizations are very concerned with how people go about solving a problem, how long it will take, and how much it will cost. Therefore, you must evolve procedures that will not create problems.

As with the other parts of the planning process, it is necessary to be very specific. You cannot just say you are going to interview employees. Instead, you are specific on the following points:

1. what employees;
2. how the employees will be selected and how many;
3. the kinds of interviews;
4. when the interviews will take place;
5. how long the interviews will last; and
6. what will be asked.

Again you can see the need to think the entire piece of research through very carefully and to be very precise. This plan is often referred to as *research design*.

What is the difference in meaning between *precise* and *concise*? (See Appendix 1.)

Consider the Scope and Limitations

The next step in preparing to write is deciding how far you want to go with your research and how far you *can* go. Considering the scope of the research means deciding how deep or how shallow you plan to go in analyzing the problem. In an analysis of "Employee Performance," for example, you may be satisfied with each employee's monthly production record. On the other hand, the scope of your research might be more detailed: monthly production for each of the last twelve months; number of items rejected each month; cost to produce each item; record of absenteeism; and other points.

You also have to consider the limitations of your research. In a laboratory, researchers can often conduct *perfect* research. Unfortunately, live organizations are not perfect, so you try to develop the best possible research procedures. But you may still have problems. For example, you wanted to obtain a perfect random sample of all employees in your company in North America for your mail questionnaire, but because of the postal strike in Canada, you cannot obtain Canadian responses. Or the research would be best if you could interview each of the supervisors who work in the six retail outlets. However, because of vacation schedules and an extremely heavy work load, you can only interview 75 percent of them. Thus, it is necessary to specify the limitations before you start your research and writing—not after you have completed the analysis.

Step Six: Decide how deep your analysis will go.

Evaluate Time and Money Constraints

Step Seven: Examine time and money limitations.

Organizations are concerned with how long it will take to obtain the answer they want and how much it will cost. Often you are given an exact date for presenting your report. It is important to consider the problem, purpose, and procedures, and to see if it is possible to accomplish all you desire within the limits of time. You may discover that although you would prefer to develop and mail a questionnaire to customers, you do not have the available time. It would take at least a month to send and receive the questionnaires and your report is due in two weeks. Therefore, you will need to alter your procedures and use a telephone questionnaire system which can be conducted in ten days.

What is the difference in meaning between *alter* and *altar*? (See Appendix 1.)

Even if you are a member of the organization, and not an outside consultant, there are many costs associated with decision making and report writing. One of the basic steps in preparing for the research and the eventual decision is to project these costs. Some of the costs are obscure, but nevertheless they are present. They include:

1. your time;
2. time of employees interviewed, surveyed, and questioned;
3. research costs—mailings, postage, charge for mailing lists, experiments, instruments;
4. computer costs to record data and carry through data analysis; and
5. report preparation and general support.

Getting a handle on costs is vital. After all, most organizations are not going to authorize a $1,500 research expenditure to solve a $500 problem.

Outline

Step Eight: Prepare a logical outline.

Before jumping into the report-writing and decision-making process, the final activity of the planning stage is to prepare an initial outline. The report outline, which indicates how the report will be organized and what will be examined, aids both you and anyone reviewing your plan. It clearly presents the building scheme. (See Chapter 1 for techniques of outlining.)

There is nothing absolute about an outline, and it will change many times before you complete the project. But it is much better to consult the road map before leaving on a journey than after going down some road and discovering you are heading in the wrong direction or are at a dead end.

These eight steps to report preparation are vital to follow before carrying through secondary and primary research. Once the data have been obtained, other steps are needed—evaluation and interpretation of data, final outline preparation, selection of visual aids, and other steps—prior to the composition of the final draft.

Gathering Information: Secondary Sources

Planning the report is one important part of the decision-making process. Another is determining who has the information you need so you can present the relevant material in the report and make the correct decision.

Secondary sources are those information sources based on the experiences, experiments, and writings of others. You were not involved in the initial gathering of the original data, therefore it is secondary. Actually there are an amazing number of resources available to aid you in gaining access to secondary sources.

Secondary sources reflect the experience of others.

Books

Books are written on every conceivable topic; dozens are published daily. In order to gain access to current and older books, you must know how to use the library book indexes, the card-catalog system, and the stacks. Most books are published once. However, in some disciplines, sequential books are published. Therefore, if you need information on current federal taxes, you certainly would want to refer to the book, *Federal Tax Course,* that is published annually.

Because there are so many books published each month, there are indexes which will assist you in finding those books with which your topic is particularly concerned: *Books in Print* (New York: R. R. Bowker Co., 1948 to date); *U.S. Catalog: Books in Print* (New York: H. W. Wilson Co., 1933 to date); *Subject Guide to Books in Print* (New York: R. R. Bowker Co., 1957 to date); and others. These indexes, like those available for magazines, reports, government publications, and other secondary sources may be found in the reference room of your library or by asking your librarian for assistance.

Many indexes and abstracts are available to help you find the secondary sources you need.

Magazines and Periodicals

Generally more current than books, various magazines, periodicals, and journals contain articles that indicate current trends and new research findings. Common magazines and periodicals that often provide overviews of business-organizational topics include: *Forbes, Nation's Business, Fortune, Time, Newsweek,* and *U.S. News and World Report.* Also, most professions have their own current periodicals.

Journals are generally considered to be more scholarly than magazines. They often present articles with more in-depth analyses. Again, most disciplines and professions have at least one journal that reports on current activities, research, and developments in the specific discipline. For instance, in the area of personnel there are publications such as *Personnel, Personnel Journal,* and *Personnel Management.*

Like books, there are indexes to assist you in finding the information you want in the thousands of magazines which are published annually. You are probably aware of the most common magazine index, the *Readers' Guide to Periodical Literature*. It indexes over 130 well-known and popular current periodicals. There are many more specialized indexes, such as: *Business Periodical Index, Index of Supermarket Articles, Engineering Index*, and the *Index to Labor Union Periodicals*. In addition to these indexes, a number of abstracts are available which present brief summaries of articles in magazines and periodicals. Some samples of periodical abstracts are: *Computer and Information Systems, New Literature on Automation, Personnel Management Abstracts, Psychological Abstracts*, and the *ABS Guide to Recent Publications in the Social and Behavioral Sciences*.

Abstracts which summarize articles can be a valuable reference for secondary sources.

Newspapers

For very current information, newspapers are an excellent source. The nation's major dailies often have the capability of providing detailed statements on current events. A few papers even publish indexes that will aid you in tracing the materials you need from their publications: *Index of the Christian Science Monitor, National Observer Index, New York Times Index, The Wall Street Journal Index, Los Angeles Times Index, Barron's Index, American Banker's Index*, plus indexes for some sixteen other major city newspapers. The indexes for the *New York Times* and *The Wall Street Journal* also provide short summaries of the articles.

Reports, Bulletins, and Brochures

Corporations, foundations, universities, professional societies, and others often produce reports, bulletins, and brochures that provide information you may need. Unfortunately, there is no overall guide that does an adequate job of indexing these publications. The *Vertical File Index* may be of some assistance. If you are aware of an organization that may have studied the problem you are investigating, you should write to it. For instance, if you are doing research in some area of education you might want to contact the Carnegie Commission which sponsors and publishes various reports on major issues facing education. In attempting to discover reports, bulletins, and brochures, you might survey *Business Pamphlets and Information Sources* and *Gebbie House Magazine Directory*.

Government Documents

The largest publisher in the world is the United States Government. The nature of the publications range from very sophisticated technical reports and translations of reports written in foreign countries to numerous simple bulletins on everyday topics. There are a variety of reference guides to aid you in selecting the correct government document for review. Also, you may want to contact particular government agencies for assistance. If you are located in a major metropolitan area, there will be a government document center that may have various reports on hand that will aid you.

Because there are so many government publications, there are numerous guides and catalogues that cite the data by specific category. There are general guides, such as the *Guide to U.S. Government Statistics* and *Manual of Government Publications.* There are specific bibliographies for the major government divisions, such as the *U.S. Bureau of Census Catalog* and the *U.S. Department of Commerce Publications.*

Finally, as you may have already guessed, since there are so many references to secondary information sources, there must be guides to the guides. Among these are E. P. Sheehy, *Guide to Reference Books* (9th ed.) R. W. Murphey, *How and Where to Look It Up—A Guide to Standard Sources of Information,* and L. M. Daniells, *Business Information Sources.*

There are even indexes to help you find the index you need!

Gathering Information: Primary Sources

As you have seen, much of the material you use to prepare a report and to make a decision may be obtained from others or from secondary sources. However, when time, money, and expertise are available, primary sources can be most helpful and very convincing in guiding a decision. A primary source is one that has not been interpreted among individuals or reported by an outside source. The primary source is firsthand material. It is not obtained in the library and is not determined from someone else's study; primary sources are obtained and determined directly by you.

Primary sources are first-hand information.

Questionnaires

A popular means of obtaining information today is via questionnaires or surveys. It is often a relatively inexpensive way to gather volumes of data. With the increased popularity of questionnaires there has also arisen increased skepticism. Some people absolutely refuse to complete them; they feel it is an invasion of their privacy. Many people feel that although you guarantee that the individual completing the questionnaire cannot be identified, they fear some secret scheme will permit tracing answers back to them. (And such schemes do exist!) Also, as the technique of administering questionnaires has increased, some people respond in very cavalier manners—they get tired of being questioned. Instead of completing the questionnaire, they report their frustration by completing it in a manner not truly reflective of their feelings. This can create problems in providing reliable answers for the researcher.

For instance, perhaps a college has students evaluate every faculty member each term. A sophisticated questionnaire is used. All evaluations are tak-

Questionnaires are a popular and inexpensive method of gathering data.

en during the last week of class. About the time students complete the fifth questionnaire in one week, the fifth professor may be receiving some very unreliable responses. It is not the professor's fault; it is just that the students have tired of so many questions and tend to rush through the questionnaire quickly. The people responding pay little attention to what they are actually reporting.

Careful questionnaire planning can help avoid potential problems.

Even with these potential problems, with careful planning and the imposition of some safeguards, questionnaires can provide excellent primary data. After all, if you are coordinator of employee communications for your large company and you are interested in knowing what your employees want to read in your firm's company magazine, which of the following would be most important to you: 1) information collected at some other company, or 2) information you gather via a questionnaire from a sample of your firm's employees?

Whom to question?   The most difficult problem in conducting your own primary research concerns the *who*. Out of the entire population of customers, vendors, employees, or townspeople, *whom* are you going to select as representatives of the population? It generally is impossible or impractical to include everyone in your project; therefore you must be selective. Selecting the sample that will be representative of the entire population, or *universe,* is complex. Entire books are written on the subject of sampling. For our purposes it is important to understand there are various kinds of samples:

Random and stratified samples are used most frequently.

1. Random Sample. The random sample assumes that every individual in the *universe* has an equal chance of being selected. Thus, if you require a sample of fifty from a population, or universe, of 500 dentists, a plan must be devised to reach the sample size in such a way that each dentist has an equal opportunity of being selected.

2. Stratified Sample. Realizing that you have 10 percent of your employees in management, 70 percent in hourly positions, and 20 percent in clerical jobs, you select a sample of 100 employees. You send ten questionnaires to managers, seventy to hourly employees, and twenty to those in clerical positions. This is usually referred to as a *proportional stratified sample.*

It is important for you to know the basic rules of sampling, to be aware that there are many different types of samples, and to attempt to do the best you can in obtaining a reliable sample. Remember also that there are experts in the field of sampling and statistics who are prepared to assist you in getting a reliable sample from the universe with which you are working. You also should be aware that you need not be concerned with obtaining a large sample to secure reliability. Many of the samples of the opinions of U.S. citizens are prepared by sampling fewer than 2,000 people out of a population that exceeds 200 million!

What kind of questionnaire?   Some questionnaires are designed to be administered individually or to a group of people. Someone must carefully explain the instructions and make sure the respondents know how to complete the instrument. The *administered questionnaire* has the advantage of reducing error, attempting to hold outside variables constant, and securing a higher percentage return. However, it requires a trained individual to administer this type of questionnaire, and it can be slow and expensive.

Another kind of administered questionnaire is the one often referred to as an *interview schedule* or *interview survey.* It is administered face-to-face on a street corner, door-to-door, or to workers picked at random at the factory gate.

Other questionnaires reach subjects through the mail. Even though postage rates have increased and some new postal regulations place greater restrictions on questionnaires, the *mail questionnaire* can be a relatively inexpensive means of obtaining large amounts of data from individuals who are geographically dispersed. And at times, a mail questionnaire can reach a top executive's desk whereas an interviewer may not get past his secretary.

Mail questionnaires are usually less expensive than administered questionnaires.

With the mail questionnaire, as with other primary techniques, you can carefully select your sample. But you have much less control on whether the recipient will return the questionnaire. Again, if you want to survey a sample of employees, customers, or vendors, put them in a room, administer the questionnaire, and you will probably get a 100 percent return. If you mail the questionnaire to the homes of the employees, you have no control over who really completes the questionnaire; you have no way to provide additional instructions if the questionnaire is confusing; and you will be fortunate if 15 percent of those receiving the questionnaire return it to you. However, the mail questionnaire is still a valuable survey instrument and is used extensively and effectively.

Designing your own questionnaire   The formulation of the questionnaire is a science and there are companies that are in the business of designing questionnaires for particular needs. Also, you can consult numerous books. Yet, there are a few basics that can aid an individual who must operate on a smaller scale without the advantage of outside support.

1. Sequence questions carefully. Do not start with the most difficult question. Also, do not ask questions later that refer to earlier answers: if Question 5 asked if the person is married, Question 12 should not ask about the number of children. Group related questions together.

Remember these six rules in designing a questionnaire.

2. Ask simple questions for easy response. Provide alternative answers which the respondent can simply circle or check. Questions using the semantic differential or a number continuum provide the respondent with a choice and provide the researcher with data easily tabulated. In both these cases, the respondent has a choice from low to high. With a semantic differential question, the respondent may be asked to select a point that he or she feels is accurate, from "unattractive" to "extremely beautiful." In the case of a number continuum question, the respondent may circle the number which he or she feels is accurate, from one to ten. One may indicate "very inexpensive" and ten would indicate "very expensive" (see Figure 12–1).

**Figure 12–1
Questionnaire
Exemplifying Numerical
and Semantic
Differential Questions**

On the following scale of 1 (no interest) to 7 (great interest)
indicate your interest in the following subjects. Specifically, would
you like to read them in the company newspaper sent to your home?
Remember, the larger the number you circle the greater your interest
in the topic.

	No						Great
Company Products	1	2	3	4	5	6	7
Executive Promotions	1	2	3	4	5	6	7
News About Retirees	1	2	3	4	5	6	7
Business Trends	1	2	3	4	5	6	7

**Numerical continuum-type
questions**

For each of the following statements indicate your opinion by circling
the appropriate answer:

    SA = Strongly Agree
     A = Agree
    NO = No Opinion
     D = Disagree
    SD = Strongly Disagree

**Semantic differential-type
questions**

The company newspaper
should be published more
than once each month.   SA   A   NO   D   SD

There is an effort made
in the company newspaper
to cover topics of
interest to the entire
family.   SA   A   NO   D   SD

3. Address only one topic in each question. The question, "Would you like more photographs and more cartoons in the company paper?" does not indicate what respondents really want—photos *or* cartoons or photos *and* cartoons?

4. Do not ask a leading question—one that leads the respondent to the answer you want—"Isn't it nice that the company magazine is printed in color?"

5. Avoid skip-and-jump questions and extensive ranking questions; they often become too difficult and discourage the respondent. It usually is unwise to state, "If you replied yes to question 3, skip 4 and 5 and go on to 6. In the event you are not married, also skip 6 and go immediately to 7." In the case of extensive rankings, a high percentage of accuracy is lost when respondents are asked to "Rank the following ten activities in order of importance beginning with 1 as the most important."

6. If you provide open-ended questions, make them specific. Otherwise you will end up with such disparity in the answers that you will be unable to analyze realistically the answers. Remember, open-ended questions take much longer to analyze than do forced-answer questions.

The attractiveness of the questionnaire and its ease of completion has much to do with gaining a satisfactory response. If you are going to the trouble to prepare a questionnaire, take some time to lay it out in a logical and pleasing manner. Often a brief discussion with a printer will pay dividends in gaining a better-looking item. A questionnaire that does not look crowded, appears easy to complete, and has plenty of open space stands a good chance of gaining the recipient's attention and response.

The design and layout of the questionnaire will play an important role in the response received.

Questionnaire introduction If you are mailing a questionnaire to individuals, it is wise to introduce it with a cover letter. The cover letter should note such factors as the reason for the survey, why the respondent was selected, the importance of the needed information, and why this person's thoughts are desired. Without being trite or overly institutional, you should seek the individual's cooperation and thank the person for replying. In addition, it is often wise to add a due date for the response and an assurance of anonymity or confidentiality, if that is in order. In many ways, the cover letter for a questionnaire is similar to a sales letter—you are attempting to *sell* the receiver on the idea of completing the questionnaire (see Chapter 8).

The cover letter must sell the reader on completing the questionnaire.

What is the difference in meaning between assurance *and* insurance*? (See Appendix 1.)*

In situations in which interviewers use a questionnaire, these administrators must be trained carefully on what to say, how to say it, and how to respond to questions. The questionnaire itself should include an introduction and thorough instructions for completion. If five administrators introduce the questionnaire in five different ways, you may receive unreliable data that can lead you to an incorrect decision.

Interviews

Interviews may be conducted face-to-face or over the telephone.

The interview has the built-in advantage of providing for a two-way exchange between the interviewer and the interviewee. The presence of the interviewer also provides an element of importance and urgency to the data collection. This urgency may not be present in other means of collecting primary data. There are basically two ways to interview: face-to-face and by the telephone.

Face-to-face interviews   Individuals or groups can be interviewed face-to-face. As noted previously, interviews are not casual chitchats. If you are going to interview a sample of people, it is necessary that you hold certain items constant during each interview. You always want to ask the same question in the same way and be particularly observant of verbal and non-verbal feedback.

Face-to-face interviewing is probably the most effective form of interviewing, and it is also the most expensive. Therefore, sometimes you may desire to use the telephone to gain contact with people. In almost all interviews, a series of questions is prepared which is often called an *interview schedule.* These questions should be devised with the same rules in mind as when a mail questionnaire is drawn up.

Telephone interviews   The telephone provides the chance to obtain quickly a diverse sample at a reduced cost, but the depth of the answer and the reliability of the answer is less than is the case in a personal interview. If the interviewees do not know you, it is very difficult to gain their confidence on the phone. Also, the amount of time the person will grant you over the phone is often minimal. The telephone interview must be structured carefully and provide clear and simple answer alternatives for the respondent.

Observation

Most managers are natural observers. But when confronted with a situation that needs to be reported, more precise observations must be used. For instance, with the problem of employee pilferage, the assistant to the director may desire to take some careful observations of the situation.

There are problems in observing. First, if more than one person is doing the observing, are all the observers looking for and recording the same things in the same way? Second, will the presence of the observer change the behavior of the individual being observed? You have perhaps noted how an observer can influence the individual or action being watched.

You have a professor in a course who generally is poorly organized, an uninspiring lecturer, late to class, and seemingly discourteous to students.

Suddenly one day you receive a well-organized lecture that is interesting and makes you want to study the topic in greater depth. Also, this day the professor is profoundly pleasant. The professor arrives at class early, jokes with students, and invites them to the office to discuss any questions individually. You wonder why this sudden change for the better. After class you note that today, members of the Faculty Teaching Evaluation Committee attended your class. Did the presence of observers make a difference?

Experiment

Too often we think of the experiment as being too complex for many of the situations we face in making decisions. But perhaps it is simpler than we have considered.

Experiments sometimes can be used to obtain primary information.

You are assistant to the manager of personnel; you and the manager direct personnel at two small factories. One factory is in the north end of town and the other is seven miles away at the south end of town. In your firm's manufacturing operations you employ many females, aged 20 to 35, and you have a high turnover rate among those employees. The company has justified the turnover by assuming that the women were not interested in regular work. Because of a recent investigation of the company by a representative of the Equal Employment Opportunities Commission, the manager of personnel has asked you to review the turnover problem and recommend alternative solutions.

You have heard about some firms having success with flex-time systems. Flex-time permits employees to arrange their working hours to fit their individual situations, so long as they work the required number of hours per day or week. Because many of the factory women must get children off to school, pack school lunches, and be at home when children are dismissed from school, flex-time would be helpful to many members of your work force. How can you determine if you should institute flex-time at your company?

An experiment may aid you in making the correct decision. At the south factory, you institute flex-time while you maintain the status quo at the north factory. After several months you can determine if turnover rates at the south factory are diminishing. It is a simple experiment, but it can be very helpful.

There are numerous situations in which experimenting would not be difficult.

You manage a real estate office. Is it best to hold open houses on Saturday morning, Saturday afternoon, Sunday afternoon or hold no open houses at all?

You are the sales representative for the All-Good Cookie Company. Traditionally you put all your cookies in the cookie department of the grocery. Would the cookies sell better if placed in a special display rack near the cash register?

As part-owner of a dental lab, you make contact with dentists to see if they are interested in your services. You can set up a simple experiment to determine if it is best to call before their office hours, during the noon hour, or after office hours?

These are simple situations where an experiment would permit you to isolate situations and try something new; the experiments could provide useful primary data. It is not necessary always to hold one situation constant while running the experiment elsewhere. The cookie sales representative, for example, could look at July sales a year ago when the cookies were placed in the cookie area of the grocery. Assuming that this July is similar, the cookies could be placed in the special display. The sales results for the two months could be compared to determine if the change in the placement of the cookies had any effect on sales.

Whether you hold one situation constant while imposing a change at another location or whether you evaluate comparable data collected at two different times, the experiment provides a way to determine if the change you imposed made a difference.

You and Your Expertise

An integral part of your writing and your eventual recommendation is your ability to comprehend the situation. Although often overlooked, you are a primary and perhaps *the* most primary source of information. You select what is to be observed, to whom it is to be written, who is to be interviewed, and many other factors. Many times you are in the middle of the phenomenon being studied; you can be a reliable source. Do not underestimate yourself as an important source in reporting and recommending a decision.

Concluding Comments

You yourself can be an excellent source of primary information.

Planning the report so that a reliable decision can be achieved is hard work. It is work that must be pursued with care or the eventual report will contain errors. Write your plan and share it with others. The process will keep you from stumbling into communication breakdowns. Select your sources of information with care. Often a mix of secondary and primary sources will provide the data you need to make the correct decision. The *correct decision*— that is what the report is all about. An attractive report that presents the

"What do you mean, I don't communicate? Didn't you read the memo I left you at breakfast?"

The written report plays a major role in the modern organization.

wrong answer is of little use, except as an example of a business or organization failure. What is needed is an attractive report that is concise, logically organized, clearly presented, and easy to read. It should contain well-documented conclusions that will substantiate the recommendations.

MEMO

To: Students
From: The Authors
Subject: Planning an effective report

Reports of all kinds play an important role in modern organizations, and you should expect to be asked to write reports at some point in the course of your career. The key to writing an effective report is the same as the key to writing any business communication: careful planning. By following the eight steps for preparing a report outlined in this chapter and making the best possible use of primary and secondary information sources, you will help insure that you achieve your objectives.

Decision

Here is the report, in memo format, which Geraldine Lipkowitz prepared for the president and board of directors of the Quality Auto-Parts Company.

QUALITY AUTO-PARTS

To: Frank T. Mancuzzi, President Quality Auto-Parts Company
From: Geraldine Lipkowitz, Regional Manager, East Coast Operations
Date: May 15, 198-
Subject: A survey of Conover, Ohio, for a possible Midwest distribution
           center

Problem
Freight charges for shipping Quality Auto-Parts merchandise to our midwestern dealers has become almost prohibitive.

Purpose of the Study
To determine if it is feasible and profitable for Quality Auto-Parts to open a midwest distribution center.

Methods of Research
Secondary: Federal, state, and local collections of statistics and information on Conover, Ohio, were reviewed carefully. Some periodicals and local newspapers also were examined.

Primary: Visits were made to the Conover area and the Ohio state capital; interviews were held with local administrative officers, business and union leaders; and a mail questionnaire was sent to retail auto-parts dealers in the Midwest.

Recommendations
1. A task force should be sent to Conover to investigate the facilities for sale. An on-site review should be made, and the one facility with the greatest economic advantages should be purchased.

2. Simultaneously, a communications program with present and prospective midwestern customers should begin. This should emphasize our new facility and products to be handled, plus the quality and service that will be available.

3. Key personnel in our East Coast facility should be interviewed and their transfer to Conover explored.

4. A distribution-center manager for the Conover facility should be selected as soon as possible.

[The next few pages would present the body of the report.]

CHAPTER REVIEW

Questions

1. Why do reports play such an important role in the decision-making process in most organizations?

2. Why do many individuals confuse the symptoms of a problem with the actual problem? Cite an example.

3. What specific factors are included in report planning? Please list and explain each very briefly.

4. Why is it important for the report writer and the report reader to agree on the terms used in the report?

5. What is meant by *scope of research*? Should this be determined before, during, or after the research process?

6. Why might the outline for the report change from the version made up prior to the research activity to the version at the conclusion of research?

7. Define the term *sample*.

8. How does a stratified sample differ from a random sample?

9. List two different interview methods for obtaining information, and explain the advantages and disadvantages of each.

10. What specific factors should be kept in mind in designing questions for an effective mail questionnaire?

Exercises

1. Using secondary sources, answer the following questions, and cite the specific source in which you found the answer:
   a. the age of the present Secretary of State of the United States;
   b. the titles, authors, and date of publication of three articles published on nuclear energy in any three-month period of last year;
   c. the number of automobiles manufactured or purchased in the U.S. last year;
   d. the full publication data on two books published last year in your major field (retailing, accounting, nursing, library science, or any other major).

2. You were asked to write a report on the availability of flight attendant jobs in the airlines and responsibilities of the position. You decided to use all of the following methods to obtain information:
   a. face-to-face interviews;
   b. books and magazines in the library;
   c. telephone interviews;
   d. airline brochures;
   e. answers to questions you posed in letters of inquiry to the personnel directors of ten airlines; and
   f. information from a film.

   Designate which of these investigative methods are primary research and which ones are secondary research. Explain your answers.

3. Offer your constructive and specific criticism of the following questions in a mail questionnaire:
   a. Do you usually purchase the most expensive cuts of meat when shopping?
   b. Do you prefer automatic transmission in low-priced cars that get good gas mileage or air conditioning in higher-priced cars that get good gas mileage?
   c. Indicate the percentage of your income donated to charitable organizations last year as compared to four years previous.

Applications

1. Write the cover letter to accompany the mail questionnaire to be sent to a sample of 500 women lawyers located in three urban centers. Your purpose is to collect their views on possible biases, based on their sex, which they feel they may or may not have encountered from juries in the past two years.

2. Draw up the questionnaire based on the problem described in Application 1. The questionnaire will be sent to the 500 women lawyers.

3. Draw up an interview schedule to be distributed in a survey of 200 food-store shoppers. The purpose of the survey is to determine if shoppers feel that the check-out procedure can be improved in any way. (Remember to obtain specific information.)

4. You are a student in the local community college and are very concerned about the general apathy among the full-time day students concerning student government and student voice in college administrative policy. You and a few of your friends have decided to survey the student population to see just how important this participation in student government really is to them. You plan to publish your findings in the school newspaper eventually. In a memo to your instructor, list the steps you will follow as you proceed with this investigation. Note in your memo the specifics of your research design.

5. Sherry Salman, an administrative assistant, has been asked by her employer to investigate the new duplicating machines on the market and prepare a short report giving her findings and her recommendations for purchase. Before Sherry begins her investigation, she decides to refer to the eight steps to prepare a report, so that they may serve as guidelines for her informational project. To help Sherry, list each step and briefly describe how each one could relate to the specific assignment her employer gave her.

6. Sam Birnbaum spent three hours in the college library gathering information for a report on life insurance. He copied all his findings in pencil in his class looseleaf notebook. His friend, Fukuko Hanaki, was working on a similar assignment, but copied her findings in ink on 5 × 7 cards. She made sure that she used different cards for each source. Sam thought Fukuko wasted supplies, time, and effort using her method of notetaking. In a memo to your instructor, list the advantages and/or disadvantages of Sam's and Fukuko's different methods of collecting data.

Dilemma

Jeremiah Calloway is the office supervisor in the legal firm of Kaper, Campbell, Kaper, and Campbell. The office is made up of eight lawyers. There are the four partners listed above plus four additional attorneys.

Jerry's staff consists of three secretary typists (four when he counts himself) plus a receptionist and a clerk. Mr. William Kaper, the senior partner, has talked to a representative from IBM about a word-processing center. However, before he makes any decision, he asks Jerry to write a short report for him on the present cost of the *average* letter which leaves the office. He already has the estimated figures on the cost per letter in a word-processing center. These estimates he obtained from the IBM representative.

Mr. Kaper wishes Jerry to find out the cost on the present system. He is to include dictation or "writing out in longhand" time by the lawyer, transcribing and final typing time by the secretary, stationery cost ($0.10 per letter), postage ($0.22), and overhead ($2.00 per letter to cover office rental, lighting, cost of equipment, and miscellaneous). The lawyer's time should be figured at an average of $55.00 per hour, and the secretary's time at $6.00 per hour.

Jerry hasn't decided, but he may break his information into two parts: those lawyers who dictate directly (three) and those who prefer to write letters out in longhand. The partners each send out about six letters each day on the average. The four staff attorneys, about eight each.

As yet, Jerry hasn't checked carefully the average time required to dictate a letter as compared to writing one in longhand. A casual observation on his part, however, indicates about twelve minutes for the former and about eighteen minutes for the latter. Typing time per letter, whether from dictation equipment or a hand-written copy, takes a typist about eleven minutes.

Please use the above information, plus any information you find necessary to assume, to write the short report for Jerry.

Decision, see page 265

The Short Report   13

Here is a list of the objectives you should understand by the time you complete this chapter. Place a check mark in the box beside each as soon as you feel ready to apply your understanding in a practical situation.

☐ The five primary methods of logical arrangement:
    Inductive
    Deductive
    Chronological
    Geographical
    Topical

☐ The basic purposes of headings in a short report:
    Outline
    Location
    "Rest"
    Organization
    Flow

☐ The basic rules for formatting short reports

☐ The different kinds of short report:
    Proposal
    Progress report
    Periodic report
    Memo report
    Letter report

Dana has worked hard as a general business major to acquire some management skills that will be marketable in business or some other kind of organization upon graduation. Dana's experience includes being a student assistant in the Department of Business Education in the college, and working summers as a substitute secretary, bookkeeper, and administrative aide for a large manufacturing company. His college courses include the functional areas of business, plus some work in psychology and sociology.

Based on this background, a large insurance company hired Dana to be a first-level supervisor for the Records Section in the Casualty Department. Dana has the college courses and the work experience that should make him a good manager. However, Dana is having substantial problems. A basic part of the job involves writing numerous short reports; the insurance company thrives on them. It seems that the college courses and his previous employment missed this major cog in the gears that move most organizations.

Dana is representative of the major complaint upper management has about young people in their organizations today. Individuals joining the organization for the first time often have problems in writing *short* reports.

Three important factors in the short report are: 1) gain attention; 2) transmit information; and 3) recommend action.

The short report must quickly capture the attention of the reader, immediately transmit information needed, and often recommend a course of action to the reader. And it must do all this concisely and clearly. The short report is not only a basic mechanism for most organizations, it is a primary key to success for new management-level employees who desire to make favorable impressions and to have impact.

Short reports can take various forms.

There can be numerous reasons for preparing a short report. It would be impossible to list all the different kinds of short reports and the standard forms for such reports. However, the major types can be noted: the letter report, the memo report, the progress report, and the periodic report.

The Logic, Headings, and Format

Each organization will have its own method and style for presenting material in reports. Although the specific formats may be altered from one organization to another, the basic structure of all will be very similar.

Logic

There are a number of different ways to organize ideas in the presentation. The determining factor concerns what will be the most effective order so that the material will be clear to the reader—perhaps even persuade the reader to agree with the material presented. Some of the most common methods of logic and arrangement are:

There are five basic methods of logical presentation.

    1. *Induction*—presentation of data followed by the conclusion;

2. *Deduction*—presentation of the conclusion and then a back-up of supporting data;
3. *Chronological*—presentation of the material in an historical-time sequence;
4. *Geographical*—presentation of the material by region, for example, eastern divisions, midwestern divisions, western divisions; and
5. *Topical*—identification of the basic categories of information and presentation of the data within those units (sales, financial, personnel, manufacturing).

Headings

If you note the headings of a report, you will see that they provide an overview of the subject. In actuality, the headings are also the various items in the outline of that report. It is almost impossible to have too many headings in a report. This does not mean that every paragraph should be introduced with a heading. But if solid page after solid page is presented without any headings, the reader will feel overwhelmed and will almost certainly react negatively or, worse yet, put the report aside to be read later—much later. Headings serve many purposes in the report:

Headings assist the reader in comprehending the report.

1. Present an outline   Headings present a quick outline of the report. The reader is provided with guides and hints as to the content without having to read the entire report. The style of the headings (capitalization, underline, and numbering) also permits the reader to note which topics are of major and which of minor importance.

2. Help location   Headings, which are actually guideposts, permit readers to remember where various materials are located in the report; they make it easy to refer to the report and identify important points. In the event the reader pulls a report from the file three years after it was written in order to review the section titled "Action Taken," it is not necessary to read all twenty-three pages of the report. The reader simply finds the heading, "Action Taken," and has the section needed. Time is saved.

Headings serve several purposes in the report.

3. Provide "rests"   Headings provide psychological rests. A reader will naturally slow down at the sign and then proceed.

4. Hold interest   Headings break up the monotony of reading a report; they can signal what material is just ahead.

5. Aid organization   Headings aid the writer by packaging the information carefully and correctly. When writing about female responses to a questionnaire under the heading, *Female Responses,* the writer will not accidentally fall into a careless error and present male responses in that section.

6. Maintain flow   Headings presented in parallel sequence will unify the report and lead the reader through the report. Note the parallelism of the headings in this text, in the short report (see Figure 13 – 1), and in the long report (see Appendix 3).

Format

Having established the logical approach and assigned the headings, it is important that the writer place the material on the typed page in a pleasing and readable format. Again, there can be many acceptable schemes, but the format should present material in an uncluttered manner; provide ample boundaries around the perimeter of the page; and use space and typing techniques to add emphasis and importance to material.

Use of space   Material on the typed page will receive greater emphasis in relationship to the amount of white space surrounding it. Therefore, the major headings should be surrounded with greater portions of open space than should minor headings. And of course, the entire page of space should be used with care. Provide adequate white space to balance typed areas. A brief segment should not be jammed at the top or bottom of a page but should be centered. Visual aids should be positioned logically as well as attractively from a space-utilization point of view.

Format of headings   The title of the report is often a first-degree heading. The major parts of the report often start with second-degree headings that are centered (see Figure 13 – 1). A third-degree heading is positioned at the margin. It has at least four vertical spaces above and three below it. A fourth-degree heading introduces a paragraph and may be underlined. It need not be a complete sentence. The fifth-degree heading is noted only by starting the paragraph with a key phrase and underlining that phrase of the sentence. Figure 13 – 1 does not show a first-degree heading because it is not the first page of a report but the fourth part.

Basic Kinds of Short Reports

As its name indicates, the short report is brief. Generally it will not exceed five pages in length and often it is one page or shorter. The short report may not illustrate some of the steps we discussed in planning the report, nor all of the possible headings we have listed. However, all of the principles of effective communication and report writing may be found, to a greater or lesser extent, in the short report.

What is the difference in meaning between *principle* and *principal*? (See Appendix 2.)

PART IV

What Employees Want to Know from

Published Materials

The Company Newspaper

The monthly newspaper, the NEWSLETTER, continues to be widely read and
accepted by virtually all segments of our employee audience. Before
the paper's overall acceptance is considered, its impact upon various
groups of employees should be noted. The responses to the newspaper
questionnaire are broken down into various demographic categories.

Responses By Age--As a general rule, the older the employee, the
greater the employee's interest in the newspaper. Although there are
some young employees who seem to take an interest in the paper, almost
all employees over 35 are very much interested in the publication.
Retirees are more interested than any other group.

Responses By Sex--With a growing number of women gaining employment in
the company, it was beneficial to note the differences among readers
on the basis of sex.

    The female responses tend to indicate an interest in social
issues, employee activities, and specific company "extracurricular"
activities. When the women-in-management positions are compared to the
men-in-management positions, their responses are strikingly similar.

    The male responses reveal a strong interest in the manufacturing
activities of the company along with the sales of company machinery.
The men are also very much interested in the profitability of the firm
and want more "hard" data concerning company finances.

**Figure 13—1
Report Format--
Headings**

Second-Degree Heading

4 Spaces above

Third-Degree Heading

3 Spaces below

Fourth-Degree Heading

Fifth-Degree Heading

The Proposal

The proposal is a type of short report.

If you studied the previous chapter, you are already familiar with the proposal. If you are asked to conduct a study to determine what the 16,000 domestic employees of your company want to read in the company's employee magazine, you would need to prepare a proposal report.

The report states your understanding of what you have been asked to do, presents precisely how you are going to do it, and addresses each of the items noted in the planning of a report (see Figure 13–2). This contract insures that everyone is agreed on what is going to be done and how it is going to be accomplished *before* the work is started.

The Progress Report

The progress report keeps the reader informed of progress made on a specific task.

If you are coordinator for employee communications and are involved in a nine-month study to determine what employees want to read, it would be reasonable that your superior would want to be kept informed, from time to time, of what is taking place concerning the study. If you report to the vice-president for personnel and industrial relations, it is likely that this person has numerous people simultaneously conducting studies. The best way for the vice-president to be kept informed of your progress and problems is via progress reports.

The progress report has five major objectives.

The progress report can accomplish one or more objectives:

1. *Emphasize Status:* highlight the progress and current status of the activity.
2. *Note Problems:* note any problems encountered in the project.
3. *Cite Changes:* cite changes in the activity since the previous report and note changes that had to be implemented since the original agreement or previous report.
4. *Indicate Schedule:* indicate if the activity is on schedule and if it is not, what is being done to catch up.
5. *Note Costs:* note any substantial deviations from the original cost estimates.

Some progress reports must be prepared from *scratch,* that is, on blank paper (see Figure 13–3). However, in many situations where more routine data are needed, the organization may provide a standard form on which the writer inserts specified information and comments.

Progress reports are an integral part of most construction projects, specialized examinations (such as an audit of a company's division), or almost any organizational activity that has a well-defined beginning and end. The progress report lets people know, from time to time, how things are going on that project.

Oftentimes, sales personnel file progress reports on how a new product is being accepted. The sales representative can fill in the data dealing with the number of cartons sold, the number ordered, and the number returned.

Figure 13–2
The Proposal Report

Proposal To Study Employee Communications

<u>The Problem</u>

The company's primary vehicle for communicating with employees is the <u>Newsletter</u>. It is published bimonthly and is sent by mail to the employees' homes. Since 1977, the company has grown, and the corporate structure has become increasingly complex. Within this context, top management questions the usefulness of this traditional vehicle and is concerned as to whether the correct messages are being carried to employees.

<u>The Purpose</u>

To determine what company employees want to know from the <u>Newsletter</u> and to recommend improvements to top management.

<u>The Definitions</u>

<u>Company Employees</u>--Exempt and non-exempt personnel who work at any of the domestic locations.

<u>Want to Know</u>--Specific topics that are of interest to employees.

<u>The Newsletter</u>--The bimonthly publication currently sent to all domestic employees.

<u>Recommended Improvements</u>--Specific and concrete actions the company can take to better employee communications.

<u>Top Management</u>--The company's executive committee.

<u>The Procedures</u>

<u>Mail Questionnaire</u>--A return-mail, postage-free instrument will be sent to the homes of all employees. The questionnaire will be covered by a letter from the vice-president of Industrial Relations.

<u>Interviews</u>--Dr. David Wilson will interview a sample of employees at the Minneapolis area plants. The interviews will be structured and employees will be selected randomly (each 97th employee from an alphabetical list will be interviewed).

Figure 13–3
The Progress Report

```
To      : H. D. Mallory, Vice-President
          Personnel and Industrial Relations
From    : Dennis Atwood, Coordinator
          Employee Communications
Date    : May 17, 198-
Subject : Status of Communications Study:  What Employees Want To Know
```

Background and Review

After the company's Communication Policy Board approved the proposal to determine what our employees desire in our employee communications, work was initiated immediately. Dr. David Wilson of Kalamazoo University has agreed to work with our staff in this study at a fee within our budgetary constraints.

Schedule

To date, the schedule has been met:

1. The employee sample has been drawn.
2. The Post Office has approved our special postcard that will be used to collect the data.
3. Dr. Wilson has completed his interviews of all personnel at level four and above.
4. The temporary slow down in our in-house printing office will not inhibit the progress of the study.

The Sample

Because the employees at our new acquisition in Peoria, Illinois, have not been merged into our computerized personnel files, we will be unable to include them as part of our sample. However, since the nature of the Peoria plant and the Evansville, Indiana, plant are very similar, we probably can obtain some clear idea about the Peoria employees' needs by noting the responses of the Evansville employees.

Next Phase

After Dr. Wilson completes his interviews, he will prepare a draft questionnaire instrument and meet with me. Once we agree on the instrument, I will send it to you for final approval. We plan to be prepared to send the questionnaire to employees with a cover letter over your signature on Wednesday, June 3, 198-.

The firm also might provide space for specific items, such as "What is the reaction of store managers?" or "Comments from the competition's sales representatives," or "Your analysis of the product's acceptability in the marketplace."

Besides being an excellent way to monitor the status of projects, the progress report serves as an important motivating device. If a manager must occasionally report on what has been accomplished and what is planned for the future, it tends to provide the manager with self-imposed goals for accomplishment. Whatever the nature of your employment, it would be highly unusual if you did not have to prepare progress reports.

The Periodic Report

One of the most common of all reports is the periodic report. Similar to the progress report, the periodic report is a routine statement concerning the activities of a manager's job. Bank cashiers prepare daily reports. Factory foremen write weekly reports. Department managers write weekly or monthly reports to their supervisors. And even the corporate president prepares a specific periodic report once each year for shareholders, which is called the corporate annual report. Periodic reports can be written on any *ongoing* activity of the organization.

The periodic report is issued on an on-going basis at specific time intervals.

Because the periodic report is routine, the format and topics covered generally will be similar from report to report. The periodic report usually starts by providing a general summary of activities. This is followed by a fairly detailed presentation of the primary topic. Often the current period is compared to some basic reference point, for example, the current period compared to the same time one year ago. Besides citing numerical data, the writer should evaluate the situation, make interpretations, and when needed, make recommendations (see Figure 13–4).

Periodic reports may be made on a pre-prepared form.

In very routine situations, the organization may prepare a specified form calling for basic data to be inserted by the reporter. Neatness and the ability to make short, clear, narrative statements are very important in completing the form (see Figure 13–5).

Today not all periodic reports are written. With modern computer technology, it is possible to assemble and report to managers via computer printouts. For instance, the status of a department budget generally is untouched by human hands. The computer generates a report indicating the original budget, amounts expended, funds encumbered, and amounts remaining in each budget line. The periodic computer report can compare where you are with your budget now compared to last year or last month, and how your performance compares with other departments within the organization. The computer periodic report, accompanied by a cover memo or a short report that analyzes the data, is a very powerful tool in the modern organization (see Figure 13–6).

A computer printout can serve as a periodic report.

**Figure 13–4
The Periodic Report
(Memo)**

```
To:       H. D. Mallory, Vice-President
From:     Dennis Atwood, Coordinator Employee Communications
Date:     August 20, 198-
Subject:  Last Month's Communications/Plans for Next Edition



Summary

Company Magazine--Last month 15,888 copies of the magazine were mailed
to domestic employees; 66 were returned for address errors.  Requests
from external organizations for complimentary copies of the magazine
continue to grow rapidly; a print run of 17,000 copies will be needed
for the November issue.

Company Newspaper--The standard 16,500 copies were printed last month;
next month will be identical.  Plant security reports that only 5
papers were found in company parking lots, and the janitorial crew did
not notice an excessive number in the waste bins.

Many employees on the third shift have commented that they appreciated
the special article on "Third Is First."

The union president made a special effort to see me concerning our new
feature series on fringe benefits.  He feels it is the union's
prerogative to provide that information to employees.  Further, he
feels that the company should not be using fringe benefits as a
"propaganda" technique to attempt to gain employee goodwill.


Future Editions

Magazine--The articles for the next issue are:

        The New Conveyor, X-10
        Our Machinery at Work in Japan
        Where to Look for Our Equipment When on Vacation

Newspaper--The primary articles for the next edition are:

        The Quarterly Profit Report
        Expansion of Plant HH
        Free Tickets to the Circus
        --all the regular features
```

Figure 13—4
(cont.)

Content Analysis

As noted in our earlier discussions, the contents of both the company
magazine and newspaper have shifted steadily in the last year. The
direction has been toward more material concerning company operations
with a consequent decline in personal news of employees. This is in
response to the survey of employees in which they indicated their
preference for articles in the area of operations rather than employee
chitchat.

CONTENT ANALYSIS

	Magazine		Newspaper	
	July 1982	July 1983	July 1982	July 1983
Employee News Promotions, retire- ments, awards, marriages, deaths, etc.	45%	20%	45%	30%
Company News Contracts, salaries, policies, acquisitions, sales, etc.	30%	55%	35%	50%
Employee Classified Ads	10%	10%	--	--
National News Social Security, politics, congres- sional action, etc.	15%	15%	20%	20%

Newspaper Printing

Webb Co., the printer for our newspaper, recently settled a new
contract with their union. The cost for producing our paper will
increase 7 percent per issue. The communications staff is currently
studying several alternatives on how we can absorb that increase and
remain within our budget. The alternatives being studied are:

a. Reduce the quality of the paper stock.
b. Stop sending the paper by mail to retirees, vendors, and
    others who request it.
c. Eliminate the free classified employee ads in the paper,
    thereby reducing the size of the paper by 2 pages.

Figure 13–5
The Periodic Report
(Forms)

Forms courtesy of University
Graphics, S.I.U.,
Carbondale, Illinois

**Note the need for short,
clear, narrative statements.**

☐ Mgmt. Systems
☐ Research
☐ Instruction
☐ Software Systems

Request for Service
from Computing Services

Complete this form and forward it (intact) to Computing Services.

Requesting Department	Campus Address	Date	Requisition Number

Requested Project Title	Name of Initiator	Phone

Account Number: Pay Acct. ☐ Yes
Maximum Dollar Limit:

Amount and source of funds available to support project

Goals Of Project:

(Attach Additional Pages if Necessary)

Brief Description Of
What Is To Be Done:

Benefit To The University
By Implementing This Project:

Desired Target Date For Completion Of This Project (Explain) _____

List of offices or general areas that would be affected by this project   Signature of Fiscal Officer Requesting

FOR COMPUTING SERVICES USE ONLY		One-Time Estimate		Annual Continuing Estimate	
	SERVICE TYPE	Hours/Days	Cost	Hours/Days	Cost
☐ Schedule & Publish	Development Man Hours		$		$
☐ Approve For Hold	370		$		$
☐ Disapproved	Plot		$		$
☐ Mark IV	Tab		$		$
☐ CMS	Data Prep.		$		$
☐			$		$
☐			$		$
☐			$		$

Divisional Recommendation   Propriety's Approval

Office of Record—Data Release   CS Director's Approval

Comments:

1670-1 041-22 Rev 9/77

GENERAL IMPROVEMENTS REQUEST
(Submit all copies to Business Services)

Number
Do not write in space above

To: Business Services   Date...

From: Department...........................Signature................................

Building Name, Number or Address...

Room Number...

Description of Project:

Do you have funds available for this project?...

Source of such funds..

Recommended by:

Major Building Representative .... Date....................................

Dean or Director .... Date.................................

(Do not write below this line)

TO: Campus Architect

FROM: Business Services .... Date....................................

Initial Priority...

( ) Proceed with preliminary sketch and preliminary estimate

( ) Proceed with working drawings

Blue Copy to: Business Services
Yellow Copy to: Campus Architect
White Copy to: Physical Plant   ....
Green Copy to: Department   Business Services
Pink Copy to: File

0935-2.041-4

TELEPHONE SERVICE REQUEST

Date _____

To:

From:

Department _____

Account Number _____

Telephone Number _____

Fiscal Officer Signature _____

WORK TO BE DONE: (location, number/types of telephones, etc.)

Type Phone: Wall ☐   Desk ☐   Toll Restriction Desired:

Yes ☐   No ☐

If New Installation, Indicate Directory Listing Desired _____

_____

(Do not write below this line)

SIU Telephone Request Number _____

Gen. Tel. Co. Service Order Number _____

Date Installation Completed _____

Distribution: (Dept. keeps yellow; mail all other to SIU Telephone Service)

White—Gen. Tel. Co. Commercial	Green—Gen. Tel. Co. Plant
Pink—SIU Telephone Exchange	Goldenrod—G. T. Co. for Return to SIU C. O.
Blue—SIU Telephone Service	Yellow—SIU Department

6955-2.041-1   Rev. 5/71

In some organizations, memos have a distasteful aura because they are used too frequently.

Reprinted by permission of the Chicago Tribune-New York News Syndicate, Inc.

Memo Report

In some organizations memos have a distasteful aura because they are used too frequently. However, in the reporting situation, the memo (such as the progress report in memo form, Figure 13–3) serves a very useful purpose.

Because of the possibility of error with oral orders and communication, many organizations prefer that all reporting be done in writing, using a memo. It is slower than the spoken word, but it increases accuracy and is more efficient.

Letter Report

What is the difference in meaning between *memorandum* and *memoranda*? (See Appendix 2.)

Some managers feel more comfortable preparing their reports in letter form. Also, some feel the letter is a bit more formal than the memorandum. It should be recognized that the letter, just like the memo, can be set up with headings, and organized to present data in a very logical manner and format. Often the letter form is used when either reporting to a high-level executive within the organization or when reporting to someone outside the organization (see Figure 13–7).

Figure 13–6
The Periodic Report
(Computer Printout)

```
USER ID 35.1
FAS-AM090
8494C20Z

ABR=61
```

SUB CODE DESCRIPTION	ORIGINAL BUDGET	BUDGET ADJ	ABR ADJ	CURRENT BUDGET	----EXPENDITURES----	
					THIS MONTH	YR TO DATE
21-0-000 SALARIES	344,253		344,253-			
21-0-010 REGULAR POSITIONS		43,468	344,253	387,722	34,996	128,263
TOT-21-	344,253	43,468	0	387,722	34,996	128,263
22-0-000 WAGES	2,400		465-	1,935		
22-0-010 STUDENT COMPENSATION			465	465	170	465
TOT-22-	2,400	0	0	2,400	170	465
23-0-000 TRAVEL	400		17-	384		
23-0-110 STAFF TRAVEL			17	17	17	17
TOT-23-	400	0	0	400	17	17
25-0-000 COMMODITIES	2,100		474-	1,626		
25-0-090 PRINTING SERVICE CHARGE			11	11		11
25-0-110 EXPENDBLE OFFICE SUPPLIE			11	11		11
25-0-130 LIBRARY SUPPLIES			5	5		5
25-0-170 TESTING SUPPLIES			18	18		18
25-0-190 INSTRUCTIONAL SUPPLIES			4	4		4
25-0-210 A/V SUP,FILM&FILM STRIPS			30	30		
25-0-380 STUDENT CENTER FOOD S/C			19	19		19
25-0-530 STU CTR BKSTR CHG EX EQ			22	22		22
25-0-560 GENERAL STORES S/C			343	343	3	343
25-0-820 U-SIGN SERVICE S/C			11	11		11
TOT-25-	2,100	0	0	2,100	3	444
26-0-000 CONTRACTUAL SERVICES	4,500		1,281-	3,219		
26-0-030 FREIGHT, EXPRESS S/C			43	43		43
26-0-560 PHYSICAL PLANT S/C			81	81		81
26-0-590 POSTAGE SERVICE CHARGE			173	173		173
26-0-660 ADVERTISING			39	39	9	9
26-0-720 COPYING PHOTO & PRINTING			10	10	5	10
26-0-750 COPY DUPLICATING S/C			250	250		250
26-0-760 PHOTOGRAPHIC S/C			8	8		8
26-0-950 COPYING-CAMPUS MACH S/C			676	676		676
TOT-26-	4,500	0	0	4,500	14	1,251
31-0-000 TELECOMMUNICATION SERV	3,500		1,223-	2,277		
31-0-120 DATA COM-EQUIP RENTAL			565	565	565	565
31-0-310 TELEPHONE SERVICE CHARGE			658	658		658
TOT-31-	3,500	0	0	3,500	565	1,223
* ACCOUNT TOTALS *	357,153	43,468		400,622	35,763	131,662

ACCOUNT	REFERENCE	DATE	DESCRIPTION	OPEN COMMITMENT STATUS	
				ORIG REQ	CUR REQ
2-10253-21-0-01-0	000001	10/28/77	ENC PER 10-31-77 SAL RPT		
* SUBTOTAL	* 2-10253-21				
2-10253-25-0-21-0	C66461	10/25/77	CORBELL ELECTRONICS		
* SUBTOTAL	* 2-10253-25				
2-10253-26-0-66-0	C64175	10/18/77	ALLIED SO BUSINESS ASSOC		
2-10253-26-0-66-0	C64229	10/07/77	CHRONICLE OF HIGHER EDUC		
* SUBTOTAL	* 2-10253-26				

Figure 13–7
The Letter Report

The Northern Company

806 Brunswick Road
Arlington, Illinois 60703

August 28, 198-

Mr. Jon Daily, Executive Director
American Association of Business
        Communicators
1010 Union Blvd. Suite 5
San Francisco, CA 94107

Dear Mr. Daily:

Your recent letter inquiring about the comprehensive
employee-communications study we are conducting is appreciated. I am
pleased to outline the basics of the study and the tentative findings.
Once all the data are gathered, I will send you a complete report.

Background

Northern has always been a company with a concern for the employee.
In many ways the firm attempts to communicate with employees--one way
is through the typical institutional communications of newspapers,
magazines, bulletin boards, etc. Our communications staff, perhaps
like others, may tend to fall into routines and ruts. Top management
started to question why certain kinds of articles were being published
in our house organs. We decided to conduct a study to determine what
kinds of topics our employees really want to read in the industrial
press.

Nature of the Research

Two primary techniques have been used to attempt to determine the
employees' communication likes and dislikes.

Mail Questionnaire--A return-mail postcard questionnaire was designed
and sent to every employee in the U.S.A. (22,500). The return rate
(45 percent) has been unusually high. We have been pleased with the
postcard approach and the relatively small number of errors employees
have made in completing the instrument.

Interviews--An outside expert aided us in developing the questionnaire
and also conducted interviews with a sample of our employees (750).
We have been pleasantly surprised at the loyalty the employees appear
to have for the company and their interest in the firm and its
activities.

Letter reports differ from business letters.

Why is the apostrophe after the last s in *employees'*? (See Appendix 1.)

Figure 13—7
(cont.)

Mr. Jon Daily
August 28, 198-
Page 2

Tentative Results

The questionnaires were designed to permit easy coding so the results
could be compiled using the computer program, SPSS. At this time I do
not have the data from our entire sample. However, based upon the
interviews and the questionnaires received from employees in the
Minneapolis area, the tentative indication is that employees are much
more interested in "hard" data than they are in "soft" data. That is,
employees are indicating they would prefer to have more information
from the company on:

        Business Trends
        Company Profits
        Company Competition   WHAT EMPLOYEES DO
        Fringe Benefits   WANT TO KNOW
        Product Uses

On the other hand, they are indicating that they do not desire
information (at least not to any great degree) on the following
topics:

        Executive Promotions
        Employee Hobbies   WHAT EMPLOYEES DO
        Social News   NOT WANT TO KNOW
        Societal Items

As indicated, these results are tentative, but a definite trend seems
to be in the making.

If this trend continues, it would seem to indicate that some companies
are spending thousands of dollars each month on so-called employee
communications but are not communicating the correct information to
employees.

Thank you for your interest in our project. I will send you our final
report when the study is completed. Enclosed you will find copies of
our current company publications, the Newsletter, which is sent to all
employees, and The Management Report, which is sent periodically to
exempt personnel.

Sincerely,

Dennis Atwood

Dennis Atwood, Coordinator
Employee Communications

Enclosures

MEMO

To: Students

From: The Authors

Subject: Short reports in your career

Most people in business today write a fairly large number of short reports. Such reports keep managers aware of what is going on at lower levels in the organization and ready to deal with any problems that may develop. By following carefully the guidelines for logic and format laid down in this chapter, you should be able to write any of the different kinds of short reports we've examined.

Decision

Here is the short report, in memo form, that Jeremiah Calloway prepared for Mr. Kaper.

Inter-office Correspondence

Kaper, Campbell,
Kaper &
Attorneys at Law   **Campbell**

```
To      :  Mr. William Kaper
           Senior Partner
From    :  Jeremiah Calloway
           Office Supervisor
Date    :  April 10, 198-
Subject :  Analysis of Correspondence Cost
```

Introduction

In response to your memo of March 15, I have carried through an analysis of correspondence costs. These figures are presented for your review to permit a comparison between our present system and a projected word-processing system.

The data given below are based on a survey conducted over a full three-week period (15 working days) from March 18 to April 8, 198-.

Cost per Letter (dicated)

```
        Dictation time         $4.00
        Typing time             1.50
        Overhead                2.00
        Stationery/postage       .25
        Total cost per letter  $7.75
```

Cost per Letter (handwritten prior to typing)

```
        Writing time           $5.20
        Typing time             1.50
        Overhead                2.00
        Stationery/postage       .25
        Total cost per letter  $8.95
```

Discussion

It should be recognized that most of our correspondence is relatively involved and is concerned with areas that are usually complex and require, because of legal implications, a very careful choice of words. This is in contrast to routine inquiry or acknowledgement letters with which many business firms are concerned.

Please let me know if you require further information or additional research.

CHAPTER REVIEW

Questions

1. Explain or exemplify what purpose(s) headings serve in short reports.

2. Why should reports use different degrees of headings?

3. Present an example of the use of the progress report in a specific organization.

4. What period of time does the periodic report usually cover?

5. Why is it wiser to originate a *form* for periodic reports and not for progress reports?

6. What difference(s) do you see in content and format between the business letter and the letter report?

7. What elements distinguish a memo report from a letter report? When is each one used?

8. Frequently, employees are asked to submit proposals for renovations, revisions, purchases, or innovations within their organizations. For each of the following jobs, give one or two situations that may arise to require them to write a proposal:
   a. supervisor of a word-processing center;
   b. project director of a nuclear energy plant;
   c. editor of a publishing company; and
   d. physical education teacher in a private high school.

9. List several methods travelling salespersons can use to report their activities when they are out of the office two weeks at a time but must report detailed information at least three times a week.

10. Explain the following in relationship to short reports:
    a. proposal;
    b. a fourth-degree heading;
    c. status in a progress report;
    d. chronological presentation of material; and
    e. form periodic reports.

Exercises

1. Visit the computer center at your college. Interview an employee who is familiar with the use of the computer for periodic reports and collect a sample of such a report. In a memo to your instructor, briefly discuss the use of the computer to produce a short report, note savings in time and cost, and attach the sample you have obtained.

Applications

1. Ira Kendrick is asked to type up a short memo report on the three-day marketing conference he attended in Monticello, New York. He has all the facts, including the names of new contacts and new ideas for promotion, increasing sales, and lowering expenses. He is prepared to give the company president all the data. Because Ira is in a hurry, he uses whatever margins and spacing are already set on the typewriter and does not bother with headings or centering his one table. The appearance of his report is unsatisfactory, but Ira is pleased with the contents. As the office manager in Ira's company, write a letter to Ira discussing the importance of the appearance of a report in a business office, being as specific as you can in your discussion and suggestions.

2. Lane Bronson, a staff accountant, has to submit a short report to a senior partner by 6 P.M. today that relates to a client's account. Many of the typists are sick and the few who are working already have assignments. Lane must type the report himself and has little confidence in setting up tables. As part of the report, he types in paragraph form the following information:

   The January sales figures for girls' skirts were 75 items with a gross take of $900 and girls' sweaters were 115 items with a gross take of $1165. The expected sales figures for skirts in February are 70 items, some on sale, with a gross take of $630 and 90 sweaters, also on sale, with a gross take of $720.

Lane realizes that the information in that paragraph belongs in a table, but he needs help in arranging the table. Set up the skirt and sweater data in table form the way it should be done for a report.

3. You are a personnel assistant for a company that has five employees in the personnel department. You have been asked to collect information relating to the weeks each person has chosen for vacation and to submit this report to the employee relations director. Your inquiry within your department resulted in the following information: T. Jones will be out two weeks beginning June 22. B. Smith is taking the weeks of March 21 and September 3. R. Brown will be out four weeks beginning August 3. You will probably take two weeks beginning July 15. You did not ask the employee relations director his vacation plans. Write a short memo report providing the vacation information, as requested.

4. For a work-study job at your college, you have agreed to be a peer counsellor fifteen hours a week. Your responsibility is to sit in an office in the student union building and advise any students wishing to discuss academic problems. Peer counseling is a popular service at your college and is under the direction of the college counseling department. You have been asked to submit a short report every Friday of your weekly activities on the job so that they can be made a matter of record and also so that you can be paid. Devise a form that you can use for this periodic report that will be acceptable to the senior counsellors.

5. Write a short letter report to the president of Midvale Bank and Trust Company on the basis of the following information.

On February 1, 198- you borrowed $5000 from Midvale Bank and Trust Company and with $9000 of your own money, you purchased 25 Fillmore M-21 Vending Machines.

You submitted your first progress report to the bank president on March 15 (reports are due every six weeks until the loan is paid off). On March 15, you listed your long- and short-term objectives, your cash position, and the names of two of your suppliers. In this past period you have finished placing your 25 machines (in 14 different recreational centers), firmed up three steady suppliers, bought a small pickup truck for transport, obtained insurance, and taken care of a great many other details.

This report is to be dated May 1. Please make any assumptions you feel are necessary concerning activities, financial income and expenditures, customer listings, problems encountered, new objectives (short- and long-range) which you have established, administrative details which you have instituted, and any other pertinent data.

Dilemma

For some time the Los Angeles Marketing Association has made every effort to secure the placement and promotion of women in all types of marketing organizations and to improve the attitudes toward women in marketing.

Two months ago, Mr. Calvin Curtis, Executive Director of the Los Angeles Marketing Association requested that two of his staff carry through a research project to determine "The Status of Women in the Marketing Profession."

Ms. Angele Forthman and Ms. Kimmie Jue were requested to complete the research and submit a detailed written report within forty-five days. The specific purposes of the study were to determine the attitudes toward women and their opportunities in the marketing fields. The findings were to be based on primary and secondary research. The final report was to include conclusions and recommendations.

Decision, see page 286

The Long Report
14

Here is a list of the objectives you should understand by the time you complete this chapter. Place a check mark in the box beside each as soon as you feel ready to apply your understanding in a practical situation.

☐ The four basic strategies for long reports:
    Information
    Persuasion
    Comparison
    Analysis

☐ The front matter elements of a long report:
    Title page
    Authorization letter
    Letter of transmittal
    Table of contents
    Table of charts and tables
    Synopsis

☐ The basic parts of the body of a long report:
    Introduction
    Discussion
    Conclusions and/or Recommendations

☐ The supplements in a long report:
    Bibliography
    Appendices

Your employer has questioned whether your department is needed in the organization. Could its activities be handled better by another department in the organization or by an outside vendor? In other words, is your function actually necessary?

The long report often is used as the basis for major decision making in an organization.

It is announced that a consulting firm will study the situation and issue a report—you know it will be a long report. The recommendations in that report will influence your job, your livelihood, and your family. The importance of the long report suddenly hits you. What is the long report? What does it contain? What does it do?

In the situation just described, the results presented in the long report are going to directly affect you. At other times, *you* will be called upon to prepare or assist in the preparation of a long report. Because of the impact the long report can have upon the organization and you, it is vital to understand this document which often is used as the basis for major decisions in business, industry, government, and other organizations.

What is the difference in meaning between *basis* and *bases*? (See Appendix 1.)

The long report can encompass virtually all of the activities described in the previous chapters in the text. It is a formally written document that concerns a situation worthy of the considerable time and effort that must go into it. Whereas the short report summarizes activities, events, and situations, the long report is more detailed. It generally presents the results of an investigation and offers conclusions and/or recommendations. The long report will be studied carefully by those involved in the decision-making process. The long report will play an integral part—if not the primary role—in formulating a decision . . . to eliminate a product, purchase a plant, acquire a company, or change the employees' hospitalization program.

The long report often presents the results of an investigation and offers conclusions and recommendations.

Alternative Strategies

There can be many reasons for writing the report. It is important for the writer to develop the most appropriate strategy in order to gain acceptance for the ideas presented.

The Persuasive Strategy

The long report may develop any one of several strategies; it may be persuasive.

After careful research, the coordinator of Internal Employee Communications determines that the department should be expanded. A long report needs to be prepared for the vice-president. The coordinator feels that the department can attain objectives beyond what is currently accomplished with its newspaper and company magazines. There is a need to expand the department; that conclusion is reached before writing the report. But now the report must be prepared in such a way as to persuade the decision maker that expansion is reasonable and acceptable. The use of primary and secondary sources, the logic, and how the ideas are supported become very important. This report is a difficult document to write because it must be clearly persuasive but not *hard* sell.

The Informational Strategy

The purpose of the information report is to present data. How the data are collected (primary and secondary sources) is as important as how the data are organized and presented. The originality of the writer in logically presenting and organizing the information is vital. As we will note later in this chapter, sometimes words can go only so far in presenting information. Therefore, it becomes important to supplement the words with tables, charts, and other visual aids. The tables will permit the decision maker to compare quantitative information, while charts and graphs will reflect trends in production and/or sales.

Why is *are* used after *data* instead of *is*? (See Appendix 1.)

The Comparative Strategy

When an organization wants to consider various solutions to a problem, it is possible to organize the report to present the alternatives and compare them. For example, the choices facing a growing small-parts manufacturing company could be presented using the comparative strategy:

The long report may compare two or more situations.

1. expand the Detroit plant;
2. expand the South Carolina plant by adding third shift;
3. expand the South Carolina plant production by addition to the current physical facility;
4. do not expand; or
5. maintain the status quo.

The comparative strategy presents the advantages and disadvantages of each alternative, compares them, and makes a recommendation.

The Analytical Strategy

The primary purpose of some long reports is to analyze a situation. Such reports often follow a four-point presentation:

The long report may use an analytical strategy.

1. identify the various problems (or supposed problem areas);
2. examine each in depth;
3. present conclusions which are justified; and
4. offer recommendations which are substantiated.

Combined Strategies

It must be recognized that it is possible for a long report to encompass one or more of the strategies. For instance, a report on the expansion of the Internal Communications Department could:

1. start with a strong information strategy that would present the history and need;
2. compare alternative solutions to the problem;
3. analyze each of the alternatives; then
4. present a recommendation in a persuasive manner.

Remember, research precedes the development of strategies and the writing of the report. You first discover and examine all the available facts. The conclusions and recommendations often become obvious when the facts have been displayed and examined. Once these steps have been taken, the strategies of the presentation can be designed. It takes careful thought and concentration not to let your mind wander to considering strategies of presentation before a fair conclusion or recommendation is determined.

Parts of the Long Report

There are three basic parts to the long report and each can have several divisions: the preliminaries, the body, and the supplements. Figure 14–1 presents a brief summary of the contents and paging of these parts (see also Appendix 3 for a sample long report).

For purposes of showing you a long report, sample parts of one will be presented in this chapter. You should realize that some companies or organizations will want to rearrange the order. But if you know the purpose of each of the parts, you will be able to adjust to the standards of any organization's format and arrangement.

The Preliminaries

The first few pages of any report are devoted to preliminary matters. Some of these are formalities which depend on company policy. Others are meant to prepare readers for the report that will follow.

Title page The title page presents the full title, and often indicates the primary readers and their titles, the primary author of the report, and his or her title. The date and place of preparation are also included (see Figure 14–2). Generally this information is spaced out over the entire page unless the cover has a cut-out opening that is designed to show the essential information.

Figure 14–1
Parts of the Long
Report and Pagination

Pagination*	Part	Division
	Preliminaries	
Small Roman "i"**		Title page
ii**		Authorization letter
iii**		Letter of transmittal
iv		Table of contents
v		Table of charts and tables
vi		Synopsis
	Body	
Arabic numeral "1"***		Introduction
All page numbers follow in sequence		Major parts of report
	Supplements	
Arabic numerals in sequence following those of body		Bibliography or list of references
		Appendices

*All page numbers are placed on the page centered at the top of the paper except where there is a centered heading at the top of the page. Then the number is centered at the bottom. Numbers are never set off with dashes, periods, or parentheses.

**These pages are counted in sequence, but it is inappropriate to place the actual page number on the page. Starting with "1" all page numbers will be Arabic numbers to the end of the report, through the supplements.

***Traditionally the number "1" does not appear on the first page.

**Figure 14–2
Title Page**

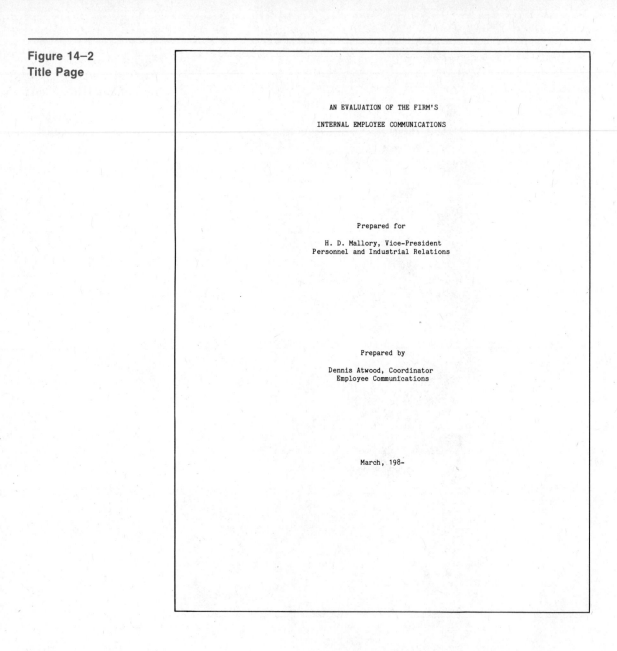

AN EVALUATION OF THE FIRM'S

INTERNAL EMPLOYEE COMMUNICATIONS

Prepared for

H. D. Mallory, Vice-President
Personnel and Industrial Relations

Prepared by

Dennis Atwood, Coordinator
Employee Communications

March, 198-

Authorization   If you received a letter authorizing you to conduct the study, that letter often becomes part of the final report. The authorization letter specifies what is to be done and establishes your authority to conduct the research. Such a letter is included in most government and other official reports, although it is found less commonly in the business report.

Letter of transmittal   The transmittal is similar to a cover letter and a sales letter. It is a key part of the report. The purpose, as the name indicates, is to transmit the report to the reader(s), but the letter can do much more. The transmittal letter establishes the initial setting for the report; it says much more than "here is the report." The letter can accomplish one or more of the following tasks:

The letter of transmittal is very important in establishing the setting for the report.

1. establish your authority to conduct the research and write the report;
2. state the purpose of the project in a brief manner;
3. cite any major limitations of the report, such as interviewing fewer people because of vacation schedules, or using a limited mail sample because of financial constraints;
4. summarize the basic findings in a cursory form and note the recommendation(s) if a synopsis is not used; and
5. acknowledge those who assisted in the preparation of the report.

The writer must select the contents of the transmittal letter carefully. For instance, if you are presenting a recommendation that initially may be received unfavorably, you should not attempt to present and explain it in two or three sentences in the letter of transmittal. You will want the reader to get the full impact by reading the entire report and noting the logical steps which you followed to reach those recommendations. In that situation, ignore the recommendation in the transmittal letter, and concentrate on such items as the research method, basic findings, and the expression of appreciation to those who assisted you.

Too often report writers spend hours writing the report and just a few seconds writing the transmittal. Most likely the transmittal letter will be the first item the reader will study carefully. As you know, first impressions are important. You often can make or break your case by the way you handle the contents of the transmittal (see Figure 14–3).

Table of contents   At the very least, the table of contents presents the major divisions of the report and indicates their respective pages. If the report is lengthy and has numerous subdivisions, those subdivisions can be noted, either with or without page notations (see Figure 14–4). Report pagination is important. Figure 14–1 notes the kinds of page numbers to be used in the report and where the numbers are to be placed on the page.

Figure 14–3
Letter of Transmittal

The Northern Company

806 Brunswick Road
Arlington, Illinois 60703

August 17, 198-

Mr. H. D. Mallory
Vice-President
Personnel and Industrial Relations
Inter-Office

Dear Mr. Mallory:

Establish authority.

Our internal communications continue to grow in importance. Since initiating the Department of Internal Employee Communications less than five years ago, we have made very basic gains in improving the delivery of information to our employees.

State purpose of research.

The study you authorized on July 10, 198- has been completed. You will recall that you requested a determination of:

1. What types of news in our company publications our employees found most interesting, and

2. What level of readership our publications enjoyed among our various employee levels.

Refer to basic findings.

Answers to those two basic questions have been obtained through the use of a questionnaire distributed to a carefully selected sample of employees. In addition, interviews were held with another segment of our work force. I feel the information obtained has produced reliable results upon which decisions may be made. For your consideration, you will find conclusions and recommendations included in the attached report.

Acknowledge assistance.

This study could not have been accomplished without the excellent assistance extended by the central management group, the functional directors, and the individual supervisors. Mr. Anthony Ray, director of Computer Services, and Ms. Carole Reynolds of Print Duplicating were particularly helpful in handling the preparation and processing of the various questionnaire items.

It will be a pleasure to present a review of these findings and recommendations to you and your staff next month. If you have any questions or would like to discuss the report before that time, I would be pleased to meet with you.

Sincerely,

Dennis Atwood

Dennis Atwood
Coordinator,
Employee Communications

Figure 14–4
Table of Contents

TABLE OF CONTENTS

Most headings in the table of contents will come from the report's basic outline.

Table of tables   If your report contains numerous tables and figures, a separate listing of tables is necessary. Because figures and tables clearly summarize important points made in the report, it is necessary to tell the reader where these representations can be found. If your report contains only a few tables, it is acceptable to include that small listing as the last item on the table of contents page.

The synopsis, when included, should contain a very concise overview of the report.

Synopsis   Reports for businesses and organizations often call for a synopsis or summary. This document is a crisply written one-page statement that gives an overview of the report and stresses the results. Think of the major findings and consider the busy executive who will have only a few moments to concentrate on your report. What are the *most* important items from the report that must be communicated? The synopsis should provide an excellent overview to the person who will read only this one page. To further aid the busy reader, it is wise to include clear topic headings in the synopsis. Of course, this same suggestion is made for the entire report.

Cover and binding   Organizations often specify how they prefer to have the report covered and bound. Numerous styles and degrees of expense are available for covering a report. Although inordinately expensive covers are not recommended, it should be remembered that some people judge a book by its cover. The data placed on the cover should present, at the least, the report's short title, the individual or department for whom the report is written, and the date.

A variety of techniques are available for binding the report. There is the simple staple and three-ring binder method to hold a report together. A bit fancier are spiral and plastic bindings. Today, many people like to be able to photocopy a report or parts of it, and thus a loose-leaf technique is often preferred.

The Body

The body of the report is made up of the introduction, the discussion, and the conclusions and/or recommendations.

The body of the report presents the major substantive materials. The organization of the body follows the outline you have prepared previously. The items contained in the body can be categorized into three major divisions: introduction, discussion, and conclusions and/or recommendations.

Introduction   Because the long report will become part of the organization's history and possibly may be referred to in a court of law, it is important to clearly state the thinking that went into the report: Why was it conducted, how was it done, and what was the context surrounding the report?

Actually, the introduction is very similar to the research proposal. The basic difference is that the proposal is written in the future tense and the introduction is written in the past tense. Generally the topics covered in the introduction include:

1. a statement of the problem;
2. a specific statement of purpose;
3. definitions of terms (working definitions);
4. research procedures; and
5. the scope and limitations of the research.

Items dealing with outlines, time schedules, and costs are usually not included in the report introduction. Those items were necessary in the research proposal, but they are not relevant in the introduction.

As it was important in the proposal to establish clearly the case for doing the research, it similarly is important to establish those factors in the writing of the introduction.

Discussion   The discussion section of the report—actually the heart of the report—takes up the majority of the total length. The strategy selected by the writer will certainly influence how the materials in the discussion are organized. All of the basic rules of communication and writing are applied in presenting the discussion. The format and generous use of headings are important. The insertion of visuals to supplement ideas also can aid the presentation.

The discussion section presents the findings and is the major portion of the report.

A review of basic writing and format will assist you in preparing the discussion section. Understanding the simple mechanics of presentation makes the actual preparation much easier.

Briefly review English usage before writing the report. Some of the common items you probably will encounter in writing the long report include: direct quotes, ellipses, capitalization, the use of numbers, and others. (These and many more items are covered fully in Appendix 1.)

Pagination is basic to the report and its organization; review Figure 14–1 for rules on the numbering and placement of page numbers on each page.

Footnotes generally appear at the bottom of the page. This can be done in the business-organization report, but it is becoming less common. However, the writer, whether a business writer or a scholar, should always cite his source for important information or data.

A footnote is used to indicate either the source of an idea or quotation or to provide greater explanation of a point discussed in the text. Footnotes may also present a critical comment on a source, compare the views of two or more authorities, or direct the reader to additional sources.

The business report also will contain a bibliography that cites all the sources used in the report. The simple citation method calls for assigning each item in the bibliography a number. In the text, when it is necessary, for example, to refer to the article by R. Wayne Pace who is assigned number 17, one just inserts (17:3). The notation means the idea came from the work by Pace, page 3.

Internal summaries and headings are items inserted by the writer which make the report more comprehensible to the reader. Each time a major section ends, it should be summarized in a paragraph or two. Of course, the basic road signs—headings—are always helpful to the reader. It is acceptable to assign the summary a heading and to call it either *summary* or *summary of* _____.

The personal pronoun is not necessary in the long report. As a matter of fact, the tone of the report should be objective and impersonal. Since the writer has written the entire report and the writer's name is on the title page, "I"s are not necessary. The only time it would be reasonable to use "I" would be for dramatic emphasis.

Figures, tables, and charts obviously can be important in the report. It is never adequate to simply write "see Figure XXX" without explaining the concept. The item should be explained as clearly as possible in words. The writer has the responsibility to tell the reader what the table or figure reveals. As has been done in this text, the reference to figures is usually parenthetical.

By reviewing these basic guides, studying the material in Appendix 1, and examining the long report example in Appendix 3, you should have a solid understanding of how to prepare the major section of the long report.

Conclusions and/or recommendations   The long report will have a conclusion. If the writer's assignment was to solve a problem, the report also will have a recommendation. Often the writer will want to include both a conclusion and a recommendation. The conclusion summarizes the major points of the total report. Even though the report may have numerous internal summaries (actually mini-conclusions), the report's major conclusion section provides the large, overall, interrelated picture.

If the report is one that calls for a recommendation, the writer may prepare a conclusion section and a separate recommendation section. Or, it is possible for the writer to briefly summarize the report's data and emphasize the solution to the problem. In the latter situation, the single section would be called either *Conclusions and Recommendations* or *Recommendations*.

Recommendations should be clear and precise. Broad multi-directional recommendations help no one. If recommendations for different areas are provided, each section should be introduced with a heading.

Because of our busy and complex society, conclusions and recommendations usually are placed at the beginning of the long report.

Optional arrangement   The traditional sequence of the organization seems to be changing from placing conclusions and recommendations at the end of the report to the beginning. Today's managers are extremely busy and often must read dozens of reports each week. Therefore, in an effort to save time and obtain an overview of the activity, the manager may simply read the introduction, the conclusions, and the recommendations. Of course, the supervisor concerned intimately with the activity must read the entire report carefully. Thus executives can read the summary or synopsis and obtain a broad overview; by referring to the conclusions and recommendations, they can obtain specific directions without having to read the entire report. If readers then want or need additional data, it is obtainable in the discussion section. Generally, managers are interested primarily in the answer or the recommendation. They assume the writer employed reliable research methodology and conducted excellent research; they want the answer. Therefore, the recommendation section before the discussion is desired by some organizations.

The Supplements

Various kinds of backup materials may be needed for the report. Literally, they *back up* the body; they are placed at the end of the report and are available to the reader on an *as needed* basis. The two basic supplements are the bibliography and appendix.

Supplements provide backup materials.

The bibliography   Sources which were used in preparing the report are listed in the bibliography. The bibliography should list both primary and secondary sources. (See Appendix 3 for bibliography format.)

The appendix   Materials that may be helpful to the reader are placed in an appendix. If an item is not absolutely necessary in understanding the report, it should be placed in the appendix, not in the text of the report. For example, your research used a questionnaire; the discussion section cited various questions and results from that instrument. One can understand the discussion section and recommendations without seeing the actual questionnaire. In such a case, the instrument would be a good item to place in an appendix. If the questionnaire is absolutely necessary in order to understand the report, then it belongs in the body of the report.

The contents of the appendix can vary.

There is really no limit as to what can be placed in an appendix — questionnaire cover letters, a list of locations visited, photographs that provide greater detail of an item studied, the full text of a government regulation, and many other auxiliary items.

In some cases one might even package a special appendix separately. Again, such an item should supplement the report. Common items that would be too bulky to place in the appendix of the normal 8½-by-11-inch report and therefore might be bound or packaged separately are product samples, newspaper advertisements, or computer printouts. You should rec-

ognize that modern photocopying machines often permit you to reduce original copy. Items that once had to be bound separately can now be reduced photographically and included in the report or in the appendix that is bound with the report.

Visuals

As best you try, your words can take you only so far. Sometimes you will find that other modes of expression beyond words may be necessary. Throughout the text you have noted forms of expression other than words—tables, figures, charts, and an occasional cartoon. These visuals are used when either one-dimensional words cannot adequately express an idea or when there is need to supplement the words.

When appropriate, use visuals to communicate ideas.

The types of visuals are almost limitless. Other forms of visuals that have not been mentioned here include bar charts, graphs, pictorial tables and charts, organization charts, map charts, photographs, and drawings. Many of these are discussed in Chapter 15.

The Long Report: An Overview

As an individual or as a member of a team, it occasionally will be necessary for you to prepare a long report. As illustrated, the report can discuss major items that will have lasting effects on the organization and the people within the organization. Therefore, not only is the report presentation important—but its success depends on the fair and detailed research that must precede the report itself.

MEMO

To: Students

From: The Authors

Subject: Long reports and your career

It is unlikely that you'll write many long reports in the course of your career. Therefore, it is especially important that the ones you do write are as effective as possible, both in accurately communicating the message you want to convey and in displaying your own talents in the best possible light.

Decision

Here is the title page of the long report which Angele Forthman and Kimmie Jue prepared for the Los Angeles Marketing Association. Refer to Appendix 3 for this long report in its entirety.

THE STATUS OF WOMEN

IN

THE MARKETING PROFESSION

Prepared for

Mr. Calvin Curtis
Executive Director
Los Angeles Marketing Association

Prepared by

Angele Forthman

Kimmie Jue

May 9, 19_

CHAPTER REVIEW

Questions

1. Explain how the long report differs from the short report in ways other than length.

2. Why are strategies important in the design of the long report?

3. Why is the letter of transmittal similar to a sales letter?

4. If you are authorized to write a report, why is it necessary to prepare an introduction for the report—after all, the person receiving the report told you to do it?

5. Explain why certain items should be placed in the appendix; a good example would be helpful.

6. In report writing, what options do you have in the placement of numbers in the body of the report and in the pages preceding and following the body of the report? When are Arabic numbers used and when are Roman numerals used?

7. Explain the purpose of the following items that may be part of a long business report:
   a. a letter of authorization;
   a. a letter of acceptance;
   a. a letter of transmittal; and
   a. an index.

8. What factors should be considered when determining the appropriate cover and binding for a business report?

Applications

1. As the Personnel Director of your company, you recently suggested to the firm's president that a training section be established in your department. You also suggested that a training director be hired, along with two support individuals.

   The president asked for a report to justify such a move. The eighteen-page report has been completed and you have just received from your assistant a letter of transmittal to accompany the report. Call your assistant in and offer some constructive criticism on the letter of transmittal which follows.

July 1, 198–

Mr. Robert Rowe, President
Foremost Plastic Company
110 South State Street
San Francisco, California 94011

Dear Mr. Rowe:

As requested and authorized by you on May 15 the attached report has been prepared to justify the position of Training Director for Foremost Plastic Company.

For well over five years we have needed an individual in this spot and now with over 1500 employees, you would be making a mistake in not approving the request made and substantiated in the attached report.

Your favorable reaction is awaited.

Sincerely yours,

Write an improved version of this letter of transmittal.

Dilemma

Yoshi Tanaka works in the personnel department of the Sav-Mor Food Chain.
Recently the vice-president of personnel requested that Yoshi complete a
detailed analysis of whether or not Sav-Mor should begin publishing a
monthly employee magazine.

Yoshi selected a sample of Sav-Mor's 1250 personnel and sent them mail
questionnaires. In his primary and secondary research, he attempted to
answer questions concerning content, distribution, cost, publication styles,
effectiveness, and other areas.

Among the data he has gathered is the information listed in the following
two areas. He has decided to present each in the form of a visual aid. How
would you present each area for maximum impact?

1. 60 males and 65 females preferred a quarterly publication, while 60
   males and 30 females preferred one issue monthly. The other 15 (10
   males) had no preference.
2. An overwhelming majority of the respondents (86 percent) felt each
   of the six districts, the headquarters, and the warehouses, should
   each have its own "reporter."

Decision, see page 305

Visual Aids for Effective Communications

Here is a list of the objectives you should understand by the time you
complete this chapter. Place a check mark in the box beside each as soon
as you feel ready to apply your understanding in a practical situation.

☐ The meaning of the *visual concept*

☐ The three main purposes of visuals in reports:
  To supplement
  To emphasize
  To clarify

☐ The basic techniques for making your own visuals

☐ The rules for placing visuals in reports

☐ The uses of visuals in business communications other than reports

Words alone may not be enough. When attempting to express an idea by using only words you may not be using the most effective means of representing an idea. In order to reach the receiver in a clear and precise manner, it is sometimes necessary to go beyond the printed or the spoken word.

The Visual Concept

Visual aids can assist communicators in expressing ideas. The term *visual aid* is very appropriate. Literally, these are *visual* materials that *aid* the communicator in expressing either a written or a spoken message. The visual aid may help to supplement, emphasize, or clarify an idea that otherwise would lack understanding.

When you are faced with a task of presenting material in narrative form, the use of some visual assistance may not only be a good idea but may be vital to the success of the communication.

At one time business-organization communications had to be dull. The use of visuals appeared too flashy. Evidently anything beyond words was inappropriate for the *conservative* business approach. No longer. Today it is recognized that the effective use of visuals is an efficient way to express an idea.

In previous chapters we have noted that clear language, good grammar, and a logical sequence of thought can each support the communication. The use of visuals is yet another way that you can support the clear transfer of information from one person to another. Visuals should support the idea you desire to communicate. The visual is not the communication. It is used to *assist* the communication. The emphasis should be on understanding, not on the visual aid.

The situation of the visual becoming the communication might be exemplified by describing how some students approach the visual-aid presentation in a speech class. There is often one student who prepares a beautiful graph or a pretty picture and simply stands before the audience and shows off the decorated poster board. This person has misunderstood the assignment. The task was not to draw a picture or a chart. The assignment was to have an idea, to transmit the idea to another's head, and to maximize understanding by using the visual to assist the communication process. In your written communications be aware of how visuals can aid in helping people understand your idea. However, this is not to suggest that every message needs a visual.

Visual aids should be used to assist in the communication of ideas.

Why Visuals?

Visuals are used by the communicator to supplement, emphasize, or clarify narrative material. Although it is impossible to represent the numerous ways visuals can be used, a few can be noted.

FIVE YEAR FINANCIAL HIGHLIGHTS (IN THOUSANDS)

Figure 15–1
The Balance Sheet

For the Year Ended	December 31				
	1982*	1981	1980	1979	1978
Gross Income	$ 249.225	$ 192.721	$ 164.375	$ 136.457	$ 114.861
Net Earnings	$ 19.346	$ 20.278	$ 16.573	$ 9.896	$ 4.515
Real Estate Lending Volume	$ 741.177	$ 728.150	$ 579.891	$ 532.306	$ 304.553
Average Interest Rate on Real Estate Loans Orig.	11.21%	9.76%	9.10%	9.09%	9.23%
Real Estate Loans Sold	$ 195.612	$ 98.414	$ 134.780	$ 133.695	$ 45.789
Average Fee on Real Estate Loans Originated	1.41%	1.37%	1.40%	1.45%	1.60%
Net Savings Increase (Includes Interest Credited)	$ 212.273	$ 151.105	$ 176.814	$ 230.085	$ 178.013
End of Year					
Assets	$2.756.029	$2.432.548	$2.126.558	$1.838.543	$1.643.268
Loans Receivable. Net	$2.340.806	$2.125.597	$1.859.029	$1.628.119	$1.429.243
Number of Loans	61.945	60.751	51.217	58.893	56.507
Savings Accounts	$2.204.710	$1.821.473	$1.661.548	$1.484.534	$1.251.334
Number of Savings Accounts	288.783	283.919	271.368	254.404	236.110
Federal Home Loan Bank Borrowings	$ 274.322	$ 208.414	$ 103.271	$ 103.246	$ 356.854
Real Estate Loan Portfolio Yield	9.04%	8.57%	8.24%	7.92%	7.74%
Interest Rate on Savings Accounts	7.82%	6.63%	6.49%	6.47%	6.34%
Interest Rate on Borrowings	10.06%	8.29%	6.98%	6.53%	8.54%
Combined Cost of Funds	8.18%	6.73%	6.57%	6.55%	6.43%
Margin on Funds	.91%	1.42%	1.53%	1.09%	.78%
Return on Retained Earnings	13.35%	16.26%	15.47%	10.02%	4.45%
Number of Operating Offices	46	46	39	36	32

*Projected

Visuals to Supplement

The accountant's balance sheet is an exact and precise piece of communication by itself. However, for some audiences, the balance sheet may not be the best way to relate important information.

For years, companies have prepared annual reports in an attempt to communicate financial data to shareholders. A brief look at these reports during the past twenty-five years indicates an increasing use of visuals. First, the audience has become diverse, and second, companies have become more concerned with good communication. Therefore, an attempt has been made to take relatively dull numbers and make them relevant to the audience by going beyond the balance sheets. Visuals are used to add a different dimension to the narrative and balance sheets of annual reports.

They can be used to supplement the idea. For example, a balance sheet can provide a snapshot of the profit picture for one year (see Figure 15–1). However, a visual, in this case a simple bar graph, can isolate the information, put it in the context of time, and dramatically supplement the balance sheet (see Figure 15–2).

Visuals can supplement the information presented.

Figure 15–2
The Bar Chart

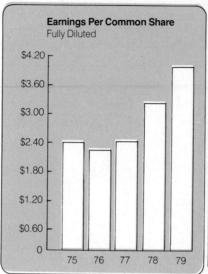

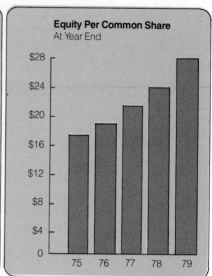

Visuals to Emphasize

Visuals can emphasize key ideas.

Which of the following emphasizes the point and will remain with you longer?

Statement #1:

> *Since the mid-1800s, we have made dramatic progress in shortening the time to cross the USA, coast to coast. In 1849 the covered wagon made the trip in 116 days; in 1870 the train made the crossing in 11 days; in 1923 an aircraft could make it in slightly more than one day; in the 1980s the Space Shuttle Orbiter will cross the country in 8 minutes.*

Statement #2:

By Covered Wagon 166 days (1849)	By Air 26½ hours (1923)
By Stage Coach 60 days (1860 s)	By DC-3 17½ hours (1938)
By Train 11 days (1870 s)	By 747 5 hours (1975)

The Space Shuttle Orbiter will cross the United States in only 8 minutes

Visuals, in addition to supporting the communication process, can also be used to add emphasis to an idea. Sometimes it is desirable to repeat a point; besides repeating it with words, a visual may be the efficient way to achieve repetition without boring the reader. In this way, visuals add life and emphasis to your materials.

Visuals to Clarify

Often tables are used because the mix and maze of numbers in a written paragraph would be so complex that it would take hours to unravel the data. In this case the visual, such as a table, clarifies information. Again, which of the following statements is clearer?

Visuals can clarify points.

Statement #1:

With the decline in the teenage population and with people living longer and retiring earlier, the student mix on college campuses may change. For instance, at Milwaukee University the 17–22 age group has been declining: 1975 = 95%, 1977 = 90%; 1979 = 87%, 1981 = 85%, 1983 = 82%, and 1985 = 80%. At the same time, in the Milwaukee area, the portion of the population reaching the age of 65 has been increasing dramatically: 1975 = 7%, 1977 = 8%, 1979 = 10%, 1981 = 13% 1983 = 15%, 1985 = 20%. Although not as dramatic as the increases in the general population, the portion of the students who are 65 or older has also been increasing.

Statement #2:

	CHANGE IN STUDENTS' AGE (Given in percent)		
Year	% of students age 17–22	% of students age 65 yrs +	% of area population age 65 yrs +
1975	95%	0.03%	7%
1977	90%	1.00%	8%
1979	87%	1.50%	10%
1981	85%	2.00%	13%
1983	82%	3.50%	15%
1985	80%	5.00%	20%

Whenever it is necessary to compare more than two items, it is generally best to discover a way to go beyond the words. The data are contained in Statement #1. But to visualize and sort out the data is rigorous. A visual, in this case a table, can clarify the matter. Tables, on the whole, permit numerical data to be easily retained, compared, analyzed, and evaluated.

Certainly, besides tables there are other visuals that can assist one's efforts to be clear. Consider, for example, a description of a mechanism that is part of everybody's life but which few people understand—the gasoline engine. It is okay to start with words:

> *Gasoline engines are known as internal-combustion engines, for the fuel is burned inside the cylinder where the piston is pushed. During the intake stroke, fuel and air are drawn in through the intake opening. Next is the compression stroke—the air and gas vapor are compressed. Next the sparkplug fires, igniting the vapor. Next is the power stroke. The burning gases force the piston downward. Last is the exhaust stroke, in which the burned gases go out through the exhaust opening.*

But a visual, in this case an illustration (see Figure 15–3), will assist the words and will aid the reader to better understand the concept.

Making Your Own Visuals

Your imagination is the only limitation to determining the kinds of visuals that can be used in written materials. For convenience, the major categories of visuals can be noted:

1. tables
2. photos
3. cartoons
4. illustrations
5. charts and graphs
   a. pie or circle
   b. bar
   c. segmented bar
   d. pictogram
   e. map

There are many different types of visual aids.

Initially you look at the list of visuals and think, "I'm not an artist—I can hardly draw a straight line with a ruler; I can't use visuals in my presentation." Wrong! You should not feel that you need to be a professional illustrator or an artist in order to use visuals in your written materials. Today, book stores

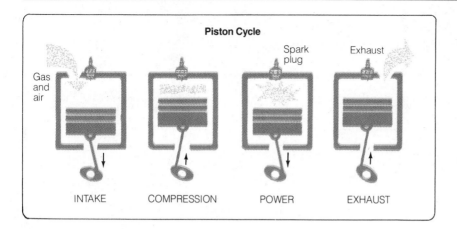

Piston Cycle

Gas and air

Spark plug

Exhaust

INTAKE   COMPRESSION   POWER   EXHAUST

Figure 15–3
Illustration Used as a Visual

and art stores carry a variety of self-sticking materials that make the design of visuals relatively easy. All kinds of adhesives are available for picture representations. Tapes come in a variety of widths and colors for use in bar charts and graphs. Transfer lettering and symbols are available to accomplish virtually any job.

Most of the materials can be peeled off a piece of plastic and stuck on your report. Others are designed to be placed over your page and then rubbed so that they will adhere permanently to your visual.

What is the difference in meaning between *peel* and *peal*? (See Appendix 1.)

When considering methods of creating and reproducing visuals, do not ignore Xerography. This process permits you to duplicate almost anything in print. Furthermore, much of the modern equipment lets you reduce automatically pictures, charts, and computer printouts so that they can be easily transformed into useful visuals in reports and other forms of communication.

Creativity and Visuals

The entire act of communication involves creativity. How can you select just the right words to draw the picture in another's mind? When words will not suffice, it is necessary to be equally creative with the use of visuals. Recognize that even the old traditional bar chart can contain a new twist and even make the presentation a bit livelier. It is possible to be creative and simultaneously very communicative.

Inject creativity into your visual aids.

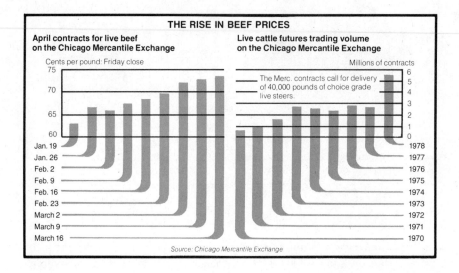

Note, if the dates were placed horizontally, the charts would become very large and much less readable.

Figure 15–4 illustrates a creative approach to the standard bar chart. It is interesting to note that in this case the artist was undoubtedly working against a deadline and had to come up fast with a finished product. The figure is an example of the use that newspapers make of visuals to supplement their news stories.

The *Chicago Tribune* had a relatively small amount of data to present, but if traditional techniques were used, the chart would become bulky. If the data notations were spread across the horizontal axis, the chart's width would be unreasonable. Note how the material was condensed and presented in a unique and informational manner.

The pie chart can be handled in a different manner. Figure 15–5 represents the rather traditional pie. If it is necessary or desirable to include additional information, data can be pulled from the pie and emphasized in larger print and in more detail (see Figure 15–6).

In addition to the visual aids already discussed in the text, you will find others illustrated on page 304, including a graph, a flow chart, an organizational chart, and a map.

Effective Placement of Visuals

A frequent question is, "Where does the visual go?" For either a written report or an oral presentation, a basic guideline is to present the visual at a time when it will not disrupt the logical flow of information.

In the written report be careful not to present a graph, chart, or pictogram until the reader has been introduced to the material. Be sure the person reading the report has received enough information so that he or she can understand the idea. If the visual is crucial to the understanding of the idea and vital to the impact you desire to make, it should be incorporated in the body of the report. If the visual is supplementary and is not needed in order to understand the idea, it may be best to place it in an appendix. And keep in mind that regardless of where in the report the visual is placed (or displayed in an oral presentation), it must always carry a concise, clear, explanatory title or caption.

In both the written and the oral presentation, do not reveal your visual until you are ready to address it. Remember, most of us are very interested in visuals. That is a major plus in using them. But do not let the intrigue of your visual be disruptive to the communication process by presenting the visual at the wrong time.

Visuals Only in Reports?

This section of the text has focused on reports and this chapter has centered on the use of visuals in reports. But are reports the only kind of business communication in which you'll want to use visuals?

During the past week you probably received at least one sales brochure in the mail. If it is holiday time or early spring, you may have received a half dozen or more. These brochures are nice to look at and they often grab our attention. Why? Because of the effective use of visuals. Be it the original Sears catalogue or the new sophisticated brochure from Nieman-Marcus, they all feature brief word descriptions accompanied by pleasing visuals. The visual may be used in any kind of communication to supplement, emphasize, or clarify an idea. Therefore, the use of the visual in a letter, a memo, or even a questionnaire may be desirable.

Visual aids can be used effectively in reports, memos letters, speeches, and in dozens of other communication situations.

Figure 15–5
Traditional Pie Chart

**ALLOCATION OF REVENUE
AND EXPENSES**

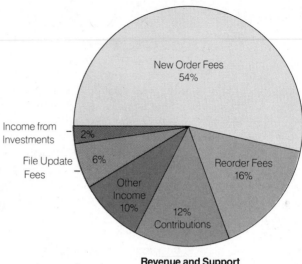

Revenue and Support

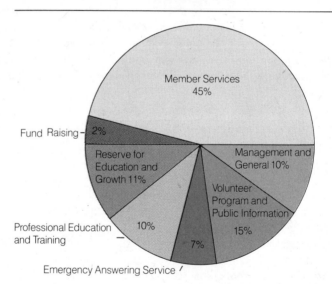

Application of Funds

Employee Compensation

For wages, salaries and benefits to employees, Rexnord paid $228,000,000. This amount is divided between direct and indirect compensation. This chart shows the major elements of employee pay and benefits.

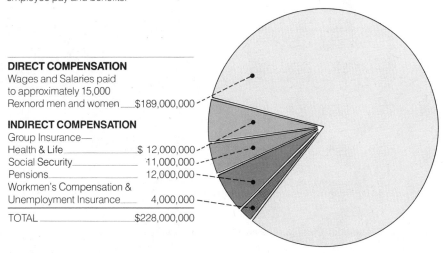

DIRECT COMPENSATION
Wages and Salaries paid
to approximately 15,000
Rexnord men and women___$189,000,000

INDIRECT COMPENSATION
Group Insurance—
Health & Life_____$ 12,000,000
Social Security_____11,000,000
Pensions_____12,000,000
Workmen's Compensation &
Unemployment Insurance_____4,000,000

TOTAL _____$228,000,000

In a letter to an editorial association in which you want to emphasize the growth in the readership of your firm's publication, a bar chart may be most appropriate, as in Figure 15–7. Note how the writer first presents background information and then makes the point by the use of a graph originally prepared for a report to a vice president of the company.

In a memo to your company's vice-president of personnel, you want to point out how various brochures and booklets would be valuable in maintaining good employee communications. You include with your memo a rough sketch that illustrates your ideas, showing clearly what you have in mind. Your attachment indicates current and projected techniques, adding emphasis to your memo and giving it staying power (see Fig. 15–8).

In a questionnaire in which you desire to gain the attention of the readers and also be very clear what it is you want them to comment on, visuals can be helpful.

One company had instituted some new magazines for employees and then wanted to determine how the employees liked the publications. The company

Figure 15–7
Visual Used in a Letter

All-Company

203 Sperry Road   Madison, Wisconsin 16303

February 4, 198-

Mr. Henry Smithy
Executive Director
Business Communications Association
1212 Winchester Street
Rochester, Minnesota

Dear Hank,

Your request for information on how company publications can increase
their readership arrived just at the right time. Recently our
department prepared a report for the vice-president of personnel that
dealt with many features of our communication program.

At All-Company, we take pride in providing our employees and members
of our community with news about our company. Therefore, we send our
publication to a variety of community leaders, high school teachers,
individuals in the labor movement and members of government. We have
also found that hospitals, doctors' offices, and auto-repair shops
appreciate receiving our publications. After all, these organizations
have many people sitting in waiting rooms who can really enjoy our
company magazine--and they can learn more about All-Company, our
products, and the contributions we make to the community.

We have had tremendous growth in our readership. The graph from our
recent report to Vice-President Montgomery clearly indicates the
increase in the readership of our company magazine since we started
sharing it with people outside the firm in 1974.

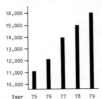

If you would like additional information on how we use our employee
publications to serve non-employees, we would be pleased to provide
additional data.

Sincerely,

Timothy Jones, Director
Employee Communications

Figure 15-8
Picture Illustration as
a Visual

was huge and it was possible for employees to receive several magazines from various segments and divisions of the firm. To add clarity and to insure that employees understood the publications involved in the survey, visuals were used (see Figure 15-9).

Visuals obviously are not limited to written communications. As visuals support the written communication process, they also give substantial assistance to the person making the oral presentation. The uses of visuals in speech are the same as in written language—to clarify, to emphasize, or to support an idea. We'll look closely at the use of visuals in oral presentations in Chapters 17 and 18.

A Concluding Comment

Visuals are a part of your communication style, and an important part of communication is to put your idea in something *other* than words. Can any of us give directions to a stranger in town without extensive use of visuals—pointing, waving, and sometimes even drawing a picture? Visual aids should be a part of the writer's and speaker's vocabulary just like language, grammar, and syntax.

**Figure 15–9
Photographs Used as
Visuals**

From ''How Do You Rate
Intercom?'' Rexnord Inc.

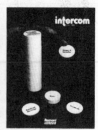

How Do You Rate Intercom?

October, 1977

Hello,

Did you ever wonder if you were talking and nobody was listening?

You recently received the seventh issue of **Intercom,** *Rexnord's corporate magazine, and our curiousity has gotten the better of us. That's why we've asked the personnel manager in your plant to give you this survey. You and several other employees at your location were chosen at random so that we can end up with a crossection of opinions about* **Intercom** *which represent all Rexnord employees.*

Please take a few minutes to fill out the survey and return it to your supervisor or personnel manager in the envelope provided. The survey will be returned unopened to the Intercom Editor. **Please do not sign your name.**

Your comments and opinions are important to us. With your help, we can make **Intercom** *a better communications tool for all employees. The survey returns will be analyzed by Rexnord's Corporate Data Processing Department, and we will publish the results in the Winter, 1978 issue of* **Intercom.**

Let us know what you really think. In appreciation, you will receive a Rexnord ballpoint pen for participating in the survey. Thanks for your help.

Sincerely,

*Joel H. Head
Intercom Editor*

Rexnord

GRAPH

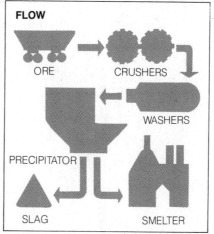

Tons Shipped

— wheat
--- corn

projected

100
90
80
70
60
50
40
30
20
10

Year 75 76 77 78 79 80

FLOW

ORE   CRUSHERS

WASHERS

PRECIPITATOR

SLAG   SMELTER

Figure 15–10
Five types of visuals

ORGANIZATION

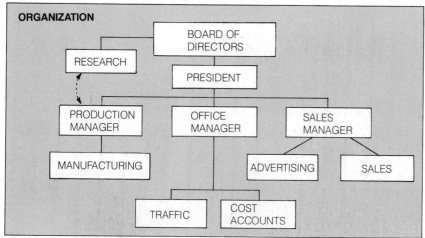

BOARD OF DIRECTORS

RESEARCH

PRESIDENT

PRODUCTION MANAGER

OFFICE MANAGER

SALES MANAGER

MANUFACTURING

ADVERTISING   SALES

TRAFFIC   COST ACCOUNTS

MAP

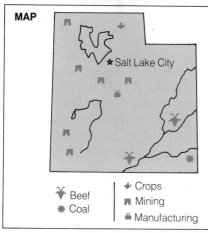

★ Salt Lake City

🐂 Beef
❋ Coal

🌾 Crops
🏭 Mining
🏭 Manufacturing

SIZE COMPARISON

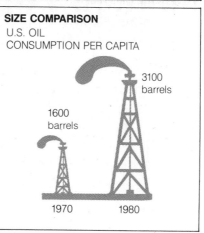

U.S. OIL
CONSUMPTION PER CAPITA

3100 barrels

1600 barrels

1970   1980

"I'm afraid I don't have any good news for you today, but I do have some real neat charts."

The visual is not "the communication."

MEMO

To: Students
From: The Authors
Subject: Visuals

Every time you turn on a TV, pick up a magazine, or look at a billboard, you come in contact with visuals. Every day, visuals of all types play a greater and greater role in our lives as devices to assist in the communication of ideas. Knowing how to use visuals effectively—in reports, in memos, in letters, and in speeches—can be a tremendous help to you in building your career.

Decision

Here are the two visual aids Yoshi Tanaka prepared for the vice-president of personnel.

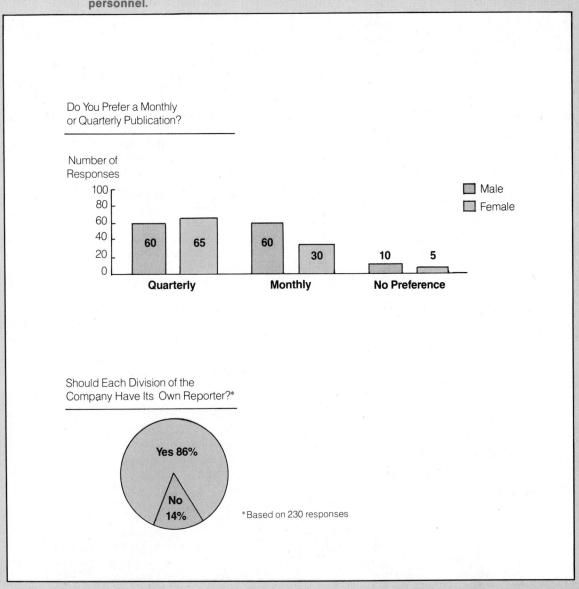

Do You Prefer a Monthly
or Quarterly Publication?

Number of
Responses

Male
Female

	Quarterly	Monthly	No Preference
Male	60	60	10
Female	65	30	5

Should Each Division of the
Company Have Its Own Reporter?*

Yes 86%

No
14%

*Based on 230 responses

Questions

1. Explain and exemplify what determines the placement of the visual aid in the written report? In the oral presentation?

2. Why are tables one of the best methods of presenting information when two or more sets of data need to be reported?

3. What types of visual aids can be used to reflect trends? Why?

4. What visual aid would you use to present information on plant productivity for the past year to the organization's department heads? What would you use to present the same data to stockholders of the company? Why the difference, if any?

5. Illustrate the following types of visual aids frequently used by business communicators. With what type and/or level of audience should each be used?

   a. pie graph;
   b. photograph;
   c. diagram;
   d. map;
   e. flow chart;
   f. line graph.

6. If you were asked to include visual aids in reports you submit to the vice-president of finance of your company (an electronics manufacturing firm that employs 2100 people), which form of illustration would you select for each of the following topics:

   a. The allocation of the tax money collected by your city;
   b. The weekly stock market fluctuation of a major oil company;
   c. In yearly intervals, the number of fatal industrial accidents in your county for each of the last five years;
   d. The new uniforms worn by the guards;
   e. The bus routes from the suburbs to your home office;
   f. The operation of a machine;
   g. The increase of personnel in your company since 1970 in each department.

Exercises

1. Obtain a corporate annual report. Study the use of visual aids in the report by judging their appearance, purpose, clarity of presenting information, and overall effectiveness. In a memo to your instructor, report your findings and evaluation. Attach the annual report to the memo.

2. Visit the office of a local newspaper or a television studio. Interview an employee who can answer five or more questions you will pose relating to the use of visual aids in presenting current news. Present your findings either in written form or in a short oral presentation as assigned by your instructor.

3. Study five persuasive communications sent in the mail. Look for one example of each one of the major categories of visual aids listed in this chapter. In a short memo report, in narrative form, describe the use of each visual aid in the persuasive communications. Include the original illustrations in the appropriate places in your assignment.

4. Compare the effectiveness of using photographs versus cartoons to communicate news, concepts, and activities of prominent political figures. You and one other classmate, as a team, should choose a political figure and collect two recent photographs and two cartoons pertaining to this person. Together, write a short narrative explaining the impact of the visual aids you have selected on a designated audience. Communicate your conclusions in a short oral presentation.

Applications

1. Lola Stores and Walter Dugan, two mechanical engineers, frequently submit reports to their project supervisors. They both know the advantages of including appropriate visual aids in their business communications. Lola places all her illustrations in the appendix of her reports while Walter prefers to intersperse them in the body of the report. In paragraph form, give the rationale for using both Lola's method and Walter's method of including visual aids in a report. Which method do you prefer? Explain your answer.

2. Present the following information in visual form to the president of the Midvale Realty Board:

    Last year, 450 homes were constructed in the city of Midvale. These homes had a first customer sale of between $44,500 and $95,000 dollars. In the case of multiple units (4 apartment to 24 apartment buildings), the figure was 85 and the cost range between $160,000 and $2,400,000. This compares unfavorably with the previous year when 560 single homes were constructed and sold at a price of $39,500 to $74,000. In the case of multiple units, 140 (4 apartments to 24 apartments) were constructed and sold at a price of $140,000 to $1,800,000.

    It should also be noted that this year 80 townhouses were constructed and sold at a price between $74,000 and $82,000 each. No townhouses were constructed in Midvale in the previous year.

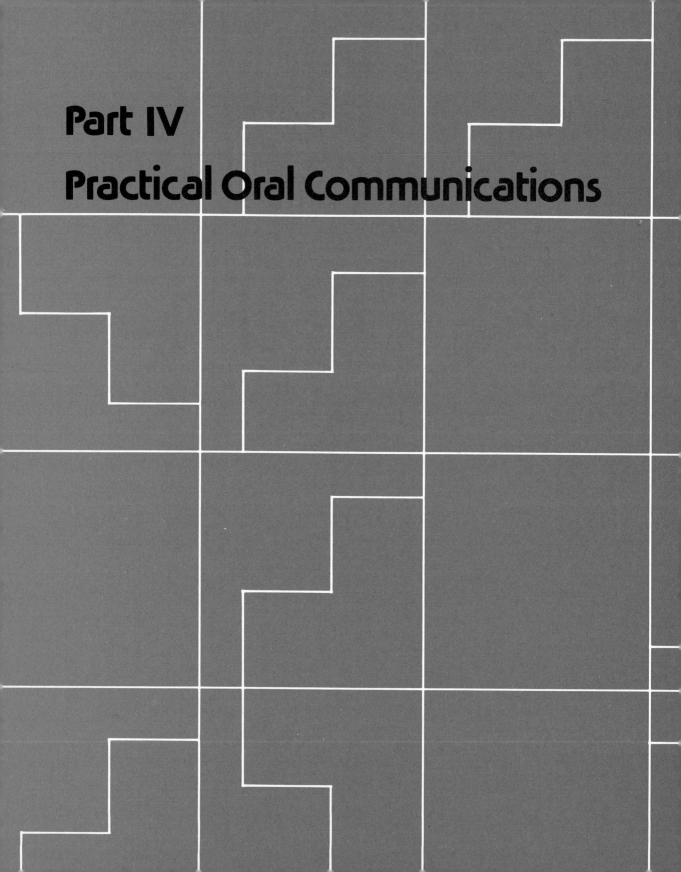

Part IV
Practical Oral Communications

Dilemma

Because of a large number of thefts and vandalism incidents at the Jackson
Yard Service Center, Corporate Security Director Elizabeth Mason
assigned her assistant, Al Foster, to investigate operations there. Only a
few days after Foster's assignment to the case, however, Mason received
an angry phone call from Yard Superintendent Bob Roberts.

Roberts complained that he had more to do than play Sherlock Holmes for
every fifteen-dollar ladder in the yard. He had half a million dollars of
expensive equipment to watch, forty-four vehicles, a staff of thirty-five
people, and a plant worth three hundred thousand dollars, and he "damn
well wasn't going to spend all his time patrolling in the hope of catching
some punk in the act of stealing a fifty-cent roll of twine." Roberts also
complained that just because Foster was Mason's assistant, he had no
right to tell Roberts, who had worked for the company for "more years
than Foster is old," how to run his yard.

Mason then called in Foster to get his side of the situation. Foster was
amazed that Roberts had called and surprised at the superintendent's
reaction. "I had no idea my suggestions upset him," said Foster. "I only
told him that it was his job to maintain security in the yard and that he's
not doing his job if he doesn't do that."

Make separate lists of the facts and feelings Bob Roberts expressed over
the phone, and try to suggest some ways that Elizabeth Mason can use
her understanding of these facts and feelings in dealing with Bob Roberts
in the future.[1]

[1]This case is adapted from Norman B. Sigband, "The Jackson Yard Case," © 1980.

Decision, see page 319

Do You Listen When You Hear?

Here is a list of the objectives you should understand by the time you complete this chapter. Place a check mark in the box beside each as soon as you feel ready to apply your understanding in a practical situation.

☐ The importance of *listening* to effective business communications

☐ The difference between listening for facts and listening for feelings

☐ The major factors behind inefficient listening:
    Competition for attention
    Failure to concentrate
    Emotions
    Evaluations
    Laziness

☐ The six basic guidelines for improving your ability to listen for facts:
    Catalogue key words
    Review key ideas
    Be open and flexible
    Evaluate without tuning out
    Resist distractions
    Work at listening

☐ The five basic guidelines for improving your ability to listen for feelings:
    Listen with the speaker
    Understand words used according to the speaker's connotations
    "Listen" to nonverbal communications
    Listen and respond to what isn't said in what is
    Listen attentively

When most of us think of communication, we usually divide the subject into verbal and nonverbal. A further division of the first area brings us to writing, reading, speaking, and listening. Most of us probably have had rather uneven exposure to the four areas listed. There were many semesters spent on learning to read and write effectively, beginning with the first or second grade in elementary school. In the case of reading, some of us even have had courses in speed reading while others have taken programs in advanced writing. As for speaking, many college students have had a semester or two of public speaking. But how many individuals reading this page have had any formal instruction in how to listen better? Recent surveys indicate the answer is about 5 or 6 out of 100. Yet most of us spend about 50–60 percent of our communication time not reading, not writing, not speaking, but listening.

How effectively do you listen?

Components of the Spoken Message

The spoken message often contains facts and feelings.

If you review the statements directed to you in the last two hours, you will probably agree that many contained *facts* and *feelings*. The facts may include the date a job will be completed, the number of people expected for dinner, the specifications for a piece of equipment, the items covered at this morning's meeting, and similar items of information.

Hearing the speaker's feelings, which are transmitted simultaneously with the facts, is more difficult. At times, a statement contains only facts and the feelings are objective, neutral, or some might even say nonexistent. But if there are no strong identifiable feelings transmitted with the facts, that in itself is a type of feeling!

In most cases, however, the individual's feelings are quite evident to the sensitive listener. Visualize the situation of a red-faced, obviously upset, college student waving his exam book at his father and shouting: "I don't know if *anything* will ever satisfy you! Here I get a B+ on an outrageously difficult exam and you ask me why it isn't an A!"

Most of us hear facts better than we hear feelings.

Obviously there are several facts contained in the message; in addition, there are some very strong feelings. To hear and respond to only the facts very well may result in a breakdown in communications. Of course, there are those who listen and retain facts and feelings better than others. But on the whole, most of us probably can do a better job in both areas. Let's first determine why we don't!

Why We Listen Inefficiently

There are several reasons why we often don't hear the facts or feelings which are transmitted to us. *Competition for attention* in a busy, complex society is certainly one factor. Although we would like to listen to the person speaking to us, there are other items competing for our attention: the stack of reports

"What? I'm sorry. I wasn't listening."

ZIEGLER

Resist distractions.

on the desk which must be read and evaluated in the next two hours; the heated conversation Mel and Bob are having just fifteen feet away; the conference we must hold with the firm's most important customer at 1:00 P.M. this afternoon, the hospitalization yesterday of a family member, and on and on. We would like to listen, but the competition is severe.

Failure to concentrate on what is being said is still another reason. It may result from competition for attention or it simply may be the situation of the moment. Nevertheless, such a failure is real. Another factor which often makes concentration difficult is the difference between speaking speed (about 150 words per minute), and listening speed (about 600 words per minute). Quite obviously this differential between speaking and listening speed permits the receiver to think about ideas other than those being transmitted. As a result, listening ability is lessened.

Emotions also may get in the way of listening. Perhaps a word, the inflection in the speaker's voice, or the point of view presented may cause the listener's emotions to turn on and his listening receiver to turn off. Of course, one of the major problems which occurs when our emotions rise is that we are most motivated to talk or shout rather than listen. Yet it is at these times, when emotions are high, that we should really listen — but so often don't.

There are many reasons why we listen inefficiently.

Frequently, as a result of our emotions, we *evaluate* the situation — correctly or incorrectly — and figuratively or sometimes literally, we stop listening. This snap evaluation may result from the speaker's appearance, dress style, beard, accent, color of skin, or a hundred other items. Whatever the cause, once we evaluate strongly and lock in our opinions, the ability to listen objectively may be lost.

Many of us just don't work at listening. We relax too much, we permit our minds to wander, we sprawl in our seats, we don't force ourselves to concentrate, we don't try to review what we've heard. We make no effort to recall key words or names. We just don't work at listening.

Do both apostrophes indicate possession? (See Appendix 1.)

Perhaps it's today's society that contributes to this. After all, most of us spend more time than we should watching television. And very often, if what we see doesn't entertain us, doesn't intrigue us, doesn't please us, we reach over and change the channel. We can carry that habit into our interpersonal communications with others. If we don't hear what pleases us, we find it quite simple to reach up into our minds and ears and "change the channel."

These are some of the reasons many of us listen inefficiently; there are others. But most readers will find that those described above sound very familiar.

Listening for Facts

We have all had the experience of missing a meeting and then approaching someone and saying, "Jimmy, I missed yesterday's meeting. You were there; what took place?"

"Well, it was an interesting meeting. You know with 780 people in the company, we have a lot of people-problems and so we talked about personnel and really got a lot straightened out," says Jimmy.

"Yes, I'm sure of that, Jimmy. But specifically, what was covered?"

"Well, like I say, we talked and discussed personnel and got some important issues settled."

"Well, I'm sure of that, Jimmy. But *what* took place?"

And then with some heat, Jimmy probably shouts, "Look, I told you. We discussed the company's personnel. If you're so interested, why in the H- don't you go to the meetings yourself?"

And now with no information and some irritation, you approach Sarah.

"Sarah, did you go to yesterday's meeting?"

"Yes, I did. And it was very worthwhile. Too bad you couldn't make it."

"Well, I'm sorry too. What was covered?"

"As you know, we have almost 800 people now and all the problems that go with that number of personnel. However, we did hit four key areas: First, on recruitment of professional personnel, we agreed not to use newspaper ads beginning March 1 but to use the college placement services at State and Franklin Technology. Also, we are going to rely on our own employees' recommendations. Second, we're going to put 80 percent of next year's training budget into supervisory and only 20 percent into management training. Third, we are going to interview every employee who leaves the firm. Whether that termination is voluntary or involuntary, there is going to be an exit interview . . . something we've never done before. I thought that was a great idea. And fourth, on fringe benefits, we changed one item and that concerned the pension plan that went from a 5 percent of base salary company contribution to 7 percent. Yup, it was a good meeting."

What a difference between the way Jimmy listens and the way Sarah listens!

But how do you listen? Like Jimmy or like Sarah?

You *can* improve your ability to listen for facts. All that is required is a little effort on your part and you will better retain the facts you hear at a lecture, a meeting, an interview, a formal presentation, or even in conversations where specific items are listed.

1. *Catalogue key words.* In the above exchange Sarah probably catalogued the key words *recruitment, training, termination interviews,* and *fringe benefits.* Remembering just these four words was all that was needed to keep in mind the major factors of the meeting.

   We can listen better for facts by following these six guidelines.

2. *Review key ideas.* In the course of the meeting, Sarah probably reviewed, from time to time, the ideas and concepts associated with recruitment, training, termination interviews, and fringe benefits. There were some ideas and concepts that supported and some that opposed the four points discussed.

   What is the difference in meaning between *review* and *preview*? (See Appendix 1.)

3. *Be open and flexible.* Listen to ideas and expand your knowledge. Even if Sarah disagreed with some of the suggestions and ideas, she still *heard* them and was sufficiently flexible to see their value or to build logical arguments of opposition.

4. *Evaluate but don't tune out.* Too often when we hear ideas with which we disagree, we tune out. And we should not. It may be that Sarah was strongly opposed to 80 percent of the training budget going into supervisory training. She felt that management training should have 80 percent of the budget. When the decision was made to put 80 percent into supervisory, she evaluated and disagreed but she did not tune out.

5. *Resist distractions.* It's true the room was warm, the lunch too heavy, and the bickering between Frank and Harry silly, but Sarah resisted that and remembered key ideas. Can you do the same with distractions?

6. *Work at listening.* Among the suggestions a noted authority makes for better listening, none is more important than his suggestion that we work when we listen.[2] Sit up straight, consciously listen, review key ideas. Work at listening; be alert mentally and physically. All facets of *effective* communications — writing, speaking, reading — require concentrated attention and effort. Listening is no exception.

What is the difference in meaning between *there* and *their*? (See Appendix 1.)

The ability to listen better for facts is an extremely valuable attribute. For students, it can add materially to their assimilation of information and therefore help their grades. For people at work it can make a major contribution to their own work effectiveness and their advancement.

Listening for Feelings

We live in a society that often inhibits many of us from saying what is in our hearts. Some individuals express their feelings more easily than others. But in the main, many people sometimes have difficulty voicing their feelings which involve deeply held emotions. As a result, Dave may say,

> *Boy oh boy; this was some job you asked me to complete by 10:00 A.M. today! I was here Thursday and Friday nights and spent most of my Saturday here. Digging out all that data on inventories for the last four years was murder. But I've got it all and one hour ahead of schedule. If you never give me another job like that, I'll be happy!*

If Dave's boss, Vern, should now reply, "*Great, now what about the sales figures for the same period?*" communication will certainly break down.

What was Dave *really* saying with his deeply expressed comments on "Thursday night and Friday night and most of Saturday"? What was he saying in what he wasn't saying?

"Give me a pat on the back?"

"You're unreasonable in your assignments."

"How about overtime pay?"

"Don't give me another job like that."

It could have been any one of these four messages or others. But one fact we do know is that Dave was not saying what he was saying. How do we know which of the four unspoken messages is the correct one? If he is praised and

[2]Ralph G. Nichols, "Listening Is a 10-Part Skill," *Nation's Business* (July 1957): 56–60.

he was looking for overtime pay, communication between Dave and Vern will still break down.

Certainly Vern can't say, "What are you *really* saying, Dave?" If he could, Dave probably would have told Vern in the first place! The answer probably lies in knowing Dave. If we *really* listen *with* people, we can determine what feelings they are expressing in what they *don't* say. Knowing our children, our friends, our fellow workers, tells us enough about them so we know what they feel in what they say. Of course we may not always be correct, but one factor we do know about Dave's message is he wasn't *really* saying what he was saying!

Because Louise knows Maurice she knows what he really is saying when he walks into the house, slumps into a chair, and says, "Boy, another killer day." And she responds correctly, "That boss of yours never lets up, does he?"

Why is the question mark inside, not outside, the quotation marks? (See Appendix 1.)

Maurice in turn knows what Louise *really* is saying when she asks, "How do you like the dress I'm wearing to the Donalds' party tonight?" He replies, "You'll be the most beautiful woman there." Interestingly enough, neither one replied to the *facts* in the statements, but both did respond to the feelings. And communication between them is effective.

How well do you listen to others' feelings? Here are a few suggestions on how your ability in this area may be improved:

1. Listen *with* the speaker. Appreciate the speaker's values, perceptions, cultural background, expectations, hopes, and desires. It isn't necessary to agree or accept those values or desires. It *is* necessary to understand them.

We can listen better for feelings by following these five guidelines.

2. Understand the words that are used—according to the speaker's connotations. What does the speaker mean by *inexpensive*, *unreasonable*, *early.*

3. Listen to the nonverbal communication. Do hands, eyes, facial expressions, tapping heels, drumming fingers, voice inflections agree or disagree with the message that is being voiced?

4. Listen and respond to what isn't said in what is! What is she thinking when she says, "I really don't mind not going out to dinner after all," or what is he thinking when he says, "Well, it really wasn't such a great return; I just happened to get it back and the ball dropped in the right spot"? Responding to what a speaker *thinks* is often more important than responding to what is said!

5. Listen attentively. Even if you don't hear the speaker's feelings, the fact that you obviously are *trying* to hear those feelings may well be all that is necessary to maintain the flow of communication.

These suggestions on more effective listening are easier to offer than to carry through. In a world that is highly competitive and where it is often necessary to think of "How can I win the game?" to get the best job, the highest test score, the best presentation, we are motivated to think of ourselves. But effective listening requires that we think of the speaker's viewpoint, hopes, and desires. To get outside ourselves in order to really listen from that viewpoint is not easy, but it is worth the effort; the rewards gained by effective communication are tremendous.

The Advantages Gained from Effective Listening

The effective listener can gain many advantages.

There is an old quotation that says you can get a reputation for being a wonderful conversationalist if you are an effective listener. But beyond the basic truth of that statement, we also gain other advantages:

1. *information* that helps us in our tasks;
2. *ideas* that will advance us on the job, in class, and in our interpersonal relationships with others;
3. *understanding* of what is said in what isn't and of people. He needs *stroking,* she doesn't. He is an introvert, she is an extrovert. He is terribly angry inside, she is confused. Such understanding may well assist in communication;
4. *cooperation.* When the other person feels you have *really* listened and understood, that individual now will listen to you—not in every instance, of course, but most of the time.

No, effective listening for facts and feelings isn't easy. No one ever said it was. It requires true sensitivity to others, hard work, and a deep desire to communicate effectively with those around us, whether we agree or disagree with them. But the rewards are worth the effort. There is little that contributes to effective communication as much as sensitive and efficient listening.

What is the difference in meaning between *whether* and *weather*? (See Appendix 1.)

In a world in which more and more people are shouting to be heard, effective listeners are not easily found. But when they are, they are not only effective decision makers, but respected husbands, wives, friends, teachers, and managers as well.

MEMO

From: The Authors

To: Students

Subject: Listening and your career

Good communicators *must* be good listeners. At your job, you can expect to spend over half your time listening—not speaking, not writing, not reading—but *listening.* No matter how well you perform the tasks that occupy the other fifty percent of your time, you'll only be spinning your wheels if you fail to listen effectively.

Decision

Here is the list of facts and feelings that Elizabeth Mason drew up to help her analyze the real message conveyed by Bob Roberts.

Facts Stated by Bob Roberts

1. He does not wish to play "Sherlock Holmes" for minor property items.

2. He is in charge of a half-million dollars' worth of property, 44 vehicles, a staff of 35, and a $300,000 plant.

3. He was not going to spend his time trying to catch a petty thief.

4. Foster can't tell Roberts how to run his yard.

5. Roberts has worked for Jackson Yard more years than Foster's age in years.

Feelings Stated by Roberts

1. Playing guard is below my dignity as a Yard Superintendent.

2. I am an important individual with heavy financial, material, and staff responsibilities.

3. It is below my dignity and position to spend time trying to catch a petty thief. I feel such a request made of me is unreasonable.

4. I absolutely won't permit a young man with no background to tell me how to discharge my responsibilities.

5. Foster is a callow, disrespectful, superficial kid who has no right or authority to give me directives in any area.

CHAPTER REVIEW

Questions

1. Select the two major reasons why *you* sometimes listen inefficiently. Can you explain the reasons for these?

2. Speculate on why most people will *not* tell you what they are *really* saying (in what they are saying) if you ask them?

3. Are there ever instances where we should probably *not* listen to what people say to us? Explain.

4. Is there a danger in trying to be *too* receptive to what people don't say? Explain.

5. Explain how the following situations can enhance or decrease a listening experience:
   a. You have a bad cold;
   b. Your seat in an auditorium is second row center;
   c. You have just had a meeting with your employer and were told that your work is commendable;
   d. Before coming to work, you and your spouse had a disagreement;
   e. The speaker is of the opposite sex and is strikingly attractive and fashionably dressed.

Exercises

1. Maintain a log, as accurately as you can, of your communication activities for one weekday. Record by the number of minutes the time you spend in reading, writing, speaking, and listening.

2. Duplicate the above assignment except select a Saturday or Sunday. Draw up a chart to compare your communication activities on a weekday with the weekend day selected.

3. Describe a dialogue involving controversy between two individuals. Quote a statement from one. Indicate the *facts* in that message, and the *feelings* in the same message.

4. Compare two lecture classes you attended this week in respect to the following:
   a. the ability of the lecturer to communicate facts clearly;
   b. the success of your active listening in each class;
   c. the results of your passive listening in each class, and
   d. the listening barriers that existed in each class.

5. Think of a situation in your past that may have had better results for you if you had listened more carefully to either instructions, directions, or suggestions of someone else. In paragraph form, describe this situation fully.

6. Elementary-school youngsters are given instruction in both reading and writing but rarely in listening. In order to prepare young people to sharpen their listening skills, some training should be offered to them. Think of an exercise that would be appropriate to teach fifth-grade youngsters the art of careful listening. Write a topical outline listing the major phases of the exercise that would be engaged in by the fifth-grade class.

7. Refer to Problem 6. Take the critiqued outline and fill in the entire listening exercise in role-playing form. Have a few of your fellow students join you in participating in the role-playing in front of your business communications class. A question-and-answer session after the role-playing will indicate whether the audience was listening carefully to your performance and will give you feedback on the merit of the listening exercise you selected.

8. We know that speaking speed averages 150 words per minute and listening speed averages 600 words per minute. List five actions you can carry through to maintain intensified listening despite the speed differential. These five factors must keep you from thinking about ideas other than those being communicated to you.

9. This chapter suggests that you can improve your ability to listen for facts by engaging in six activities. In an attempt to improve your listening, apply each one of these activities to the very next class you attend. In a memo to your business communications instructor, a) fully explain what you did to improve your listening ability, and b) note what success if any you achieved. Attempt to be as specific as possible.

Applications

1. As a management trainee, Trygve Thoreson was asked to attend an hour lecture on the "Implications of the changes in the 198- income tax form." He was determined to listen very intently so that he could give a report to his supervisor. Unfortunately, the following conditions arose while he was trying to listen attentively:
   a. The two men next to him conversed with one another;
   b. Three latecomers sauntered down the aisle temporarily blocking his view of the speakers;
   c. An attendee behind him was continually rattling papers;
   d. On three occasions, the speaker pointed to a blackboard behind her and looked at the board as she spoke;
   e. A floor fan, positioned near Trygve, hummed incessantly.

   Trygve grasped as much as he could of the lecture. Study each of the listening barriers that he experienced. In a memo to your instructor, discuss the action Trygve might have taken to alleviate the effect of some or all of these distractions to him.

2. Read the following quotation by Michael O'Rourke, secretary to Doris Donald, president of the Donald Textile Corporation. Indicate under the heading "Facts" what specific facts he voiced, and under "Feelings" what attitudes or feelings he was attempting to convey in addition to the facts.

   "Of course I'm upset, Ms. Donald. You would be too if you had been typing a report for three hours steady under a deadline and then been told it had to be redone. And now I've got to complete it by 8:30 A.M. tomorrow for the Board of Directors meeting!

   "This would never have happened if the sales department had planned more carefully. But they don't and I'm the only one who can type it because of my background. But I'll be typing until 9:00 or 10:00 P.M. which of course means I won't be able to attend my dad's sixtieth birthday party tonight. And it's all because of those unthinking people in sales!"

Dilemma

Raj Singh, research assistant at Detroit Edison, has been asked to make fifteen-minute presentations on "Methods of Energy Conservation." He has collected most of the facts to be used in the two presentations scheduled for today, but he does not have the introductions.

Write the introductions to each presentation (approximately three minutes for each introduction) for the two groups:

1. A luncheon for businessmen and businesswomen. Raj's talk is scheduled for 12:45 P.M.
2. A Parent-Teacher Association meeting scheduled for 7:30 P.M.

Decision, see page 338

Oral Communication: Short Talks and Presentations

17

Here is a list of the objectives you should understand by the time you complete this chapter. Place a check mark in the box beside each as soon as you feel ready to apply your understanding in a practical situation.

☐ The five basic types of short presentations:
   Introductions
   Briefings
   Informative talks
   Recognitions
   Welcomes

☐ The advantages and disadvantages in the four basic methods of delivering a short presentation
   Reading the speech
   Memorizing the speech
   Presenting the speech extemporaneously
   Making an impromptu speech

☐ The six fundamental principles for preparing an effective short speech:
   Know your subject
   Know your audience
   Be well organized
   Involve your listeners
   Plan your conclusion
   Maintain poise

☐ The seven basic guidelines for presenting a short speech:
   Look at your audience
   Vary your volume and speed
   Speak clearly
   Use appropriate gestures
   Check your posture and appearance
   Make clear transitions
   Watch and listen for feedback

As a manager, a shop owner, a professional assistant, an artisan, a nurse, or an engineer, you are constantly involved in communication.

You may *inform* your secretary about the urgency of transferring Mr. Casey's telephone call directly to you when he telephones.

You may *meet* for a moment in the corridor with your boss concerning the situation at the warehouse.

You may *discuss* informally with your associates the governor's requests on fuel allocation.

You may *confer* with the section heads on the preferred method of progress report preparation.

You may *explain* to a group of Middle Eastern visitors the functions of your department.

You may *answer* a wide range of questions posed by three new employees.

You may *introduce* a newcomer to the community at the town's service club meeting.

You may *present* to the city zoning board your petition for a variation in construction regulations.

The list of daily oral communications goes on and on.

If you were to keep a precise diary of your oral interactions during the normal working day, you would find the list to be lengthy and made up of tremendous variety. The examples above are very real and they include only the typical interactions which are brief. Add to those examples the several formal presentations concerning departmental projects you might be called on to make to company executives and the times you are asked to speak to community and professional groups and the number of situations increases. It is easy to see the important role oral communication plays in your life and success as an employee, a manager, or the owner of your own firm.

In actuality, most of your oral communications are not formal speeches. However, if you can identify and apply the basic guidelines for a speech, your effectiveness in all oral communication situations—formal and informal, short and long—will be improved. In other words, if the principles for good oral presentations are followed, you will be a better oral communicator.

Types of Short Presentations

Before exploring how to give a speech, it is beneficial to step back and ask, "What kind of short presentations are people in organizations called on to make?" Once we can identify the typical kinds of presentations, then we can discuss how to be more effective in those situations.

Introductions

From time to time, you will be called on to introduce people and concepts. Whether introducing a person or an idea, it is your job to quickly familiarize the audience with the person or idea and to attempt to encourage the audience to accept what follows.

Introducing people   A creative introduction will make an individual feel welcome and will heighten the audience's interest in that person. In this situation, it is your responsibility to gain some familiarity with the individual and to go beyond the data sheet or resumé you received. Generally the person you introduce will be making a speech. Know the audience and the speaker and then strive to match their mutual interests. It is always polite to ask the person being introduced if there are some specific items that should be included or avoided in making the introduction. Finally, avoid all the trite nonsense that we have heard too often: "This person needs no introduction . . ." "It is a pleasure and an honor . . ." "I am pleased . . ." "Without further ado . . ." "Last but not least . . ." Remember that the listeners are present to hear the speaker, not the introducer. Yet, the introduction sets the stage for the presentation. Your sparkling and interesting words may perk up the audience and motivate the speaker.

> In introducing a speaker, match the speaker's background with the interests of the audience.

The introductions just described concern formal speech situations. On the other hand, you may be asked to introduce people around a conference table or at a panel discussion. In such situations, help all involved to get to know one another's name. Pronounce each person's name slowly, clearly, and distinctly. Attempt to relate the individual to the group by indicating what the person does or by telling something about the person. These techniques permit people to associate names and faces. In following these hints you not only will be effective, you also will assist in making people feel very comfortable.

Introducing concepts or projects   It is common to divide long presentations into several component parts. For instance, the parts promotion department of a tractor company has been researching the ways in which parts sales personnel can be made more effective. The department would like to create a new sales-training module for the sales-training program. A presentation is to be made to a group consisting of the company's director of national marketing, the head of the marketing department, the assistant marketing head, the company's training director, and representatives of the college recruiting department. The presentation has been divided into several sections and a different person will speak on each part: introduction, background, basic findings, alternative solutions, recommendation.

You may introduce the entire concept with a very short presentation and say a few words before each of the speakers begins. In this way, you link one presentation with the next and add coherence to the total package.

The introducer should whet the appetite, gain the audience's interest, and provide the group with enough information so that the listeners will appreciate fully the materials that are to follow. The introduction is a short presentation that can set the stage for success.

Briefings

The oral briefing is concise and clear; its primary purpose is to be informative.

The oral briefing is described very well by its name, *brief-ing.* It is short, to the point, and very concise. In the business context you may be asked to brief people who are somewhat familiar with an operation, a project, an idea, or an event. Generally the committee report is identical to the briefing. As a representative of a committee, you are asked to summarize concisely the transactions of a committee. Your purpose is to update the information of others and to allow them to put your information into the context of their particular interests.

In a briefing, attempt to limit your comments to a background statement of the project and then provide the new information. A business organization uses the briefing as an integral method to keep busy managers and employees informed of the variety of projects which are being carried through at any one time. It would not be unusual in a department's weekly or monthly meeting to ask the managers to present briefings on the projects they are currently conducting.

By definition the briefing does not get into specific details of the project. However, it keeps people generally informed. Those listeners who feel they need additional information then will have the opportunity to visit personally and informally with the individual concerned in order to go over items in greater detail.

The ability to give short, concise, and interesting oral briefings identifies the employee in the organization as a person who knows what is going on and is able to differentiate the important data from the unimportant.

Informative Talks

Informative presentations generally are longer than briefings and usually provide the audience with information on a specific topic.

A common category of oral presentations is the short informative talk or speech. A list of situations calling for a speech to inform is almost endless. You may be called upon to inform high-school students about careers; new company personnel about the products and services of your organization; older employees about the firm's retirement options; customers about a new service; individuals in your profession about new concepts; a city service

club such as Rotary about new government regulations; a citizens' group about new health care policies . . .

All in all, the purpose of the informative talk is to provide individuals with information they previously did not have. The speech to inform is different from the briefing in that generally it will be presented to a group not informed to any great degree on the topic, and usually the informative presentation will be somewhat longer than a briefing.

In order to relate the informative speech to the particular audience, it is vital to know their current understanding. Certainly a presentation on new state regulations concerning education of handicapped children will be different when given to a citizens' organization as compared to making the presentation to the Association of Teachers of the Handicapped. We all are annoyed when speakers do not tell us anything new or when speakers present data we cannot understand.

Recognitions

In various situations, and at many points in your career, you will be called upon to present an award or special recognition to an individual or group. There are numerous presentation situations: the Employee of the Month Award, the Annual Safety Award to the foundry foreman; the United Fund's 100-percent Award to a company; 25-Year pins to employees; a company scholarship to an outstanding student. It is assumed that a group of people will be present when the award or honor is presented.

Recognition presentations must be brief and sincere.

Remember that the people assembled are there not to recognize the presenter but to honor the recipient. It is appropriate to note the reason for the award, to suggest why it is important to the organization, and to indicate some of the attributes of the individual or group receiving the recognition.

Presentations are very important to the recipient. Yes, the individual may feel a bit embarrassed at the moment, but that person has done something beyond the norm. The recipient probably has devoted many hours and made individual sacrifices in achieving the award. It is important that the presenter consider these aspects in making the formal presentation and do so with sincerity and enthusiasm. One of the greatest failings of the modern organization is in not recognizing individuals. Therefore, when the opportunity arises to turn the spotlight on accomplishment, it is important that it be handled in an enthusiastic and professional manner. Both the recipient and the audience should come away with an impression that the company is truly appreciative.

Welcomes

In your service club, in your organization, and in your individual department, frequently someone is called upon to welcome guests. As an administrative assistant in the business affairs department of a major hospital, you are to welcome a group of college juniors majoring in health care; as an executive secretary in a major corporation, you may be called on to welcome high-schools seniors in secretarial studies who are touring your company today; as vice-president of a service club, you are to welcome a group of high-school merit scholars to the weekly luncheon meeting; as head of your organization's word-processing division, you are called upon to welcome a group of executives from other companies who are going to observe your word-processing center.

The welcome presentation should convey information in a friendly, sincere manner.

If you are called upon to welcome people to your department, organization, or club, strive to gain their interest. Know why the people are with you and let them know that you hope they will be able to learn from their experience. Indicate an interest in them and relate a sincere enthusiasm about who it is you are representing.

Besides providing a spirit of friendliness and interest, the welcome also may convey information that must be transmitted clearly to the group. Such information may include telling people that they are not permitted to take pictures, that it is absolutely necessary to wear safety goggles in the factory, or that employees are not permitted to visit with the group as they tour the facilities.

Modes of Delivery

There are four basic ways that an individual can present a speech: read it, memorize it, present it extemporaneously, or simply make the presentation in an impromptu manner.

Reading the Speech

Reading the speech is a common technique, especially in business. However, if a manuscript is prepared and all the presenter does is stand up, look at the paper, and read it to the audience, we have to ask: "Why wasn't the speech just duplicated and sent to us?"

There are times when it may be appropriate to read a speech. The statements, statistics, and policies presented are so vital that they must be absolutely accurate. Presidents of the United States usually read their speeches. What they say often has tremendous impact. And an unfortunate slip of the tongue or a side comment could be subject to gross misinterpretation and could lead to domestic and international problems.

If the speech is written in a conversational manner and delivered informally, it can be very effective when read. The speech should be typed in large print. (Very large-sized type—often referred to by the typewriter manufacturers as "orator-style"—is available.) It is also a good idea to leave plenty of space on the paper between lines and paragraphs. Key ideas can be underlined in red to remind the speaker to give those points emphasis. Green marks can be noted here and there in the margins to remind the speaker to look up and at the audience. At appropriate places, the marginal note *smile* may be written. And most important, go over and over the pages so that you can read with force and clarity, knowing precisely what comment and idea is coming up next. The pre-preparation items can aid in making the read speech acceptable communication. Certainly there is never an excuse for speakers to bury themselves in fifteen pages as they slowly and monotonously read the material.

It *is* possible to read a speech effectively.

Memorizing the Speech

Memorizing the speech is probably a dangerous technique. First of all, it takes a great deal of time to memorize. It was okay to memorize Lincoln's Gettysburg Address for a public-speaking class, but why memorize welcoming comments to a group of high-school seniors or an introductory statement at the departmental conference? Second, just like reading the speech, the act of memorization may pull the speaker away from interaction with the audience. When presenting a memorized speech, the speaker may be saying, "I figured out exactly what I am going to say, and regardless of the blank looks on your faces, I'm forging ahead."

There is another danger in memorizing a speech: What happens when you forget what to say next? People have a tendency to memorize words and not ideas or thoughts. If a word is forgotten, where does that leave you? Memorizing an entire speech is not recommended. However, that is not to say that memorization is completely out of line. The memorized statement can be very

There is always a danger you may forget a memorized speech.

effective. For instance, a speaker may be able to establish just the right mood in memorizing and presenting a poem, a quotation, or a segment of scripture as part of a speech. This may serve to unshackle the speaker from notes and the podium and present an idea in a very special manner. Used in this way, memorization may add emphasis to the presentation. But this is substantially different from memorizing the entire speech!

Presenting the Speech Extemporaneously

Extemporaneous speeches are carefully planned in advance.

The extemporaneous presentation is probably the preferred way to relate to people when called upon to give a brief talk. *Extemporaneous* means that the speaker has given careful thought to the presentation, probably has outlined what is going to be said, but is not going to present something memorized. The key phrase that is often used to explain the extemporaneous speech is *conversational mode.* Having given careful preliminary thought to the speech, having made up an outline and drawn up notes, the speaker presents the speech to achieve close interaction with the audience. All of the language is not established precisely beforehand. But the speaker knows the basic ideas to be presented, knows the order in which topics will be revealed, and has developed a clear introduction and a meaningful conclusion.

The extemporaneous speech allows you to adjust the presentation to the situation. Audience feedback tells you to expand on the point or eliminate it, tell the joke or not, cut the talk short or lengthen it, poke fun at the guest of honor or not. It is all extemporaneous, but thoughtfully so. Extemporaneous does not mean "spur of the moment," "off the cuff," or "winging it." The extemporaneous speech is a well-prepared presentation.

Presenting the Speech Impromptu

Impromptu speeches don't need to be intimidating or difficult if you do some impromptu planning beforehand.

The impromptu talk actually refers to a situation where the speaker is given little or no time to prepare. On the spur of the moment, the individual quickly must develop a presentation and begin. The basic guidelines of speech still apply, but they are substantially telescoped. In the business organization, the impromptu speech would be used most frequently in conference situations. Because the issue has just emerged in the discussion, it must be presented immediately. Perhaps you will have a few moments to jot down some notes and sketch a rough outline . . . then, you are on your feet and talking. But never begin speaking without thinking and deciding the order in which your points will be presented.

As noted, there are advantages to each of the four presentation methods listed above. You often may find that a combination of modes will be used in one presentation. For instance, you may present the speech extemporaneously, but you may read some specific figures, memorize a summarizing quotation, or respond to impromptu questions.

Guidelines for Preparing the Speech

Preparing a speech seems like a chore to most people. It need not be difficult, though, if you follow a few simple rules.

Remember these six basic rules for preparing an effective speech.

Know Your Subject

If you do not know the topic, you should not be talking about it. Thorough knowledge is needed. That knowledge will give you confidence and motivation to speak in a forceful manner. Many times this means that you will have to do some research in order to have the information you need to make an interesting and knowledgeable presentation. Knowing your subject permits you to anticipate objections and answer questions that members of your audience may bring up.

Know Your Audience

The effective speaker is often successful because of how the topic is related to the receivers. As has been emphasized in writing letters, it is vital to know the receiver. The job of the speaker is more difficult because the receiver is plural. But by discovering all you can about the audience, by identifying what it is they will want and need to know, and what will motivate them, you can relate the information directly to them.

Be Well Organized

The oral presentation does not gel *after* you are on your feet. It must be organized logically in your planning process. If you have six points to cover, what order should be followed? Clearly set down the basic ideas you want to express, look at them, and consider different ways of arranging them. Always ask what the audience knows, what the audience wants to know, and how the materials can be ordered best to satisfy both the information and interest needs of the audience. (See Chapter 2 for techniques of outlining and organization.) If you are going to discuss a problem, process, or project, state it clearly. Note your objectives.

Involve Your Listeners

Involve your audience.

Tell the members of the audience how they personally are involved. This can be done through various means.

1. *Tell a real story.* Reviewing an actual incident that relates to the point you want to make can be very interesting. A story is an effective way to establish a base of information in an exciting manner. The story may be serious or humorous; it may be a situation from your personal experience or a story you learned from someone else. The telling of a story may not only gain the attention of the audience but may also put you at ease.

2. *Tell a hypothetical story.* By relating a situation that may not be real, it is possible to capture the attention of the audience. This is the use of a story that is believeable and actually could happen. The hypothetical story and the license that goes with it provide a useful tool in exemplifying ideas to an audience.

3. *Present statistics.* The use of numbers can put ideas in perspective. However, numbers just presented by themselves can be confusing and impersonal. It is important to relate the numbers to the audience. For instance, which of the following statements will most likely get the attention of the audience and also be remembered by them?

This year 1,500,000 people in the United States will be hospitalized.

Three of you in this audience will be hospitalized this year.

4. *Use a quotation.* The incorporation of interesting statements from others often can be a focal point for an idea. The quotation provides the audience with something to remember; it may also capsulize a complex concept in an interesting way so that you can further explain the idea.

5. *Tell a joke.* A joke or a humorous situation that illustrates an idea can be a good way to help the audience think about the idea you are explaining. Of course, good taste must always prevail.

Plan Your Conclusion

Plan your conclusion to be effective.

At times you want your audience to take specific action; at other times you may want them to clearly remember your key ideas. Whichever the case may be, a strong conclusion can help accomplish your objective. Perhaps a quotation from a recognized authority will accomplish your objective, or a dramatically revealed visual aid, or simply restating your key idea by using carefully chosen words. The point is, don't let your talk die out. Prepare your conclusion so that it will be effective and perhaps even memorable.

Maintain Poise

Often people do not think about stage fright until after they are standing before an audience. Then it is too late! Although various patent medicines have been suggested over the years to alleviate stage fright, there *is* a cure: be knowledgeable, be well-organized, be honest, and be prepared. In other words, plan, prepare, and practice. Know your audience. Speak to their needs, their wants, their desires.

Preparation is vital for the inexperienced speaker. Good speeches do not happen by accident. The impressive speaker meticulously has prepared, planned, organized the materials, analyzed the audience, and practiced. Having accomplished these pre-speech duties, you can approach the podium with confidence and poise.

Nervousness can be eliminated or alleviated if you are prepared.

Guidelines for Presenting the Speech

In presenting the speech, a different set of guidelines is needed. Up to this point, with the exception of practice, the speech is an item on paper or a series of thoughts in the mind. To implement the oral presentation and to aid you in actually making the speech, there are some very practical guidelines.

Look at Your Audience

The first way to make the written paper different from the oral presentation is to involve yourself in the presentation. The easiest way to do this is to look at the audience. This does not mean periodically glance at the group; it means talk with them and look at them. We have all been in situations where someone came and either read a speech to us or presented it while looking at the podium or over our heads. We felt that the speaker was leaving us out. Look directly at individuals in the audience. Be alert to audience feedback and make adjustments as necessary. Maintain good eye contact. All this will permit you to relate your information *to* them instead of *at* them.

Good eye contact helps to build a link between the speaker and the audience.

Vary Your Volume and Speed

Inexperienced speakers often do not speak loudly enough. It is important to speak up! Let your voice bounce off the back wall. Of course, don't turn up the volume to the point that your voice is an irritant. On the other hand, the audience cannot believe what it cannot hear.

Some ideas need to be stated rather forcefully; others should be noted softly, respectfully, or sympathetically. Like a good piece of music that is

A droning speech may put your audience to sleep.

"Speak slowly. You know I don't understand gobbledygook."

Pronounce fully every necessary sound in every word.

fast, slow, high, low, loud, or soft, so a speech should reflect changes to match the content of the ideas. How boring and monotonous is a piece of music or a speech that proceeds at one volume level and one speed!

Speak Clearly

Be sure to enunciate clearly and distinctly.

As you practice—perhaps with a tape recorder—listen to yourself or have someone else listen also. Do you hear yourself saying "comin'," "goin'," dontcha"? Enunciate every necessary sound in every word. It is just easy to do it correctly as to drop a syllable here and there. Check the pronunciation of words; are you placing the correct emphasis on the correct syllable?

Use Appropriate Gestures

Use appropriate and natural gestures to add interest to your talk.

A broad smile, a clinched hand, a fist hitting the rostrum, hands on hips, all can communicate very specific information to the audience. In preparing your speech, analyze the ideas and the feelings you want to express. Then determine what gestures will aid in communicating the idea to the audience. Standing before a group with both hands in your pockets while reading a speech obviously is not making the best use of the oral situation.

Gestures can be used in many ways:

to aid in picturing the speaker's words—"The economy has been like a roller coaster . . ." (the speaker moves a hand and arm in a waving motion);

to add emphasis to a point—"We should clearly understand . . . (the speaker strikes the podium);

to help the audience know that a new piece of information is going to be introduced—"Second, let us turn to the foreign market implications . . ." (speaker holds up two fingers and makes a turning motion to the audience).

Gestures should come naturally. But many effective speakers must plan carefully and practice diligently to incorporate them into the speech. Regardless of how the gestures get into the speech, whether as natural expressions or calculations to provide special emphasis, they are an important element in the *live* oral communication situation.

Check Your Posture and Appearance

Obviously a speaker will dress and stand in a manner appropriate for the presentation. Just as the sales letter is typed neatly on company stationery, the sales speech is presented by a neatly dressed representative of the organization. However, there is another important aspect of appearance—distracting gestures.

As noted earlier, when used appropriately to supplement the spoken words, gestures can add substantially to the presentation. At the same time, watch out for and eliminate unnecessary and distracting gestures. If you are continually putting a hand into your coat pocket or jingling coins or keys, such action will prove distracting. Don't let your appearance, posture, or distracting gestures override your message. It is important for you to dress properly, stand correctly, and bring the focus of the audience to your message and not to distractions.

Check your posture and appearance to eliminate distracting mannerisms.

Make Clear Transitions

It is very possible to cover topics faster than the audience can follow them. Therefore, it is vital that you watch your transitions. At the end of a major point, slow down or pause for a moment. Then, instead of abruptly stating the next idea, clearly tell the audience that you are now moving from your explanation of "customer reaction to advertising," to "customer credit accounts." Statements like this are called transitions and they tell the audience to switch gears and prepare for the next item in the speech. Transitions provide a rest for the listener and also give a clear signal of where you are and where you are going. Some common transitions that might be used are, "Now let's turn to another point . . ." or "However, there is another aspect that we should look at today . . ." or "Now with our understanding of _____ we can move to a discussion of _____."

Use transitional phrases or sentences to move from one topic to another.

When the transition is stated slowly, when you look at the audience and incorporate an appropriate gesture with the transition, the audience will understand what is being said and will know where you are going.

Watch and Listen for Feedback

Regardless of how much you plan and practice the speech, the actual presentation will be different from thinking about the speech. The alert speaker will be on the lookout for feedback. If the audience looks confused on a particular point, you can assist by interjecting a statement—for example, "Let me repeat that . . ." or "Perhaps I can state this concept in another way . . ." Besides helping the audience to understand the message, these statements indicate that the alert speaker is paying attention to the audience. Also, if the audience laughs longer than expected at a humorous comment, the speaker who is tuned in to feedback just does not plow ahead; instead, the speaker pauses and permits the audience to catch up. The oral presentation allows you to actually interact with the audience. By looking at the people in the audience and interpreting their feedback, you can keep the message on target. If you do not react to the audience's feedback, the speech might as well have been sent to the audience on tape.

The good speaker is alert to non-verbal feedback from the audience.

Successful interaction with the audience is, to a large extent, the element that makes your listeners glad they have come to hear you. It is the element that is missing when they listen at home on television to even the most polished and charming of speakers.

Concluding Comments

Although we engage in oral communication many hours each day, most people are hesitant to stand before an audience and make the simplest announcement. It should be recognized that most of the presentations made by the new employee or manager are brief. These situations provide you with ideal opportunities to hone your speaking abilities. After making several short presentations, you will become more and more comfortable before an audience. But regardless of how short or how long the speech is or how many are made, the steps in the preparation and the presentation guidelines always are vital to follow.

It is not proposed that these guidelines for speech preparation and presentation will automatically make you become a silver-tongued orator. But by studying, applying, and practicing these guidelines, it is possible to reflect credit on yourself in oral communication and simultaneously advance yourself in your job and/or profession.

MEMO

To: Students

From: The Authors

Subject: Short talks and your career

Although most of the business communications we've studied so far have involved writing, the truth is that nearly all the communicating you'll do on the job will be oral. The ability to deliver effective short talks can be a major asset in your career. In order to develop that ability, don't shy away from opportunities to give short talks in your organization. Make as many as you can. You will improve your own speaking abilities and you will make yourself known to your employer as someone who can be counted on when the need for a short talk arises in the future.

Decision

Here are the two different introductions to the same short talk that Raj Singh prepared on the topic "Methods of Energy Conservation."

Audience 1: Businessmen and businesswomen

How long will your company be able to remain in business if the cost of energy increases by ten times within the next three years?

Yes, you did hear correctly! There is a distinct possibility that the $1000 per month charge that your firm presently pays for electricity or natural gas will skyrocket to $10,000 in just three years . . . if we don't do something about it today!

And we must do something about it--not only for the benefit of our individual companies but for our schools, homes, and commercial establishments. If we don't, the American way of life, as we know it, will undergo almost catastrophic changes.

Let me suggest a solution; a solution that is simple; a solution that is workable; a solution that is a must.

Audience 2: Parent-Teacher Association meeting

Can you visualize a school system that is closed from November through March; that may use its electric lights for only one hour each day; that may not utilize projectors; that must close all shops? all science rooms?; that eliminates all bus transportation for regular and handicapped children--in short, an educational system that is permitted to run at only a 15 or 20 percent level of efficiency because there is almost no electric, coal, or gas energy available for use?

It can happen . . . and sooner than you think . . . to your children and mine!

Frightening? Yes! Possible? Yes! Upsetting? Yes!

But there is a solution.

CHAPTER REVIEW

Questions

1. Present a list of different types of short presentations in which most of us frequently are involved.

2. Define a *briefing* in the context of oral presentations.

3. How does an informative talk differ from a briefing?

4. List the four modes of speech delivery. Under each, indicate the advantages and disadvantages.

5. Are there ever situations in which a combination of two or more modes of delivery would be used in delivering a speech? Explain.

6. What factors may vary in your speech based on your knowledge of the audience?

7. What exemplification techniques can be used for personally involving your audience in your speech? Describe one.

8. Why is eye contact an important guideline to keep in mind in oral presentations?

9. What vocal factors should be remembered when giving an oral presentation? Explain one in detail.

10. What four factors will greatly assist any speaker in overcoming nervousness?

11. Several statements or terms were used in this chapter pertaining to short interactions in the organization environment. Explain the meaning of each of the following and give an example if applicable.
    a. Whet the appetite of the audience.
    b. Oral briefing.
    c. Avoid trite expressions when introducing a speaker.
    d. Indicate the attributes of an individual receiving a company award.

Exercises

1. Name a television personality and comment on his or her use of a) mannerisms and b) gestures. How does each add to or detract from the total presentation?

2. Name a group and a situation in which people will be visiting your organization. Prepare and deliver an extemporaneous two-minute welcome to the group.

3. Choose a school organization of which you are a member. Brief the Faculty Advisory Committee to School Organizations on your group's objectives, membership, activities, and responsibilities.

4. After you have given a presentation, attempt to view it on videotape. Whether or not that is possible, write a brief, constructive criticism of your presentation.

   Divide the two major categories of a) content and b) delivery into sub-categories. (*Content* may be subdivided into organization, logic, introduction, and substantiation. *Delivery* may be subdivided into use of visual aids, volume, rate, enunciation, gestures, and mannerisms.) Write a closing statement indicating your major strength in your presentation.

5. Interview the business manager at your college or at a local company. Ask about the role short interaction or speech plays in the managerial job and the jobs of the people in his or her department. Record your findings in a memo report to your instructor.

6. Name an award that an employee in your academic or business department could win. Assume you are the department head. Establish the setting for the presentation and then give a three-minute talk to present the award.

7. As mentioned in this chapter, if you were to

keep a precise diary of your oral interactions during a normal day, you would find that they were many and quite varied. Experiment with this statement, by selecting a few hours at your part-time job or time spent in classes or meetings at the college. Jot down a brief summary of all your short oral interactions, noting the following:

a. persons involved;
b. general topic discussed; and
c. your primary role in the oral communication.

Bring your diary to class and compare your list with the items written by your classmates. In a discussion session, examine the diversification of short interactions engaged in by the members of your class.

Applications

1. The vice-president of your company has been invited to speak to your professional club (for example, personnel association, nursing association, public relations group, or secretarial society). You are to introduce the vice-president. Describe the situation and present a brief extemporaneous introduction.

2. Prepare a briefing for a group of managers in your future profession. They all are from different companies and are visiting your school. Brief them on the preparation you and your fellow students are receiving for entry into the field. Remember to organize carefully.

3. A group of regional business people are visiting your campus. The dean of your college wants to provide these representatives with a wide variety of information about the various academic programs. Give a five-minute presentation on your major and inform the business people about the types of jobs students are getting who graduate with your major.

4. Refer to Application 3. Once again, you are asked to give a presentation on your academic major and discuss the kinds of jobs students are getting who graduate from the program you have selected. This time, however, your audience is different. You will be speaking to 100 high-school seniors who are in the process of selecting a college and a program to meet their needs. In your five-minute speech, attempt to sell them on the benefits of attending your college and enrolling in your program.

5. You have been asked to introduce the speaker at the Future Business Leaders of America meeting which is being held in the auditorium. You know that eye contact is important, but you don't know how it is applied when you address a large group from a stage. Interview three people at your college who are adept at giving oral presentations, and ask them for their practices on the use of eye contact to enhance their presentations. In a letter to your instructor, relate your findings.

6. A local professional club (nursing association, computer programming society, dental technician club, or any other) has asked several students to come to a dinner meeting. Each student is to speak for five to seven minutes on why he or she chose the field and then to highlight the strong points in the modern curriculum. Prepare and deliver such a speech and include at least three different forms of exemplification in your presentation.

7. Gerald Long, a car-leasing salesman, has been asked to present a ten-minute speech on the advantages of car leasing and the benefits of dealing with his company. Briefly describe how he will vary the contents of his presentation in order to reach the following audiences:
a. prospective auto-leasing customers;
b. representatives from General Motors who sell the cars to his leasing company;
c. a class of sixth-grade youngsters learning

about different occupations; and

d. customers who are uninformed about leasing and are planning to buy a car.

8. You are a newly hired administrative assistant at a local bank. At a conference meeting with the vice-presidents and department managers you are asked to give an impromptu talk on the word-processing system used by the insurance company which you have just left. Unfortunately, your previous job had nothing to do with the word-processing system, and you know very little about it.

You believe, however, that you may give the wrong impression if you do not give the talk as requested. What would be the correct way to handle this situation?

9. You have been asked to speak for ten minutes to induce your classmates to vote for your candidate in this year's primary election. What methods could you use to warm your audience to accept the ideas that will follow? Think of three to five ways to make your listeners receptive to you and convey these thoughts to your instructor in a memo.

Dilemma

Mario Aguilar, as representative of the South Los Angeles Community
Association, has been scheduled to make a ten-minute presentation to
the Los Angeles City Council next Wednesday. His purpose is to persuade
the council to purchase a square block of property to be used for
community recreational purposes. The property is located in a heavily
populated Latin area which currently affords the neighborhood almost no
recreational activities.

The property is now selling for $140,000. In addition, it is estimated that
landscaping, recreational equipment (for adults and children), and
necessary sanitation facilities will cost the city approximately $110,000.

In preparing his speech, Mario wants to begin by accomplishing the
following three tasks:

1. Define the purpose and the audience.
2. Write a brief outline of the speech (details to be filled in later).
3. List visual aids that may be appropriate in proving his points.

Decision, see page 365

Oral Communication: The Long Presentation

Here is a list of the objectives you should understand by the time you complete this chapter. Place a check mark in the box beside each as soon as you feel ready to apply your understanding in a practical situation.

☐ The three main purposes of the long speech or presentation
   To inform
   To persuade
   To convince

☐ The importance of audience analysis in the process of preparing an effective speech

☐ The role of the introduction in a long speech
   To indicate your topic
   To establish a relationship with the audience
   To define the terms you will use
   To get the audience to trust you

☐ The four keys to an effective body of the long speech
   Make the right appeals
   Organize your materials
   Make effective transitions
   Use variety

☐ The purpose of the conclusion of a long speech
   To summarize
   To make recommendations or suggest alternatives

☐ The advantages and disadvantages of different kinds of notes in presenting your speech

☐ The keys to handling questions effectively

☐ The advantages and disadvantages of different types of visual aids to supplement a long speech

As organizations become more complex and deal with many community, government, and business groups, there is a greater demand on managers, supervisors, and technical personnel to make oral presentations. This does not diminish the value and place of the written report. It is simply that the organization is probably making more use of both written and oral presentations today than at any time in history. Intelligent management and decision making are largely dependent on a base of reliable information. And that information must be communicated.

The long oral presentation is primarily a communication vehicle used inside the organization; it provides a way of exchanging information, fostering discussion, and focusing on issues that are of importance to the organization. Whether the session is called an internal meeting, conference, discussion, presentation, or something else, the point is that employees are spending more time in meetings listening. And, besides listening, there are times when an employee will have to make a long presentation. Therefore, there is a need to understand the use, the strategies, and the techniques for effectively delivering the long oral presentation.

What we have said in the previous chapter on the short talk concerning guidelines for preparation and guidelines for speaking applies equally to the long presentation. It goes without saying that following those principles of effective organization, eye contact, volume, and use of visual aids applies to *every* talk.

There are a variety of reasons and purposes for the long presentation. The speech may inform, persuade, convince, compare, or recommend. The long oral presentation is differentiated from the short presentation in three ways:

1. It is lengthy; it probably will be at least ten minutes long and can often run between a half hour and an hour.

2. It permits the speaker to develop complex ideas. Whereas the short presentation is often general and cursory, the long presentation provides greater depth for analysis and detail.

3. It provides the opportunity for exchange and closure. Actually, the short presentation is more one-way oriented and sets forth a single definitive message for the receivers. The long presentation generally will provide ample opportunity for exchange, discussion, and debate. These discussions can aid in the resolution of problems.

There are many ways an organization might use the long presentation, such as:

Calloway Inc. has had an outside consultant looking at its internal employee communication situation for over a year. Today, the top managers of the corporation are gathered to hear the consultant present the findings of his research and to listen to the corporation's director of internal communications indicate how he plans to implement the consultant's recommendations.

The assistant director of compensation for Norbert and Norbert is to report to an executive committee on the advantages and disadvantages of the firm instituting a cafeteria-style fringe benefit package.

Central Illinois University has decided to switch from the academic quarter system to the semester system. A special committee has been appointed to oversee the complicated transition. Today a member of the special committee is reporting to the top university officers on a laundry list of items that will need to be changed and the effect of those changes upon various functions. A technical formula for scheduling the transition will be proposed.

The director of manufacturing and the director of personnel for a company are both presenting their departments' budget requests for the next fiscal year to the firm's finance committee.

The list can go on and on. But it is obvious that most organizations today have dozens of studies, projects, problems, and recurring situations that all call for the long oral report.

It should be understood that often much of what is presented in the long oral report has been written previously in memos, letters, and reports. The advantage of the oral report is that it gets the involved people together in one room and provides the opportunity for immediate exchange of ideas. The immediacy, the give-and-take of ideas, and the benefits of hearing other people's points of view are tremendous advantages of the effective oral presentation.

The long oral report provides an opportunity for the exchange of ideas.

It is clear that the meeting to hear the long report can be a very convenient means of exchanging information. Also, it is possible for you to present ideas to an organization's leaders and influence their thinking. Therefore, in some very important respects, the long oral report can directly influence your career path. It is for these reasons and many others, that we see how beneficial it is to learn how to properly prepare and deliver this type of presentation.

Presenting a long report effectively may have some influence on your career path.

The Purpose of the Presentation

If you have been asked to make a presentation at one of your organization's meetings, the individual who requested you to speak had a specific purpose in mind for you to accomplish. In many situations, you have been supplied an agenda for the entire meeting, of which your talk is one portion, or you have received an announcement of the meeting that explains to the audience why you will be making the presentation. Overall, the long report has three major purposes:

The long report has three main purposes.

1. *To Inform.* One reason for the presentation is to inform the group concerning an item about which you are knowledgeable. The topic is important to those assembled. As differentiated from the briefing, the long informative presentation is lengthy, provides greater depth, and will probably include

time for oral exchange—questions and discussion—between the presenter and the listeners.

2. *To Persuade.* There often are a variety of alternatives facing a company and there will be differing points of view and perspectives. The persuasive presentation attempts to win the listeners over to your point of view but not necessarily to immediate action.

3. *To Convince.* The presentation to convince attempts to move the audience to some immediate action. The persuasive speech wins the audience over, the convincing speech seeks specific movement. In the business context, examples of a speech to convince could be to move

    a. the group to vote to extend an offer to Ms. Carol Pursell as Assistant Finance Officer;

    b. the group to establish a special committee to study the implications of new labor legislation on the company;

    c. the listeners to vote for the acquisition of a small firm that will contribute to the growth of your organization.

It is possible to have more than one purpose in a long presentation. For example, before attempting *to convince* the group to establish a committee to study the impact of the new labor legislation, the speaker may want *to inform* the audience about the background and implications of the legislation. Of course, how much time is spent informing depends on the audience's knowledge of the topic. Therefore, the speaker has a deep responsibility to carefully analyze the listeners—their knowledge, their attitudes, and their possible responses to a particular type of presentation.

Why is the apostrophe in *audience's* before and not after the *s*? (See Appendix 1.)

Analyzing Your Audience

Prior to making a long presentation, the speaker should analyze the audience.

After deciding on the purpose of your presentation, you must give careful consideration to the audience. If the report is internal, you probably have the advantage of knowing the members of the audience individually or at least knowing them by reputation. But it is still important to take time to look at this particular group of people in light of this presentation.

1. *Who will be in attendance at the meeting?* The listeners obviously will influence what will be presented. Also, it is important to know how many people will be present—this has a substantial influence on the kinds of visual aids that can be used.

2. *What does the audience know?* The knowledge of the audience concerning the subject of your presentation is a crucial part of planning the speech. You do not want to bore knowledgeable people with data they already know. However, you do not want to confuse those present by skipping over important information.

"I SEE OUR NEXT SPEAKER NEEDS NO INTRODUCTION ····"

© William P. Hoest

3. *What does the audience* want *to know?* It is possible to be in situations where the group will want you to recommend that your budget be increased only 6 percent and you are going to request a 10 percent increase. With this knowledge you then can consider carefully how you will structure your presentation in an attempt to convince the group to accept your proposal. In other situations the audience may want to learn specific pieces of data. Those items should be carefully noted and strategically placed in the presentation.

4. *What are the prevailing attitudes in the audience?* How have key members voted on similar topics in the past? How have others reacted to a situation like this? Have these committee members been consistently conservative or liberal in their approach?

5. *What is your objective/purpose?* In considering the audience and your purpose, give thought to what kinds of data will be important to the audience and to the kinds of arguments that will be most appealing.

By giving careful thought to your purpose and by putting it in the context of the audience, you can develop a presentation that will match the interests and attitudes of the audience, be interesting, and simultaneously achieve your objectives.

Parts of the Presentation

There are three basic parts of any long presentation.

Long presentations and speeches have three basic parts: the introduction, the body, and the conclusion. Understanding the purposes of each of these sections can aid you in formulating a speech that will be acceptable to your listeners.

Introduction

The introduction of a long presentation or speech must prepare the audience for what is to come. In writing your introduction, you should try to accomplish several different tasks.

Indicate your topic   Never assume that the entire audience understands why you are at the podium. There can be any number of reasons why even a small group of people may include one or two persons who are confused as to why you are making the speech. Therefore, one point of the introduction is to clearly indicate your purpose and precisely explain the topic of your presentation.

With the fast pace of modern business, it is not uncommon to have substitutes sitting in on meetings or to have department heads bring along assistants to gain understanding by hearing your speech. You may be unaware of these changes in advance. Therefore, if you start your presentation by assuming that everyone knows everything, you may be leaving part of your audience in the dark.

Establish a relationship with the audience   Your presentation is going to be long. The assembled people are going to have to listen to you for some time. Therefore, take immediate steps in your introduction to win the audience over to you—not to your ideas—but just to you. Try to establish a good rapport with the audience; attempt to be friendly and considerate. A few moments spent building your relationship with the audience can be time very well spent. After all, if you start your presentation on the wrong foot, you may be wasting your time when it comes to asking the group to be interested in your topic, to accept your recommendations, or to consider your suggestions.

What is the correct pronunciation of *rapport*? (Check your dictionary.)

Define your terms   Generally the long presentation will involve a very specific concept or a technical area. It may be necessary to use a special set of jargon to accompany the ideas. It is a good idea to define your terms in the introduction and then explain how those terms are used in the context of your work or procedures. This is sometimes referred to as the *operational* meaning of the terms.

Gain the audience's confidence   A knowledgeable person who is in command of the situation, is prepared and well organized, but who also displays an air of humility and understanding may win the audience over very rapidly. The nonverbal attributes of communication that permit the audience to first gain confidence in *you* will permit them later to have confidence in your ideas.

In exemplifying the aura of confidence and to indicate its importance, some very poor ways of presenting an introduction can be cited. What is your reaction to a speaker who starts as follows:

Speaker #1:
I don't quite know for sure how to present my ideas to you, but if you will just bear with me, we will be able to discuss some information.

Speaker #2:
You know, I just do not understand why Mr. Shaw asked me to speak on this topic. I know that some of you know more about this subject than I do. However, here goes . . .

Speaker #3:
Pardon my lack of organization, but with so many things happening around here, I don't often get everything I need to these meetings. You were each to have a schematic of the R-1 system but the copier wouldn't cooperate. Now, somewhere here are my notes for today's presentation.

We have all heard speakers start out in one of these ways. Very clearly they are telling the audience not to have confidence in what is going to be presented. The first words of a speech are very important. Start out in a positive way, indicate that you are in charge, reveal to the audience that you have given careful thought to what is going to be said—these actions all exude confidence. The three speakers cited above exemplify a lack of confidence; we would not blame any person in the group who, after deciding there were better things to do, got up and left.

Because the introduction is so vital to the overall success of the presentation, some speakers prefer to write out all or part of it. This may insure that you get the presentation off on solid footing. It is permissible to read the introduction as long as it is presented in a manner that does not appear to be read—that is, presented in a conversational style. Also, if you write an introduction, leave room in the manuscript for comments or directions to yourself which you may desire to insert later. This technique will be explained in a later section of this chapter. Do not trap yourself into casting your introduction in concrete and then not altering it to take advantage of the situation. For in-

The introduction is vital to the success of a speech.

stance, as you wait to start your speech, a vice-president tells a story that can be related to your topic. Or, prior to your presentation, another speech was given that ties into your subject beautifully. You may want to take advantage of these events in relating your introduction to the audience.

Throughout this text we have emphasized the significance of the first impression as it relates to communication. The introduction to the long oral presentation is where you are making your first impression concerning the topic. Strive to be positive and to get the audience with you from the first moment, otherwise you will be facing an uphill battle throughout your long presentation.

For some reason, many people feel that a speech should start with a joke or humorous story to "set the audience at ease." This is nonsense. If you have a humorous comment that is related to the talk, use it. On the other hand, if the topic is a serious one, a story that is meant to be funny can turn out to be thoroughly out of place. Remember, a presentation of this type is not the same as one made to a relaxed, informal group after an evening of eating, drinking, and conviviality.

The Body

The body of the presentation provides most of the discussion and the examples that the listeners will need to make decisions or take action. Following a few simple guidelines will make the body of your presentation more effective.

Make the right appeals   In considering the audience and the nature of the topic(s) being discussed, think about what appeals will be most effective. Will this audience be won over with appeals to logic, statistics, authority, humor, emotion, detailed data, research, or some combination of these? Recognizing what appeals to your audience will aid you in selecting your material and organizing it in the correct sequence.

Organize your materials   There are a variety of ways to arrange materials in a presentation. Before automatically settling on your "traditional way," consider the options and give careful thought to the audience and what will be most effective in this particular situation. Many business presentations are arranged easily around a series of topics that the speaker has identified. However, there are other ways to arrange materials: by chronology, by space or geography, by induction, by deduction, going from simple to complex, complex to simple, and by many other methods (see Chapter 13).

Make transitions effectively   In a long presentation in which several major topics and subpoints are going to be discussed, the transition is crucial. Be sure to summarize each point and then carefully, slowly, and explicitly move the audience to the next point. Remember, you have practiced the presenta-

Good transitions from one topic to another are vital in the body of the long report.

tion, you know the material, and you know what is coming next in the speech—the audience doesn't. Therefore, envision that you literally have to move the audience from one point to another graciously and gently. Of course, an excellent idea is to use a visual aid where your audience can *see* the topics or ideas displayed on a chart as they *hear* you go from one to another.

What is the difference in meaning between *vision* and *envision*? (See Appendix 1.)

Use variety   The body of the long presentation will be the longest portion of the speech. You do not want to tire out in presenting it and you do not want to exhaust your audience by dragging them through a dull, repetitious, and monotonous litany. There are a number of ways you can add variety to the body of the long presentation. The purpose is to keep the audience alert and also to provide the speaker with some changes of pace. Some of the options include:

Variety in material and presentation prevents a speaker from boring the audience.

Visuals. The use of various techniques that take the audience beyond just the words of the speech can add variety. (Visuals are explained in Chapter 15 and later in this chapter.)

Exemplifications. As indicated in Chapter 15, there are different ways of attempting to explain a concept to an audience. In the long presentation, it is very important to change the pace of the speech by altering the way in which you exemplify ideas. The analogy, the story, and the statistics, for example, can all be used to add variety to the presentation.

Vocal Expression. A monotone will put the audience to sleep and kill your chances of gaining acceptance of your ideas. Variance in the tone, loudness, and rate of delivery can keep the attention of the audience.

Word Choice. The language you use and how synonyms and alliterations are injected can add variety to the presentation. Also, be careful of using slang. It may distract the listeners from hearing your message. In presenting your ideas, beware of substituting non-words such as *em, un, jist,* and *yeah* for *them, and, just,* and *yes.*

Participation. Involve the audience by asking a question now and then or have a specific individual or two contribute data. These should be limited and you should always remain in control.

There is no rule of thumb on how long the body of the presentation should be. Sometimes you will be given an absolute time limit for your long presentation and that limit will place restrictions upon you. But the crucial question is: has the material in the body of the speech adequately explained the concept to the audience? And, has it provided the audience with enough information to permit each listener to follow through on the purpose you established for the speech?

The Conclusion

The conclusion has several positive purposes.

The conclusion can take several forms. Like other parts of the speech, it must be considered carefully. Also, it must be presented to the audience with special care.

Often we hear speakers come to the end of the speech and announce, "In conclusion . . ." Truly, we are often pleased to hear those words—the end of an atrocious speech is in sight. Actually, the use of the words *in conclusion* is trite and overused, as is, "Well, I guess that about ties it all together unless anyone can think of anything I left out."

The conclusion is vital. Many members of the audience will remember your final comments. Make them memorable! Write them out. Choose key words; use personal terms; try to evoke a response—a reaction. "Therefore, if you, your children, and your children's children are to live in peace, every one of us in this room must . . ."

Summary   Often the purpose of the conclusion, especially in an informative presentation, is to summarize the major points that have been presented. Or the speaker may want to re-emphasize some particular points. But keep in mind that the summary can be more than just a re-hash of what has been said previously. Sometimes a quotation, a story, or a specific example can provide an interesting twist in summarizing the major points, or leading the audience to your goal.

Recommendations/alternatives   In the business context, the conclusion of the speech often consists of presenting various recommendations to the audience. For instance, the body of the speech outlines the history of the problem and how the problem has grown within the company. In the conclusion, you now want to suggest various recommendations and alternatives to the audience. Perhaps your purpose was not to select a recommendation but to explain the problem and present options. Often a company is not going to accept one solution on the spur of the moment. That will come later. In these situations the purpose of the concluding portion of the presentation is to present the options.

It is not enough to feel that if you do a good job of relating the data in the body of the speech, somehow the conclusion will fall automatically into order when you get there. In the conclusion, give the listeners something that they can take with them to add to their knowledge or to be used for decision making.

Using Notes

In most speaking situations, and especially in the long presentation, you are going to take some materials to the podium—an outline, detailed notes, or a manuscript. As the presentation has been planned very well, it is also important to handle the note materials in a professional manner. After putting hours of preparation into a presentation, you do not want to end up at the podium fumbling with notes.

There are three basic reasons why it may be necessary to take some kind of note material to the podium:

There are three main reasons for using notes.

1. To insure that you keep on the topic and neither wander (add unnecessary materials) nor drop needed materials.
2. To jog your memory so that there will be a natural flow of information. You do not want to stand before the audience hemming and hawing or struggling to remember the next point.
3. To allow you to make precise statements when they are necessary and to relate some information in one exact way.

What is the difference in meaning between *precise* and *concise*? (See Appendix 1.)

Choice of Notes

The need for notes can be readily understood. They are an integral part of the presentation and need some special care of their own. As stated, the purpose of using notes is to aid you in delivering the message—they should not be used as a crutch nor as a substitute for not preparing and becoming familiar with the presentation. There is a wide variety in format you can use in the preparation of your notes. The selection of format depends upon the type of presentation you must make and what you are most comfortable with.

Manuscript   In some situations it may be necessary to speak from a manuscript or at least to present part of the long presentation by reading. It may be imperative that specific data be presented or the exact wording in a piece of legislation be read.

The speaker's notes may be made up in many ways.

Whenever reading a speech or a portion of a speech, be absolutely sure that it is possible for you to see the material. If the speech is typed single spaced on thin, light-weight paper, you will be in trouble. Use a heavy bond paper and prepare the final copy by using orator-style type. Use very wide margins and double- or triple-space between lines. Indent the paragraphs substantially and leave more space between the paragraphs than between the lines of each paragraph. Also, attempt to group phrases together and do not prepare the final copy in such a manner that it will be necessary to turn pages at crucial points in the presentation.

Even though you are speaking from a well-prepared manuscript, you may desire to make some changes before the speech. The wide margins and other extra space will permit you to write in additional items. Some speakers find it convenient to provide themselves with various clues in the manuscript. A clue could be: "turn the flip chart," "bring up the next slide," or "pause for a moment." In a neatly prepared manuscript there is plenty of room for inserting these added notes (see Figure 18–1).

Figure 18–1
Manuscript Notes with Clues

WHAT INTERESTS EMPLOYEES???

    IN OUR BROAD DISCUSSION WE ARE JUST HITTING THE HIGH POINTS. ACTUALLY, OUR EMPLOYEE AUDIENCE IS VERY DIVERSE AND ATTEMPTING TO CREATE A SINGLE MESSAGE THAT IS GOING TO BE MEANINGFUL TO THAT WIDE SPECTRUM OF EMPLOYEES IS DIFFICULT ----THE AUDIENCE IS DIFFERENT IN AGE, SEX, KIND OF WORK, ATTITUDES, AND VALUES.

    BUT . . . .DOES THAT MEAN THAT WE CANNOT MEANINGFULLY PROVIDE EMPLOYEES WITH THE INFORMATION THEY WANT AND NEED TO KNOW? *pause – look at audience*

    AS WE HAVE SEEN, IT APPEARS THAT EMPLOYEES ARE OFTEN MIS-UNDERSTOOD.

    NOT REALLY UNDERSTANDING THE EMPLOYEE AUDIENCE, MANAGEMENT MIS-READS THEM AND THEN SENDS THEM THE <u>WRONG</u> MESSAGES. *emphasize!*

Note cards   Often in presenting materials you will find that note cards are very handy. In some situations it may be convenient to prepare a manuscript speech entirely on cards instead of on 8½-by-11-inch paper. In other situations, the note cards may contain an outline, some basic notes of the major points, a quotation or some statistical data.

Don't fool yourself by attempting to use small 3-by-5-inch note cards. The audience will know you have the cards, so why limit yourself to such a tiny item? The 5-by-8-inch cards are substantially larger, more sturdy, and permit you much more flexibility.

Whether you use typing paper or some size of note card, be sure to number your materials sequentially. If an accident happens and your cards fall during your presentation, you do not want to have to take a great deal of time to figure out which card goes where.

Notebook   It is sometimes very convenient to prepare your notes on 8½-by-11-inch bond paper and then place them in a three-ring notebook. The advantage of this approach is that the materials will not fall, slip out of order, or slide about on the podium as you speak.

Another advantage of the notebook is that if you plan to use a few overlays or transparencies, it is possible to have them in the ringed notebook. In this way you have everything that is needed for the presentation in one place in a very orderly manner.

The disadvantage of the notebook is that it may tend to tie you to the podium. This may inhibit your movements and deter you from using gestures and from generally interacting with the audience. However, there is a way to combine the 8½-by-11-inch paper and the large note cards in order to provide the speaker with greater flexibility. As we have already suggested, the material can be first prepared on 8½-by-11-inch paper. Then unified sections of the material can be xeroxed and placed on 5-by-8-inch cards. The cards will exactly match segments of the material on each notebook page. With the cards laid upon each page the speaker has the option of using the manuscript and/or the cards.

By leaving the rings of the notebook open, it is easy to lift the materials out of the way as you speak. If you desire to move from the podium, just take the appropriate cards with you. Now you have the speech with you in a convenient manner and your mobility is not hampered by the podium. Since the cards and the manuscript match exactly, there is no danger of the speaker getting lost in the materials and not being able to find the place when returning to the notebook.

"Hidden" notes   There are some less obvious ways to use notes that may be helpful once in a while. In some situations, you may use an overhead projector throughout the presentation. On the overhead transparency, an evolving outline of the speech can be projected or principal ideas noted in key words. Because you want the audience to clearly understand, the audi-

"Hidden" notes are especially helpful when you are speaking extemporaneously.

ence is provided with the projected outline or the major points. And it is possible to expose the outline point-by-point by simply using a piece of opaque cardboard. This then can be moved as you proceed down your list of points. The key, of course, is that the outline or the principal ideas are also there for you, and with your knowledge, you can elaborate on the projected information. This technique is especially helpful when speaking extemporaneously.

Another type of "hidden" note is the kind that can be placed on the large flip chart. The large chart will have the material to be communicated to the audience placed in large print and/or pictures or diagrams. However, in using the chart, you may want to insure that several basic points under each heading are conveyed. To make sure that materials are not forgotten, you can list the basic points in pencil on the chart. These usually will not be seen by the audience; but even if they are, no harm is done. Everyone recognizes the need for notes at times. The point is, these notes are clearly visible to *you* as you speak and having them *on* the flip chart in small letters frees you from running back and forth between your notes on the podium and the easel stand. Using this method insures that vital and necessary data are communicated to the audience.

Tips on Using Notes

Always try to prepare for the unexpected surprises that may occur when using notes.

Generally, you will be in familiar surroundings to give your speech, and you will have ample time to check out the room. The podium, the lighting and any other material can be arranged to satisfy you. Remember, it is your responsibility to make sure the needed materials are prepared properly. There are all kinds of things that potentially can go wrong. By preparing for various disasters and by checking out the arrangements in advance, it is possible to substantially reduce problems. Just a partial list of items that may not be the way you expect them are as follows:

1. You have practiced your presentation using a podium that tilts the manuscript toward you; the podium provided when you arrive is flat.

2. You will have to turn down the lights for the presentation of your twelve slides . . .where are the light switches?

3. The offices have soft music on constantly. Is there a switch in the conference room that will turn the music off?

4. Your flip chart sheets do not match the stand in the conference room. What to do?

5. You practiced your presentation in a well-lit room at a podium with a light. You are provided a room that is relatively dark and the podium has no light.

6. The overhead projector works fine but goes out during the talk. Do you know where the replacement light bulb is?

Granted, these are small items. But if they make you uncomfortable, cause you to lose concentration, or interfere with the effectiveness of the presentation—they are major considerations to be remedied in advance. Each of the six items above—and dozens of others—can be taken care of easily with a little forethought and five minutes spent in the conference room prior to the presentation.

Preparation is the key. Preparation of the speech, of notes, of visuals, of key ideas, of the concluding statements, of the conference room equipment, of everything! Prepare, prepare, prepare.

Answering Questions

A major advantage of the oral presentation is that it can provide the opportunity for some open exchange between you and the audience. It is assumed that there will be questions and that you will provide some answers. As you took considerable time to prepare the presentation and its many facets, preparation should also be devoted to the question and answer portion.

Answering questions in the long presentation is very important.

Anticipate Questions

If you are a careful and thorough speaker, you will anticipate the kinds of questions that might be asked. Of course, you cannot anticipate all possible questions, but you should take time to list potential questions and think through reasonable answers.

In handling questions, it is very important to listen carefully to the actual question being asked. As noted in Chapter 16, the good listener does not cut the questioner off and start answering. The anticipated question and the actual question may be very different.

Establish the Ground Rules

There are three basic ways to handle questions when making a presentation. In all cases, you are wise to establish the ground rules immediately. Those rules should be conveyed to the audience by your introducer or by you. In that way the audience will know that you will answer questions in any one of the three following ways.

There are three basic ways to handle questions.

Laissez faire Take questions at any point in the presentation. This means you stop where you are and provide an answer. The advantage of this approach is that it may keep the audience with you, and it can provide you with the opportunity to clear up misunderstood items on the spot. A disadvantage is that you may get waylaid by poor questions or by questions from eager beavers asking about items that will be covered later. Or you may even have someone who wishes to ask a question but who goes on to make a speech.

Question breaks   At one or two points during the presentation, take a break for questions. These breaks should be made when moving from one major point to another. The approach is to summarize the one section and then ask for questions before moving to the next topic. The advantage of this approach is that it gives you some control, and it still provides for direct audience interaction during the presentation. The major disadvantages are very similar to those noted in the laissez faire approach — you may be taken out of the mainstream of the idea by extraneous questions.

The end   Another way to handle the questions is to hold them all until the end of the presentation. If you are provided with a definite time limit, it may be best to hold the questions until the end of your presentation, after you have related the material that needs to be covered. If you take questions during your presentation, you may cover only one-third of the data and spend the remainder of your time attempting to answer questions, making a mess of the presentation.

Whichever way you decide to handle the questions, it is generally your decision. But keep in mind that the question period is usually an important aspect of your presentation.

Using Visual Aids

At various points in this text, the use of visual communications has been introduced. When it comes to the long oral presentation, the visuals may be an integral part of the speech, as they are in the report and in the proposal. Most people are not, by themselves, captivating speakers. It is difficult for many people to hold an audience's attention for forty-five minutes while presenting the pros and cons of establishing a new program or explaining a method for producing a product. However, visuals can aid the speaker in making materials clear and adding variety to the presentation. The variety that is achieved with visuals can be an important factor in maintaining the audience's interest.

Use effective visual aids to complement the message in the long report.

Like so many aspects of communication, it is not possible to absolutely prescribe what visuals should be used in each situation. However, by becoming familiar with the types available, knowing the pitfalls and advantages of each, and knowing the audience, you can make decisions on the use of them.

Besides knowing that the visuals must complement the spoken message and be of interest to the audience, don't forget the physical nature of the room. Where the presentation will be made definitely influences the visuals selected. Carefully consider such items as: room size, electrical outlets, availability of projection screen and chalk board, and the ability of the speaker to easily control and dim the lights. Let's look at various items that can be classified as visuals that will assist us in communicating our ideas.

Handouts

Many different items can be handed to the members of the audience. However, we generally think of the handout as some special material that has been arranged on an 8½-by-11-inch sheet of paper. It may be a table, a chart, or a listing. It is material that you think the audience needs to better understand the presentation.

If the material can be distributed easily and if the data assist the presentation and do not detract, handouts can be very beneficial. Handouts get the material directly into the hands of the listeners and generally will be the most visible kind of item that can be used.

Use handout materials in the long presentation with caution.

If, during the presentation, several handouts are going to be used, it may be convenient to print the materials on different colors of paper. This will permit you to identify easily the material and also allow you to make sure that when you want the audience to look at the pie chart (on yellow paper) that everyone is actually looking at the pie chart on the yellow paper and not the bar chart on blue paper.

Do not let the handouts get in the way of the presentation. Work out in advance how they can be distributed; generally it is best to have a person distribute the handouts at the precise time you will refer to them. If the materials are distributed at the beginning of the speech, some members of the audience will begin to study them and not listen to you. Thus, what was supposed to have been an aid becomes a distraction.

If you happen to use a handout and a projection at the same time (such as a slide or overlay), be sure that the item projected matches *exactly* what the people in the audience have in their hands. If the two items differ, you will get numerous questions and comments about the difference. This breaks the continuity of the presentation and detracts from your credibility.

Reports

The report is actually a handout, but it is much more than a single piece of paper. Sometimes the audience will have received a written report or a detailed summary of your data prior to the presentation. In this case, it is assumed that the audience will be informed and that the oral presentation will consist of more than just reading from materials that have already been provided.

When using reports, be sure to keep the audience's attention on the relevant material.

The written report can be an excellent piece of source material when giving the oral report. If the written report contains various tables, charts, and other visuals, have the audience turn to these items as they are explained in the context of the oral report.

If twenty people all have a fifty-page report in their hands, it will be very difficult to get all of the people on the same page at the same time. Also, people are naturally curious, and at the time you are attempting to direct their attention to a point you are making with the aid of the overhead projector, some will be flipping through their reports to see how some idea relates to an interesting table in the written report.

In a courteous manner ("Let's all focus on the vital statistics on page 12"), attempt to keep the audience's attention directed on the relevant material. Also, when referring to the report, beware of reading too much material from it. It is best to speak extemporaneously about materials in the report and to look directly at the audience.

Chalkboards

Using the chalkboard or whiteboard in the long presentation can be an effective tool.

The chalkboard can be helpful in a number of different ways. First of all, the boards are not just blackboards any longer. The color of the board may be green, white, or yellow. With the colored board and the varieties of colored chalk, the board can be a useful way to quickly list materials and categorize data.

Some conference rooms will have white chalkboards. The advantage of the white board is that it may serve as a projection screen. It is then possible to project items like a balance sheet or a procedure form; the speaker can literally write the materials on the white chalk boards, using colored chalk. The new white boards can be written on with special colored felt tip markers.

If there is a series of boards, each on its own track, it is possible to prepare materials in advance, keep the boards covered, and then slide out the appropriate board when you want it in your presentation. The chalkboard also may be helpful particularly during the question and answer period when it is necessary to quickly illustrate an item.

If the speaker is in a neat dress or business suit, sometimes working with a chalkboard and different colors of chalk can become messy. Also, if the chalkboard cannot be covered, the speaker is forced to either place the information on the board before the presentation and let everyone look at it before it is presented, or stop the speech and work on the board. Both of these options are distracting.

Usually the boards are placed at a height convenient for the speaker—not the audience. If there is a relatively large group, it may be difficult for them to see the material on the board.

Slides

With fast and colorful photography, slides can be prepared on almost any subject. The slide can project actual photos of materials, can present lists of items, and can be artistically done to project interesting collages when the speaker is attempting to summarize several points.

When using slides, check all mechanical aspects carefully.

Sometimes a speaker may desire to use the slide as the focal point at a particular time in the presentation; at other times the slide may be used as a supplementary item. When using slides, it is possible to represent complex ideas pictorially, and the slide often can provide just the dynamic boost your presentation needs.

There is a potential sometimes to let the slides become too overpowering in making the presentation. Be sure that they do not detract from the major points. When using slides, give careful consideration to when you will switch from one to another. It is very distracting to be projecting a picture concerning product use in snowy Wisconsin when speaking about the use of products in hot Florida. Slides often call for dimming the lights. If you are presenting material that will require the audience to take notes, slides may be inappropriate.

What is the difference in meaning between *detract* and *distract*? (See Appendix 1.)

Practice with the slides and be sure they are in the correct order. Also, insert blank slides when you prefer to project nothing. The blank slide that reveals a mild subtle color is not distracting. However, to project white light may be visually upsetting to the audience.

It is generally best to have an arrangement where you can adjust the focus and movement of the slides. Take time to learn how to push the right buttons on the control. If someone else is going to run the machine, try to work with him or her in advance, and make sure the individual knows when to change pictures.

Large Flip Charts

The large flip chart consists of large sheets of paper, often about 3-by-2-feet, fastened together and hinged on a tripod in such a manner that each page can be flipped over and out of the way, thereby exposing the next page. The pads of paper can be purchased and the sheets are thrown away after use.

The large flip chart is useful in providing a listing, an outline, a basic graph or a diagram, or in developing a progression of ideas—one page to the next. The material placed on the flip chart will be drawn or printed by hand. Using felt tipped markers, you can prepare materials in different colors to subtly highlight specific items. As compared to fancy overlays and slides that can take days or weeks to prepare, the flip chart does not call for much lead time. To prepare charts, you need only a few minutes, the pad, and several colored markers.

The large flip chart affords the speaker easy control.

"Could you go over that once again, Gene? Just in case any of us don't understand it."

The flip chart provides you with many advantages because it gives you so much control. It is easy to alter the sequence of materials presented or to refer to items previously cited. The flip chart is one of the oldest and yet one of the most practical means of relating visual materials to a small group.

If there is any doubt in your mind about whether the data should be placed on one chart or perhaps two, it is usually better to use two. Keep the charts simple; don't put more information on a chart than can be easily assimilated.

Table Flip Charts

The table flip chart is effective for small groups (six to eight people).

For a small group seated close to the speaker or around a table, the table flip chart is a convenient way to visualize materials. Much smaller than the large flip chart, the table model can be placed on the conference table and is very easy to flip.

Generally the table flip chart is used when a presentation is given several times and there is a need to carry a compact package from one place to another. The table flip chart is very suitable for presenting charts and graphics that have been prepared in advance; it is not a handy device to attempt to draw on during a speech.

The most common use of the table flip chart is probably in sales presentations. If a sales representative is going to make a similar presentation a number of times in a number of different places to small groups, the table flip chart can be very handy.

The major limitation of the table flip chart is its size. It would not be appropriate for a group that is larger than six or eight people, and it should not be used in a situation in which individuals are going to be seated more than ten or twelve feet from the chart. The table flip chart is excellent for indicating a progression of ideas or thoughts. However, be sure that those ideas progress correctly on the chart and that they match identically the context of the spoken materials.

Overhead Projectors

One of the most versatile pieces of visual equipment is the overhead projector. It can project images of items the speaker writes on the spur of the moment, and it can project drawings, tables, charts, and other visual examples that have been prepared in advance. The overhead has the advantage of being used in a well-lit room; you can stand next to the machine and introduce transparencies when you want.

The overhead can be used in several ways:

1. *Acetate Roll.* Some overheads have rolls of acetate attached; this makes it possible to draw anything on the roll with a grease pencil or a transparency pen, and project it.

2. *Thermo-Fax Transparencies.* Printed and typed materials or drawings can be reproduced onto single pieces of acetate with a copy machine that has this capability. This technique is handy when you wish to prepare material in advance; it is a good idea to type the materials using orator-style type so the print will be large enough for the audience to see. Of course there are machines available that print large-size letters, numbers, and symbols specifically for use on transparencies.

3. *Overlays.* You may wish to develop an idea in a series of related steps, and it may be distracting to keep switching individual transparencies. In this situation the overlay, which is a series of hinged transparencies, is useful. For instance, a company has altered its stationery, and the new stationery and letter format are being explained in a presentation.

    The first transparency would show the piece of stationery, the second transparency would be laid over the first to show where to place the date, the third shows the salutation, and the fourth adds the body of the letter and so on. The overlay permits you to develop an idea in steps by adding material in sequence.

The overhead projector is a versatile and effective aid in long presentations.

In using any of the three techniques noted above, you have two ways of pointing to the materials being projected. You may use a pencil and point to the materials on the transparency or acetate; the shadow of the pencil will be projected. Or you may go to the screen and point to the material there.

Among the many advantages of the overhead are that it permits you to 1) face the audience in a room that need not be darkened, and 2) control carefully the progress of your presentation.

Other Visuals

As has been noted, visuals can bring an interesting dimension to the long oral presentation and can be a substantial aid in adding variety to the material. Besides the techniques noted, there are other forms of visual and audio media. Generally, if you were to use these other forms, your organization would have experts to assist you in appropriately preparing and integrating the materials into the presentation. These include motion pictures, film strips, opaque projectors, audio tapes, and videotapes. Today, with the increasing ease of videotaping, this medium is becoming more widely used. You generally would use videotape to represent clearly items that cannot be brought into the room; or for example, to show how a product is used, to illustrate a new production procedure, or to bring testimonials from individuals who cannot be present for the speech.

All in all, good visual aids that supplement and emphasize your oral comments add a powerful dimension to your presentation. You actually are communicating on two levels with your audience: the listeners *hear* your message and, simultaneously, *see* your key points. Presenting your speeches in this manner assures you of delivering—as a skilled boxer would say—a "knock-out, one-two punch."

MEMO

To: Students

From: The Authors

Subject: The long presentation and your career

You probably can count on the fingers of one hand the number of long presentations you have made. In the coming years, however, these formal talks will play a more and more important role in your life. While making a long presentation, you are at your most visible in the organization; you are given a chance to put your best foot forward for your employers. In short, the ability to make a successful long presentation can be a basic key to career success.

Decision

Here is the organization sheet Mario Aguilar used to prepare his long presentation for the Los Angeles City Council.

PURPOSE : To persuade the City Council to allocate $250,000 to create a new recreational facility for the community.

AUDIENCE: City Council of Los Angeles (16 members)

OUTLINE :

    I. Introduction: Equal rights and privileges for <u>all</u> citizens

   II. Neighborhood Analysis and Comparison
       A. Population statistics
       B. Crime, vandalism, and theft rate
       C. Parks and recreational facilities available

  III. What Will Be Achieved by the Expenditure
       A. Social advantages
       B. Neighborhood advantages

   IV. Return of Investment for City of Los Angeles
       A. Financial
       B. Social
       C. Political

    V. Conclusion

Visual Aids:

1. Pie charts to compare South Los Angeles with Westwood and Beverly Hills in terms of a) population; b) crime, vandalism, and theft; and c) parks and recreational facilities available.

2. Table and bar charts to show a) projected expenditure in dollars; and b) projected savings as a result of decline in vandalism, theft, and cost of law enforcements, as well as increase in tax return as a result of rise in property values.

3. Pictogram of bags of money, one bag for "Costs" and two bags for "Long-Term Savings."

Questions

1. Explain what a speaker can do to establish his or her confidence on the subject of the presentation.

2. Identify a topic that you might be asked to report on in a long presentation, and then list and explain how each of the following aids could be used:
   a. handouts;
   b. chalkboard;
   c. slides;
   d. flip chart (large or table);
   e. overhead projector; and
   f. video tape.

3. For each of the purposes of a long presentation (to inform, to persuade, and to convince), list four topics on which you could be asked to speak as part of your job.

4. For the type of job that you hope to assume in an organization, name four situations in which you could be called upon to make a long presentation. Explain each.

Exercises

1. Select one of the situations you named in Question 4 and develop it as follows:
   a. clearly state the purpose of the presentation;
   b. identify and analyze the audience;
   c. outline the long presentation;
   d. write the introduction, manuscript style;
   e. prepare the actual notes for the conclusion and include various clues that would be helpful;
   f. indicate in the outline where visuals would be beneficial; name and briefly explain each visual;
   g. develop one of the visuals so that it could actually be used in a presentation; and
   h. list seven questions that you would expect the audience to ask.

2. Based upon a long business-type presentation you have seen (or one that you can make arrangements to see), prepare a 500-word critique. Evaluate the presentation and specifically note the content and delivery. Point out what was well done, and why, and what could be improved and how.

3. Make a long presentation on the basis of the topic selected in Exercise 1 above. (Attempt to have your presentation videotaped for your own viewing and/or make your presentation in front of a group who will offer constructive criticism.)

4. Interview the sales manager of a large local company. Ask this person five to ten prepared questions on the use of the long oral presentation in the company you visited. Also, request any additional information that would be helpful. Write your findings in memo report form.

5. Refer to Exercise 4. Convert your findings to a format that can be presented orally to your class. Give a ten-minute presentation relating to the information you received at the interview. Be prepared to respond to any questions students might pose about your interview.

6. Make a ten-to-twenty-five-minute presentation on one of the following topics. You are required to use visual aids. Obviously, careful preparation and research will be required. (Attempt to have your presentation videotaped for your own viewing and/or make your presentation in front of a group who will offer constructive criticism.)
   a. Why Nuclear Energy Must (Must Not) Be Developed More Aggressively in the U.S.
   b. National Health Insurance Is (Is Not) the Answer in the U.S.
   c. How to Study for an Examination
   d. How to Water Ski (Bowl, Play Chess, Scuba Dive, or . . .)
   e. Why You Should Contribute to . . .
   f. A topic of your choice

Application

1. You are the vice-president of your college's student government. The president was to have presented a thirty-minute speech before the Board of Trustees and executive officers of your university. Unfortunately, she had an emergency at home, and you were called upon to present her speech, "Student Government Activities During the Past Year." You have one hour to prepare your delivery from the typewritten speech that was handed to you. List several things you can do to refrain from just standing in front of the group and reading the speech.

Dilemma

For some time now, the Trojan Corporation has been considering starting up a physical fitness program for employees. The personnel department, in which Elisabeth Duncan works as assistant to the director, has been pushing for the program.

One reason that the program hasn't yet got off the ground is that the meetings of the Fitness Committee have been poorly attended by key decision makers, have tended to ramble on and on without reaching any conclusions, and have often neglected questions. After the last meeting, one committee member (a supporter of the program) had this comment: "I'd rather drop the program altogether than go through another meeting like that one."

George Hitchcock, the director of personnel, feels that one reason the meetings have been unproductive is that no formal agenda was drawn up in advance. Therefore, he has asked Elisabeth to examine the issues that must be discussed in order to reach a consensus and to draw up an agenda for the next meeting. The agenda should be in the form of a memo which will be distributed to all committee members.

Decision, see page 383

Conducting Effective Interviews and Meetings

19

Here is a list of the objectives you should understand by the time you complete this chapter. Place a check mark in the box beside each as soon as you feel ready to apply your understanding in a practical situation.

☐ The role of interviews in the modern organization

☐ The eight basic kinds of interviews
    Information interview
    Employment interview
    Appraisal interview
    Counseling interview
    Disciplinary interview
    Persuasive interview
    Technical exchange interview
    Exit interview

☐ The basic steps to follow in preparing for, conducting, and following up on interviews

☐ The importance of meetings to organizations

☐ The basic steps to be taken in planning a meeting

☐ The basic procedures for holding a meeting

☐ The various steps to be taken during the post-meeting period

Much of organizational activity is transacted through people. At times, it is on a one-to-one basis: buyer-seller; job candidate-personnel officer; engineering director-production supervisor; company officer-government representative; and on and on. In each case, an interview takes place.

Also held with equal frequency is the one-to-group relationship: the meeting or conference. Here a group of people sit together to explore, inform, or compare ideas, concepts, and data to solve mutual problems.

This face-to-face interaction, either on a one-to-one or a one-to-group situation, takes place daily behind the counter of a small retail operation as well as in the walnut-panelled conference room of a giant corporation. Let's examine these areas of communication.

Interviews

What is the difference in meaning between *personal* and *personnel*? (See Appendix 1.)

As a manager or employee you frequently will assume the role of interviewer or interviewee. As a job seeker you will be an interviewee; as a manager looking for a competent employee to fill an opening, you will be the interviewer. As a buyer or seller or prospect, you will be in one position or the other. And as a husband or wife, a child or parent, you also must be, from time to time, an interviewer or interviewee. What all this means is simply this: understanding the interview process and being competent as an interviewer or interviewee can make a vital contribution to your business and personal life.

Often individuals think of the interview as a situation involving two people—one asking questions and the other answering. It is that, but it is also much more. The interview is an *exchange* of thoughts, feelings, and attitudes, in which ideas, goodwill, and understanding can grow as a result of the efforts of the individuals involved. Each person must receive (listen) as well as send (talk) in the exchange.

The interview is an exchange of ideas, concepts, feelings, and attitudes.

The interview is an effective communication method for sending and receiving information and for gaining understanding and acceptance of ideas. The interview is also an excellent device for developing and changing attitudes and behavior, and for motivating individuals to work toward common goals.

The interview has many purposes.

Types of Interviews

There are many types of interviews.

There are many different types of interview. They can be distinguished by the goals they are meant to accomplish and the strategies needed to make them succeed.

Information interview   Here the primary purpose is to obtain or give information, as in a buyer-seller interview in which prices, weights, delivery schedules, and other information are of vital importance. But obviously the information interview takes place in a hundred situations beyond a buyer-seller relationship: patient-physician, teacher-student, parent-child, lawyer-client, and on and on. As in all interviews, you must *listen* carefully for facts and feelings to determine what information has been omitted, avoided, distorted, or expanded.

Listening is a vital factor in the information interview.

The employment interview   Here, the interviewer wishes to get as much information as possible about the prospective employee. The job seeker wants to learn as much as possible about the organization. This obviously means that both must enter the interview with a list of specific questions and goals to be achieved.[1]

Preparing questions prior to the employment interview is wise.

It is probably wise to write out the questions and test them *before* the interview so that a carelessly chosen word does not derail the interview. The job seeker should inquire about promotion, but to phrase the question, "When do I get promoted?" is obviously foolhardy when he or she hasn't been offered the job yet! If, however, the job seeker first writes the question out *before* the interview, it will be determined that "What is your firm's policy on advancing employees?" is a much more acceptable choice of words than "When do I get promoted?"

The same is true for the interviewer: careful preparation of questions is always wise. There is also a further consideration for the interviewer. With the new Fair Employment Practices legislation, Equal Employment Opportunity regulations, and other laws, there is a whole series of personal questions concerning age, marital status, race, and religion, which, if asked, would be cause for legal action.

What is the difference in meaning between *farther* and *further*? (See Appendix 1.)

Thus both the job seeker and the organization's representative should prepare carefully for the interview. In this way, the interviewer will secure the information needed on the applicant's qualifications, personality, and attitudes. At the same time, you, the job seeker, will learn enough about the company to help you decide whether you should pursue the opportunity further.

Appraisal interview   Most organizations require that all managers at all levels periodically interview subordinates. The review periods occur most frequently quarterly or semiannually. The purpose is to mutually appraise performance in such areas as production, efficiency, responsibility, creativity, initiative, and judgment. This interview should also review how well previously established goals have been met and establish new objectives for the interviewee.

What is the difference in meaning between *semiannual* and *biannual*? (See Appendix 1.)

In almost every instance, a form is completed during the course of this interview which both parties sign or initial. This is done to indicate mutual agreement.

---

[1]The subject of employment interviews will be discussed in greater detail in Chapter 22.

Counseling interview   One of the obligations of the supervisor is to offer suggestions and advice to subordinates. In an interview situation, the boss may wish to counsel one of the workers on various methods of motivating others, arranging a production operation, mediating a problem, setting goals, dealing with suppliers, or increasing production. At other times a supervisor may wish to counsel the subordinate, if appropriate, on personal problems such as finances, participation in overtime, or health-care plans.

What is the difference in meaning between *counsel*, *consul*, and *council*? (See Appendix 1.)

It is vital, however, for interviewers to recognize that they usually are not professionally equipped for counseling in depth or in many areas: alcoholism, marital affairs, and drug abuse, among others. For this reason, many employers have a professional psychologist on the staff or on a retainer basis for such cases.

Disciplinary interview   Here the interviewer (whether a manager or parent) wishes to correct a situation while retaining the goodwill of the interviewee. In most cases, it is possible to review the action of the interviewee and criticize *that action* rather than the individual. Thus, the interviewer dwells on the action of leaving a work station fifteen minutes early rather than "*You* cut out before *your* time was up even though we pay *you* for a full eight hours."

It is better to criticize an action than a person.

If the negative and detrimental action is frequent, however, a more forceful approach may be needed. Each case will determine the action selected. In no case should carelessly chosen words be used which arouse antagonism and do not solve the problem. Rather than saying, "You failed to . . . ," it is usually wiser to say, "When you do it this way, you will achieve . . ." Instead of saying, "I was disappointed to learn that you . . . ," it is better to say, "I learned that you . . ." This is never an easy interview to hold, but problems don't go away by themselves. A well-conducted interview brings problems into focus and permits solutions to be reached while goodwill is maintained.

The choice of words is especially important in the disciplinary interview.

Persuasive interview   This interview commonly is thought to occur primarily in buyer-seller relationships. However, there is an element of persuasion in almost every interview. You should keep in mind that you usually can't persuade others; you only can supply them with information in such a way that they will persuade themselves. Most of us resent a hardsell approach simply because someone else tries to push ideas on us.

Remember our discussion on listening: supply the facts, listen from the other person's point of view, listen with understanding, and listen with empathy. Your receiver may accept your views.

The technical exchange interview may involve two or more individuals.

Technical exchange interview   Although two individuals may be involved here, it is also quite possible that several may be. This interview usually takes place when a problem is defined that can be solved only by the technical skills and performance of several different individuals and their support groups.

For example, the government is looking for a method to inoculate twenty million people in a very limited time period to avoid a potential epidemic.

Obviously we need medical technicians and engineering, production, logistics, planning, transportation, and financial personnel involved in an effort to solve the problem. They must all exchange technical information as a solution is sought. No area can be ignored and all must recognize the problems of the others.

Exit interview   Much can be learned from employees who voluntarily or involuntarily leave firms. Such information may help future operations. However, to be successful, this interview must be structured carefully. If it is not, it may become a gripe session in which an employee who is disgruntled disparages the actions of his former boss or fellow workers in an effort to relieve his guilt or make himself an undeserved hero.

Normally the interview should be conducted by an objective individual from the personnel department. Personalities, if at all possible, should be avoided. The focus should be on the manufacturing or office process: the methods of production, sales, distribution, transportation, or other areas. What specific actions *were* followed? What should be done? How could it be done? What specific recommendations does the interviewee have?

Steps in the Interview Process

Regardless of the type of interview, there are some basic steps which should be carried through for each interview.

Preparing for the interview   Few activities can be conducted successfully without preparation. Certainly the interview requires careful preparation. It is a good idea not only to prepare but to actually write out key items such as background data, objectives to be achieved, critical questions, and possible courses of action.

Most interviews can be divided into three basic steps.

The following checklist should be reviewed prior to the interview:

1. Obtain the necessary background information to successfully conduct the interview.
2. Establish goals or objectives for the meeting.
3. Design or formulate critical questions or points for discussion.
4. Determine, to the best of your ability, the interviewee's needs and personality and make provisions to adapt to them.
5. Determine possible solutions, courses of action, and appropriate reactions to specific proposals or alternatives.
6. Select a satisfactory interview site.

What is the difference in meaning between *course* and *coarse*? (See Appendix 1.)

Conducting the interview   Your goal in the interview is to gain the information you need. The following guidelines should help ensure your success in achieving that goal.

1. Establish a comfortable climate by choosing a satisfactory and comfortable place for the interview. Begin at the time scheduled, cordially greet the interviewee, provide handouts, reference materials and/or refreshments if appropriate.
2. Listen effectively to gain active participation.
3. Have at hand and supply relevant information.
4. Ask key questions.
5. Be aware when crucial periods arise; these may be signals for closure, new directions, agreements, or compromise.
6. Observe, evaluate, and note the interviewee's comments, nonverbal communications and reactions.
7. Establish key items for action (commonly called *action items*) and a schedule for follow-up.
8. Close the interview in a thoughtful, appreciative way. Don't permit a jangling phone call or an interruption to break in and cause the interview to be closed.

Following up on the interview   The interview has been prepared for and held. However, the circle has not yet been closed. It is now necessary to follow up to make sure that the agreements reached and the decisions made are completed. The steps listed below are designed to help follow up an interview:

1. All action items accepted by the interviewer as his or her responsibility should be carried through.
2. The interviewer should assist the interviewee in achieving the action items designated as the latter's responsibility.
3. The interviewer should also assist the interviewee by obtaining materials or by taking those steps needed to achieve agreed-upon goals.
4. The interviewer should maintain contact and communication with the interviewee. Certainly meetings should not be held at the quarterly or semiannual review periods only.
5. The interviewer should be available for discussion and communication as a follow-up to the interview.

Obviously the interview is a vital communication activity. It can be the vehicle for problem solving, goal setting, information exchange, and, most important, the opportunity for building goodwill. Because people are involved—and people never react according to a precise formula—every interview will vary. Nevertheless, it is an activity in which you should be proficient. As a manager, an employee, a clerk, an artisan, a parent, a friend, a wife, a husband, a son, or a daughter, you frequently will have occasion to be an interviewer or an interviewee. Make the most of the opportunity.

Meetings and Conferences

One of the most costly communication activities in an organization—and seldom recognized as such—is the meeting. Visualize twelve to fifteen men and women in a room for over two hours. Each earns around $18.00 per hour (salary plus overhead costs). The meeting continues for two hours and thirty minutes. How much has the company spent? Now multiply that figure times one thousand or five thousand or ten thousand meetings held each year throughout the organization. The total yearly cost is staggering.

Meetings that are not productive can be extremely costly.

But the expense may be worthwhile if decisions are reached and goodwill among the participants increased. The problem, however, is that most meetings seem to result in individual frustration, confusion, and irritation. Too often, the most frequently heard comment after meetings is: "What a waste of time that was!"

And that is because most meetings are not conducted properly. If you are a conference leader or a conference participant, you have a responsibility for contributing to a successful meeting. Here are some concepts, suggestions and a plan for achieving that goal.

Policy for Meetings

An effective meeting is a forum where knowledgeable individuals come together to solve organizational problems through participative and open communication. It is a group session where plans are made, goals established, and problems solved. It should be conducted in a climate where goodwill is increased and personnel are permitted to grow.

Management (or company) policies should be established and followed for attaining effective meetings.

Meetings will have a much better opportunity of succeeding if management establishes policies for their conduct. Some of these should be:

1. Only those individuals should be invited to attend who can make a contribution. Individuals should not be invited because of past protocol, politics, or the fear of offending "good old Harry."

2. An agenda should be prepared for every meeting. It should be distributed prior to the session or posted at the beginning of the meeting.

3. A set of minutes or a meeting recap sheet should be distributed within twenty-four hours after the meeting close. This should list items for action and the name of the person responsible for completing the action stated.

4. Every meeting should begin and end precisely at the times announced.

"We may as well go home. It's obvious that this meeting isn't going to settle anything."

Most meetings seem to result in individual frustration, confusion, and irritation.

The Pre-meeting Period

Meetings usually will not be successful unless they are planned carefully in advance. During the pre-meeting period, you should be sure to carry out a number of specific steps.

Establish the need for the meeting   It is true that enough activities take place in some organizations to warrant a meeting "each Wednesday at 2:00 P.M." However, at many firms, meetings are held each week — or day, or month — simply because someone set it up that way.

If there is no need for a meeting, it should not be held even if the specified day and time have arrived. Meetings are just too expensive.

Define the purpose   What is the primary purpose of the session? Is it to gain consensus for a course of action on a problem? Is it to define a problem? Is it to hear the opinions of knowledgeable people? Is it simply to disseminate information and answer questions? Is it to exchange technical data to determine a course of action?

Of course, a meeting may have several purposes and they all can be achieved. But we must define those so we can accurately identify the type of meeting, who should be invited, and what the specific agenda items should be.

Decide what type of conference should be held   If we know our purpose, we can determine which of the following types, or combination of types, our meeting will be: informational; problem solving; training; technical exchange; idea discussions; or decision making.

Don't try to conduct several different types of meetings at the same time.

Once we have selected the type or types, we then can determine if we are being too ambitious. It is certainly possible to accomplish in one meeting one, two, or three of the above. A problem is encountered when the meeting leader tries to complete them *all* in one session.

Decide who should participate and who should lead   All persons should be invited who can make necessary contributions to achieving the meeting goals. As stated on page 375, no one should attend because of politics, hurt feelings, or "I think he would like to be represented."

Finding a leader is a critical decision. Conference leaders should be excellent listeners, rather than speakers; they should be arbitrators, mediators, facilitators, and chairmen. They should be objective, sincere, honest, and respected and liked by those who attend. They should be able to draw forth the reticent, motivate the silent, and silence the rambler. They should be analytical, decisive, impartial, patient, quick thinking, and thoroughly articulate.

Where does one find such a paragon?

Of course it is most difficult, but it is possible for us to study these qualities and improve our abilities in those areas where improvement is needed.

Select topics and distribute an agenda   The selection of items for discussion should be made with care. To choose those which are not thoroughly relevant or more items than can be discussed easily in the time frame provided can be frustrating to the serious participant.

Making up an agenda and distributing it prior to the meeting is a vital and necessary step (see Figure 19–1). The agenda should include:

1. Date, time, and place of meeting;
2. Topic for discussion;
3. Subtopics to be examined;
4. List of participants; and
5. Materials (if applicable) to be reviewed prior to the session.

In the event a sudden meeting is called to handle a crisis, and there is no time to reproduce and distribute an agenda, there is still a solution. The agenda may be penned on a flip-chart pad or on a chalkboard three minutes before the meeting opens.

An agenda will accomplish several valuable services. It tells the participants what will be discussed so that they may prepare and avoid the comment, "If I'd known we were going to discuss that, I would have . . . " An

An agenda is a critical factor in attaining effective meetings.

Conducting Interviews and Meetings   **377**

Figure 19–1
A Meeting Agenda

JONO COMPANY

To: Mr. Roger Sherman, Vice-President, Personnel
From: Ms. Betsy Seamans, Office Manager
Date: December 3, 198-
Subject: Recruitment and Training of Personnel Meeting:
          1:00 to 3:00 p.m., Conference Room A

Topic for Discussion:

Shall the Jono Company revise personnel recruitment and
training procedures?

Specific Items for Discussion:

1. Possible use of Technical Recruiting Services, Inc.
2. Use of local college placement offices
3. Use of newspaper classified ads
4. Brief overview of training objectives established:
    Policy C-124
5. Shall we engage a training director?
6. Cost effectiveness of #5
7. Other business

Meeting Participants Invited

A.L. Arthur
B.T. Bastin
C.C. Charmay
L.M. Fornier
T.O. Gardener
M.M. Hightower
T.T. Kite
B.A. Seamans
R. Sherman

agenda gives the meeting leader an opportunity to interrupt and cut off the rambler with "That's a good point, Joe, but right now let's get back to item three on the agenda." It forces the meeting leader to plan and prepare. It tells participants who will attend, and that enables them to plan strategy if necessary.

Make all necessary physical preparations This step seems so obvious, but it is often overlooked. Yet if the details are not taken care of, the entire meeting can be derailed. Nothing, for example, is so irritating than to have twelve people assemble for a meeting in Room 10 and find the room already being used and no other facility available!

The best way to handle the details is to use a checklist:

The room: Reserved? Table? Chairs? Podium?
Audio-visuals: Charts? Projectors? Recorders? Mikes? Translation
　　equipment?
Handout materials: Number needed? Complexity?
Refreshments: Coffee? Sandwiches?
Miscellaneous: Pads? Pencils? Name Cards? Reference materials?

Now that all these steps have been taken care of, we're ready for the meeting itself.

Meeting Procedures

Although the pre-meeting details are important, the meeting itself is the vital activity. It is the meeting leader who plays a major role in the success of the session. A leader should have the ability to involve all participants, keep the meeting on course, reach consensus, and promote goodwill. In every instance the meeting leader should:

1. Obtain participation;
2. Move through the agenda;
3. Begin and end on time;
4. Secure decisions when needed; and
5. Thank the participants for their preparation, participation, and attendance.

Meeting leaders should remember that their primary role is to serve as a catalyst. They should bring a variety of views together, analyze them, and offer possible solutions. Leaders never should dominate but should listen and encourage discussion.

Meeting leaders should choose their space with care. If they sit alone they will be "in charge." They might be wiser to sit among the participants. Being sensitive to the climate and having everyone relaxed is important. The leader should respect everyone and honestly believe that the group can accomplish more than an individual.

"There's another meeting in five minutes, Ed. Did you hear me, Ed? Ed?"

Yes, there are problems when one calls a meeting.

The meeting leader should appoint someone to take notes and, at times, may wish to ask a knowledgeable participant to lead the meeting. Obviously, this is a device for the leader to move out of the spotlight, to permit another individual to assume a leadership position, and, overall, to develop personnel.

As the time approaches for the meeting cut-off, the leader may wish to have a vote or a consensus opinion on key issues, establish action items, and designate who will carry them through (or secure volunteers), and, finally, offer a summary of the key areas discussed and the decisions reached.

> The meeting leader and the activities are critical in securing an effective meeting.

The Post-meeting Period

Although the meeting has been held and the participants have dispersed, the session is not yet over. The decisions which have been reached must be carried out, the action items implemented, and the next steps taken. Almost invariably other problems surfaced during the meeting, new opportunities were recognized, and old issues continued. All this requires some follow-up.

Almost all of these situations can be handled with the distribution of a set of minutes of the meeting or a recapitulation sheet (see Figure 19–2). It

Figure 19–2
A Set of Minutes from
a Meeting

JONO COMPANY

MINUTES OF MEETING

To: All participants, meeting December 3, 198-
From: Mr. Roger Sherman, V.P., Personnel
Date: December 4, 198-
Subject: Minutes of meeting, December 3, 198-,
          1:00-3:00 P.M., Conference Room A

Present: Arthur_____, Bastin_____, Charmay_____,

         Fornier_____, Hightower_____, Kite_____,

         Seamans_____, Sherman_____.

Summary of Discussion:
    Item one General dissatisfaction with current procedures
    Item two Current recruiting is haphazard, directionless
    Item three Possible need to hire training director

Agreements Reached:
    1. Need for thorough review of recruiting techniques
    2. Possibility of a coordinated company-wide
       training program should be explored

Action Items:

Item No.	Action Item	Individual Responsible	Due Date
1.	Which college placement offices should be used	C.C. Charmay	Dec. 10, 198-
2.	Cost effectiveness of our classified ads; June 1 - December 1	T.T. Kite	Dec. 9, 198-
3.	Review of training policies of Martex, Kelly, and Blake companies.	B.A. Seamans	Dec. 10, 198-
4.			

Every meeting participant
should receive a
recapitulation or set of
minutes of the meeting.

normally should be in the hands of each participant within twenty-four hours of the meeting's conclusion. Obviously, if any participant feels corrections or additions are in order, he or she should let the meeting leader know. The leader then most probably will issue a corrected set of minutes.

The advantages of preparing and distributing a set of minutes are:

1. Everyone who attended the meeting receives the same set of minutes and thus the same set of perceptions of what took place. It avoids the comment, "But that isn't the way I heard the vote go." If the minutes need to be corrected, that can be done easily. In any event, the decisions reached are noted clearly and specifically.

2. Items to be investigated, researched, evaluated, or secured (action items) are clearly noted along with the individual's name who is responsible for completing the task. This avoids the argument: "But I didn't know *I* was supposed to obtain that information."

3. The minutes become a matter of record. They may be used for review by those who attended the meeting, for study by those who were absent, and for reference by those who may need the information months or years later.

The post-conference period is as important as the pre-meeting period and the actual conference. Completing a good job on it assures that the session is finished neatly.

Concluding Comments

Yes, there are problems when one calls a meeting. Yet, it is an extremely valuable communication device for motivating others through participatory management. The conference is an outstanding method for developing personnel, and it is an excellent forum for permitting and encouraging others to voice opinions and for keeping the lines of communication open.

MEMO

From: The Authors

To: Students

Subject: Interviews, meetings, and your career

Anyone who has ever looked for a job or who ever expects to look for a job realizes the importance of interviews to a successful job search. But there are many other kinds of interviews, and an ability to conduct *any* interview effectively will help to ensure success in your career.

In many organizations, poorly conducted meetings can cause a great deal of complaint and low employee morale. Your ability to hold effective meetings that get the job done with a minimum of fuss and bother will make you stand out as something special in the eyes of your employer.

Decision

Here is the agenda that Elisabeth Duncan prepared for the upcoming meeting on a company physical fitness program.

```
To:      _____
From:    _____
Date:    _____
Subject: _____


Topic for Discussion:
     Should the Trojan Corporation move into a company-wide physical fitness
     program?


Questions for Discussion:
     1.  Should this question be discussed in relationship to only a
         specific group or level of employees at Trojan or all employees?

     2.  Positive aspects of such a program.

     3.  Negative aspects of such a program.

     4.  Conducted by outside agency or Trojan?  On Trojan Corporation's or
         employees' time?

     5.  Impact on Trojan Corporation's Medical Department?  Insurance
         coverage?

     6.  Financial aspects of such a program?

     7.  Other factors.


Distribution List:

     _____      _____
     _____      _____
     _____      _____
     _____      _____
     _____      _____
```

CHAPTER REVIEW

Questions

1. Of the four elements of communication (reading, writing, speaking, and listening), which do you feel is most important in the interview and why?

2. Explain why almost every interview is a combination of two or more of the types listed in the text.

3. What factors should the interviewer keep in mind while conducting the interview? Briefly illustrate one of the factors.

4. What factors should the interviewer follow up on *after* the interview? Explain why it is important to do so.

5. Why is it a good idea for firms to have policies on meetings?

6. What factors should be considered in the premeeting period? Explain the rationale.

7. What specific value(s) does an agenda for meetings have?

8. Why is it wise to have a set of minutes or a recap sheet distributed to each participant after the meeting has been concluded? Explain why this just isn't adding more paper work when the goal is to decrease paper work.

9. For a meeting that you will attend, discuss the advantages and disadvantages of receiving the agenda as follows:
   a. You receive it one week prior to the meeting.
   b. You receive it three weeks prior to the meeting.
   c. It is handed to you as you walk into the meeting room five minutes before the meeting is ready to start.
   d. It is printed on the flip-chart pad in front of the room where the meeting will be held.

Exercises

1. a. Select two classmates; among the three of you, choose a position: manager, worker, and observer. Have the manager and worker conduct an interview concerning the latter's problem of excessive absenteeism from work and late arrival at the starting time. Except for these two faults, the worker maintains very high productivity on the job.

      At the conclusion of the interview, the observer should offer his constructive criticism.

   b. Switch roles and repeat the above.

2. Interview the personnel director of a local company. Inquire about the effects of the Equal Opportunity Employment regulations on the interviewing procedures followed by the company visited. What restrictions have these regulations placed on the hiring practices? Submit your findings to your instructor in a memo report format.

3. Select eleven individuals. Prepare all materials and hold a mock meeting on any one of the following topics:
   a. Should our *company* underwrite a physical fitness program for all employees?
   b. Should a committee from each class have input on the grade the instructor awards to each student in the class?
   c. What role, if any, should students play in the design of course content?
   d. Should a student committee determine the after-class assignment load?

Applications

1. You are an experienced employment interviewer for a utility company and have been asked to evaluate the mock interview just

completed by a newly hired employee in your department. The female applicant was applying for the job of typist-transcriber in the mock interview. Comment on the appropriateness of each of the following questions asked by your colleague in the mock interview:

a. Does your religion prohibit you from working on Saturday or Sunday?
b. What grades did you earn in your typewriting and business English classes in school?
c. Who will take care of your new baby?
d. Have you ever been arrested?
e. Why did you leave your last job?

2. Today, you will be conducting a meeting of department managers. Unfortunately, your secretary is ill and will not be available to take the minutes. Your colleague, George Bell, suggested using an available tape recorder instead. Another employee, Geraldine Kay, offered to ask her secretary to take the minutes. Evaluate these two suggestions and consider the advantages and disadvantages of using either one, or perhaps both of them.

3. Prepare an agenda for a committee meeting that you have been asked to chair. The student members of the committee were appointed by the Dean of Students who is unhappy about student apathy in getting involved in college extracurricular activities. In preparing the agenda, designate the date, time, and place of the meeting, and include a list of five to ten topics to be discussed by the committee members.

Readings in Communication

YOUR PERSONAL LISTENING PROFILE

The following questionnaire was prepared for the Sperry Corporation by Lyman K. Steil, Ph.D., chairman of the Speech Communication Division, Department of Rhetoric, at the University of Minnesota. Dr. Steil specializes in scientific research on listening and serves as a corporate consultant on listening programs.

HOW WELL DO YOU LISTEN? *(. . .A Personal Profile)*

Here are three tests in which we'll ask you to rate yourself as a listener. There are no correct or incorrect answers. Your responses, however, will extend your understanding of yourself as a listener. And highlight areas in which improvement might be welcome . . . to you and to those around you.

When you've completed the tests, please turn to page 388 to see how your scores compare with those of thousands of others who've taken the same tests before you.

QUIZ #1

A. Circle the term that best describes you as a listener.

Superior   Excellent   Above Average   (Average)   Below Average   Poor   Terrible

B. On a scale of 0–100 (100=highest), how would you rate yourself as a listener?

<u>   60   </u>
(0–100)

QUIZ #2

How do you think the following people would rate you as a listener?

<u>   </u>
(0–100)

Your Best Friend ___70___

Your Boss ___80___

Business Colleague ___75___

A Job Subordinate ___70___

Your Spouse _____

QUIZ #3

As a listener, how often do you find yourself engaging in these 10 bad listening habits? *First,* check the appropriate columns. *Then* tabulate your score using the key below.

Listening Habit	Almost Always	Usually	Some-times	Seldom	Almost Never	Score
1. Calling the subject uninteresting			✓			6
2. Criticizing the speaker's delivery or mannerisms					✓	10
3. Getting *over*-stimulated by something the speaker says					✓	10
4. Listening primarily for facts				✓		8
5. Trying to outline everything					✓	10
6. Faking attention to the speaker					✓	10
7. Allowing interfering distractions				✓		8
8. Avoiding difficult material			✓			6
9. Letting emotion-laden words arouse personal antagonism			✓			6
10. Wasting the advantage of thought speed (day-dreaming)				✓		8

TOTAL SCORE 82

Key
For every "Almost Always" checked, give yourself a score of   2
For every "Usually" checked, give yourself a score of   4
For every "Sometimes" checked, give yourself a score of   6
For every "Seldom" checked, give yourself a score of   8
For every "Almost Never" checked, give yourself a score of   10

PROFILE ANALYSIS

This is how other people have responded to the same questions that you've just answered.

QUIZ #1

A. 85% of all listeners questioned rate themselves as *Average* or less. Fewer than 5% rate themselves as Superior or Excellent.

B. On the 0–100 scale, the extreme range is 10–90; the general range is 35–85; and the *average rating* is 55.

QUIZ #2

When comparing the listening *self-ratings* and projected ratings of others, most respondents believe that their best friend would rate them highest as a listener. And that rating would be higher than the one they gave themselves in Quiz #1 . . . where the average was a 55.

How come? We can only guess that best-friend status is such an intimate, special kind of relationship that you can't imagine it ever happening unless you *were* a good listener. If you weren't, you and he or she wouldn't be best friends to begin with.

Going down the list, people who take this test usually think their bosses would rate them higher than they rated themselves. Now part of that is probably wishful thinking. And part of it is true. We *do* tend to listen to our bosses better . . . whether it's out of respect or fear or whatever doesn't matter.

The grades for colleague and job subordinate work out to be just about the same as the listener rated himself . . . that 55 figure again.

But when you get to spouse . . . husband or wife . . . something really dramatic happens. The score here is significantly lower than the 55 average that previous profile-takers gave themselves. And what's interesting is that the figure goes steadily downhill. While newlyweds tend to rate their spouse at the same high level as their best friend, as the marriage goes on . . . and on . . . the rating falls. So in a household where the couple has been married 50 years, there could be a lot of talk. But maybe nobody is *really* listening.

QUIZ #3

The average score is a 62 . . . 7 points higher than the 55 that the average test-taker gave himself in Quiz #1. Which suggests that when listening is broken down into specific areas of competence, we rate ourselves better than we do when listening is considered only as a generality.

Of course, the best way to discover how well you listen is to ask the people to whom you listen most frequently. Your spouse, boss, best friend, etc. They'll give you an earful.

10 KEYS TO EFFECTIVE LISTENING

These keys are a positive guideline to better listening. In fact, they're at the heart of developing better listening habits that could last a lifetime. [See page 389.]

FACTS ABOUT LISTENING

1. *First of all, you should know what we mean by "listening."*
It's more than just hearing. That's only the first part of listening . . . the physical part when your ears *sense* sound waves. There are three other parts equally important. There's the *interpretation* of what was heard that leads to understanding, or misunderstanding. Then comes the *evaluation* stage when you weigh the information and decide how you'll use it. Finally, based on what you heard and how you evaluated it, you *react*. That's listening.

10 Keys to Effective Listening	The Bad Listener	The Good Listener
1. Find areas of interest	Tunes out dry subjects	Opportunizes; asks "what's in it for me?"
2. Judge content, not delivery	Tunes out if delivery is poor	Judges content, skips over delivery errors
3. Hold your fire	Tends to enter into argument	Doesn't judge until comprehension complete
4. Listen for ideas	Listens for facts	Listens for central themes
5. Be flexible	Takes intensive notes using only one system	Takes fewer notes. Uses 4–5 different systems, depending on speaker
6. Work at listening	Shows no energy output. Attention is faked	Works hard, exhibits active body state
7. Resist distractions	Distracted easily	Fights or avoids distractions, tolerates bad habits, knows how to concentrate
8. Exercise your mind	Resists difficult expository material; seeks light, recreational material	Uses heavier material as exercise for the mind
9. Keep your mind open	Reacts to emotional words	Interprets color words; does not get hung up on them
10. Capitalize on fact, *thought* is *faster* than speech	Tends to daydream with slow speakers	Challenges, anticipates, mentally summarizes, weighs the evidence, listens between the lines to tone of voice

2. *Before we can become good listeners, it helps to know why people talk to each other.*

There are four basic types of verbal communication. There's the "getting-to-know-you" or the "building of relationships" kind of talk which is called *phatic* communication. Next, there's *cathartic* communication which allows the release of pent-up emotion and often amounts to one person spilling his or her troubles on concerned, caring ears. Then there's *informative* communication in which ideas, data or information is shared. Last of all is *persuasive* communication where the purpose is to reinforce or change attitudes or to produce action.

3. *Listening is our primary communication activity.*

Studies show that we spend about 80% of our waking hours communicating. And, according to research, at least 45% of that time is spent listening. In schools, students spend 60%–70% of their classroom time engaged in listening. And in business, listening has often been cited as being the most critical managerial skill.

4. *Our listening habits are not the result of training but rather the result of the lack of it.*

The chart shows the order in which the four basic communication skills are learned, the degree to which they are used and the extent to which they are taught. Listening is the communication skill used most but taught least. [See chart at bottom of the page.]

5. *Most individuals are inefficient listeners*

Tests have shown that immediately after listening to a 10-minute oral presentation, the *average* listener has heard, understood, properly evaluated and retained approximately half of what was said. And within 48 hours, that drops off another 50% to a final 25% level of effectiveness. In other words, we quite often comprehend and retain only one-quarter of what is said.

6. *Inefficient and ineffective listening is extraordinarily costly.*

With more than 100 million workers in America, a simple ten-dollar listening mistake by each of them would cost a billion dollars. Letters have to be retyped; appointments rescheduled; shipments reshipped. And when people in large corporations fail to listen to one another, the results are even costlier. Ideas get distorted by as much as 80% as they travel through the chain of command. Employees feel more and more distant, and ultimately alienated, from top management.

7. *Good listening can be taught.*

In the few schools where listening programs have been adopted, listening comprehension among students has as much as doubled in just a few months.

And a final word about listening.
We at Sperry feel strongly that listening is an important . . . and often neglected . . . communication skill.

Listening is just as active as talking, although most people believe the primary responsibility for good communication rests with the speaker. But think how much better we could communicate if both the listener and the speaker took at least 51% of the responsibility for successful communications!

	Listening	Speaking	Reading	Writing
Learned	1st	2nd	3rd	4th
Used	Most (45%)	Next Most (30%)	Next Least (16%)	Least (9%)
Taught	Least	Next Least	Next Most	Most

YOU AND YOUR TELEPHONE

New York Telephone Company

The following article was a service message of the New York Telephone Company, designed to help the company's customers use that indispensable instrument to their own best advantage. Although it was written a number of years ago, when all secretaries and switchboard operators were women and all business executives—as well as all telephone linemen—were men, and there weren't even any pushbutton telephones, its advice is still valid.

"Oh yes, I know the company well. That's a good outfit to do business with—I've talked with them by telephone."

With people whose business starts and ends over the telephone that kind of recognition builds reputations.

When you talk on the telephone you become a public relations committee of one. Every time you pick up the telephone, you make a definite impression—good, bad, or indifferent—on the person at the other end of the line. Your voice, what you say and how you say it, is what reveals you to others. A pleasant personality is like a share of stock, and a cordial voice pays dividends.

The art of getting results by telephone—meriting good will, having people enjoy telephoning you—is largely a matter of dealing with others as you would have them deal with you. "Phone as you would be phoned to," is the way one successful salesman put it.

This booklet outlines methods of applying that principle.

Phone as you would be phoned to

The telephone provides communication by voice—the natural and quickest way of making your thoughts and personality known to others. You like to deal by telephone with people whose voices and telephone manners show them to be courteous, interested and alert.

Business people have become keenly aware of the value of good telephone habits. One company tells its employees, "The telephone, if properly used, will foster a spirit of friendliness within and toward our organization."

In a newspaper article which carried the headline "Pleasing Voice Now An Important Business Asset," correct telephone speech and cordial manner are rated *the foremost requirement* of employees who have telephone contacts with customers.

Charm schools now stress a pleasant speaking voice as one of the first requisites of natural poise.

It *pays* to have a good telephone personality. Whether you are an executive, secretary, switchboard attendant, salesman, clerk, or in some other position where you deal with people, success depends largely upon how you treat customers, make friends, create good will.

The voice with a smile

If you were able to call yourself up, do you think you would be satisfied with what you hear?

If not, it's high time for you to try to improve your telephone personality.

If you train yourself to speak clearly and distinctly, you can make a good impression from that one feature alone.

You'll want to study your voice and speech.

Think about using *the voice with a smile* and putting it to work effectively every time you make or answer a call.

Are your callers welcomed?

Do you want to hear how those voices at the office sound to others? Just call up your headquarters once in a while and listen with an attentive ear to the kind of welcome you get. If you were the head of the business, you'd find it helpful to rate the voices representing *you*. For instance, are they: Pleasing? or Curt? Helpful? or Indifferent?

If you are aware of the importance of a good *telephone reputation,* you'll be pleased and rewarded with the results. Your callers will too.

Let's look at some of the specific situations in telephoning.

How to meet your caller

Never underestimate the power of a first impression. Remember you don't know who's calling. It may be one of the company's best clients, a prospective customer "shopping around," or a good friend. You'll want to make sure callers feel they are welcome—as you would if you met them face-to-face.

The welcome you offer is the promptness and pleasantness of your answer, the friendly attitude shown in your first greeting, even before you know who your caller is. This is good business. Time and again it actually determines the attitude of the caller and assures an agreeable tone to the interview.

People don't like to be kept waiting. Some of your callers may grow impatient with a delayed answer, and give their business to firms who will answer more promptly.

It's an interesting fact that a minute, while talking, flits by in no time at all, but those 60 seconds, while waiting, seem agonizingly long.

Get right to the point

When you answer, don't use such old-fashioned and time consuming words as "Hello" and "Yes?" The best way to answer is to identify yourself with your name, your company, department, or your telephone number—or combinations of these—depending upon what will be most helpful to the person calling:

"Mr. Brown," or "Brown" ("Mr." is optional).
"Duane Roberts and Company."
"Phillips Brothers, Mr. Johnson."
"Rug Department, Mr. O'Brien."
"MUrray Hill 4-9970."

Much can be accomplished simply by the tone of these few words of identification. The important welcome is conveyed by a tone of helpful cordial interest. A slightly rising inflection will imply "May I help you?" without actually saying the words.

The person calling responds by identifying himself. The conversation can then proceed with no time wasted on annoying questions like, "Who's this?" or "What company do you represent?"

Suppose you are answering someone else's telephone or a firm telephone. You'd want to say:

"Mr. Brown's office, Miss Smith."
"Phillips Brothers, Mr. Johnson."

Some facts about tact

When you answer another's telephone, it's often wise to find out who's calling—if the caller does not identify himself. The best way to do this, without appearing inquisitive and to make it clear that the information is for the other person, is to ask a question like this:

"May I tell him who's calling?"

Very often the person called may be talking on another extension or be busy with other pressing office business. At such times, steer clear of such remarks as: "Mr. Brown is busy right now." You'll earn a better response if you say:

"I'm sorry but Mr. Brown is talking on another extension. May I take a message for him, please?"

"Mr. Brown is at a meeting this morning. I'll have him call you as soon as possible."

This method indicates your willingness to serve. Incidentally, whenever you take a message for someone, be sure to write it down and leave it where the right person will see it.

Occasionally, when you answer your telephone, the caller may not give his name. If that's the way he wants it, don't make an issue of it. He'll call again if it's important. Avoid abrupt questions like: "Who are you?"

Phrasing of a question can change it from one that may be resented to one that is willingly answered.

"May I ask who's calling, please?"

Attending another's calls

If you are employed by a firm which has its telephones served by a private switchboard, remember that being transferred from one telephone to another is annoying to the person calling. No one likes to repeat the same message to several different people before reaching the one who can take care of him. If you can attend to a call yourself satisfactorily, always do so instead of transferring it. If this is not possible there are ways to handle it:

(1) You should offer to transfer the calling party to someone who can take care of him.

"I'm sorry, but I don't have that particular information. Our credit department is familiar with that problem. May I transfer you?"

(2) You may say that you'll refer the matter to the proper person. In some cases you will want to indicate that the proper person will call back. For instance:

"You want Mr. Brown's department. Shall I have him call you?"

When transferring calls be sure that the caller knows what you're doing. Signal the switchboard attendant *slowly* to get her attention. Explain the situation to her so she will not have to ask the person calling to repeat.

This saves time and assures the caller that he is getting courteous and efficient treatment.

"Will you please transfer this call to Mr. Brown in the credit department?" (Or use extension, if known.)

Wait for the attendant's reply to make sure she understands you.

Earning your welcome

Up until now you've been on the receiving end of a call. Now let's put you on the other end of the line. The situation is reversed, but the courtesy doesn't change. Your first job is to make a good impression to earn that welcoming answer.

Your self-introduction must be effective. You are the caller. You are in the position of wanting something or selling something. In either case, your success will be spurred by genuine, well-expressed courtesy.

If you're doing your job, you'll make every second count in your introduction.

Promptly give your own name and firm:

"This is Mr. Wood of Curtis and Sons."

If the one who answers the telephone is not the person you want, or does not identify himself, ask politely for that person.

"May I speak to Mr. Baker, please?"

If you're not interested in any particular person, simply state your wishes in a cordial way in the form of a request.

"The accounting department, please."

Incidentally, it's always helpful to speak politely to switchboard attendants, secretaries, and others upon whom you depend for further assistance. They—like everyone else—respond to *the voice with a smile.*

Bad impressions

Perhaps you've had this experience—and annoyance. Your telephone rings. You answer, and a secretary's voice says, "Just a moment, please, Mr. Jones would like to talk to you." Then a wait. Finally, long lost Mr. Jones comes to the telephone.

Presumably Mr. Jones is busy and thinks he can save time by telling his secretary to get you on the telephone and then call him back. But he somehow forgets that he is the one who asks the favor of your time. Actually he *requires* you to waste your time, waiting for him.

Always being ready at the telephone, ready to greet the called person when he answers is the courteous way to telephone. It reflects favorably on you and your company.

A busy executive said recently: "My time is precious. The time of the people with whom I usually talk is just as valuable. They don't like to have me keep them waiting and I share the sentiment when the situation is reversed. So the only sensible and fair thing is to be at my best, ready for the answer of the person I'm calling."

Conversation accessories

Few things sour a pleasant telephone conversation more than unnecessarily excusing yourself from your caller. Always have a pencil and paper within arm's reach of your telephone. If you have to get some business records on file, first request permission from your caller and explain what you are going to do. Make it a point to justify your absence with:

"I'll check our files. Would you hold the line a moment, please?"

"Will you wait, please. I'll check our records."

When returning to the telephone, if there has been some delay in doing so, apologize for it and thank your caller for waiting. Add a few words of explanation if it seems necessary.

In some instances, it might require considerable time to get the information or to take required action. If so, offer to call back.

"I'm sorry but it may take some time to get that information. I'll be glad to call you back in an hour."

Absence without leave

When you expect to be away from your telephone, it's a good plan to leave word where you are going and how you can be reached — with the telephone number and extension — and when you will return. This is especially advisable if those who answer the telephone in your absence are not qualified to speak for you.

Sorry — wrong number

Nobody likes wrong numbers. To operators they mean work to be done over again, work that could be devoted to handling another call. To the dial apparatus it means machinery that could be occupied with someone's "right" number. Everything possible is constantly being done by your telephone company to reduce the number of wrong connections.

Telephone users can help greatly by pronouncing telephone numbers distinctly, by dialing carefully and by obtaining telephone numbers from directories, private lists and letterheads, rather than trusting to memory. Keep your own personal list of telephone numbers.

When you are called by mistake, be quick to correct the person calling to avoid a prolonged waste of time on both ends of the line. A smart way to do this is to reply:

"I'm sorry, but this is not *Phillips Brothers*."

Tell the caller politely that he has the wrong number or extension.

If you sense you've reached the wrong number, verify it immediately. Don't say, "What's your number?" or "Who are you?"

If it's evident that some error has been made, express regret in some way, even if you were not responsible:

"I'm sorry. Please excuse it."

Easy does it

When you have finished your visit, replace the telephone gently. Slamming it might cause a sharp crack in the ear of the person with whom you have been talking. All the personality pluses you have chalked up during a telephone conversation can be erased by such carelessness. Since you wouldn't slam the door after a face-to-face visit, be just as mindful in closing your "telephone door."

There's a method to good manners

People like to be addressed by their names, together with titles when appropriate. In your conversations, sound the personal as well as the courteous note. Time-honored expressions of consideration, like "Thank you," "I'm sorry" and "I beg your pardon" are jewels when properly used in the art of making good impressions. So are such things as letting the other person finish what he has to say without interruption, avoiding argument or signs of impatience.

As to other details, such as the general character of your speech—the avoidance of slangy and careless expressions, and the use of good English—they are matters for each person to decide for himself. The most effective speech is correct speech, natural and unaffected. The best manners are those which are in good taste and prompted by a genuine consideration for others.

Your telephone number

Your telephone number is as vital as your calling card. It should be featured as prominently as your address, on your business stationery, on billheads, promotional booklets, folders and in newspaper and other advertising.

Your telephone number is needed by the reader of your letter or advertising material, when he has the impulse to reach for the telephone.

For your own convenience you should keep a list of the telephone numbers you often call.

A partner—yours for success

Your success by telephone takes thoughtful effort and intelligent observance of certain basic principles. It also takes a lot of *common sense* to develop a pleasant telephone attitude.

Keeping these factors in mind, make your telephone a "junior partner" in your business activities. It's a small investment, and the returns are big.

Part V
Communication in Action: Getting a Job

Dilemma

Marcia Goldberg has grown up hearing about the health care field. Her father is a pharmacist, her mother is a pediatrician, and her brother is now in his last year of dental school.

Marcia will be completing her second year of junior college in just three months. She wants to work this summer and then transfer to the four-year state university in the fall. Ideally, she'd like to find a summer job in the health care field.

When the school placement director asked to see her resumé, Marcia was flustered. "I haven't got one!" she said. Yet Marcia has a good background: she has held three part-time jobs, taught Sunday School, served as a volunteer for two summers at a camp for deaf children, acted as assistant editor of the college newspaper, received several awards, plays the piano, and worked as a "candy striper" for two years at a local hospital.

But how to organize all this material? The school placement director has suggested to Marcia that the first step in putting together an effective resumé is to draw up a personal background inventory. The inventory should list Marcia's objective, the jobs she has held, awards received, education, and special talents and interests.

Decision, see page 407

The Right Job for You 20

Here is a list of the objectives you should understand by the time you complete this chapter. Place a check mark in the box beside each as soon as you feel ready to apply your understanding in a practical situation.

☐ The need for detailed planning prior to your job search

☐ The various personal qualities about yourself that you must know well before beginning your job search
    Physical
    Intellectual
    Personality

☐ Your attitudes toward various aspects of all jobs

☐ Various formal sources of job information
    Classified advertisements
    Employment agencies
    Books and other reference sources

☐ Various informal sources of job information

There are two items you should have a great deal of information on *before* you start to think about employment: you and the job. When you really know yourself and have a clear understanding of the kind of job you want, you are better equipped to bring about a successful work relationship. If, on the other hand, you misjudge yourself and your attributes, and you aren't sure of the duties of a particular position, you may place yourself in a situation that is not good for you or your employer.

When you consider the time you spend on the job, it involves more hours during the day than any other single activity in life. Therefore, it is vitally important that you find the right job for yourself.

Plan for your job.

Today we often hear how unhappy many people are with their jobs. There are estimates that at least 20 percent or more of the full-time work force are disgruntled about their positions. Therefore, it is important for you to take a wise and thoughtful first step in order to gain pleasant and satisfying employment for the many work years ahead of you.

One reason many people may not be pleased with their jobs is that they are poor planners. They left the choice of the job until the last minute and took the wrong position for their talents and objectives. Thus, before you seek employment—by sending resumés, completing application forms, interviewing—you should have a clear understanding of yourself, the job requirements, and the employment climate into which you are going. With this understanding, you can make a better job decision. Here are several suggestions which will assist you in securing the right job.

Assess yourself and your job wants honestly.

Think Job . . . Now

Think carefully about the type of job you want.

Years ago individuals joined the job market in their teens. A specified job was identified early and obtained. Or a son or daughter followed in a parent's footsteps. Today, people are finding full-time employment at a later age; there are infinitely more fields, and consequently more job titles available. Just think of the many new areas in health care, electronics, communication technology, management information systems, computers, transportation, and so on, that are available today that were not a generation ago.

It is because of these many opportunities that the problem of job selection has arisen. If you are one of those students who still aren't sure about "what I'm going to do when I enter the job market," don't worry. Of course it's frustrating and a bit frightening when four of your friends know exactly what they are going to do, when, and how . . . and you don't. Just think of the situation as an opportunity to determine where you are going. This you can achieve when you know yourself and the job you want.

If you are in a quandary about the job you want, you may wish to review the following:

If You Don't Know Where You're Going You'll Probably End Up Somewhere Else, by David Campbell (Argus Communications, 1974).

The author provides various ways to rate your abilities and relate your skills to jobs.

College to Career: Finding Yourself in the Job Market, by John Shingleton and Robert Bao (McGraw-Hill, 1977). The book is aimed at college students who are seeking to better understand themselves.

The Career Game, by Charles G. Moore (National Institute of Career Planning, 1976). Moore emphasizes how people can select a career that is best suited for them.

There are many reference sources which will help you decide on a job or a career.

On Your Own, by Kathy Matthews (Vintage Books, 1977). The author explains more than 100 jobs designed for people who don't want to work for someone else but are interested in their own businesses.

Working, by Studs Terkel (Avon Books, 1975). Terkel indicates how one's job is part of one's life; he emphasizes the importance of getting jobs that permit individuals to feel good about themselves.

These sources will help you to develop a realistic and practical individual audit of your abilities, wants, and aspirations. In addition, you will want to carry through the individual and job audits suggested below.

The Individual Audit

It is not selfish for you to think first about yourself when considering your future job. If you know what you want and need in a job, and you can obtain them, then your relationships with your employer, your family, and your friends will probably be satisfying because of your own contentment.[1]

For your job, you are #1.

Take a few moments and become familiar with the primary communicator in your job search—*you.* This self-analysis will aid you in discovering your *traits,* your *strengths,* and your *weaknesses.* Think about what it is that you have to offer the potential employer and what it is you like and what you dislike in a job. What are you specifically qualified to do? Writing these down, even in the form of lists, will help you inventory yourself.

Review your own attributes to discover your assets and liabilities.

The specific qualities of people can be placed into three basic trait categories: physical traits, intelligence traits, and personality traits. Different kinds of employment call for people with different traits.

There are three basic trait categories.

Perhaps like the computer dating analysis, it is necessary for you to match your individual traits with the characteristics that go with a particular job. If your traits do not fit a specific job, it does not mean you are a failure. It just means that you need to select a type of employment that calls for the traits you possess.

Match your personality traits with a job's demands

[1] A very valuable article that will help you in your self-assessment and job evaluation is "How to be an Employee" by Peter Drucker, reprinted in the *Readings on Communication* on pp. 453–460 of this text.

For example, an individual notes his or her traits as follows:

Physical
    Excellent coordination
    Good health, but needs nine hours of sleep each night
    Chronic asthma
Intelligence
    Average IQ
    Doesn't like to read a great deal
    Enjoys meticulous work
Personality
    Prefers to work alone
    Does not make "small talk" easily

It is not necessary to make a value judgment as to whether those traits are good or bad. But it can be helpful to recognize honestly your traits and attempt to match them with a job you want.

The individual with the traits cited above is not going to be able to perform or enjoy a job that calls for locating in a smoggy metropolitan area, working odd hours day and night, reading volumes of material, and interacting constantly with fellow workers. But the traits listed might match very well with jobs that call for independent work, a steady work day, and intricate types of activities.

Before you ask an employer to hire you — make sure you know yourself and your work-related interests. You should also ask yourself how you feel about:

Determine your own requirements for a job.

1. The size of the organization: do you prefer working in a large or in a small organization? Would you prefer being a small fish in a big pond, or would you like to become a big fish in a small pond?
2. What are your salary needs? Now? In the future?
3. How do you feel about the length of the working day? Overtime?
4. How do you feel about evening and weekend assignments?
5. Travel? How frequent?
6. Company dress regulations?
7. Fringe benefits offered?
8. Time spent in commuting?
9. Opportunities for advancement?
10. Types of people you like to work with?
11. Potential for transfer to other cities?
12. Level of job security offered?

Although all these are not involved directly in the job, they are items better thought about first and then discussed at the interview rather than after the job has been accepted. There is no point in locking yourself into a job that you will keep for only a few months . . . and being unhappy with in the bargain.

The Job Audit

It is good to know yourself; but when considering employment, you do not operate in isolation. It is necessary to know and to understand the job marketplace as well as the requirements of specific jobs.

The job market depends upon many things, such as the nature of the economy, the number of people employed, the number of people in the job you want, the forecast for economic growth, and the changes in technology. With many factors influencing the job market, there are many excuses available to people who cannot find the job they want. But, with careful preparation and planning, there are no valid excuses for not landing a job. There are many opportunities for matching your qualifications with the wants of a prospective employer.

Why is *who* and not *whom* used here? (See Appendix 1.)

Again, planning must be emphasized. It is estimated that about 90 percent of college students get jobs. But, almost one-fourth of them do not get the jobs they want. To avoid becoming one of the unhappy 25 percent, it is necessary to look at employment opportunities, your traits, and job requirements as early as possible.

The problem is getting the job you *want*.

In the initial job search, exactness is necessary. Remember, there are thousands of exact job titles. Your chance of getting the right job is increased if you are very clear in identifying the job you want. When seeking employment and advancement, vagueness is not a virtue.

Name your job specifically.

The *Occupational Outlook Handbook* (U.S. Bureau of Labor Statistics, U.S. Government Printing Office) and the *Dictionary of Occupational Titles* (U.S. Department of Labor, U.S. Government Printing Office) list thousands of exact job titles. Review these titles or a similar list. Remember, employers rarely hire just managers, technicians, administrators, or other generalists. The employer hires a person for an exact job; for example:

garage mechanic;
assistant editor, company magazine;
keypunch operator;
training coordinator, shop personnel;
production coordinator, plastic housewares;
dental laboratory technician;
assistant buyer, men's wear;
legal secretary.

Once you have the job title, determine the specific skills needed, the responsibilities attached, and the duties involved.

Speak to friends in specific areas. Question your instructors. What are the duties of this specific position? That particular job? What tasks are involved? How much responsibility is attached? What does the job pay? What future does it hold?

Where Are the Jobs?

Is your job available?

Lists are published each year that report the current and future status of various jobs. Reviewing these lists provides you with a good start in attempting to understand the nation's future employment needs. For instance, in the 1980s and probably for the remainder of the century, Kiplinger and Ford Motor suggest that there are expected to be many job opportunities in the following job categories:

accountant/bookkeeper;
computer programmer;
dietician;
health services administrator;
insurance actuary;
management trainee;
occupational therapist;
public relations copywriter;
social worker.

Formal Sources of Job Information

Check current information sources; there are many that can lead to excellent jobs.

Your local newspaper, state employment agency, and private employment firms are places to learn about job opportunities. In addition, very valuable sources are colleges and university placement offices that work closely with students and alumni in obtaining employment.

Read classified ads with care.

When you read the classified ads, examine them with care. Don't be taken in by the ad that promises "a minimum of $50,000 each year for the right person" but goes on to describe in vague terms the job requirements. Such ads often are designed to have you come in and work on a straight commission basis selling items to a very limited market.

Choose the ad that carefully lists the specific qualifications needed and says something about what the organization has to offer. In selecting ads to reply to, shoot a little high. Answer those that will require you to stretch a little to do a good job. On the other hand, if you are twenty-one years old, and have only part-time experience, don't waste your time (and the employer's) replying to an advertisement that calls for " . . . a minimum of ten years' experience as a financial officer for a major corporation . . . salary to $60,000 based on qualifications."

Why is the apostrophe after the *s* in *years'*? (See Appendix 1.)

Use employment agencies with caution.

Employment agencies can be helpful. On the other hand, be careful what agreements you sign and what arrangements you make. Many agencies charge the applicant no fee but do bill the firm. In other cases, the applicant is charged. Certainly there are many excellent agencies. However, few can do a better job in writing a resumé for you than you can. There is no magic to composing a good resumé. All that is required is knowledge and hard work. This knowledge you can find in this chapter and the next. The hard work you must supply.

Other useful places to gain clues about job openings are Northwestern University's annual Endicott report and books such as *Who's Hiring Who* by Richard Lathrop (Ten Speed Press, 1977), *The Uncle Sam Connection* by James Hawkins (Follett Publishing Co., 1978), and *Guerrilla Tactics in the Job Market* by Tom Jackson (Bantam Books, 1978).

Additional sources that are published in a recurring sequence are:

1. *National Business Employment Weekly.* Published each Sunday by *The Wall Street Journal,* the tabloid contains career-advancement positions in organizations throughout the nation. The jobs listed in the weekly are not available in any regional edition or single issue of the *TWSJ.* The publication is available by subscription or on newsstands.
2. *Occupational Outlook for College Graduates.* This is published periodically by the Government Printing Office and contains employment information on jobs for which some education beyond high school is needed.
3. *Occupational Outlook Handbook.* This book is published frequently by the Government Printing Office and highlights the employment outlook for about 300 occupations in thirty-five industries.
4. *The Encyclopedia of Associations.* Available in most libraries, this book lists trade associations and organizations. These groups can provide up-to-date information on the job outlook in their fields.
5. *College Placement Annual.* Produced annually, the directory contains career information supplied by about one thousand employers. The *Annual* is published by the College Placement Council and is generally available free of charge at all college placement offices.

Informal Sources of Job Information

There are also numerous informal sources of information available about the job market. Some are in published form and others involve interacting with people. Do not overlook the informal sources of job information such as talk-

Talk with people who are working; sometimes they are good leads for jobs.

ing with your instructors, meeting with employers that come to your campus, and calling former students who have gotten jobs. In looking for a position that will afford a good income in satisfactory surroundings, you are playing for high stakes involving your future happiness. Use every possible source for your benefit.

Concluding Comments

Finding the right job, but finding it a month after someone else has been hired is frustrating. Planning ahead is becoming increasingly vital to college-aged job seekers.

The nature of recruiting and the length of the employers' recruiting year have changed substantially since 1975. Prior to that time, employers often hired graduating students in the spring to begin work in June. Companies are now making offers in the late fall and early winter, a full six to eight months prior to starting the job. Today, those students who wait until spring to find a job that begins in June may find that many organizations will have already filled their available positions.

For a variety of reasons, the old May and June hiring time has been pushed back in the year considerably. This is especially the situation with managerial-type positions. If you truly want to find the right job, your chances are increased significantly by starting the job search well in advance of college graduation.

MEMO

To: Students
From: The Authors
Subject: The right job for you

For many students, the toughest stage in the job hunt is deciding exactly what kind of job they want. You can make this decision easier by first looking closely at *yourself*—your likes and dislikes, your talents and interests, and the particular aspects of a job (salary, travel, organization size, formality, and so on) that are important to you. Once you've done this, you will be prepared to look closely at the kinds of jobs available in order to find those best suited to your particular preferences. This kind of fit between your personality and the "personality" of the job can be the key to your long-term satisfaction in your chosen career.

Decision

Here is the personal background inventory Marcia Goldberg put together to help herself find a job.

<u>Personal Background Inventory: Marcia Goldberg</u>

Career Objective: Professional participation in the health-care field

Education: Completed high school, science major
                       Completed junior college (two years);
                       introductory courses with science electives

Experience: Sales clerk, Fohrman's Department Store
                       September 1980 to June 1981 (evenings and Saturdays)

                       Clerk, Ice Cream Igloo
                       Christmas season 1979

                       Information receptionist, Conover Community Hospital
                       Summer 1981

                       Camp counselor, Conover Camp (for deaf children)
                       Summer 1980 and summer 1981

                       Assistant editor, Conover Community College Newspaper
                       1981

                       Teaching assistant, Jewish Community Center Sunday
                       School, January-May 1980

                       "Candy striper," Conover Community Hospital
                       Weekends 1979-1981

Awards: Academic Torch Award, Conover High School
                       Dean's List, Conover Community College, 1980
                       Counselor of the year at Conover Camp

Personal Attributes: Plays piano
                       Likes people
                       Gets along well with others
                       Appreciates responsibility
                       Excellent health

Education areas
  enjoyed: Biology, Science

Vocational areas
  enjoyed: Health care, music

References: Ms. Phyllis Carleton, R.N., (work)
                       Mr. Albert Fohrman, (work)
                       Dr. Robert Fisher, (academic)
                       Dr. Mervyn Morter, (academic)
                       Judge Harry Volpon, (personal)

CHAPTER REVIEW

Questions

1. Compare the advantages and disadvantages to the job applicant of these types of employment ads:

   a. An ad for a "fee paid by company" job placed by an employment agency.

   b. An ad placed by the company soliciting the applicant and listing the name and address of the company.

   c. An ad for which the fee is not paid by the company. The ad was placed by an employment agency.

   d. An ad placed by the company, but the name of the company is missing and the only address given is a post-office box number.

2. Why is it so vital for us to *plan* for our jobs?

3. Are you going to look for a job in which you are a "little fish in a big pond" or a "big fish in a little pond"? Why? What are the advantages and disadvantages of each situation?

Exercises

1. Prepare a self-analysis audit of what you have to offer as a job applicant. Divide your analysis into logical categories.

2. Read the classified advertisements carefully and then select three ads to which you feel qualified to respond. Attach those three to a sheet of paper, and then indicate *why* you feel one of those would be your first choice to respond to.

3. Select ten entry-level classified ads from your Sunday newspaper in the career field of your choice. Examine each ad to see the precise skills requested by the advertiser. Compile a list of the skills and indicate them in rank order according to the number of ads mentioning them.

4. Visit your college placement office and interview a placement counselor. Inquire about the number and types of jobs available to students graduating in your major. Ask for suggestions on how to enhance your chances of securing employment. Report your findings orally or in writing as assigned by your instructor.

5. In this chapter pages 400–401, five books are mentioned that might be helpful in selecting a career and a job. Refer to one of these books or any other book available to you on this topic. Search for some new and different ideas relating to the job search that had not occurred to you previously. In memo-report format, communicate these new ideas to your instructor.

6. Interview two people, one male and one female, who appear to have successful careers in the field of your choice. Ask them seven to ten questions relating to their education, reason for choosing the field, responsibilities of their position, and any other topics that interest you. Convert the information you received from the interviews into a short oral presentation. In your speech, you will want to convey the differences and similarities of the responses given by the interviewees.

7. Refer to a copy of the *Encyclopedia of Associations* in your college library. Choose the names and addresses of two or three associations involved in your chosen career field. Write a letter of inquiry to them asking several questions about the opportunities and other particulars pertaining to your field.

Application

1. Barbara Jenson will graduate from a local community college in May with an Associate Degree in Management. She is interested in full-time employment. She wants to use every method at her disposal to find out about exist-ing opportunities for which she is qualified. Prepare a list of sources not cited in the text that she could tap for information on job openings.

Dilemma

Marcia's search for a summer job in the health care field did not go well at first. It seemed that nearly all the jobs available required more experience than Marcia had or else wanted someone who would continue to work year-round.

But one day, just as she was about to close her local newspaper in frustration, something caught Marcia's eye. A small "Help Wanted" advertisement seemed to have slipped into the "Musical Instruments for Sale" section. The ad read as follows:

> BRIGHT, ENERGETIC YOUNG PERSON wanted to work as assistant to health director at Sunnybrook Home for the Aged. Summer only. Some health care experience preferred. Send resumé to Health Director, Sunnybrook Home, 6 Plover Road, Conover, Ohio 23546.

Using the background inventory she has already written, Marcia now wants to put together an effective resumé. She feels that if she can customize her resumé to fit the job for which she is applying, she will have a better chance of obtaining an interview.

Decision, see page 426

Effective Resumés

Here is a list of the objectives you should understand by the time you complete this chapter. Place a check mark in the box beside each as soon as you feel ready to apply your understanding in a practical situation.

☐ Procedures for making up a data sheet to help organize your selling points

☐ The purpose of a resumé in securing you a job

☐ The seven basic sections of most resumés and the contents of each
Career Objective
Major Qualifications
Education
Experience
Activities and Interests
Personal Data
References

☐ Techniques for shortening an overlong resumé
Page reduction
Change of format

Perhaps you are now holding or have held a full-time job. Perhaps it was obtained through a family member or a friend. Or maybe the extent of your employment has been a part-time position. Whatever the situation *has* been, let us assume you are now going to plunge into the job market seriously.

Your future income depends on the position you select. How well you and your family will live is related directly to your job: whether you will be able to afford one car or two; a weekend out of town, or a month on the beach of Hawaii; a one-bedroom apartment or a three-thousand-square foot home. But even more than the income from the job, you are interested in the satisfaction you will have.

For these reasons, and dozens more, you want to secure the best position possible from the point of view of challenge, growth, advancement, satisfaction, and income. But it does take effort that only you can supply.

Whether you decide to seek a job through the mail, on recommendation of others, or through cold calls on companies, you should prepare a resumé. That process of preparation will force you carefully to consider exactly what major and minor qualifications you have to offer a prospective employer.

Organizing Information

The data sheet is a valuable device for obtaining a self-inventory of qualifications.

Prior to making up the formal resumé, many individuals find it very helpful to first organize their marketable qualities. This data collection may then be set down on a data sheet. Usually the data sheet is divided into four broad categories: education, experience, personal, and references. Each of these, in turn, can be subdivided:

Education
    Schools attended and dates
    Academic major
    Certificates and licenses
    Grade point average(s)
    Honors, awards, scholarships (if name of award does not describe it, explain in a brief phrase)
    Extracurricular activities
    Amount of educational expenses earned

Experience
    Jobs held (that relate to the desired employment) and the responsibilities of the job
    Jobs held (that do not relate to desired employment)
    Volunteer activities that provided experience (leadership, responsibility, group interaction)

Personal
    Age
    Marital status

Health
Travel desires (geographical location preferred)

References
    Professional references
    Educational references
    Personal references

The data sheet can be used in making an inventory of what you have to offer. It is a way to gather and organize facts and have them readily at hand. In preparing the data sheet, you don't have to be selective; this preparation is a means to pull together the information that can be strategically used for letters, interviews, resumés, and application forms.

Now that you have your inventory, you can turn to the preparation of the piece of communication which will be submitted to the potential employer: the resumé.

The Purpose of the Resumé

The resumé is a detailed statement that neatly, precisely, and clearly provides a potential employer with a quick, convenient, and favorable overview of you and your job qualifications. In a limited amount of space, you attempt to represent yourself in the way that you want the receiver to see you.

The resumé provides the potential employer with a summary of your qualifications.

As you begin to prepare your resumé, always keep in mind that the resumé is a piece of sales literature. It represents a very important commodity—*you*. In one or two neatly typewritten pages, it presents a clear and well-organized statement of your abilities, qualities, accomplishments, and job aspirations. The subject—you—is interesting and complex, and therefore you want to represent yourself in the best light possible.

Resumés reflect, to a degree, our society and its emphases. Therefore, what is to be included in a resumé, or excluded, changes from time to time. For instance, prior to the anti-discrimination legislation of the 1960s and 1970s, the first item generally addressed in a resumé was one's personal characteristics. Today, some authorities recommend that the personal items be left off completely. In the 1980s, the trend seems to be to emphasize the applicant's career objectives and factual qualifications for the job; there is a lessening emphasis on personal characteristics (height, weight, physical condition, sex, health, and marital status.)

Why use the word *emphases* and not *emphasis*? (See Appendix 1.)

What is the difference in meaning between *martial, marital,* and *marshall*? (See Appendix 1.)

Format and Length

As the examples in this chapter indicate, there are various formats that can be used in presenting your information. Use the format that represents you best and that fits your employment strategy. Probably the most popular format today is to have all headings in the left-hand margin (see Figure 21–1).

Figure 21–1
Resumé with headings in left-hand margin

```
                          ELIZABETH BROWN

                       3636 South Kellogg Drive
                        Indianapolis, IN 55451
                          (314) 892-2090

JOB              General office position with growing real estate
OBJECTIVE        management company.  Eventual objective is managerial
                 position.

MAJOR            College education in business management and real
QUALIFICATIONS   estate.  Work experience in clerical work, including
                 bookkeeping, typing, and other office duties.

EDUCATION        Glenvale Community College, Glenvale, IN
                    Associate of Science Degree (Real Estate major),
                    June 1981.

                    Real estate courses include:  Real Estate Analysis,
                    Residential Real Estate Analysis, Commercial and
                    Investment Real Estate, Advanced Appraisal.

                    Management courses include:  Accounting, Management of
                    Small Businesses, Business Communications.

EXPERIENCE       Memorial Medical Center, 110 Long Street,
                    Indianapolis, IN
                    Part time, April 1980 to present.
                    Responsible for bookkeeping, correspondence,
                    payroll accounting, and other clerical work.

HONORS           National Honor Society, High School
                 Treasurer, Alpha Phi Sorority
                 Dean's List, Spring and Fall 1980

PERSONAL         Age:  21
DATA             Marital Status:  Single
                 Health:  Excellent
                 Interests:  Reading, skiing, swimming

REFERENCES       Dr. Marcus T. Mann, Manager    Ms. Edith Krol
                 Memorial Medical Center        Instructor, Management
                 110 Long Street                Glenvale Community College
                 Indianapolis, IN 55451         Glenvale, IN 55450

                 Mr. Lester Zarnowitz
                 Assistant Professor, Real Estate
                 Glenvale Community College
                 Glenvale, IN 55450
```

For college students, a one-page (8½-by-11-inch, typewritten) resumé is almost always adequate. It is possible, however, to find situations in which it would be necessary to make the resumé longer. If, for instance, you have extensive work experience, your resumé may have to be two or even three pages long so that your experience and related responsibilities can be represented properly. Obviously, a prospective employer who will pay a salary of $16,000 to $26,000 a year should not object to reading an extra page or two. The investment in the applicant is so large that the length of the resumé becomes relatively unimportant.

Unless absolutely impossible try to keep your resumé down to one page.

Nonetheless, it is a good idea to make your resumé as compact as possible. One device that is sometimes used to cut the number of pages is *page reduction*. The resumé is typed on two or four pages and then reduced by 25 or 35 percent on a copier. The reduced pages, which are clearly legible, can then be cut and pasted together. A two-page resumé now fills one page; a four-page resumé becomes two.

The length of a resumé can be reduced by a copier or by changes in format.

You should also keep in mind that the format of your resumé will affect its length. Often it is possible to fit a two-page resumé onto one page just by changing to a slightly tighter format, as in Figures 21 – 2 (a – b).

Sections of the Resumé

It must be emphasized that there is no one perfect resumé model for you that can be presented in a textbook. Each individual must develop her or his own strategy. There are, however, certain basic resumé parts that are common to nearly all resumés.

Career Objective

The *Career Objective* section tells the reader what your present and long-term goals are. Don't hesitate to indicate a desire to reach top levels. Executives like to hire people who are ambitious. They know that as you advance so will the organization.

Career Objective:
To begin as an accounting trainee and eventually become the controller or top financial officer in a dynamic, growing company as a result of my hard work and contributions.

The *Career Objective* section reflects your long-range goals and immediate job objectives.

Career Objective:
To serve as a legal secretary in a major law firm and to eventually rise, as a result of hard work, to a position of administrative assistant to one of the firm's officers or partners.

Figure 21–2a
First page of a
two-page resumé

MARGARITE PALMER

1050 Stormcroft Avenue
Westlake Village, CA 91707
(213) 512-5111

CAREER OBJECTIVE

Entry-level position in growing advertising firm. Eventual
objective is to become manager of either the creative or the
business department.

MAJOR QUALIFICATIONS

Junior college background in business administration, advertising,
and art. Work experience in sales, marketing, and art.

EDUCATION

East Los Angeles Junior College: Associate of Science (Marketing
major), June 1981.

Marketing Courses

Basic Marketing
Retailing
Principles of Advertising
Market Research
Marketing Management
Marketing Strategy

Art Courses

Drawing and Painting
Drawing, Beginning and Intermediate
Design, Beginning and Intermediate
Fundamentals of Commercial Art

EXPERIENCE

Kelly & Kelly Advertising, Inc.
1515 South 6th Street
Los Angeles, CA 90007

Part time: May 1980-January 1981
Duties: As assistant in Art Department, worked on preparation of
art work, copy, and design for potential campaigns.

Figure 21–2a *(cont.)*
Second page of
the resumé

Bank of America
Graphics Department
1000 Wilshire Blvd.
Los Angeles, CA 90010

Full time: May–September, 1979
Part time: September 1979–April 1980
Duties: Assistant to graphics director with special assignments for
   newspaper and magazine advertisements.

ACTIVIES AND INTERVIEWS

Member of Sigma Phi Sigma honorary society and of American Marketing
Association. Special interest in fencing, Georgian architecture,
and local politics.

PERSONAL DATA

Age: 21
Marital Status: Single
Health: Excellent

REFERENCES

Mr. Art Hamilton, Creative Director
Kelly & Kelly Advertising, Inc.
1515 6th Street
Los Angeles, CA   90007

Ms. Jackie Cates, Director
Graphics Department
Bank of America
1000 Wilshire Blvd.
Los Angeles, CA   90010

Dr. Frank Palmer
Professor of Marketing
East Los Angeles Junior College
100 Westwood Blvd.
Westwood, CA   90024

Figure 21–2b
The same resumé
retyped to occupy
just one page

MARGARITE PALMER

CAREER
OBJECTIVE

Entry-level position in growing advertising firm.
Eventual objective is to become manager of either the
creative or the business department.

MAJOR
QUALIFICATIONS

Junior college background in business administration,
advertising, and art. Work experience in sales,
marketing and art.

EDUCATION

East Los Angeles Junior College, 1979–1981. Associate
of Arts (Marketing), June, 1981.

MARKETING COURSES
Basic Marketing   Principles of Advertising
Retailing   Marketing Management
Market Research   Marketing Strategy

ART COURSES
Drawing and Painting   Drawing, Beginnning and Intermediate
Industrial Design   Fundamentals of Commercial Art

EXPERIENCE

Kelly & Kelly Advertising, Inc., 1515 South 6th Street, Los
Angeles, CA 90007. Part time, May 1980–June 1981.
As assistant in Art Department, worked on preparation of
art work, copy, and design for potential campaigns.

Bank of America, Graphics Department, 1000 Wilshire Blvd.,
Los Angeles, CA 90010. Full time, May–September, 1979.
Part time, September 1979–April 1980.
Assistant to graphics director with special assignments for
newspaper and magazine advertisements.

ACTIVITIES
AND
INTERESTS

Member of Sigma Phi Sigma Honorary Society and of
American Marketing Association. Special interest in
fencing, Georgian architecture, and local politics.

PERSONAL
DATA

1050 Stormcroft Ave.
Westlake Village, CA 91707   Age 21
(213) 512-5111   Single
                                    Excellent health

REFERENCES

Ms. Jackie Cates, Director   Dr. Frank Palmer
Graphics Department   Professor of Marketing
Bank of America   East Los Angeles Junior College
1000 Wilshire Blvd.   1010 Westwood Road
Los Angeles, CA 90010   Westwood, CA 90024

Mr. Art Hamilton, Creative Director
Kelly & Kelly Advertising, Inc.
1515 South 6th Street
Los Angeles, CA 90007

"*My résumé, sir, is what you see sitting before you.*"

Obviously, this section must be written with care. There is a danger that it may sound *hard sell,* self-serving, or even insincere.

Major Qualifications

Here is a seldom-seen part of a resumé that has much to recommend it. A concise statement here serves as a summary of your major qualifications:

Major Qualifications:

Three years of part-time sales experience, extensive college education in marketing, and an ability to work with others, should all contribute to the continued growth of your company.

Be positive that your phrasing indicates how your qualifications can assist the organization, not you. Obviously the *you* attitude is a vital factor in this section as well as throughout the resumé.

The *Major Qualifications* section provides a one- or two-sentence capsule of key selling points.

Education

In the *Education* section, begin with your most recent schooling and work backwards.

It is wise to list first your most recent school or degree and work back. Don't start your listing under *Education* with the elementary school you attended ten years ago. Begin with your most recent school. It is wise to note under *Education,* courses or programs that tie into the job requirements. At times, it is also helpful to have a short statement or two indicating how relevant your education is or was to the demands of the job.

In some cases, there is no need to list the high school you attended. This might be the case if you graduated many years ago and have a good deal of work experience. However, if your high school did have, for example, a good technical or secretarial program called for by the advertisement you're responding to, you would want to list that school.

Experience

In the *Experience* section, begin with your current or most recent job and work backwards.

Under the heading *Experience,* many of the same principles hold true. List your most recent job first and then work back. The exception here is obvious: If you held a job four years ago which is associated closely to the one you're applying for today, you will list that job first.

Under *Experience,* list the company or organization name, whether full- or part-time, dates of employment, and duties. It is a good idea to indent all information under the company name so the reader can see easily where one listing ends and another begins.

Which section is listed first on the resumé sheet: *Education* or *Experience*? Here again, common sense dictates the answer. Obviously if your long suit is experience and the advertisement states "Individual with background in cost analysis with multinational firm needed," and you have such experience, then of course, this section would precede education. Figure 21–3 shows a resumé that emphasizes the education of the applicant. Figure 21–4 shows a resumé that emphasizes experience.

Extracurricular Activities and Interests

Most resumés certainly list awards, items of recognition, scholarship, and activities. Many of these will reflect very favorably on you and perhaps indicate that you are well rounded. If your grades are good, make a general statement about them under education. If they are not excellent, skip them.

Personal Data

What is the difference in meaning between *data* and *datum*? (See Appendix 1.)

This section includes marital status, health, age, physical data, and other pertinent information. Many of these items may be listed. They serve to give background on you which some prospective employers will find valuable.

Figure 21-3
**Resumé emphasizing
applicant's education**

BRADLEY BOSTON

(HOME)
1101 North Park Drive
Peoria, IL 61606
(309) 676-1909

(SCHOOL)
Merir Hall 333
Andrews University
Berrien, MI 49104
(616) 529-1776

Objective

Position as electronics technician with a major electronics firm.
Eventual objective is to obtain managerial position on engineering
staff.

Education

Bachelor of Science (Electronics), Andrews University, 1981.

Program included course work in advanced circuitry, computer
programming, systems analysis, and technical drawing. Cumulative
grade point average: 3.66 (A = 4.0).

Associate of Science (Electronics), Riverside Junior College, 1979.

Program included course work in basic circuitry design, pulse
circuits, technical writing, physics, and calculus. Cumulative
grade point average: 3.8 (A = 4.0).

Experience

Supreme Radio (Division of Motorola), Peoria, Ill., summers, 1976-80.

As electronics technician, serviced and aligned all portable and
pager equipment for the central Illinois area. Also helped to
install mobile telephones and commercial two-way radios.

Andrews University, Berrien, Mich., September 1979-April 1981

As electronics department lab assistant, assisted professors in
teaching lab and grading papers and projects.

Licenses

Hold a valid F.C.C. second class radio telephone license and amateur
extra class license with the call of WB9LPX.

Personal

Born 26 February 1959, Height: 5'11"; Weight: 172 lbs.,
Health: Excellent

Interests

Building electronic equipment, civil defense radio, tennis, skiing

References

References available upon request.

Figure 21–4
**Resumé emphasizing
applicant's experience**

```
                              ROBERTO FRANCESCO

                              1210 Magil Avenue
                              Chicago, IL  60661
                              (312) 887-5454

   CAREER          Entry-level management position with progressive retailing
   OBJECTIVE       firm.  Eventual objective to serve as senior manager.

   MAJOR           Diversified experience in food sales and distribution.
   QUALIFICATIONS  Educational background in marketing and management with
                   emphasis in foods distribution.

   EXPERIENCE      Kroger Company, Skokie, Ill., June 1979-present.

                     Served as produce manager; responsible for maintaining
                     proper supply levels, keeping spoilage records, and
                     supervising five general produce clerks.

                   Safeway Corporation, Evanston, Ill., 1975-79.

                     Served as assistant warehouse manager (produce),
                     responsible for supervising eight loaders and maintaining
                     careful inventory records.

                   Jewel Tea Company. Rock Island, Ill., 1971-74.

                     Served as assistant store manager with full
                     responsibility for inventory maintenance, sales
                     promotion, and supervision of clerks.

                   United States Army, 1969-71.

                     Served as warehouse manager (produce & perishables);
                     responsible for procuring, distributing, and accounting
                     for foodstuffs and non-durable goods.

   EDUCATION       Central States Community College, Rockford, Ill.  Associate
                   of Arts Degree (Food Marketing), June 1981.

                     Program included course work in marketing and
                     distribution, retailing, advertising, and business
                     ownership and management.

   PERSONAL        Age 31               Height 5' 9"
   DATA            Married, no children Weight 185 lbs.
                   Health excellent

   REFERENCES      Dr. Estella Zuno              Mr. Jack Washington, Manager
                   Associate Professor, Marketing Kroger Company
                   Central States Community College 5959 Whitehall Road
                   Rockford, IL  64378           Skokie, IL  60302

                   Mr. Alfred Kim
                   Instructor, Management
                   Central States Community College
                   Rockford, IL  64378
```

There is much confusion today about what an employer may ask you without violating discrimination laws. You should keep in mind, however, that *you* may submit any data you wish. Employers, on the other hand, are limited by law on what they can ask you to provide. Therefore, if you feel that some personal activity or attribute which you possess will assist you, certainly you should list it.

References

Most experts in personnel feel that the listing of references is vital. The rule seems to be noting a minimum of three and a maximum of four references. The most effective type are work references, probably because 1) the comments made about you by a former employer are accurate, and 2) the prospective employer is usually very interested in your work record. A second set of references that usually is well accepted is from your teachers. Most personnel managers agree that comments received from instructors about an applicant usually may be relied on. You should not list three or four personal references. Most prospective employers feel—usually with good foundation—that you have told your personal reference sources what to say about you, and they say it.

The *references* section can contribute to the proof that you are a qualified candidate for the job.

Perhaps the most important point to remember about references is to list individuals who will take the time and trouble to respond in some detail about your qualifications. Of course, you should obtain permission from those concerned before you list their names as references. In any event, choose with care and attempt to select those people who are concerned and conscientious.

Be sure to get permission to use names as references.

Instead of listing references, you may wish to use an alternate course and simply state, "References furnished on request" or "References available." If you can call on several impressive references, you should list them.

Miscellaneous Items

Salary: Do not note your salary requirements unless the advertisement specifically asks for such a listing. An item as sensitive as salary is usually better left to the interview. At such a discussion, you can quickly determine that a $12,000 per year salary with a generous benefit package might be superior to a $14,000 salary with few benefits.

Don't include salary requirements in your resumé.

Photograph: Although photographs frequently were included in the past, they are not used very often today. With heavy emphasis on equal opportunity, some individuals may feel you are saying something when you enclose a

It is not necessary to attach a photograph to your resumé unless you are asked specifically to do so.

photo. You should, however, have a supply available. They are needed when you complete your final job application or your personnel record forms.

As you can see, there are many factors to consider in preparing your resumé. Once you determine your employment strategy, you can answer the questions as they relate specifically to your situation. However, every individual has different qualities and is looking for a different job; therefore, resumés necessarily must be different.

Your resumé is part of your overall job strategy.

Developing your job strategy is the key in resumé construction. To this point, the pieces have been assembled—now some intelligence must be applied so that the resumé can be constructed creatively. You want to present yourself honestly, in the best possible light, to gain the job you want. Your strategy should concentrate on what the potential employer needs to know to make a favorable evaluation of your ability to successfully perform the job.

MEMO

To: Students

From: The Authors

Subject: Your resumé and your career

At certain times in the course of your career, your resumé will probably be the single most important document in your life. A resumé that is prepared hastily, contains typographical errors, is laid out poorly on the page, or fails to include the information potential employers need to make a decision—such a resumé can be the surest road to failure in a competitive job market. On the other hand, a clean, crisp resumé that presents the facts concisely and accurately while at the same time presenting *you* in the best possible light can be the key to a successful career.

Decision

Here is the resumé Marcia Goldberg prepared to answer the newspaper ad.

```
                          MARCIA GOLDBERG

                         4242 Larch Avenue
                         Conover, OH 23546
                          Tel. 493-0217

Objective

    Summer position as assistant to health director at the Sunnybrook Home
    for the Aged.

Health-Care Experience

    CONOVER COMMUNITY HOSPITAL, 1979-1981:  Worked weekends as "Candy
       Striper," assisting registered nurses in a wide variety of nursing
       activities.  Also served as information receptionist for the
       hospital fifteen hours a week during 1981.

    CONOVER DAY CAMP FOR THE DEAF, 1980, 1981:  Worked as summer camp
       counselor, both summers.  Assisted head counselor in planning and
       organizing activities, including the first "Conover Day Softball
       Tournament," summer 1980.  Received Counselor of the Year Award,
       1980.

Other Experience

    Have also worked in a variety of part-time positions, including
    assistant editor, Conover Community College Newspaper; teaching
    assistant, Jewish Community Center Sunday School; and sales clerk at
    Fohrman's Department Store and at the Ice Cream Igloo.

Education

    A.A., CONOVER COMMUNITY COLLEGE, 1981:  Majored in community health,
       minored in biology.  Dean's List, 1979-1981.  For second-year course
       on "Aging and the Aged in American Society," wrote paper on "HMOs
       and the Elderly," 1981.

    DIPLOMA, CONOVER HIGH SCHOOL, 1979:  Received Academic Torch Award,
       Senior Year.

Outside Interests

    Community health, piano, sports.

References

    Dr. Anna Swokowski              Phyllis Carlton, R.N.
    Professor of Biology            Director of Nursing
    Conover Community College       Conover Community Hospital
    Conover, Ohio 23477             Conover, Ohio 23546
```

Questions

1. What are some of the specific ways you can establish contact with prospective employers?

2. Do you feel a resumé should be any specific number of pages in length? Justify your answer.

3. Write two different career objectives for your resumé.

4. Which of the items listed below should be included on your resumé and which items should be omitted?
   a. date resumé is written;
   b. religious preference;
   c. work experience, giving job titles and a summary of job duties;
   d. a statement telling why you left your past employment;
   e. a career objective;
   f. your education, including the dates and names of your grammar school and junior or middle school;
   g. hobbies.

5. You have written an impressive two-page resumé to be sent to ten insurance companies for an entry-level job as a claims adjuster. In paragraph form, discuss the advantages and disadvantages of each of the following:
   a. each resumé is an original copy which you typed on twenty-pound bond paper.
   b. you typed two original resumés and made four carbon copies with each original.
   c. you duplicated your original resumé on the ten-cent duplicating machine in your college library. The copies are clear, but the paper is off-white and light weight.
   d. you paid Copy Cat Duplicators four cents per copy to run off twenty-five copies on twenty-pound bond paper.

Exercises

1. Choose two careers you could pursue as a result of your education, interests, and past part-time or full-time employment. Look at several want ads for jobs pertaining to these careers. For each career, write a concise statement of your major qualifications.

2. In this chapter you read, "Developing your job strategy is the key in resumé construction." How did you interpret this statement? In a memo to your instructor, describe your job strategy for creating a resumé and eventually obtaining full-time employment.

3. Name an industry and a firm within that industry for whom you might like to work. Obtain background data on that organization. Briefly list that information *and* the sources from which you secured that information.

Applications

1. You are a marketing major who will graduate from college this May. A representative from a well-known insurance company has asked you to join his firm after graduation to begin a career as an insurance salesperson. The job requires an individual who is ambitious and doesn't mind devoting long hours to a job that could eventually pay a substantial salary and commissions. It calls for evening interviews, close contact with people of all ages, and an extrovert personality. Analyze yourself to see if you have the attributes required for a successful career in insurance sales. List all of your strengths and weaknesses pertaining to this career choice.

Dilemma

Ever since he took his first class in bookkeeping in secondary school, Robert Hill has been intrigued by the world of numbers. Throughout his junior college and college career, he held part-time positions in the field of accounting. In college, he majored in accounting and will receive his degree in just three weeks.

For the past two months, however, he has been involved in his job search for a full-time position. So far he has interviewed for an accounting position with a food manufacturer, an electronics firm, two of the "Big Eight" accounting firms, and a medium-sized accounting company.

It is the last one that has really excited Bob. He had a one-hour interview with the Personnel Director, Mr. Kenneth Moskowitz, two weeks ago and has just come from a second visit to the firm. In that time, he spent one hour with each of the two partners.

They told him the firm intends to expand within the next year, move more heavily into the area of accounting for retail firms, and design a program for employee profit-sharing. The salary offered to Bob was competitive with that being paid by the "Big Eight" companies and the fringe benefit package was most attractive.

Bob knows he is in competition with two other candidates for the job. However, he really would like to be selected. He decides to write a follow-up letter to the interview to Mr. Moskowitz.

Decision, see page 444

Selling Yourself through Employment Letters and Interviews

Here is a list of the objectives you should understand by the time you complete this chapter. Place a check mark in the box beside each as soon as you feel ready to apply your understanding in a practical situation.

☐ The six basic techniques of contacting employers
   Walking in cold
   Using an employment agency
   Using your college or state placement service
   Making contacts through friends and associates
   Starting a mail campaign
   Responding to advertisements

☐ The four basic goals of any employment letter
   Arouse interest
   Describe your abilities
   Prove your claims
   Request an interview

☐ The different kinds of employment letters and the qualities and purposes of each
   Solicited cover letter and resumé
   Unsolicited cover letter and resumé
   One-part employment letters

☐ Techniques for preparing for an effective employment interview

☐ The purposes and qualities of various other employment communications
   Follow-up letter
   Inquiry
   Job offer acceptance
   Job offer refusal

Now that you have expended the effort in the pre-job steps — analyzing the job market, looking at yourself and at the individual requirements for the job, and preparing an effective resumé — you are ready to establish contact with potential employers.

There are a variety of ways to get in touch with someone who may have a job for you. You may, for example:

There are many possible job sources.

Walk into the organization and ask for an interview;

Go to an employment agency and ask them to find you a job (the fee may be paid by you or the hiring organization);

Use a free employment service (state agency or college placement service) to put you in contact with potential employers;

Make your employment desires known to teachers, friends, and associates so they might call to your attention a job opening which exists;

Start a mail campaign in which you send your qualifications to potential employers even though they did not seek your services;

Monitor and respond to the help wanted advertisements in the local or regional newspapers; read advertisements in trade and professional journals of your occupational choice.

You may find it beneficial to use a combination of several of these methods to make contact with someone who has a job you want.

Employment Letters

You only need look at the classified ad section of your newspaper to note that employers seek employment letters as a device for obtaining new employees. The newspapers of major cities carry hundreds, and sometimes thousands, of advertisements asking individuals to reply by letter to indicate their interest in filling specific positions. Companies also are accustomed to receiving letters from persons who are not replying to an advertisement but are simply prospecting to determine if a specific company has an opening.

The employment letter is often the key to obtaining the job which will give you personal satisfaction, economic security, and challenging and enjoyable experiences.

Goals of the Employment Letter

Employment letters are very similar to sales letters. In this case you are not attempting to sell a product to a buyer but yourself to a potential employer. Like the sales letter (see Chapter 8), these letters should accomplish four main purposes.

The typical employment letter usually has four goals.

1. Arouse interest   Without being cute or loud, you want to gain the interest of the potential employer. Avoid leading off with a dull statement that may convince the reader you also are dull. Do not start with a statement that reflects concern for only *your* benefit—not the reader's. The following are examples of how to turn you reader off:

> *I will get my A. A. degree this month and I will be ready to take a job.*

> *This letter is in reply to your ad which recently appeared in the News. I think I would be interested in the job you listed.*

> *Up, up, and away! I'm "Sky King" and I'm ready to put my piloting skills to work for Airgot Airlines. Call me today and I'll fly for you tomorrow.*

> *After four years of hard work and intensive effort, I'm ready to take a position with your firm.*

Instead, provide the reader with a quick statement of your qualifications. Immediately come to the issue of how the organization might benefit from your abilities. But at the same time, remember you are not going to save the organization. Start your letter with the *you* attitude instead of the *I* or *we* attitude illustrated in the examples above.

> *Two years of part-time experience as a bookkeeper, a college degree with a major in accounting, and a desire to work hard are the qualities which I have to fill the position opening you advertised.*

The opening of your letter should indicate how you can contribute to the organization.

> *Your employment announcement calls for an individual with an engineering-technical background and business experience; this description matches the qualifications I possess.*

> *Work experience as a part-time private security officer, an associate's degree in Law Enforcement, and an ability to work with others are probably the attributes you seek in the "Security Deputy" for which you advertised.*

These approaches of introducing yourself to the potential employer are fresh and attempt to indicate how your abilities can help the organization. Note that the introductory sentence provides a summary of your selling points: education, special abilities, training, and experience.

2. Describe your abilities   As best you can, attempt to match requirements of the job with your experience and abilities. If a particular technical skill is required, and you have it, this point should be emphasized in your letter. The letter should do much more than just say "here I am" or "here is my resumé." You should emphasize your abilities and your experience and comment on your accomplishments.

3. Prove your statements   Provide the potential employer with evidence of your abilities. There are various kinds of evidence: references (former employers, teachers, service organization sponsors), course work, jobs (indicating your duties and responsibilities), and leadership positions as exemplified in religious, school, or civic organizations.

Ask for an interview in a positive and direct manner.

4. Request an interview   The purpose of writing the letter is to get a job. To get the job, you will need to be interviewed. Therefore, it is important that your letter gets you the interview. Do not be fuzzy or hesitant on this matter. Your request for an interview should be straightforward and positive. Indicate in your request that you have told only a part of your story. The interview will give you an opportunity to tell the prospective employer about the additional attributes you possess. A statement in the last paragraph such as the following is helpful:

> *I would appreciate an opportunity to meet with you so we can discuss in greater detail my education and experience backgrounds, plus other details.*

Cover Letters

Cover letters usually are divided into *solicited* and *unsolicited* types.

The cover letter literally covers a resumé you are sending. Cover letters may be either *solicited* or *unsolicited.* Solicited cover letters are those that are sent out in response to an advertisement in a newspaper or trade journal, an announcement on the school's placement office bulletin board, or a personal request. The unsolicited employment letter is sent out cold to a firm for which you would like to work.

The cover letter can be the key factor in the evaluation of the resumé.

The solicited cover letter   The solicited cover letter is sent when an employer has requested material. You may be responding to an advertisement or to an oral request for a resumé. In this case you know that the employer has an opening and is expecting to receive resumés.

If you are responding to an individual who requested you to send a resumé, you obviously will know the person's name and be able to respond to him or her by name. For example, Mrs. J. F. Morton, Personnel Director of Banyon Company. Sometimes too, an advertisement seeking resumés will identify the potential employer and name a person to write (see Figure 22–1).

Frequently, however, firms advertise employment opportunities and do not identify themselves. These are *blind* advertisements. You are required to respond to a newspaper's box number, not to an individual. Traditionally, blind employment letters have been addressed "Dear Sir" or "Dear Sirs." However, the male gender cannot be assumed. Therefore, some people start the letter with "To Whom It May Concern," "Dear Sir or Madam," "Dear Personnel

nd ot accntg.,
spondence, and
to work closely

and looking for a change? A position is now available for an experienced manager or supervisor with an accounting background. Send resume and salary expected.

OFFICE MANAGER

Some EDP Experience with background of accntg., collection, correspondence, and office mgmnt. to work closely with Pres. of top rated NW side mfr. Estab. 1934, 250 employees, office of 12. Send resume and salary expected. Jan Walker, P.O. Box 5566, Chicago, Ill. 60615

OFFICE MANAGER

Some EDP Experience with background of accntg., collection, correspondence, and

OFFICE MANA(
Are you now in
and looking fol
position is now a
experienced mai
visor with an
background. Mu
relocate after lo
6-12 months.
    SNAP-ON T(
Irene Loftus

OFFICE M.

Auto dealership
Must have ref;
Mr. Neal betwe
374-7600
        7600 S. STO(

OFFICE MANA(
Are you now in
Auto dealership
Must have ref
Mr. Neal betwe

GER TRAINEE
management
r a change? A
available for an
nager or super-
    accounting
st be willing to
cal training of

)OLS CORP
            437-6112

ANAGER
. Experienced.
erences. Call
:en 9-12 only.

VY ISLAND

Figure 22–1
Classified ad
that gives a name
to write to

Manager," or "Ladies and Gentlemen" (see Figure 22–2). But this kind of all-inclusive terminology may be awkward or overly condescending for you.

There is another technique that is slowly coming into practice. The salutation is a short *you*-oriented phrase that greets the recipient and states the reason for writing (see Figure 22–3). Use the form and format that is most comfortable for you. But be aware of the alternatives; there are ways to avoid the stereotyped "Dear Sir."

The unsolicited letter   The requirements of the unsolicited cover letter are the same as for the solicited cover letter; but your task is somewhat more difficult. In this case, you are writing to a person or an employer who has not asked to be contacted. In this instance, it may be much harder to secure the individual's attention and be able to sell yourself. The unsolicited letter should emphasize immediately your interest in the firm and clearly indicate you are familiar with the organization. Your qualifications to perform a specific job should be highlighted.

Never send an unsolicited letter to just an organization or to an office. To send an unsolicited letter "To whom it may concern" is to engage in a wasteful fishing expedition. Take the time and effort to write to a specific person by discovering that individual's name and title before writing. Determining that name (and the correct spelling) and title is simple. A phone call to the firm's switchboard or to the individual's department is usually all that is needed.

The unsolicited cover letter and resumé can be a valuable device for getting a job interview.

Figure 22-2
Letter answering
a blind ad

3636 S. Kellogg Drive
Indianapolis, IN 55541
April 5, 198-

General Manager
BOX 999
Indianapolis Press Telegram
Indianapolis, Indiana 55542

Dear Sir or Madam:

Your ad in the Indianapolis Press Telegram, April 4, 198- requests a
general office worker with experience. My degree in real estate,
experience in bookkeeping, clerical duties, and working with the
public, along with my knack for detail, sounds just like what you're
looking for.

For the past year, I have been employed by Memorial Medical Center in
Indianapolis and have been responsible for their payroll accounting.
I've always been delighted to take on new office duties. This
experience, along with my sincere interest in this kind of work, would
be a valuable asset to your company.

In June of this year, I will graduate from Indianapolis Community
College with an Associate of Science degree in real estate. I have
also minored in business management and have taken several courses in
that area. As property management has always been an interest of
mine, your company is one for which I have an extreme desire to work.

I would be pleased to meet with you and give you a more complete
picture of my background. I can come in at your convenience; just
telephone 892-2090 any evening or write to the above address.

Sincerely yours,

Elizabeth Brown

Elizabeth Brown

Figure 22–3
Letters that skip
the traditional
salutation

```
                                    1716 Ridge Avenue
                                    Ada, Minnesota 56510
                                    January 29, 198-

Bloomington Eagle
1010 Main Street, Box 11-A
Bloomington, IN 67601

You Need RN's with Experience.

. . . having completed five years of work at a major university
hospital and having also been employed in a small community hospital,
I feel well qualified to fill the position you describe

- - - - - - - - - - - - - - - - - - - - - - - - - - - - - - - - - -

                                    903 West Main Street
                                    Burbank, MO 74633
                                    September 3, 198-

St. Louis Post
1003 Missouri Avenue
Box 17-D
St. Louis, MO 63103

Your desire to hire chemists is exciting.

. . . with a B.S. in chemistry and a minor in marketing, I am
interested in your need to expand your Chemical Sales Division.
```

There can be any number of reasons why you would be interested in working for an organization for which you have not seen an employment notice. For example: 1) This specific company is in the industry in which you would like to work; 2) you want to live in a specific geographic region or metropolitan area; or 3) your spouse has accepted employment in the area and you also desire employment. The best reason is, of course, the first.

It is wise to be honest and state why you are writing when the firm has not asked to be contacted. With employee turnover and potential expansion, you may very well be the kind of person the employer is seeking. Also, many firms will retain your letter for several months just in case an opening occurs. Therefore, do not be hesitant to send the unsolicited letter. But understand that it must incorporate all the requisites of a positive sales letter. Your unsolicited employment letter is just like the unsolicited letter you may have received today from Visa Card encouraging you to apply for one of their credit cards. Visa wants to get your attention, acquaint you with their attributes, and get you to take a positive action. That is exactly what you want your employment letter to accomplish for you when it lands on the desk of a potential employer (see Figure 22–4).

With knowledge of the content of the cover letter and resumé, you are now ready to put the package together. Whether you are replying to an ad (solicited) or simply prospecting (unsolicited), carefully write the cover letter and resumé. Together, they form the two-part letter which will assist you in securing the position you desire.

Figure 22–4
Unsolicited
employment letter

1050 Stormcroft Avenue
Westlake Village, California 91707
May 20, 198-

Mr. Morris Obeta
Personnel Director
Able-Kelly Advertising Agency
1681 S. Wilshire Blvd.
Los Angeles, California 90207

Dear Mr. Obeta:

An outstanding agency such as yours probably has need for an
individual with a marketing background who is creative and experienced
in the graphic arts and likes to work with people. My practical job
experience, creativity, and my educational training can definitely be
an asset to your company.

I received my Associate of Science degree from the East Los Angeles
Junior College, where I majored in marketing and took classes in art.
The courses in advertising, commercial, and advertising art were all
carefully integrated to prepare me for a position with a firm such as
yours. Details of my education and job experience as well as other
information can be found on the attached data sheet.

For the past two years I have been working at various jobs that
brought me into contact with the public. These included graphics
assistant at a major agency and work with the creative art director at
Bank of America. These jobs also gave me valuable experience in art
and marketing.

I feel that I would be an asset to your organization. I would like an
opportunity to meet with you at your convenience to discuss in detail
my qualifications and possible future with your company. I can be
reached at the above address or at (213) 512-5111.

Sincerely,

Margarite Palmer

Margarite Palmer

Enclosures

One-Part Employment Letters

The one-part employment letter, or application letter, is sent without enclosing a resumé. It is a total package in *one part* because it combines the features of both the cover letter and resumé. The one-part letter is preferred when you want to make the maximum impression in a minimum of space.

The one-part employment letter is a combination of cover letter and resumé.

Much of the basic information that would appear in a resumé is included in the application letter. However, the format changes substantially, and many of the specific details are not included. You may find in writing firms that have not asked to be contacted, the application letter (in this case unsolicited) has several advantages:

1. It establishes interest and, in summary form, highlights your abilities.

2. It interests the receiver without the need to provide detail relative to your references, educational data, personal items, etc.

3. It provides the employer with the opportunity to contact you to obtain more detail; this can be a good gauge on how your job search is progressing.

Figure 22 – 5 shows an example of an effective one-part employment letter.

The employment letter, the vehicle often used to make your initial contact with an organization, is probably one of the most important communications you will ever prepare. Whatever type of employment letter you use, be sure it gains the positive attention of the reader and presents you in a positive way.

Employment Interviews

The purpose of the application process is to get an interview. To some degree, the letter and resumé are one-way communications. The employment interview is very much a two-way communication. In preparing your cover letter and resumé, you were able to draft and rewrite your presentation. In the interview situation, there is no such thing as a redraft. It will be necessary for you to respond to questions and indicate that you have a pleasant personality, can communicate effectively, have knowledge of the job and organization, and are familiar with topics of professional, socio-economic, and cultural interest.

The interview is the critical factor in having a job offer made.

Preparing for the Interview

In gaining knowledge of the job and the organization and by preparing the employment letter and resumé, you have the basic bits of information needed for an interview. However, the interview can be considerably less structured than your resumé. Therefore, perhaps one of the best ways to prepare for the interview is to do what is often done in preparation for an oral examination or

Figure 22–5
One-part
employment letter

Morir Hall, 339
Andrews University
Berrien Springs, MI 49104
February 17, 198–

Mr. Rodger M. Jennings
Employment Director
Motorola Corporation
Box 7272
Chicago, IL 60606

Dear Mr. Jennings:

Motorola's progress in the electronics industry, your electronic
systems and your product developments are most familiar to me. For
the past five summers I've been employed by your Peoria Division,
Supreme Radio. Now about to complete the B.S. degree in Electronics
Technology, I am prepared to enter the electronics industry. Because
of the positive experiences with your corporation, the potential of
employment at Motorola is exciting.

Besides the hands-on work at Supreme, I've also been fortunate to
receive some managerial experience and theoretical assignments in
electronics technology. This has provided the background enabling me
to assume such full-time positions as manager of electronic-systems
inventory, electronics trouble shooter or electronics supervisor.
Related activities that could be of interest to you include:

   Completed electronics curriculum at Andrews University and took a
   variety of computer and technical writing courses.

   Licensed F.C.C. second class radio telephone; amateur extra
   class.

   Teaching/supervisory experience as a lab assistant at Andrews
   University.

Although location is not a primary consideration, a position in the
midwest in a metropolitan area would be excellent. I have no
reservations about locating in Chicago.

Because Andrews is on spring vacation April 2-7, I could conveniently
come to Chicago for an interview at that time. Can we arrange a
meeting during that week?

                         Sincerely,

                         Bradley Boston

                         Bradley Boston

the way in which presidents prepare for news conferences. List the questions that might be asked. Carefully think through how you would answer each one. The possible categories of questions are your background, your personal interests, your knowledge of the organization, your family, your previous employers, people with whom you have worked, civic activities, your personal and professional goals, and your attitudes on leadership.

In preparing for the interview, anticipate questions and design those which you should ask.

You also have a responsibility to be well informed about the organization that has asked to interview you. Do your homework. If the organization is a local concern, you can gain information by talking to employees, picking up literature at the company or by reviewing the files at your college placement office. If you are interviewing with a large regional or national firm, you can obtain information from some of the following sources:

1. *The firm's annual report.* Many libraries have recent annual reports of major organizations. The modern annual report, besides providing basic financial data, presents detailed statements concerning the markets, the emphases, and the direction of the company.

You can obtain information about an organization from numerous sources.

2. *Dun and Bradstreet Million Dollar Directory.* This publication lists over 30,000 companies that each have a net worth in excess of $1 million. Information includes addresses, product lines, and names of top company officials.

3. *Dun and Bradstreet Middle Market Directory.* Similar to the *Million Dollar Directory,* it provides information on over 33,000 companies whose worth is estimated to be between $500,000 and $1 million. Both Dun and Bradstreet publications are handy because they provide specific names of people, addresses, and telephone numbers.

4. *Fortune.* The magazine annually lists rankings of U.S. and foreign firms. The listings provide information on sales, profits, number of employees, and gains or losses compared to the previous year. (May, largest 500 U.S. corporations; June, second 500 largest U.S. corporations; July, 50 largest companies in insurance, utilities, banking, services, and others; August, the 300 largest corporations outside the U.S.)

5. *College Placement Annual.* Published annually by the College Placement Bureau, it contains basic information about job opportunities in hundreds of companies and organizations.

Making a Good Impression

First impressions are vital in most situations—especially in the interview setting. Through your mode of dress, conversation, courteousness, alertness, and enthusiasm, you will provide the interviewer with ample verbal and nonverbal cues about your ability to fit the employment position.

What is the difference in meaning between *principles* and *principals*? (See Appendix 1.)

What is the difference in meaning between *prohibit* and *inhibit*? (See Appendix 1.)

The first impression is a lasting impression, and it often will color the recipient's interpretations of everything you say. There are hundreds of recent studies and books dealing with how to dress and act for success. These studies and principles are often just basic common sense — be neat, be courteous, be interested, and be communicative. That is, this is not the time to clam up and have nothing to say. Conversely, it is not the time to dominate the conversation and to prohibit the interviewer from conducting a satisfactory interview.

You, the interviewee, can have a definite effect on the verbal and non-verbal interview setting. Obviously you should sit up straight, maintain good eye contact, watch your enunciation, and be aware of other details. You know, of course, that you should not slouch, drum on the desk top, or wear a T-shirt in an interview. *You* can influence the nature of the interview and obviously the end result — getting the job.

Generally, interviewees should remember that they have a responsibility to provide the interviewer with information about themselves and to aid the interviewer in obtaining the necessary information in a comfortable manner.

Other Employment Communications

The basic employment communications have been introduced. It may be necessary to initiate other kinds of communication.

Inquiries

A letter of inquiry may be sent if no response to a resumé is received.

If you wait a reasonable period of time after sending an organization your resumé, and if you have had no response, it is acceptable to write an inquiry letter. It could be that your materials have been misplaced. Certainly you would not want to miss the chance for an interview through no fault of your own. Your letter — which basically inquires about the status of your materials and the potential of getting an interview — should follow the basics for inquiry communications. (See Chapter 5.)

One approach would be to send a short letter to a person (not an office) at the organization in the employment area or to the person you originally wrote. Simply state that you previously wrote (cite the date) about potential employment. You are interested in the organization and are concerned that you have had no word from them.

Another way to establish contact when you have not heard from the organization is to send a copy of the original materials. Include a note indicating that you still are interested in the organization and that you are concerned about not having received any response.

It is possible that you would like to be hired by organization *y*. But before you have a chance to interview with them, you receive an offer from company

x. It is acceptable to contact *y* and inform them of your problem. Be straight-forward. Indicate you would like an interview with them before making an employment decision, if they are interested in talking with you. You may want to either phone or write company *y* depending upon the time limits you are facing.

In this type of inquiry you will have better success if you write to a specific individual; that person will follow through on your inquiry. To write an inquiry letter to an office increases the chance for inaction.

The Follow-Up Letter

If you had a lengthy interview for a position, a follow-up thank-you note is always appropriate. This type of letter thanks the interviewer for the time spent together, briefly reviews your qualifications, and indicates your serious interest in the position. The letter can be especially effective if it refers to some high point in the interview or an area of common interest between you and the interviewer. It should be mailed the same day or the day following the interview. Figure 22–6 is a good example of a follow-up letter.

A follow-up letter to the interviewer can be a very positive piece of communication.

Figure 22–6
Follow-up letter
after an interview

```
                                          1100 S. Ballview Court
                                          Chicago, IL 60011
                                          February 11, 198-

          Mr. Frank Palmer
          Personnel Director
          Kaplan and Kaplan, CPAs
          One South Madison Avenue
          Chicago, Illinois 60020

          Dear Mr. Palmer:

          Thank you very much for spending time with me recently
          regarding the accounting trainee position you have open.

          Needless to say, I was very impressed with your firm and its
          long-range goals.  I do feel my background--two years of
          part-time experience in accounting as well as educational
          training--can contribute to the attainment of your firm's
          objectives.

          I shall be pleased, Mr. Palmer, to visit your office again to
          supplement the data on the resume I left with you or to
          answer questions that have come up.

          Cordially yours,

          Robert Carpenter

          Robert Carpenter
```

Accepting a Job Offer

If you are offered a position, you should accept the position in writing. If the job offer is extended orally, your letter of acceptance can restate such important facts as the type of position you are accepting, the salary, any special benefits or fringes that were extended, and when and where you plan to report to work.

It is wise to accept a job offer in writing.

Declining a Job Offer

If an organization is kind enough to offer you a job and you cannot accept the position, you should be courteous enough to respond in writing. This brief letter can thank the organization for the offer, point to the attributes of the organization, and state why you are declining the offer. Be positive and polite. At a future date you may want to be considered by the organization for another position.

It is courteous to decline a job offer in writing.

Some of the most exciting and, at the same time, frightening kinds of communication are those dealing with employment. With careful planning, you can eliminate many of the elements of fear and concentrate on your objectives and qualifications.

MEMO

To: Students
From: The Authors
Subjects: Employment letters and interviews

A good resumé alone rarely will get you a job. To do that, you have to write employment letters that will convince employers to read your resumé and grant you an interview. Succeeding in this, you also have to make an excellent impression at your employment interview. Acquiring the skills necessary to sell yourself effectively through employment letters and interviews is no easy task. But the rewards you will reap most certainly are worth the effort.

Decision

Here is the follow-up letter Robert Hill wrote Mr. Moskowitz, expressing interest in working for the accounting firm.

1480 South Kimberly Avenue
San Francisco, California 94111
April 20, 198-

Mr. Kenneth Moskowitz, Personnel Manager
Stevenson and Emmons, Inc.
Professional Accounting Services
1400 South Fourth Street
Suite 210
San Francisco, California 94111

Dear Mr. Moskowitz:

This is a brief letter to once again tell you how much I appreciated the time you, Mr. Stevenson, and Mr. Emmons spent with me this past week.

From the description of your firm's activities, as well as its long range goals, I believe very strongly that I can make a significant contribution if selected for the opening which you have available.

My degree in accounting, part-time experience in the field, and my interest in retailing, all make me feel that I will be able to integrate quickly into your firm and become a valued--though junior--team member.

Mr. Stevenson indicated that travel to clients in various parts of the state would be required. Because I have no family obligations and am not married, I would look forward to this aspect of the position.

Again, Mr. Moskowitz, I want to emphasize that I feel very well qualified for the position and will certainly give my all to becoming a strong employee on your team. I do hope to receive a favorable response from you within the next few days.

Cordially yours,

Robert P. Hill

Robert P. Hill

CHAPTER REVIEW

Questions

1. It often is said that the sales letter and the employment letter (or cover letter to the resumé) are similar in many respects. Specifically, what are those similarities?

2. "It is absolutely vital to have a strong *you* attitude in employment letters." Explain and justify that statement.

3. List the advantages and disadvantages of using:
   a. the solicited letter and resumé, and
   b. the unsolicited letter and resumé.

4. How does your one-part employment letter differ from your cover letter and resumé?

5. What specific areas should you concern yourself with in your preparation for the interview?

6. List and answer five questions that you feel are most likely to be asked of you by the interviewer in a job interview.

7. List several questions *you* should ask at the interview if the topics with which they are concerned are not brought up. How would you word such questions? (Watch your tact and word choice.)

8. Why is it often wise to send a follow-up letter after the interview has taken place?

You also may search your trade or professional journals for such an advertisement. Write a cover letter and resumé in response to that specific advertisement. Make *no* assumptions that are not true except your completion of the educational program in which you are now enrolled. You may assume that you will receive the certificate or degree for your program in one month. All other data must be accurate: experience, references, age, and so on.

3. Refer to Exercise 2. Exchange and read the cover letters and resumés of two other students. Now set up teams: interviewer, job applicant, and observer. After each job interview, the observer should offer feedback. That feedback should be specific and should comment on the a) entrance, b) word choice selected, c) questions' asked, d) questions answered, e) poise, f) nonverbal communication, and other factors which have an effect on the total situation.

4. After carrying through the assignment in Exercise 3, write a follow-up letter to the student who acted as your prospective employer. Assume you would like very much to receive a favorable response from him or her regarding the job available. Remember to express your appreciation for the time the interviewer spent with you.

Exercises

1. Contact a personnel interviewer at your college or at a local company. Seek information that will describe the "ideal applicant" for a job. Ask questions relating to dress, personality, mannerisms, communication ability, job qualifications, and any other factors pertinent to the candidate at an employment interview. Relate your findings in a memo to your instructor.

2. Go through the classified advertisements in your Sunday (or any day) newspaper and select an ad to which you would like to respond.

Applications

1. Martha Gray is interested in an entry-level data processing job. She did not take a business communications course, but a friend lent her a book filled with resumés and cover letters. Martha selected a cover letter that applied to her career field and copied it almost verbatim from the book. She was convinced that the professionally written letter would impress any prospective employer. In paragraph form, give your opinion on the advantages and disadvantages of copying letters found in textbooks.

2. This morning, you were interviewed for the job of administrative assistant to the hospital administrator, George Woloski, at County Memorial Hospital, 325 East Marshall Street, Pennsauken, New Jersey 18337. He described the secretarial and management skills needed for the job and intimated that you were highly qualified and a choice candidate. Two other people also are being considered to fill the vacancy. Since you are very much interested in this job, you should write a follow-up letter to Mr. Woloski; add any information that will strengthen your position.

3. Lawrence Mead, a business communications professor claimed that since all resumés are similar, most recent graduates appear to be too much alike. He contended that the cover letter, not the resumé, allows for individualization, and more effort should be spent writing the cover letter than the resumé. Do you agree with Dr. Mead? In a memo, give your opinion of the relative importance of the employment cover letter versus the resumé and justify your stand.

4. You will graduate from a four-year college as a finance major with a career interest in banking. Distinguish between the approach you will take to apply for a) solicited positions, and b) bank openings that are unsolicited. Discuss this in detail in a memo report.

5. You sent an unsolicited cover letter and resumé to a midwest electric company three weeks ago. You have received no response. Write an inquiry letter concerning your application.

Readings in Communication

SELLING YOURSELF IN INTERVIEWS   David Gootnick

Job-Interviewing Process

The intelligent job seeker views job interviewing as a logical process consisting of five stages: (1) Pre-Interview, (2) Interview Opening, (3) Interview Development, (4) Interview Closing, and (5) Post-Interview. To progress successfully through the job interview process, the job seeker must demonstrate various skills at each stage.

Stage 1: Pre-interview.   While an invitation to interview is a well-earned accomplishment, it is not the signal to start celebrating and stop campaigning.

Arriving at the right location at the designated time is essential. Plan to arrive about five to ten minutes early so that you may relax for a few moments in the outer office, collect your thoughts, and be refreshed when you are called in to interview.

Arriving late for the job interview is one of the worst things you can do. If for any reason you must be delayed, call the interviewer and explain the problem and ask for permission to arrive a little later or on another day. If you fail to call and explain and simply show up late, you may not be seriously considered further. Reliability is a critical trait that is first demonstrated by your punctuality on the job interview.

Look businesslike when you arrive at the office and carry an attaché case or briefcase that includes your job-getting documents, paper, and pen. Introduce yourself courteously to the secretary and state the purpose of your business. If you are not absolutely certain of the pronunciation of the interviewer's name, ask the secretary.

Stage 2: Interview Opening.   In your greeting, use the interviewer's name and apply a firm handshake. A favorable first impression can help a great deal in the interview. On the other hand, an unfavorable first impression can hurt. Do not smoke in the interview, even if asked.

Show the interviewer that you recognize and respect his or her authority and position by allowing him or her to open the conversation. The interviewer may attempt to put you at ease with "small talk" about your trip, some news events, or the weather. Respectfully react with agreement or appropriate thoughts of your own on the subject. Or, the interviewer may directly launch into business with a question about you. The interviewer may start telling you about conditions, needs, or problems around the company. Listen closely to this valuable information for a few minutes. Then, as soon as the opportunity allows, begin to inject your thoughts into the conversation.

Stage 3: Interview Development.   After a few minutes of opening remarks, you should begin to develop your sales presentation and score points. You have limited interviewing time in which to present your case. Therefore, find an appropriate opportunity to begin talking about those things you want the interviewer to hear.

Throughout this stage of the interview, maintain a positive frame of mind and demonstrate your grasp of job-getting interview techniques.

Stage 4: Interview Closing. As soon as you sense the interview coming to a conclusion, start to close out the session on a "high note." Use these last few minutes to (a) summarize a few key credentials in a final statement, (b) express enthusiasm about working for the company, and (c) express appreciation to the interviewer for an interesting time.

The interviewer will probably tell you the next step in the procedure. If nothing is mentioned by the interviewer, however, you may raise the subject by saying, "What is the next step?" or "I would like to continue our discussion again soon if you feel there is a basis for another meeting!" Such closing comments encourage commitment.

The interviewer may offer you a brief take-home project. If offered such a project, willingly and graciously accept it, for this is a sign that the interviewer is interested in you and your thoughts.

Before you leave the meeting, be certain that you have all the correct information concerning the next step in the selection procedure: Where, when, and with whom is the next interview? When can you expect to hear any word? Or, when is your brief project needed, if one is requested?

Stage 5: Post-interview. Immediately following an interview, record the key points of the discussion—important and interesting remarks made by both you and the interviewer. Note the names and key comments of all other people you talked with while you visited the company.

On another sheet of paper, evaluate the success of your interview. Note your strengths and weaknesses. What things said by you interested the interviewer, and what things bored, irritated, or disappointed him? How could you improve your next interview presentation based on this session? Keep this evaluation sheet.

Five to seven days following the interview, send a "thank-you" letter to the interviewer. In it express appreciation, comment on key points of the discussion, allude to others you met in a complimentary manner, reiterate key credentials, and if new events have occurred during the intervening period, provide a brief update on these accomplishments. Such a follow-up letter shows thoughtfulness, perseverance, and motivation.

Desirable and undesirable traits

During the job interview, the interviewer makes a series of judgments or evaluations about your ability to do the job. All these judgments go toward forming the overall impression that plays a crucial role in the selection procedure.

Three factors are particularly important in the forming of the overall impression: appearance, oral communications skill, and social skill.

Another factor that is seriously considered in the job interview is "personality." This factor, however, is more complex, less evident, and more subjectively judged by interviewers than the three factors just mentioned. The employment representative wants to know your attitude toward, and feelings about, yourself, your past, the company, the job, and the profession so that a prediction about your future performance with the company can be made.

Whereas a candidate's underlying motivations, attitudes, and feelings may not be clearly revealed in resumés and letters, these personality traits are sought out and frequently discovered within the face-to-face exchanges of the interview. A technique for exploring one's personality is referred to as depth interviewing. Broad, open-ended questions are put to the interviewee, and the resulting responses are followed up by probing questions that elicit more details, revealing feelings and attitudes. Probing questions often deal with reasons behind an act and the feelings associated with the act. Here is such a depth-interviewing exchange:

Broad, Open-Ended Question:
"Tell me about yourself at Murphy's Store."
Probe 1:
"How did you go about getting your promotion to assistant section supervisor?"
Probe 2:
"Why did you handle it that way?"
Probe 3:
"How did you feel when you received the promotion over Judy Stickler, who had been there three years longer than you?"

Depth-interviewing techniques have the appearance of casual conversation but actually reveal much information to the skilled interviewer about the inner workings of one's personality. In any such conversation, be careful to reveal attitudes, feelings, and motivations that are desirable.

Do not be deceived by the cordiality of an interested and curious interviewer; such behavior is essential to place you at ease, get you to talk, and make you reveal *everything* about yourself. Be as honest and frank as possible in revealing positive personality traits that will help on the job. But before uttering a negative, cynical, pessimistic, resentful, or antagonistic remark, think twice. The fact is that the prospective buyer will decide to buy your talents for your positive qualities and will decide to reject your talents for your negative qualities.

The following list contains many desirable traits:

Professional appearance
Good speaking skills
Good listening skills
Adaptability
Enthusiasm and determination
Self-confidence
Practical and realistic approach
Courtesy, appreciativeness,
   and consideration

Believability and persuasiveness
Willingness to work hard and assume responsibility
Imaginativeness, creativity, and resourcefulness
Good sense of humor
Conscientiousness and dedication
Insightful, thoughtful, and analytical
Alert and attentive
Honest and truthful
Logical and well organized

The following list contains many undesirable traits:

Poor appearance
Inability to express oneself
Poor listening skills
Lack of common courtesy
Lack of preparation for interview
Lack of confidence, interest, and enthusiasm
Passiveness and indifference.
Conceit and overconfidence
Negative, apologetic, and insecure
Evasive, deceitful, and dishonest
Contradictory
High-pressure selling
Long-winded or abrupt

The likelihood is that you now possess many of the positive traits needed to make that favorable personal impression. Try not to be shy, meek, overly modest, or embarrassed in expressing your desire for the job and your reasons for qualifying. Only you can state your case.

Fifteen important questions

Much of what you say in job interviews is in the form of direct replies to important interviewer questions. This section deals with 15 of the most frequently asked questions.

In addition to answering these important questions, you may be asked to verify and clarify parts of your resumé, letter of application, or application blank. The interviewer's attention will especially be drawn to "delay statements," such as "To be discussed during interview," written on the application blank. Therefore, have a thorough knowledge of all facts and figures submitted before the interview.

Key Question 1:
"Tell me about yourself!"

Reply Hints
A common opener, this broad question throws many unprepared interviewees. It is, in fact, a "sell-me" invitation. Impress the interviewer by expressing your interest in and desire to work for the company. Offer to discuss a number of your qualifications. Then present a few of your functional selling points and ask the interviewer to choose the ones he or she is interested in hearing about. You can also mention how you learned about the position and company.

Key Question 2:
"Why are you interested in working for this company?"

Reply Hints
Emphasize that you are very interested in working for the company, that you've considered joining the company for a while, and that your decision to seek employment here is based on sound reasons. Then produce those reasons, supported by facts and figures from your Company Data Sheet.

Key Question 3:
"Why do you want to leave your job?"

Reply Hints
One of two conditions prevails: you're either employed or unemployed. Obviously, being employed is the preferred condition, especially if you're happily employed and are merely investigating possibilities for even greater achievement. Being unemployed detracts from your bargaining position, especially if you were fired for incompetency, negligence, or other serious reasons.

If you have already left or plan to leave a position due to poor working relationships, one of the worst interviewing errors you can make is to respond to this question by ventilating your negative feelings, accusing superiors, claiming unfair treatment, or condemning people with whom you've worked. By leveling personal charges against others in your self-defense, you make the interviewer conclude that you were unable to handle an interpersonal job situation to the point of separation, that you may have been the cause of the trouble, and that, after some period of invested time with your employer, you are displaying disloyalty and could be as disloyal to your new employer.

You can sell yourself more effectively when you associate with successful people, programs, and companies. Build the image of your employer and you will be building your own.

Respond to this question as positively as possible by stating new job objectives rather than old job failures.

Key Question 4:
"Why have you chosen this particular field?"

Reply Hints
Here is a perfect opportunity for impressing the interviewer with your interest, knowledge of the field, and ability to perform successfully on the job. Explain that this type of work gives you a strong sense of purpose, identity, and accomplishment, a feeling that you could not derive from other types of work. Avoid discussion of fringe benefits. Emphasize your feelings for and knowledge of the work itself. Mention key functions of the job and claim that you are interested in and possess competency in them. Develop this claim and support your beliefs by presenting functional selling points.

Key Question 5:

"Why should we hire you?"

Reply Hints
This question is the most important question any interviewer can ask. Whether it is asked directly or indirectly, be certain that it is uppermost in the interviewer's mind throughout the interview. It is a direct invitation from the interviewer to you to "sell me" and requires extra attention.

Key Question 6:

"What are your long-range goals?"

Reply Hints
This question is very popular in interviewing because it gathers a lot of useful information:

(1) maturity, foresight, and realistic outlook; (2) degree of preparation in career planning; (3) knowledge of yourself, the occupation, and the company; and (4) commitment to the company and profession.

In your reply, reveal a career plan. In your research, determine what position you could reasonably expect to reach in five years and in ten years. Read about and speak to others who have successfully advanced themselves in your field and with this company, if possible. In your answer note that you have the potential and capability, possess the knowledge and desire, and will acquire the necessary skills for growth within the organization.

Key Question 7:

"What is your greatest strength?"

Reply Hints
This is a direct "sell-me" question. Select one key quality you possess that you know to be in great demand on this job. State the quality, then support your claim with past achievements.

Key Question 8:

"What is your greatest weakness?"

Reply Hints
This is a "suicide question" that has probably caused the downfall of many qualified but thoughtless interviewees. Interviewers pose this question to you in a fair-play manner, implying, "Well, everyone has weaknesses as well as strengths; it's only human!" You will be coaxed and prompted to answer this question. But before you volunteer anything negative, remember this important rule: "You are screened in because of your strengths and screened out because of your weaknesses."

In stating your reply to this question, emanate self-confidence, express a desire to further improve the good credentials you now possess, and possibly point to a relatively unimportant, non-job-related area that needs some improvement.

Key Question 9:

"What is your current salary?"

Reply Hints
There is a wrong time and a right time to discuss salary matters. The wrong time is before you've had the opportunity to sell yourself in person during the interview. The right time is after the interviewer tells you that a specific job is available and that he or she wants you for the opening.

Who should initiate the first figure in discussing salary, you or the interviewer? It is generally to your advantage to get the interviewer to throw out the first figure.

Key Question 10:

"What is important to you in a job?"

Reply Hints
The interviewer wants to hear that the things that satisfy you personally are the same things

that contribute to the organization's programs and objectives. One effective reply is, "What really motivates me at work is the personal pleasure and feeling of accomplishment I can derive from doing a good job in an organization where my opinions and contributions really count!"

Play down the importance of salary and fringe benefits in response to this question. First, impress the interviewer with your desire to do a good job; then, after you receive the job offer, you can negotiate for fair compensation.

Key Question 11:
"What do you do in your spare time?"

Reply Hints
From your reply, you want the interviewer to realize that:
1. You use your time wisely;
2. You are well rounded and have diverse interests and involvements in cultural, recreational, and civic affairs;
3. You would get along well with others in the company;
4. You are a participant and not just a spectator; a leader and not just a follower; a doer and not just a sitter.

To make a favorable impression here, find out the preferences of successful people in your field as to sports, magazines, and books. If you are involved in these activities, emphasize them in your reply. Also, if you have a unique or special talent, hobby, or skill, mention it. This will make you more memorable and add to the uniqueness of your image.

Key Question 12:
"Which feature of the job interests you least?"

Reply Hints
This is another "suicide question," as was Key Question 8. It can, however, be converted into a positive selling opportunity.

Tell the interviewer that all aspects of the job interest you, which is the reason you have chosen this line of work. Do not admit that anything about the job bothers you, no matter how much you are coaxed to do so. If the interviewer mentions that the work is difficult and could require frequent overtime, unpredictable work schedules, or hard-to-handle customers, reply in a positive manner.

Key Question 13:
"How do others describe you?"

Reply Hints
Tell the interviewer that you get along well with your co-workers, have the respect of your subordinates, and are respected by your boss. Your ability to work well with other people is extremely important to the interviewer; therefore, paint a positive picture of your social relationships on the job.

Key Question 14:
"What are your plans for continued study?"

Reply Hints
Convey your desire for continued growth and self-improvement. Indicate that your studies will help you stay current and be better prepared to cope with the new and changing techniques of your profession.

Key Question 15:
"Tell me about your schooling!"

Reply Hints
The key to this question is to keep your reply positive. Speak well of your alma mater, for you are, in part, a product of your school's educational programs. If you praise the programs, you indirectly praise yourself; and if you condemn its programs, you indirectly condemn yourself.

If you are asked to explain some low grade,

avoid being defensive or blaming others. Follow up with a reasonable explanation of your priorities, indicating that you had to work 30 hours a week to help support yourself and family, if this was the case. Then add that whatever grade you earned, you learned a great deal from that course, much of which you still use today.

HOW TO BE AN EMPLOYEE

Peter F. Drucker

This vintage article by a well-known writer on business subjects was originally published in the May 1952 issue of Fortune *magazine. It reflects the attitudes of the immediate post-World War II era, when the business world was still very much a man's world, and it must be read with those attitudes in mind. The content, however, is not dated. Drucker's advice still holds good, and for that reason the article is reprinted here.*

Most of you graduating today will be employees all your working life, working for somebody else and for a pay check. And so will most, if not all, of the thousands of other young Americans graduating this year in all the other schools and colleges across the country.

Ours has become a society of employees. A hundred years or so ago only one out of every five Americans at work was employed, i.e., worked for somebody else. Today only one out of five is not employed but working for himself. And where fifty years ago "being employed" meant working as a factory laborer or as a farmhand, the employee of today is increasingly a middle-class person with a substantial formal education, holding a professional or management job requiring intellectual and technical skills. Indeed, two things have characterized American society during these last fifty years: the middle and upper classes have become employees; and middle-class and upper-class employees have been the fastest-growing groups in our working population — growing so fast that the industrial worker, that oldest child of the Industrial Revolution, has been losing in numerical importance despite the expansion of industrial production.

This is one of the most profound social changes any country has ever undergone. It is, however, a perhaps even greater change for the individual young man about to start. Whatever he does, in all likelihood he will do it as an employee; wherever he aims, he will have to try to reach it through being an employee . . . .

Being an employee is . . . the one common characteristic of most careers today. The special profession or skill is visible and clearly defined; and a well-laid-out sequence of courses, degrees, and jobs leads into it. But being an employee is the foundation. And it is much more difficult to prepare for it. Yet there is no recorded information on the art of being an employee.

The first question we might ask is: what can you learn in college that will help you in being an employee? The schools teach a great many things of value to the future accountant, the future doctor, or the future electrician. Do they also teach anything of value to the future employee? The answer is: "Yes — they teach the one thing that it is perhaps most valuable for the future employee to know. But very few students bother to learn it."

This one basic skill is the ability to organize and express ideas in writing and in speaking.

As an employee you work with and through other people. This means that your success as an employee—and I am talking of much more here than getting promoted—will depend on your ability to communicate with people and to present your own thoughts and ideas to them so they will both understand what you are driving at and be persuaded. The letter, the report or memorandum, the ten-minute spoken "presentation" to a committee are basic tools of the employee.

If you work as a soda jerker you will, of course, not need much skill in expressing yourself to be effective. If you work on a machine your ability to express yourself will be of little importance. But as soon as you move one step up from the bottom, your effectiveness depends on your ability to reach others through the spoken or the written word. And the further away your job is from manual work, the larger the organization of which you are an employee, the more important it will be that you know how to convey your thoughts in writing or speaking. In the very large organization, whether it is the government, the large business corporation, or the Army, this ability to express oneself is perhaps the most important of all the skills a man can possess.

Of course, skill in expression is not enough by itself. You must have something to say in the first place. The popular picture of the engineer, for instance, is that of a man who works with a slide rule, T square, and compass. And engineering students reflect this picture in their attitude toward the written word as something quite irrelevant to their jobs. But the effectiveness of the engineer—and with it his usefulness—depends as much on his ability to make other people understand his work as it does on the quality of the work itself.

Expressing one's thoughts is one skill that the school can really teach, especially to people born without natural writing or speaking talent. Many other skills can be learned later—in this country there are literally thousands of places that offer training to adult people at work. But the foundations for skill in expression have to be laid early: an interest in and an ear for language; experience in organizing ideas and data, in brushing aside the irrelevant, in wedding outward form and inner content into one structure; and above all, the habit of verbal expression. If you do not lay these foundations during your school years, you may never have an opportunity again.

If you were to ask me what strictly vocational courses there are in the typical college curriculum, my answer—now that the good old habit of the "theme a day" has virtually disappeared—would be: the writing of poetry and the writing of short stories. Not that I expect many of you to become poets or short-story writers—far from it. But these two courses offer the easiest way to obtain some skill in expression. They force one to be economical with language. They force one to organize thought. They demand of one that he give meaning to every word. They train the ear for language, its meaning, its precision, its overtones—and its pitfalls. Above all they force one to write.

I know very well that the typical employer does not understand this as yet, and that he may look with suspicion on a young college graduate who has majored, let us say, in short-story writing. But the same employer will complain—and with good reason—that the young men whom he hires when they get out of college do not know how to write a simple report, do not know how to tell a simple story, and are in fact virtually illiterate. And he will conclude—rightly—that the young men are not really effective, and certainly not employees who are likely to go very far.

The next question to ask is: what kind of employee should you be? Pay no attention to what other people tell you. This is one question only you can answer. It involves a choice in four areas—a choice you alone can make, and one you cannot easily duck. But to make the choice you must first have tested yourself in the world of jobs for some time.

Here are the four decisions—first in brief outline, then in more detail:

1. Do you belong in a job calling primarily for faithfulness in the performance of routine work and promising security? Or do you belong in job that offers a challenge to imagination and ingenuity—with the attendant penalty for failure?

2. Do you belong in a large organization or in a small organization? Do you work better through channels or through direct contacts? Do you enjoy more being a small cog in a big and powerful machine or a big wheel in a small machine?

3. Should you start at the bottom and try to work your way up, or should you try to start near the top? On the lowest rung of the promotional ladder, with its solid and safe footing but also with a very long climb ahead? Or on the aerial trapeze of "a management trainee," or some other staff position close to management?

4. Finally, are you going to be more effective and happy as a specialist or as a "generalist," that is, in an administrative job?

Let me spell out what each of these four decisions involves:

The decision between secure routine work and insecure work challenging the imagination and ingenuity is the one decision most people find easiest to make. You know very soon what kind of person you are. Do you find real satisfaction in the precision, order, and system of a clearly laid-out job? Do you prefer the security not only of knowing what your work is today and what it is going to be tomorrow, but also security in your job, in your relationship to the people above, below, and next to you, and economic security? Or are you one of those people who tend to grow impatient with anything that looks like a "routine" job? These people are usually able to live in a confused situation in which their relations to the people around them are neither clear nor stable. And

they tend to pay less attention to economic security, find it not too upsetting to change jobs, etc. . . .

The difference is one of basic personality. It is not too much affected by a man's experiences; he is likely to be born with the one or the other. The need for economic security is often as not an outgrowth of a need for psychological security rather than a phenomenon of its own. But precisely because the difference is one of basic temperament, the analysis of what kind of temperament you possess is so vital. A man might be happy in work for which he has little *aptitude;* he might be quite successful in it. But he can be neither happy nor successful in a job for which he is *temperamentally* unfitted.

You hear a great many complaints today about the excessive security-consciousness of our young people. My complaint is the opposite: in the large organizations especially there are not enough job opportunities for those young people who need challenge and risk. Jobs in which there is greater emphasis on conscientious performance of well-organized duties rather than on imagination—especially for the beginner—are to be found, for instance, in the inside jobs in banking or insurance, which normally offer great job security but not rapid promotion or large pay. The same is true of most government work, of the railroad industry, particularly in the clerical and engineering branches, and of most public utilities. The bookkeeping and accounting areas, especially in the larger companies, are generally of this type too—though a successful comptroller is an accountant with great management and business imagination.

At the other extreme are such areas as buying, selling, and advertising, in which the emphasis is on adaptability, on imagination, and on a desire to do new and different things. In those areas, by and large, there is little security, either personal or economic. The rewards, however, are high and come more rapidly. Major premium on imagination—though of a different kind and coupled with dogged persistence on details—prevails in most research and engineering work. Jobs in production, as supervisor or executive, also demand much adaptability and imagination.

Contrary to popular belief, very small business requires, above all, close attention to daily routine. Running a neighborhood drugstore or a small grocery, or being a toy jobber, is largely attention to details. But in very small business there is also room for quite a few people of the other personality type—the innovator or imaginer. If successful, a man of this type soon ceases to be in a very small business. For the real innovator there is, still, no more promising opportunity in this country than that of building a large out of a very small business.

Almost as important is the decision between working for a large and for a small organization. The difference is perhaps not so great as that between the secure, routine job and the insecure, imaginative job; but the wrong decision can be equally serious.

There are two basic differences between the large and small enterprise. In the small enterprise you operate primarily through personal contacts. In the large enterprise you have established "policies," "channels" of organization, and fairly rigid procedures. In the small enterprise you have, moreover, immediate effectiveness in a very small area. You can see the effect of your work and of your decisions right away, once you are a little bit above the ground floor. In the large enterprise even the man at the top is only a cog in a big machine. To be sure, his actions affect a much greater area than the actions and decisions of the man in the small organization, but his effectiveness is remote, indirect, and elusive. In a small and even in a middle-sized business you are normally exposed to all kinds of experiences, and expected to do a great many things without too much help or guidance. In the large organization you are normally taught one thing thoroughly. In the small one the danger is of becoming a jack-of-all-trades, master of none. In the large one it is of becoming the man who knows more and more about less and less.

There is one other important thing to consider: do you derive a deep sense of satisfaction from being a member of a well-known organization—General Motors, the Bell Telephone System, the government? Or is it more important to you to be a well-known and important figure within your own small pond? . . .

You may well think it absurd to say that anyone has a choice between beginning at the bottom and beginning near the top. And indeed I do not mean that you have any choice between beginner's jobs and, let us say, a vice presidency at General Electric. But you do have a choice between a position at the bottom of the hierarchy and a staff position that is outside the hierarchy but in view of the top. It is an important choice.

In every organization, even the smallest, there are positions that, while subordinate, modestly paid, and usually filled with young and beginning employees, nonetheless are not at the bottom. There are positions as assistant to one of the bosses; there are positions as private secretary; there are liaison positions for various departments; and there are positions in staff capacities, in industrial engineering, in cost accounting, in personnel, etc. Every one of these gives a view of the whole rather than of only one small area. Every one of them normally brings the holder into the deliberations and discussions of the people at the top, if only as a silent audience or perhaps only as an errand boy. Every one of these positions is a position "near the top," however humble and badly paid it may be.

On the other hand the great majority of beginner's jobs are at the bottom, where you begin in a department or in a line of work in the lowest-paid and simplest function, and where you are expected to work your way up as you acquire more skill and more judgment.

Different people belong in these two kinds of jobs. In the first place, the job "near the top" is insecure. You are exposed to public view. Your position is ambiguous; by yourself you are a nobody—but you reflect the boss's status; in a relatively short time you may even speak for the boss. You may have real power and influence. In today's business and government organization the hand that writes the memo rules the committee; and the young staff man usually writes the memos, or at least the first draft. But for that very reason everybody is jealous of you. You are a youngster who has been admitted to the company of his betters, and is therefore expected to show unusual ability and above all unusual discretion and judgment. Good performance in such a position is often the key to rapid advancement. But to fall down may mean the end of all hopes of ever getting anywhere within the organization.

At the bottom, on the other hand, there are very few opportunities for making serious mistakes. You are amply protected by the whole apparatus of authority. The job itself is normally simple, requiring little judgment, discretion, or initiative. Even excellent performance in such a job is unlikely to speed promotion. But one also has to fall down in a rather spectacular fashion for it to be noticed by anyone but one's immediate superior.

There are a great many careers in which the increasing emphasis is on specialization. You find these careers in engineering and in accounting, in production, in statistical work, and in teaching. But there is an increasing demand for people who are able to take in a great area at a glance, people who perhaps do not know too much about any one field—though one should always have one area of real competence. There is, in other words, a demand for people who are capable of seeing the forest rather than the trees, of making overall judgments. And these "generalists" are particularly needed for administrative positions, where it is their job to see that other people do the work, where they have to plan for other people, to organize other people's work, to initiate it and appraise it.

The specialist understands one field: his concern is with technique, tools, media. He is a "trained" man; and his educational background is properly technical or professional. The generalist—and especially the administrator—deals with people; his concern is with leadership, with planning, with direction giving, and with coordination. He is an "educated" man; and the humanities are his strongest foundation. Very rarely is a specialist capable of being an administrator. And very rarely is a good generalist also a good specialist in a particular field. Any organization needs both kinds of people, though different organizations need them in different ratios. It is your job to find out, during your apprenticeship, into which of those two job categories you fit, and to plan your career accordingly.

Your first job may turn out to be the right job for you—but this is pure accident. Certainly you should not change jobs constantly or people will become suspicious—rightly—of your ability to hold any job. At the same time you must not look upon the first job as the final job; it is primarily a training job, an opportunity to analyze yourself and your fitness for being an employee.

In fact there is a great deal to be said for being fired from the first job. One reason is that it is rarely an advantage to have started as an office boy in the organization; far too many people will still consider you a "green kid" after you have been there for twenty-five years. But the major reason is that getting fired from the first job is the least painful and the least damaging way to learn how to take a setback. And whom the Lord loveth he teacheth early how to take a setback.

Nobody has ever lived, I daresay, who has not gone through a period when everything seemed to have collapsed and when years of work and life seemed to have gone up in smoke. No one can be spared this experience; but one can be prepared for it. The man who has been through earlier setbacks has learned that the world has not come to an end because he lost his job—not even in a depression. He has learned that he will somehow survive. He has learned, above all, that the way to behave in such a setback is not to collapse himself. But the man who comes up against it for the first time when he is forty-five is quite likely to collapse for good. For the things that people are apt to do when they receive the first nasty blow may destroy a mature man with a family, whereas a youth of twenty-five bounces right back.

Obviously you cannot contrive to get yourself fired. But you can always quit. And it is perhaps even more important to have quit once than to have been fired once. The man who walks out on his own volition acquires an inner independence that he will never quite lose.

To know when to quit is therefore one of the most important things—particularly for the beginner. For on the whole, young people have a tendency to hang on to the first job long beyond the time when they should have quit for their own good.

One should quit when self-analysis shows that the job is the wrong job—that, say, it does not give the security and routine one requires, that it is a small-company rather than a big-organization job, that it is at the bottom rather than near the top, a specialist's rather than a generalist's job, etc. One should quit if the job demands behavior one considers morally indefensible, or if the whole atmosphere of the place is morally corrupting—if, for instance, only yes men and flatterers are tolerated.

One should also quit if the job does not offer the training one needs either in a specialty or in administration and the view of the whole. The beginner not only has a right to expect training from his first five or ten years in a job; he has an obligation to get as much training as possible. A job in which young people are not given real training—though, of course, the training need not be a formal "training program"—does not measure up to what they have a right and a duty to expect.

But the most common reason why one should quit is the absence of promotional opportunities in the organization. That is a compelling reason.

I do not believe that chance of promotion is the essence of a job. In fact there is no surer way to kill a job and one's own usefulness in it than to consider it as but one rung in the promotional ladder rather than as a job in itself that deserves serious effort and will return satisfaction, a sense of accomplishment, and pride. And one can be an important and respected member of an organization without ever having received a promotion; there are such people in practically every office. But the organization itself must offer fair promotional opportunities. Otherwise it stagnates, becomes corrupted, and in turn corrupts. The absence of promotional opportunities is demoralizing. And the sooner one gets out of a demoralizing situation, the better. There are three situations to watch out for:

The entire group may be so young that for years there will be no vacancies. . . .

Another situation without promotional opportunities is one in which the group ahead of you is uniformly old—so old that it will have to be replaced long before you will be considered ready to move up. Stay away from organizations that have a uniform age structure throughout their executive group—old or young. The only organization that offers fair promotional opportunities is one in which there is a balance of ages.

And finally there is the situation in which all promotions go to members of a particular group—to which you do not belong. Some chemical companies, for instance, require a master's degree in chemistry for just about any job above sweeper. Some companies promote only engineering graduates. . . . Or all the good jobs may be reserved for members of the family. There may be adequate promotional opportunities in such an organization—but not for you.

On the whole there are proportionately more opportunities in the big organization than in the small one. But there is very real danger of getting lost in the big organization—whereas you are always visible in the small one. A young man should therefore stay in a large organization only if it has a definite promotional program which ensures that he will be considered and looked at. . . .

But techniques do not concern us here. What matters is that there should be both adequate opportunities and fair assurance that you will be eligible and considered for promotion. Let me repeat: to be promoted is not essential, either to happiness or to usefulness. To be considered for promotion is.

I have only one more thing to say: to be an employee it is not enough that the job be right and that you be right for the job. It is also necessary that you have a meaningful life outside the job.

I am talking of having a genuine interest in something in which you, on your own, can be, if not a master, at least an amateur expert. This something may be botany, or the history of your county, or chamber music, cabinetmaking, Christmas-tree growing, or a thousand other things. But it is important in this "employee society" of ours to have a genuine interest outside of the job and to be serious about it.

I am not, as you might suspect, thinking of something that will keep you alive and interested during your retirement. I am speaking of keeping yourself alive, interested, and happy during your working life, and of a permanent source of self-respect and standing in the community outside and beyond your job. You will need such an interest when you hit the forties, that period in which most of us come to realize that we will never reach the goals we

have set ourselves when younger—whether these are goals of achievement or of worldly success. You will need it because you should have one area in which you yourself impose standards of performance on your own work. Finally, you need it because you will find recognition and acceptance by other people working in the field, whether professional or amateur, as individuals rather than as members of an organization and as employees.

This is heretical philosophy these days when so many companies believe that the best employee is the man who lives, drinks, eats, and sleeps job and company. In actual experience those people who have no life outside their jobs are not the really successful people, not even from the viewpoint of the company. I have seen far too many of them shoot up like a rocket, because they had no interests except the job; but they also come down like the rocket's burned-out stick. The man who will make the greatest contribution to his company is the mature person—and you cannot have maturity if you have no life or interest outside the job. Our large companies are beginning to understand this. That so many of them encourage people to have "outside interests" or to develop "hobbies" as a preparation for retirement is the first sign of a change toward a more intelligent attitude. But quite apart from the self-interest of the employer, your own interest as an employee demands that you develop a major outside interest. It will make you happier, it will make you more effective, it will give you resistance against the setbacks and the blows that are the lot of everyone; and it will make you a more effective, a more successful, and a more mature employee.

You have no doubt realized that I have not really talked about how to be an employee. I have talked about what to know before becoming an employee—which is something quite different. Perhaps "how to be an employee" can be learned only by being one. But one thing can be said. Being an employee means working with people; it means living and working in a society. Intelligence, in the last analysis, is therefore not the most important quality. What is decisive is character and integrity. If you work on your own, intelligence and ability may be sufficient. If you work with people you are going to fail unless you also have basic integrity. And integrity—character—is one thing most, if not all, employers consider first.

There are many skills you might learn to be an employee, many abilities that are required. But fundamentally the one quality demanded of you will not be skill, knowledge, or talent, but character.

Appendices

A Brief Guide to English Usage

In preparing a speech, writing a report, or composing a letter, all of us, from time to time, have to stop and check on the correct use of a punctuation mark, the spelling of a word, or the grammar of a sentence. Should it be *continual* or *continuous? Farther* or *further?* Does the question mark go inside or outside the period in this direct quotation? Should it be *who* or *whom?*

The sections which follow may be used as a quick reference guide to answer these and other common questions. There are English-usage manuals and handbooks available which offer a more comprehensive discussion of the following areas of diction and grammar should you need more information pertaining to standard English usage.

PUNCTUATION

Use a COMMA

1. To set off an introductory word, introductory phrase, or subordinate clause from an independent statement.

   Examples
   a. Meanwhile, I am reading my History 101 assignment. (introductory word)
   b. While waiting for a train, James Johnson read the editorial section of the morning newspaper (introductory phrase)
   c. Since we have no job openings now, we are not accepting applications for summer jobs. (introductory subordinate clause)
   d. When I entered the crowded assembly hall, I immediately noted the presence of armed guards seated in the gallery overlooking the stage. (introductory subordinate clause)

2. Before coordinating conjunctions *(for, and, nor, but, or, yet)* joining two independent clauses. If the independent clauses are very short, omit the comma.

   Examples
   a. Mary dictated the letter and John typed it. (no comma needed)
   b. Barry shouted and Carlota turned. (no comma needed)
   c. My parents had hoped that their three children would enter the family furniture business, but my two sisters and I decided to open a small boutique in Greenwich Village.
   d. Key management personnel in the large organization should be care-

fully selected, and all managers should be informed of their specific responsibilities.

3. To set off nonrestrictive (nonessential) phrases or clauses.

    Examples
    a. The new procedure, as we mentioned in our telephone conversation, will begin the first of next month. (nonrestrictive)
    b. That new procedure we discussed yesterday will begin on Monday. (restrictive so no commas are needed)
    c. Dr. John Kelly, who taught philosophy for twenty-five years, received frequent commendation from students and faculty. (nonrestrictive)
    d. A professor who taught philosophy for twenty-five years is speaking to our class this Friday. (restrictive so no commas are needed)

4. To set off phrases or words in apposition.

    Examples
    a. My new graduate student, Manuela Ortega, is interested in doing an independent study on "Women in Management."
    b. Mrs. Spear, fashion director for Century Clothes, was elected president of the Designers' Association.
    c. Our first customer, a man about sixty-five years old, bought two sleeping bags and a knapsack.
    d. His sister Marijean teaches in a community college. (Marijean is essential to complete the message — he has more than one sister — so commas are omitted)

5. To set off a name directly addressed.

    Examples
    a. Mr. Barclay, write me at your earliest convenience so I may arrange a tour for your group. (the name is at the beginning)
    b. Write me at your earliest convenience, Mr. Barclay, so I may arrange a tour for your group. (the name is in the middle)
    c. Write me at your earliest convenience so I may arrange a tour for your group, Mr. Barclay. (the name is at the end)

6. To set off a mild interjection.

    Examples
    a. Oh, I didn't want you to purchase a new one.
    b. Well, well, so we finally finished that project.

7. When two or more adjectives separately modify a noun, and a conjunction is omitted.

    Examples
    a. Our minister is a kind, considerate, hardworking person.
    b. I have a dark blue suit. (omit comma as dark explains blue not the suit)
    c. My nephew is a tall, thin teenager.

8. To separate words or short phrases in a series.

   Examples
   a. The very contemporary design had lines and patterns of red, green, blue, yellow, violet, and white. (series of words)
   b. The sofa was clean and uncluttered, inexpensive but not cheap, and colorful but not gaudy. (series of phrases)
   c. Typewriting I, Shorthand I, and Business Communications I are required courses for first-semester secretarial science students. (series of words)
   d. Will the conferences be held in Spokane, in New Orleans, or in Philadelphia? (series of phrases)

   Note—Do not use a comma to separate the parts of one measurement or one weight.
   It took him 1 hour 35 minutes 15 seconds to jog around the park.
   The measurement you requested is 1 yard 2 feet 7 inches.

9. To set off a quotation from the reference source in a sentence.

   Examples
   a. "I shall arrive in Los Angeles before midnight," said Mrs. Kelly.
   b. Mr. Fujikawa commented, "I will be unavailable for any Saturday meetings."
   c. The memorandum read, "Our sales representative will send you a mailgram when the contract is signed."

10. To indicate the omission of a word or words that are understood.

    Examples
    a. Buckingham Way has been renamed Washington Street; Devonshire Place, Adams Avenue; and Kavenaugh Way, Jefferson Street.
    b. Binswanger Realtors sold our home; Cross Realtors, our office building; and Johnson Realty Company, our apartment building.

11. Before *etc.* in a series. Place commas before and after *etc.* in the middle of a sentence.

    Examples
    a. An accounting student should be familiar with working papers, profit and loss statements, balance sheets, etc.
    b. A personnel interviewer judges skills, personality, work experience, etc., when offering employment to a job applicant.

12. To offset a parenthetical (nonessential) word or phrase.

    Examples
    a. The most important item on the agenda, I believe, is the discussion of word-processing equipment.

b. I understand, however, that the management consultant disagrees with the comptroller of your company.

c. Let me say, at the very start, that you will find this lecture series to be very helpful when taking your graduate examinations.

Use a SEMICOLON

1. Between coordinate, independent clauses not joined by a coordinating conjunction *(for, and, nor, but, or, yet)*.

   Examples
   a. Ms. Sigowitz submitted her monthly report to the board; it was accepted without comment.
   b. Some of our secretaries take dictation from the executives; other secretaries use transcribing machines.
   c. The full-time faculty asked for the advanced classes; the part-time faculty settled for the freshman classes.

2. Before a conjunctive adverb *(nevertheless, moreover, therefore, however)* joining two coordinate clauses.

   Examples
   a. I thought his report was much too long; therefore, I read only his summary of findings.
   b. The girls enjoyed their vacation; however, their funds were badly depleted by the end of the second week and they had to return home.
   c. My cousin graduated first in his law school class; moreover, he has enrolled for the fall term in Jefferson Medical College.

3. Before a coordinating conjunction joining two independent clauses if the clauses are very long or have commas in them.

   Examples
   a. When the race, which has been held every year since 1955, was scheduled, we had twenty-two contestants; but five additional entrants paid their fees to the official registrar, who immediately issued a qualifying certificate.
   b. After studying business communications, John realized that effective written and oral communications are necessary for a successful business; and the mastery of the skills needed to write acceptable letters and memos will assist all business persons.

4. To separate a series if any of the items in the series already contain commas.

   Example
   Attending the ABCA international conference were Florence Walks, executive director; Louis Fineman, president; Reginald Bankenshire, first vice-president; and Gary Dunkins, journal editor.

Use a COLON

1. To introduce a list, a statement, a question, a series of statements, a long quotation, and in some cases a word.

    Examples
    a. Each person should bring the following equipment: one sleeping bag, hiking boots, rainwear, a small shovel, and heavy outdoor clothes.
    b. The needlecraft skills that are necessary for this job are these: crewel stitchery, knitting, needlepoint, and crocheting.
    c. The following suggestions are important when typing a title page for a report:
        1. Center each line.
        2. Type the title of the report in capital letters and all the other lines in initial capitals.
        3. Include the name of the writer, the date, the course, and the title of the report.
    d. Dr. Lindquist said: "My medical conference is in Chicago on May 19. I will attend that first, and then I will travel to Los Angeles to deliver my speech at the medical college."

2. Before or after a specific illustration of a general statement.

    Examples
    a. In the first week he broke a turning rod, dropped a glass test kit, and tore a rubber protection sheet: he was an extremely negligent worker.
    b. Winter arrived with a sudden fury: the temperature dropped to fifteen degrees below zero, six inches of snow fell, and the wind howled violently.
    c. The vacation you describe sounds very inviting: the cost is low, the accommodations are comfortable, the mountain scenery is beautiful, and the fishing is the best in the Southeast.

3. Following the salutation in a business letter.

    Examples
    a. Ladies and Gentlemen:
    b. Dear Mr. Jamison:
    c. Dear Sir:

Use a DASH

1. To set off and emphasize parenthetical (nonessential) material.

    Examples
    a. James Rolsted—you know he worked for us since 1955—retired in June this year.

b. We plan to see that our faculty—some of whom have been with us since our college opened—receive cost-of-living raises in the next contract.

2. To indicate when the idea in a sentence has been broken off sharply.

Examples
a. Do you believe that—
b. Here is an excellent textbook—economical, too!

3. To indicate a sudden change in thought within a sentence.

Examples
a. Do you believe that—no, I'm sure you would never accept it!
b. The spring meeting is at Indiana University in Bloomington, Indiana—or is it at Indiana State University in Pennsylvania?

4. To precede a summarizing statement at the end of a sentence.

Example
Magazines were everywhere, the record player was on, clothes were tossed helter-skelter, food disappeared like magic, laughter filled the air—the girls were home for the weekend.

Use PARENTHESES

1. To enclose ideas not directly related to the main thought of the sentence.

Examples
a. The politician heard from only a few (three) of his many followers.
b. I received a letter from Loretta Lawson (formerly Loretta Lyman) just last week.
c. Zorniatti's periodic reports (following the format recommended by the National Trade Council) were submitted by all department managers to the general superintendent.

2. To enclose a numerical designation of a verbal statement—sometimes found in legal documentation.

Example
The deposit of five hundred dollars ($500.00) will not be refunded except through court order.

3. To set off references and directions.

Examples
a. The information appears in the appendix (see pages 181–183).
b. Because of the present renovations to our hospital (see the enclosed newsletter), we must postpone using your window-washing service until spring.

Use BRACKETS

1. To enclose an explanatory comment within a quotation or to insert a correction into quoted material.

   Examples
   a. In her article on political upsets, Sarah stated, "Martin was defeated in the election of 1966 [he was defeated in 1962] and this marked the end of thirty-six years of Democratic treasurers in Wade County."
   b. The newscaster stated, "The Iranian hostages are all safe [the local newspaper questioned the location of one hostage] according to the visiting diplomats."

Use QUOTATION MARKS

1. To enclose direct quotations.

   Examples
   a. Sally said, "People don't change; their basic characteristics remain the same throughout their lives."
   b. "I don't agree," said Frank.

2. To enclose slang words or expressions.

   Examples
   a. My teenager said it was a contemporary-style "pad."
   b. He may or may not know the facts, but I notice he just "ain't sayin' nothin'."

3. To enclose a quotation within a quotation. The initial quotation is enclosed in double quotation marks; the quotation within that in single; and a quote within that in double.

   Examples
   a. Stevenson said, "If we are to live in peace, we must, as the Israeli representative has indicated, 'Appreciate the dignity of all people at all times.'"
   b. "Men's cologne and other cosmetics are 'in' for 'today's man.'"
   c. The professor said, "All groups have the same pleasure values, although Johnson disagrees with this when he says, 'Entertainment values are not the same for all age groups; a "trip" to some is attractive; to others, repulsive.'"

4. To enclose titles of articles, chapters or sections of a book, lectures, essays, sermons, paintings, poems, and sculptures.

   Examples
   a. Picasso's "Guernica" will be shipped from the Museum of Modern Art to a museum in Madrid.

b. Thomas Carton wrote the article, "The Problems of International Finance," which recently appeared in *The Financial Quarterly.*

c. The poet saw his finished work "The Light-Hearted Lass" in the *Ladies Home Journal.*

5. To define terms.

Examples

a. A "television addict" is someone who automatically turns the set on when waking up and leaves it on until nighttime when he or she goes to sleep.

b. A "principal" is the head of a school while a "principle" is a rule or precept.

6. Other punctuation marks are used with quotation marks in the following way:

a. Question marks and exclamation points are placed inside the quotation marks if they refer to the quoted material and outside the quotation marks if they refer to the statement as a whole.

Examples

1. Dr. Martinez asked, "Isn't that their usual performance?"
2. Did Dr. Martinez ask, "Is that your usual performance"?
3. A voice exclaimed, "Stand up!"
4. What a disgraceful example of "goofing off"!

b. Commas and periods are placed inside quotation marks.

Examples

1. I just read Shirley Jackson's famous story, "The Lottery."
2. "I will see you on Saturday," he said.

c. Colons and semicolons are placed outside quotation marks.

Examples

1. When I saw her, she said, "I will arrive at 10 P.M. on Tuesday"; however, she is still not here.
2. Take the following books from the box marked "History 321": *Ancient Civilization, The Old World,* and *Egypt Versus Greece.*

Use a HYPHEN

1. To divide a word at the end of a line between syllables. Divide hyphenated words *(self-assurance)* only at the hyphen. Do not divide the last word of a paragraph or page.

2. To form compound nouns, verbs, and adjectives.

Examples
a. Mrs. Lubichek was my mother-in-law. (compound noun)
b. He was angry when he saw that I had double-spaced the letter. (compound verb)
c. He is not a well-known artist. (compound adjective)

Use an ELLIPSIS

1. To indicate the omission of a part of a sentence. Use three periods if the omission is within the sentence. If the omission is at the end of the sentence, use three periods and the terminal punctuation mark.

Examples
a. The transaction was completed . . . and provided for Garson to receive the car plus miscellaneous items . . . .
b. Is anyone able to explain why . . . ?

Use an EXCLAMATION POINT

1. After interjections of very strong or sudden emotion.

Examples
a. "I will not!" he shouted.
b. Be quiet!
c. No! It isn't true!
d. Hush! Hush! She is asleep.

2. See also the section on quotation marks.

Use a QUESTION MARK

1. After a direct question.

Examples
a. Have you completed your analysis of the Compton Company case?
b. He asked if we were coming. (indirect question—omit question mark)
c. The client asked, "Is my case ready for suit yet?"

2. In a series of questions.

Examples
a. Are you opening a branch office in Newark? in Albany? in Princeton?
b. Who is making the speech—the president? the dean? the business manager?

3. See also the section on quotation marks.

Use a PERIOD

1. After a complete declarative or imperative sentence.

   Examples
   a. Your merchandise will be delivered tomorrow. (declarative)
   b. Return the defective iron to us. (imperative)

2. After a request phrased as a question.

   Examples
   a. May we hear from you within two weeks.
   b. Will you please call us tomorrow.

3. To indicate an abbreviation.

   Examples
   a. He worked for Kingston, Inc., for over ten years.
   b. Dr. George Krishnamurti lives at 1346 Landview Drive.

Use an UNDERLINE

1. To indicate a foreign expression that is not part of the English language if it is likely to be unfamiliar to the reader.

   Example
   There was a true spirit of gemütlichkeit at the family reunion.

2. To indicate titles of complete works that are published as separate items, such as books, pamphlets, magazines, newspapers, films, and plays.

   Examples
   a. Every typist will find the handbook Typing in Business a necessary reference book.
   b. The Philadelphia Inquirer has a very large classified section.

Use an APOSTROPHE

1. To indicate the omission of one or more letters in a contraction or one or more digits in a numeral.

   Examples
   a. He hasn't been home since he graduated in '70.
   b. Our motto is "Don't call us; we'll call you."

2. To form the possessive case of nouns.

   Examples
   a. The three boys' jackets were red.
   b. He purchased a dollar's worth of candy.

c. That was my aunt's coat.
d. The men's tools were left behind.

Note — If the word in question already ends in s (plural), add only an apostrophe; if it does not end in s (singular), add apostrophe s ('s). The girl's coat was green. (singular possessive) The girls' coats were green. (plural possessive)

Note — It is best to avoid the use of possessives with inanimate objects; e.g., sink's top, lamp's cord, or chair's leg. Sink top, lamp cord, and chair leg are standard usage.

Additional uses of the APOSTROPHE to indicate possession

1. If two or more persons or objects own one item, possession is indicated on the last-named only. If the writer wishes to indicate individual possession, an apostrophe is used with each name or object.

Examples
a. Robin and Shelley's car (Robin and Shelley own one car in partnership)
b. Robin and Shelley's cars (Robin and Shelley own more than one car in partnership)
c. Robin's and Shelley's cars (Robin and Shelley each own one or more cars individually)

2. In compound words, an apostrophe is added to the second or last word to indicate possession.

Examples
a. My brother-in-law's car was damaged in the accident. (singular possessive)
b. My brothers-in-law's cars were all parked in front of the house. (plural possessive)
c. You are using somebody else's dictionary. (singular possessive)

3. Certain phrases involving time that seem to express possession use the apostrophe.

Examples
a. A month's pay was granted.
b. Three hours' time is not adequate for the job.
c. His dream was to take four weeks' vacation in Hawaii.

4. The apostrophe is used to indicate possession with indefinite pronouns.

Examples
a. One's thoughts are sometimes private.
b. Anybody's ideas are acceptable in this brainstorming session.

5. Possession is indicated on the *Jr., Sr.,* or *Esq.*

   Examples
   a. Martin Kelly, Jr.'s coat was a plaid.
   b. Thomas Fonveille, Sr.'s store was sold.
   c. Lawrence McDonald, Esq.'s briefcase was stolen.

6. To indicate possession. For names ending in *s,* practice varies. Either *'s* or simply an apostrophe can be added, according to which stylebook you follow.

   Examples
   a. Mr. Jones's car
   b. Mr. Williams' car

7. Where an appositive is used, possession is indicated on the appositive, rather than the preceding noun.

   Examples
   a. That is Mr. Carson, the maintenance man's, responsibility.
   b. This was Marie Locke, our ex-employee's, personnel file.

   Note — Pronouns in the possessive case do not use the apostrophe to indicate ownership; such words are already possessive.
   > The radio is ours.
   > The chair is yours but the radio is ours.
   > Its surface was scratched, but it's (contraction of *it is*) really of no great importance.

SENTENCE CONSTRUCTION

1. Avoid pieces of sentences or fragments by having a subject and a predicate in each sentence.

   Examples
   a. In the mail she found a check. Which came as a complete surprise. (fragment)
   b. In the mail she found a check, which came as a complete surprise. (sentence)
   c. On the train I met a neighbor. Also a friend of mine. (fragment)
   d. On the train I met a neighbor who is a friend of mine. (sentence)

2. Avoid run-on sentences. (two independent clauses merged together)

   Examples
   a. Warren was the lawyer's son he was an accountant. (incorrect)
   b. Warren, the lawyer's son, was an accountant. (correct)
   c. Warren was the lawyer's son; he was an accountant. (correct)

d. Those two books are on the shelf the other two are on the chair. (incorrect)

e. Those two books are on the shelf; the other two are on the chair. (correct)

f. Those two books are on the shelf, but the other two are on the chair. (correct)

3. Avoid comma splices. (two independent clauses separated by a comma without a conjunction)

Examples

a. Suzanne graduates from nursing school now, John will graduate next year. (incorrect)

b. Suzanne graduates from nursing school now, and John will graduate next year. (correct)

c. Suzanne graduates from nursing school now; John will graduate next year. (correct)

Subject-Verb Agreement

1. A predicate (verb) must agree in number and person with the subject.

Examples

a. The typists who work in our office *have* excellent skills.

b. Behind the chairs *was* the trunk to be sent to the children's camp.

c. Walter and Nancy *are* students at the Sorbonne.

d. There *is* a speaker on the platform.

e. There *are* speakers on the platform.

f. The house, together with the furnishings, *is* very desirable.

2. If the subject is a word that means a part of something (*some, half, one-third*), the number of the predicate is determined by asking, ''Part of what?''

Examples

a. Some of the report *is* well written.

b. Some of the reports *are* well written.

3. The words *each, every, neither, either, somebody,* and *anybody* are singular in meaning and require a singular predicate.

Examples

a. Each of us *has* his or her own closet.

b. Everybody *has* to wear a cap and gown on the stage at the graduation ceremony.

c. Neither of the proposed suggestions *is* acceptable to us.

4. When a compound subject has words joined by *or* or *nor*, match the predicate with the word preceding (closest to) the verb.

Examples

a. Neither the student nor her professors *were* satisfied with her academic performance.

b. Neither Jane's professors nor Jane *was* satisfied with her academic performance.

c. Either Marvin or the two auditors *were* asked to revise the balance sheet.

d. Either the two visiting auditors or Marvin *was* asked to revise the balance sheet.

Pronouns

Pronouns take the place of nouns and permit us to avoid constant repetition.

1. A basic rule for the use of pronouns is that they agree in person, number, and gender with the word to which they refer (antecedent).

Examples

a. *Joan* gave *her* **coat** to the WAITER and HE took **it** to the check stand.

b. The *boys* ran down the road to the oak tree and then *they* cut across the field.

c. *Cecilia* got *her* car from the parking lot attendant right away; the other **girls** had to wait for **theirs.**

2. Use a singular pronoun for antecedents connected by *or* or *nor*. The pronoun refers to one or the other antecedent singly, not to both collectively.

Examples

a. Shelley or Claudine will give you *her* key if you arrive before noon.

b. A rake or a hoe will serve no purpose if *its* handle is broken.

c. Neither Mr. Carleton nor Mr. Frankenheimer will give you *his* advice without an assurance of confidence.

3. The pronoun should be plural if the antecedents are connected by *and*.

Examples

a. The car and the train blew *their* horns simultaneously.

b. Barnes and Blackwell gave *their* briefcases to the messenger.

c. My cousin and I visited *our* grandparents.

4. When two antecedents are simply different names for the same person, the pronoun is singular.

Examples

a. The professor and conference leader received a scroll for *his* efforts.

b. I missed my dog and best friend when *he was* placed in a kennel.

5. When two antecedents refer to different persons, the pronoun is plural.

Examples

a. The professor and the conference leader received scrolls for *their* excellent contributions.

b. I missed my dog and my best friend when *they* went to the park together.

6. When two or more antecedents are closely associated by usage or practice, a singular pronoun is used.

Examples

a. Tea and toast has *its* place in a convalescent's diet.

b. Pie and ice cream is delicious. *It* is my favorite dessert for dinner.

7. Antecedent nouns take either a singular or plural pronoun, according to the sense of the sentence or the idea to be conveyed.

Examples

a. The jury reached *its* verdict. (one verdict coming from one jury)

b. The jury put on *their* hats and coats and left for home. (the members of the jury are considered to be acting separately)

8. The following words, when used as antecedents, should take singular pronouns:

anybody	everybody	nobody
neither	someone	any
either	everyone	one
each	somebody ·	another

Examples

a. Neither of the men paid *his* bill.

b. Everybody in the room has *his* own opinion.

Note — the sentences above say, Neither one of the men; Every one in the room.

Personal Pronouns

The choice between *I* and *me*, *she* and *her*, *they* and *them* sometimes causes confusion. Each explanation which follows includes the standard grammar rule as well as a short-cut method. Here is a review of the pronouns in the objective and nominative cases:

	Singular	*Plural*
Nominative	I, you, he, she, it	we, you, they
Objective	me, you, him, her, it	us, you, them

Nominative case

1. A pronoun takes the nominative case when it serves as the subject of a sentence or a clause.

   Examples
   a. Betty, Dorothy, and *I* (not *me*) have made arrangements for the party.
      Short-cut method: Would you say, "*I* have made arrangements" or "*me* have made arrangements"? You would choose the former. Therefore the sentence must be "Betty, Dorothy, and *I* have made arrangements for the party.
   b. Mr. Kelly and *I* (not *me*) were selected.
      Short-cut method: Would you say, "*I* was selected," or "*me* was selected"? Certainly you would choose "*I* was selected." Therefore the sentence must be "Mr. Kelly and *I* were selected."

2. A pronoun following a connective verb or predicate complement (*am, is, are, was, were, be, been,* or *will be*) should be in the nominative case.

   Examples
   a. It was *he* who was selected.
   b. I believe it is *she* who should receive the award.

3. When the pronoun is the subject of an implied verb, the nominative case should be used.

   Examples
   a. He is quicker than *I* (not *me*).
      Short-cut method: Would you say, "He is quicker than *me* am quick," or "He is quicker than *I* am quick"?
   b. He did more for the Church than *they* (not *them*).
      Short-cut method: Would you say "He did more for the Church than *they* did for the Church" or "He did more for the Church than *them* did for the Church"?

Objective case

1. A pronoun in the objective case is chosen when it is the object of a verb or a preposition or when it serves as an indirect object.

   Examples
   a. He mailed the books to Bob, John, and *me* (not *I*).
      Short-cut method: Would you say, "He mailed the books to *I*" or "He mailed the books to *me*"? Certainly it is the second; therefore, the sentence must be "He mailed the books to Bob, John, and *me*."
   b. He called Miss Johnson, Miss Short, and *me* (not *I*).
      Short-cut method: Would you say, "He called *I*" or "He called *me*"? Obviously the second sounds better; therefore, the sentence must be "He called Miss Johnson, Miss Short, and *me*."

Relative Pronouns

Some of the more frequently used relative pronouns are *who, whom, which, what,* and *that.* The two that are often confused are *who* and *whom.*

Nominative—WHO

1. *Who,* like personal pronouns in the nominative case, is used as the subject of a sentence or a clause.

   Example

   Miss Costello is a girl *who* (not *whom*) I am sure will do well.
   Short-cut method: Would you say, "I am sure *she* will do well" or "I am sure *her* will do well"? Certainly "*she* will do well" sounds better than "*her* will do well." Inasmuch as *she* and *who* are both in the nominative case, the sentence must be "Miss Costello is a girl *who* I am sure will do well."

Objective—WHOM

1. *Whom,* like the personal pronouns in the objective case, is used as the object of the verb or preposition or an indirect object.

   Examples

   a. The soldier *whom* (not *who*) she loved has been sent overseas.
      Short-cut method: Would you say, "She loved *he*" or "she loved *him*"? Obviously "She loved *him*" sounds better than "she loved *he*." Because *whom* and *him* are both in the objective case, the sentence must be "The soldier *whom* she loved has been sent overseas."
   b. Miss Colgate is the girl to *whom* (not *who*) we gave the award.
      Short-cut method: Would you say, "We gave the award to *she*" or "we gave the award to *her*"? The second choice is preferable and because *her* and *whom* are both in the objective case, the sentence must be "Miss Colgate is the girl to *whom* we gave the award."

WHOEVER and WHOMEVER

1. *Whoever* is the nominative case and *whomever* is the objective case. Their use follows the same principles as for *who* and *whom.*

   Examples

   a. The company will award contracts to *whomever* (not *whoever*) they find acceptable.
      Short-cut method: Would you prefer "They find *they* acceptable" or "They find *them* acceptable"? The second choice is better and because *them* and *whomever* are in the objective case, the sentence must be "The company will award contracts to *whomever* they find acceptable."
   b. Mrs. Taylor, Miss Weinberg, and *whoever* (not *whomever*) else is selected will vacation in England.
      Short-cut method: Would you say, "*She* is selected" or "*her* is select-

ed"? Certainly it would be "*she* is selected" and because *she* and *whoever* are in the nominative case, the sentence must be "Mrs. Taylor, Miss Weinberg, and *whoever* else is selected will vacation in England."

Capitalization

1. Capitalize the first letter in the opening word in a sentence, a direct quotation, or each line of verse.

   Examples
   a. He was an outstanding student.

   b. Mr. Boynton said, "Effective communication is the executive's primary management tool."

   c. My heart leaps up when I behold
       A rainbow in the sky:
   So was it when my life began;
   So is it now I am a man:
   So be it when I shall grow old,
       Or let me die!
   The Child is father of the Man;
   And I could wish my days to be
   Bound each to each by natural piety.

2. Titles associated with proper names are capitalized.

   Examples
   a. Senator Birmingham
   b. President Adams
   c. Aunt Anna
   d. Commissioner Baxter

3. Names of national groups, races, languages, religions, or similar designations are capitalized.

   Examples
   a. Blacks or Afro-Americans
   b. French
   c. Israelis
   d. Canadians
   e. Americans
   f. English

4. Names of holidays, days of the week, holy days, and months of the year begin with a capital letter.

   Examples
   a. Veterans' Day

b. Wednesday
c. Good Friday
d. Rosh Hashanah
e. June

5. Capitalize the first letter in words which designate names of historical periods, treaties, laws, government departments, conferences, commissions, and so on.

Examples
a. Renaissance
b. the Monroe Doctrine
c. Clayton Act
d. United States Supreme Court
e. Bill of Rights

6. Capitalize the first letter in words which refer to names, national or international organizations, or documents.

Examples
a. House of Representatives
b. Drug Council of the International Medical Association
c. World Council of Churches

7. Capitalize the first letter of a word referring to a deity, a Bible, or other religious reference sources.

Examples
a. The Bible, the Koran, and the Torah . . .
b. Allah
c. God, Lord, and Almighty
d. the Congregation of the Missions

8. The first letter of each important word is capitalized in titles of magazines, books, essays, plays, and so on. Short prepositions, articles, and conjunctions in such titles are not, except for the first and last words.

Examples
a. *Journal of Business Communication*
b. *An Analysis of Government Taxation*
c. *The Taming of the Shrew*
d. *The Decline and Fall of the Roman Empire*
e. *My Fair Lady*

9. Capitalize a general term that is part of a name: Santa Fe Railroad.

Examples
a. Southern College of Arts and Sciences
b. Baptist Church

c. New Horizons Psychedelic Temple
d. Green Street
e. Temple University

10. Although words which refer to directions are not capitalized, words which are derived from directional terms are. Names of specific geographical areas or directional terms which have reference to parts of a nation or the world are also capitalized.

Examples
a. A path directly northwest of the tower.
b. He lives in the Northwest.
c. Far East
d. Wild West
e. Orient
f. a Southerner

Expressing Numbers

Should numbers be expressed in figures or words in written communication? To help solve this question, a number of general rules have been established.

1. When several numbers are used in one sentence and they are all above ten, use figures. If they are below ten, write them out. If a sentence begins with a number, write it out. If the number beginning a sentence is long when written out, it is usually wiser to revise the sentence.

Examples
a. We shipped 75 chairs, 90 tables, 32 lamps, and 32 pictures.
b. You have requested two rugs, three TV sets, and eight area rugs.
c. Seventy-five chairs, 90 tables, 32 lamps, and 32 pictures were shipped on December 3. (see below for improved sentence)
d. On December 3, we shipped 75 chairs, 90 tables, 32 lamps, and 32 pictures.

2. When numbers are below ten, write them out; when they are above, use numerals. When some above and some below are used in one sentence, follow one pattern for consistency. Round numbers over ten are usually written out.

Examples
a. He owned three shares of AT&T, seven shares of Sears, and fifty-five shares of Zenith.
b. The scouts consumed 8 pies, 7 chickens, 8 quarts of milk, and 32 bottles of soda.
c. He made two great throws, one of sixty feet and the other of fifty-five.

3. When one number immediately follows another, spell out the first number unless the second number would make a significantly shorter word.

   Examples
   a. He purchased five 59-cent notebooks for use in his spring quarter classes.
   b. Please get me 65 fifteen-cent stamps.
   c. I ordered 36 eleven-foot boards for the building project.

4. Place a comma between two unrelated numbers when they immediately follow each other.

   Examples
   a. On March 12, 32 new policemen were hired in New York.
   b. In 1975, 96 supersonic aircraft should be available for commercial use.

Dates

1. Write out the month when expressing a date.

   Examples
   a. June 27, 1979
   b. 27 June 1979

   Note—It is recommended that numerals for both month and day not be used. Although North American custom is to place the month first and then the day, the reverse is true in many countries of the world. Confusion in interpretation can thus easily result.
   1-4-78—Preferred: January 4, 1978 or 4 January 1978
   3/7/78—Preferred: March 7, 1978 or 7 March 1978

2. Only use *d, st,* or *th* with the day of the month when that day precedes the month or stands by itself.

   Examples
   a. She became engaged on the 4th of January.
   b. In your order of the 2d, you did not list the colors desired.
   c. Your shipment of the 1st was lost in transit.
   d. Please mail your check by March 28.

3. Well-known years in history and reference to class graduation years may appear in abbreviated form.

   Examples
   a. The class of '51 was honored.
   b. The blizzard of '88 was the worst storm of the century.

Addresses

1. House numbers should always be expressed as numerals except *one*, which should be written out.

   Examples
   a. One East Wilshire
   b. 10 North Roscomare Road
   c. 215 South Kansas Street
   d. 2157 South Topeka Avenue

2. Use words for streets from one to ten inclusive; use numerals for streets after eleven. The letters *d, st* or *th* may be used with numerals.

   Examples
   a. 2115 West Fifth Avenue
   b. 1115 West Tenth Street
   c. 210 North 19th Street
   d. 400 East 121st Avenue

   Note — The latest practice is to omit the *th* and *st* in examples such as (c) and (d) above.

3. When a number is used as a street name, use a dash to separate it from the street number only if a street direction is not included.

   Examples
   a. 210 — 10th Street
   b. 2100 — 7th Avenue
   c. 2111 West 45 Street
   d. 206 North 41 Street

Amounts of Money

1. All sums of money, domestic or foreign, should be presented in figures.

   Examples
   a. Johnson paid $155.60 for the merchandise.
   b. It is difficult for me to convert £275 into dollars.

2. For sums of less than a dollar, follow the figure with the word *cents.*

   Examples
   a. It cost 25 cents.
   b. It wasn't worth 65 cents.

3. In a sentence with a series of amounts, to be consistent use the dollar sign with a decimal point to indicate cents.

Example

Tom paid $.75 for the sponge ball, $5.00 for the baseball bat, and $14.95 for the baseball glove at the discount store.

4. The symbol ¢ for cents is used in price quotations and in technical communications.

Examples

a. 150 slats at 99¢
b. 5 bags of cement at 98¢

5. When expressing even or round sums of money, do not use the decimal and zeros.

Example

His payment was $275.

6. In legal statements the numerals should be enclosed by parentheses and sum written out.

Example

A firm offer for the car of seven hundred forty dollars ($740) is hereby made.

7. Money in round amounts of a million or a billion may be expressed partially in words.

Examples

a. The school board's budget increased by $2 million.
b. The youngster could not understand how the government could allocate $5 billion.

Decimals and Fractions

1. When a decimal begins with a zero, do not place a zero before the decimal. If the decimal begins with a number other than zero, precede the decimal with a zero.

Examples

a. .04683
b. 0.1746 (The zero prevents the reader from overlooking the decimal point.)

2. Simple fractions are written out. When whole numbers and fractions make up one unit, a decimal may or may not be used.

Examples

a. It took him one-half hour.
b. I gave him three-quarters of my allowance.

c. It was 25.5 feet long.

d. It was 25 ½ feet long.

3. Spell out a mixed number only if it begins a sentence.

Example

Three and one-half of the five boxes were used.

Miscellaneous Quantities, Units, and Measurements

1. Distance: Use numbers unless the amount is less than a mile.

   Examples

   a. We were one-third of a mile from the house.

   b. It is 9 miles to Kingston and 350 miles from there to Prampton.

2. Financial quotations: Use numbers.

   Example

   American Telephone and Telegraph hit 56 ⅞ this afternoon.

3. Arithmetical expressions: Use numerals.

   Example

   Multiply 70 by 44 and you will have the area of the house in square feet.

4. Measurement: Use numerals.

   Examples

   a. The land produced approximately 95 bushels per acre.

   b. He quickly found that 15 kilometers did not equal 16 yards.

5. Specific numbers: Use numerals.

   Examples

   a. The engine number was 4638147.

   b. Write for Training Manual 255.

6. Time: Use numerals with A.M. or P.M. Use words with o'clock. When expressing time on the hour without A.M., P.M., or o'clock spell out the hour.

   Examples

   a. The plane leaves at 7:17 P.M.

   b. We leave for work at 8:30 A.M.

   c. He is due to arrive at ten o'clock.

   d. They prefer having dinner at seven. (not 7)

7. Dimensions: Use numerals with either *x* or *by*.

   Examples

   a. The room measured 10 × 15 ft.

   b. The trim size of the annual report was 8½ by 11 inches.

8. Age: Use numerals except where approximations are used.

   Examples
   a. She became 21 and got engaged on the same day.
   b. I would say that he's about seventy years old.
   c. For your information, Bob is exactly 3 years and 6 months old today.

9. Government units: Write out such expressions as congressional units or districts.

   Examples
   a. He served in the Eighty-seventh Congress and represented the Tenth Congressional District of the state.
   b. James Jones represents the twenty-third ward.

10. Book or magazine references: Major units or divisions are indicated by Roman numerals; minor units by Arabic numbers.

    Examples
    a. He found the reference in Volume XX, number 4.
    b. You will find Figure 4 next to Table 7 on page 83 of Section 4.

100 Frequently Misspelled Words

accommodate	conscientious	extension	occurrence	receipt
acquaintance	conscious	familiarity	omission	receive
advertise	convenient	February	omitted	recommend
aggressive	criticism	foreign	opportunity	reference
all right	deceive	forty	original	referred
already	deferred	fourth	paid	repetition
analysis	definite	government	pamphlet	schedule
analyze	develop	grammar	personnel	separate
apologize	difference	grateful	possession	similar
appearance	disappoint	guarantee	practically	sincerely
attendance	discrepancy	incidentally	precede	stationery
beginning	eligible	inconvenience	preferred	strictly
believe	embarrass	its	prejudice	tomorrow
benefited	endeavor	laboratory	privilege	too
business	envelope	legible	probably	transferring
calendar	equipped	loose	procedure	truly
canceled	especially	necessary	proceed	unnecessary
chief	exceed	ninth	professor	until
committee	existence	occasion	quantity	using
confident	experience	occurred	questionnaire	Wednesday

Words Frequently Confused

Accent: to stress or emphasize; a regional manner of speaking.
Ascent: a rising or going up.
Assent: to agree; agreement.

Accept: to receive, to give an affirmative answer to.
Except: to exclude; to leave out; to omit.

Access: admittance or admission.
Excess: surplus or more than necessary.

Accidentally:
Incidentally: in both these cases, the *-ly* ending is added to the adjective forms, *accidental* and *incidental,* and not the noun forms, *accident* and *incident.*

Ad: abbreviation for *advertisement.*
Add: to join; to unite; to sum.

Adapt: to accustom oneself to a situation.
Adept: proficient or competent in performing a task.
Adopt: to take by choice; to put into practice.

Advice: counsel; a recommendation (noun).
Advise: to suggest; to recommend (verb).

Affect: to influence (verb).
Effect: result or consequence (noun).
Effect: to bring about (verb).

Aggravate: to increase; to intensify; to make more severe.
Irritate: to exasperate or bother.

All ready: prepared.
Already: previously.

All right: completely right.
Alright: an incorrect usage of *all right.*

Allusion: a reference to something familiar.
Illusion: an *image* of an object; a false impression.
Delusion: a false belief.

Almost: nearly; only a little less than.
Most: an informal use of *almost;* correctly, it means greatest in quantity or the majority of.

Altar: a place to worship or pray.
Alter: to change.

Altogether: completely or thoroughly.
All together: in a group; in unison.

Alumnus (sing.): male graduate.
Alumni (pl.)
Alumna (sing.): female graduate.
Alumnae (pl.)

Among: refers to three or more.
Between: refers to two only.

Amount: quantity without reference to individual units.
Number: a total of counted units.

Anxious: upset; concerned about a serious occurrence.
Eager: very desirous; anticipating a favorable event.

Anyone: any person in general.
Any one: a specific person or item.

Balance: as an accounting term, an amount owed or a difference between debit and credit sums.
Remainder: that which is left over; a surplus.

Being as, being that: should not be used for *since* or *because.*

Beside: by the side of.
Besides: in addition to.

Biannually: two times a year.
Biennially: every two years.

Borne: past participle of *bear* (to carry, to produce).
Born: brought into existence.

Can: refers to ability or capability.
May: refers to permission.

Canvas: a coarse type of cloth.
Canvass: to solicit; survey.

Cannon: large gun.
Canon: a law; church official.

Capital: a seat of government; money invested; a form of a letter.
Capitol: a government building.

Carat: unit of weight generally applied to gem stones.
Caret: mark showing omission.
Carrot: vegetable.
Karat: unit for measuring the purity of gold.

Cease: to halt or stop.
Seize: to grasp or take possession.
Censer: an incense pot.
Censor: a critic.

Sensor: an electronic device.
Censure: to find fault with or to blame.

Cereal: any grain.
Serial: arranged in successive order.

Cite: to quote from a source.
Sight: act of seeing; object or scene observed.
Site: a place, such as ''building site.''

Coarse: composed of large particles; unrefined.
Course: a direction of progress or a series of studies.

Collision: a clashing of objects.
Collusion: a conspiracy or fraud.

Command: to direct or order; an order.
Commend: to praise or laud.

Complacent: satisfied, smug.
Complaisant: obliging.

Complement: that which completes or supplements.
Compliment: flattery or praise.

Confidant: one who may be confided in.
Confident: positive or sure.

Consensus of opinion: redundant; *consensus* means ''general opinion.''

Continual: taking place in close succession; frequently repeated.
Continuous: no break or letup.

Council: an assembly of persons.
Counsel: to advise; advice; an attorney.
Consul: a resident representative of a foreign state.

Councillor: a member of a council.
Counselor: a lawyer or adviser.

Core: a center.
Corps: a body of troops; a group of persons in association.
Corpse: a dead body.

Credible: believable or acceptable.
Creditable: praiseworthy or meritorious.
Credulous: gullible.

Critic: one who evaluates.
Critique: an analytical examination of.

Currant: fruit.
Current: timely; motion of air or water.

Deceased: dead.
Diseased: infected.

Decent: correct; proper.
Descent: going from high to low.
Dissent: disagreement.

Decree: a proclamation of law.
Degree: difference in grade; an academic award.

Defer: to delay or put off.
Differ: to disagree.

Deference: respect.
Difference: unlikeness.

Deprecate: to express disapproval of.
Depreciate: to lessen in value because of use and/or time; to belittle.

Desert: to abandon.
Desert: a barren geographical area.
Dessert: a course at the end of a meal.

Differ from: to stand apart because of unlikeness.
Differ with: to disagree.

Disapprove: not to accept.
Disprove: to prove wrong.

Disburse: to make payments; to allot.
Disperse: to scatter.

Discreet: prudent; good judgment in conduct.
Discrete: separate entity; individual.

Disinterested: neutral; not biased.
Uninterested: lacking interest; not concerned with.

Disorganized: disordered.
Unorganized: not organized or planned.

Dual: double or two.
Duel: a contest between two antagonists.

Dying: in the process of losing life or function.
Dyeing: changing the color of.

Each other: refers to two.
One another: refers to more than two.

Either:
Neither: refers to one or the other of two. With *either* use *or*; with *neither* use *nor*.

Elicit: to draw forth, usually a comment.
Illicit: unlawful; illegal.

Eligible: acceptable; approved.
Illegible: impossible to read or decipher.

Elusive: difficult to catch.
Illusive: deceptive.

Emerge: to come out.
Immerge: to plunge into, immerse.

Emigrate: to travel out of one country to live in another.
Immigrate: to come into a country.
Migrate: to travel from place to place periodically.

Eminent: outstanding; prominent.
Imminent: impending, very near, or threatening.
Immanent: inherent.

Envelope: container for a communication.
Envelop: to surround; cover over or enfold.

Exceptional: much better than average; superior.
Exceptionable: likely to cause objection; objectionable.

Expansive: capable of extension or expansion.
Expensive: costly.

Extant: living or in existence.
Extent: an area or a measure.

Extinct: no longer living or existing.
Distinct: clear, sharply defined.

Facet: a small surface of a cut gem stone; aspect of an object or situation.
Faucet: a spigot.

Facilitate: to make easier.
Felicitate: to greet or congratulate.

Faint: to lose consciousness (verb); feeble, weak (adjective).
Feint: to pretend or simulate; a deceptive movement.

Farther: refers to geographical or linear distance.
Further: more; in addition to.

Fate: destiny.
Fête: to honor or celebrate (verb); a party (noun).
Feat: an act of unusual skill.

Flair: natural ability.
Flare: a signal rocket; a blazing up of a fire.

Formally: according to convention.
Formerly: previously.

Genius: unusual and outstanding ability.
Genus: a grouping or classification, usually on a biological basis.

Healthful: giving or contributing to health.
Healthy: having health.

Hoard: to collect and keep; a hidden supply.
Horde: a huge crowd.

Holey: having perforations or holes.
Holy: sacred, saintly.
Wholly: entirely; completely.

Human: pertaining to man.
Humane: kindly, considerate.

Imply: to hint at or to allude to in speaking or writing.
Infer: to draw a conclusion from what has been said or written.

In: indicates location within.
Into: indicates movement to a location within.

Incite: to stir up.
Insight: keen understanding; intuition.

Incredible: extraordinary; unbelievable.
Incredulous: skeptical; not believing.

Indignant: angry.
Indigenous: native to an area or country.
Indigent: needy; poor.

Ingenious: clever, resourceful.
Ingenuous: frank, honest, free from guile.

Inside of: informal use for *within* as "inside of five minutes."
Outside of: informal use for *except* or *besides* as "outside of those three members . . . ."

Its: a possessive singular pronoun.
It's: a contraction for *it is*.

Later: refers to time; the comparative form of *late*.
Latter: refers to the second named of two.

Learn: to acquire knowledge.
Teach: to impart knowledge.

Less: smaller quantity than, without reference to units.
Fewer: a smaller total of units.

Let: to permit.
Leave: to go away from; to abandon.

Likely: probable.
Liable: legally responsible.
Apt: quick to learn; inclined; relevant.

Load: a burden; a pack.
Lode: a vein of ore.

Loath: reluctant; unwilling.
Loathe: to hate; to despise; to detest.

Lose: to cease having.
Loose: not fastened or attached; to set free.

Magnate: a tycoon; important official.
Magnet: a device that attracts metal.

Marital: used in reference to marriage.
Marshal: an official; to arrange.
Martial: pertaining to military affairs.

Maybe: perhaps (adverb).
May be: indicates possibility (verb).

Medal: a badge of honor.
Metal: a mineral substance.
Meddle: to interfere.

Miner: an underground laborer or worker.
Minor: one who has not attained legal age; of little importance.

Moral: a principle, maxim, or lesson (noun); ethical (adjective).
Morale: a state of mind or psychological outlook (noun).

Notable: distinguished.
Notorious: unfavorably known.

Observance: following or respecting a custom or regulation.
Observation: act of seeing; casual remark.

Oral: by word of mouth.
Verbal: communication in words whether oral or written.

Ordinance: a local law.
Ordnance: military weapons; munitions.

Peak: top of a hill or mountain; topmost point.
Peek: a quick look through a small opening.

Peal: sound of a bell.
Peel: to strip off.

Percent: should be used after a numeral (20 percent).
Percentage: for quantity or where numerals are not used (a larger percentage).

Persecute: to subject to harsh or unjust treatment.
Prosecute: to bring legal action against.

Personal: private; not public or general.
Personnel: the staff of an organization.

Plaintiff: the complaining party in a lawsuit.
Plaintive: sorrowful; mournful.

Plane: to make smooth; a tool; a surface.
Plain: area of level or treeless country; obvious, undecorated.

Practical: not theoretical; useful, pragmatic.
Practicable: can be put into practice (not used in reference to people).

Precedence: priority.
Precedents: cases that have already occurred.

Proceed: to begin; to move; to advance.
Precede: to go before.

Principal: of primary importance (adjective); head of a school; original sum; chief or official.
Principle: a fundamental truth.

Provided: on condition; supplied.
Providing: supplying.

Quite: almost; entirely; positively.
Quiet: without noise.

Recent: newly created or developed; near past in time.
Resent: to feel indignant.

Respectfully: with respect or deference.
Respectively: in order named.

Resume: to begin again.
Resumé or résumé: a summing up.

Rise: to move upward; to ascend (rise, rose, risen).
Raise: to elevate; pick up (raise, raised, raised).

Sit: to be seated.
Set: to put in position (set, set, set).

Sometime: at one time or another.
Sometimes: occasionally.

Stationary: not moving; fixed.
Stationery: writing paper or writing materials.

Statue: a carved or molded three-dimensional reproduction.
Stature: height of a person; reputation.
Statute: a law.

Straight: direct; uninterrupted; not crooked.
Strait: narrow strip connecting two bodies of water; a distressing situation.

Than: used in comparison (conjunction): "Joe is taller than Tom."
Then: relating to time (adverb): "First he ran; then he jumped."

Their: belonging to them (possessive of they).
There: in that place (adverb).
They're: a contraction of the two words they are.

To: preposition: "to the store."
Too: adverb: "too cold."
Two: number: "two apples."

Toward:
Towards: identical in meaning and used interchangeably; *toward* is preferred.

Vice: wickedness.
Vise: a clamp.

Waive: to give up; relinquish.
Wave: swell of water; a gesture.

Weather: climate or atmosphere.
Whether: an alternative.

Who's: a contraction of the two words *who is*.
Whose: possessive of *who*.

Your: a pronoun.
You're: a contraction of the two words *you are*.

Style, Format, and Mechanics of Business Letters

There really is no correct or incorrect set of letter mechanics. However, each piece of correspondence—regardless of style selected—should reflect key information that permits accurate processing.

Letter Placement and Format

What is the difference in meaning between *stationery* and *stationary*? (See Appendix 1.)

Because the visual appearance of the letter is important, the typist should make an effort to carefully place the words on the stationery. It really is a simple matter to center the letter, to provide attractive and adequate white space on all four sides, and to maintain a fairly even right-hand margin.

In terms of format, there are several different letter styles that can be used. The most popular today are the *full block, modified block,* and *modified block with indented paragraphs* forms. These are illustrated in Figures A2–1, A2–2, and A2–3.

Every letter should be centered on the sheet of stationery with adequate margins provided.

Readers are influenced by a letter's appearance. If the initial reaction to the letter is poor, that impression may be retained as the letter is read. Certainly a ten-line letter jammed at the top or bottom of a page does little to build a positive image of the firm. A similar reaction is achieved when the reader looks at a sheet of paper with two heavy block paragraphs, one forty-two lines long, the other forty-four lines long.

On the other hand an attractive, well-balanced page with plenty of white space may indicate a company which takes pride in its effort, is well organized, and is carefully administered.

The Sections of the Business Letter

The usual business letter consists of six parts: the heading which includes the letterhead and the date; the inside address; the salutation; the body of the letter; the complimentary close; and the signature. These six parts are labeled in Figure A2–2.

Heading

The stationery letterhead should answer *who, where,* and *what.*

The letterhead usually answers the questions of who, where, and what. The *who* is the organization's name. The *where* is the address, and the *what* gives the reader some indication of the organization's operations. It is somewhat

M MC Markham Metals Corporation

1420–28 West Jefferson Boulevard
Los Angeles, California 90007

213/467-7400

October 5, 198-

Ms. Betty Borman
Office Manager
Farmer Food Company
1418 East LaSalle Street
Chicago, Illinois 60024

Dear Ms. Borman:

Thank you for your request for our new catalog. You will
find the items about which you inquired described in the
enclosed catalog.

Steel desks:	pages 81-5
Filing cabinets:	pages 110-12
Mail carts:	page 75

Most of our merchandise is available for immediate delivery.
And our "complete refund policy if you are not satisfied"
guarantee covers every item. All orders accompanied by a
check or sent C.O.D. receive a money-saving 5 percent
discount.

We hope you will join thousands of satisfied customers by
sending in your initial order immediately. If you have any
questions, Ms. Borman, or desire additional information,
please call me collect.

Cordially yours,

Robert Castlewood

Robert Castlewood
Sales Manager

RC/tm

Enclosure

CAPITAL
CARTON 12100 South Calvin Drive   St. Louis, Missouri 22562
CORPORATION

October 20, 198–

Mr. Ralph Russek
Personnel Director
Campbell Manufacturing Co.
4241 South Harvard Street
St. Louis, Missouri 63109

Dear Mr. Russek:

Thank you very much for your recent request and inquiry
concerning our #510 line of cartons.

Yes, it is possible for us to manufacture our items #510A,
B, and C, with an inner waterproof aluminum foil liner.
However, we must be assured of a minimum manufacturing run
of 20,000 cartons for each item. Of course, you can
appreciate the need for this quantity requirement: the
change in assembly line operation required, the set-up time
involved, and the machine modifications needed for each of
the different units.

The charge for manufacture will be as quoted in our latest
price list plus an addition of $0.145 per carton. This cost
is fixed for all runs between 20,000 and 30,000 cartons. The
additional charge will drop to $0.125 for quantities between
30,000 and 50,000 units. Over 50,000, the cost will run
$0.105 per carton.

If you will call me collect, Mr. Russek, I will have a half
dozen samples made up and sent to you within two weeks. And,
as is our custom, we guarantee delivery of all merchandise
within 30 days of receipt of order.

                              Sincerely yours,

                              Martin Varon
                              Sales Manager

MV/tm
cc: Alice McHenry
Midwest Sales Representative

Foreman's Fine Furniture

1933 Cally Road
Lewistown, West Virginia 04321

May 15, 198–

Ms. Carole Finer
1468 South Carleton Ave.
Peoria, Illinois 61699

Dear Ms. Finer:

We can certainly understand your recent frustration with
our delivery of the Contemporary coffee and lamp tables
which you purchased.

We know delivery was promised for February 27; we had
scheduled delivery for February 27; and delivery was to be
made on February 27. But it was not.

And we apologize.

There is good reason why the delay occurred forcing
shipment on February 28. However, I'm sure you're not very
interested in hearing about truck problems, the
unavailability of a substitute driver, etc., etc.

The fact is, delivery was not made. But we promise to do
better in the future, and we do hope you will accept with
our compliments the imported crystal vase (mailed today) for
display on your coffee table.

Cordially yours,

Merilyn Lynch

Merilyn Lynch
Customer Relations

ML/gb

disconcerting to receive a letter from the T. R. Fiji Corporation requesting information on a former employee of yours. Regardless of how carefully you examine the sheet of paper, there is no way of telling whether the T. R. Fiji Corporation manufactures thumbtacks, exports locomotives, or is involved in employee security.

Of course, the *who* should reflect the exact legal name of the company (not *Corp.* if it is really *Inc.*) And the *where* should indicate not only the street address, but also city, state, and zip code.

The letterhead design is usually selected very carefully by most organizations. There can be no doubt that the reader derives a portion of his or her image of the firm from the letterhead. If it is highly stylized, it may convey one image; if it is very formal, still another. Color, pictures, and graphics all convey ideas both liminally and subliminally to the reader. Obviously a photograph which includes a picture of a fifteen-year-old car or van and a blaring "We aim to satisfy" will evoke one reaction. On the other hand, a modern design with the address carefully printed across the bottom of the sheet of stationery may give the reader another image.

Part of the reader's image of the firm is derived from the letterhead design.

Paper companies, advertising agencies, and communication consultants are available to give counsel and advice on letterhead design and preparation. The key consideration is the image which the letterhead conveys in addition to the who, where, and what.

What is the difference in meaning between *counsel, council,* and *consul*? (See Appendix 1.)

The date should be written using either of the following formats:

May 3, 1982

3 May 1982

It is usually recommended that the date not be typed or written 5/3/82 or 5-3-82. This may cause some confusion because of the possible interpretation. In the United States, 5/3/82 would be read as May 3, 1982, whereas in Latin America and much of Europe, this date would be interpreted as March 5, 1982.

In the event an individual does not have letterhead stationery, but simply uses plain white paper, the format used in Figure A2–4 is correct. The address in the upper right corner is that of the writer.

The Inside Address

The inside address should duplicate the information on the envelope and should be derived from the letterhead of the correspondence to be answered. The company designation, name and title of addressee, and street address, should be reproduced exactly as indicated on the original letter. If the firm is designated as *Inc.,* that should be used and not *Corporation.* If the street is listed as *Fourth,* the reply should not use *4th.*

The recipient's name in the inside address should always be preceded by a

The inside address always includes basic information.

```
                                        1565 West First Street
                                        Tyler, Texas 75701
                                        April 15, 198-



          Mr. Robert Murphy, President
          The Farnsworth Corp.
          121 Canal Street
          Houston, Texas 77002

          Dear Mr. Murphy:
```

Appropriate titles should be used in all inside address sections.

title (Mr., Ms., Mrs., Miss, Dr., Colonel, Reverend) If the individual holds a supervisory position, both title and position should be stated:

Dr. James Stevenson, Director
Food Industry Management Program
University of Southern California
University Park
Los Angeles, California 90007

Where the degree designation (initials) is the same as the individual's title, only one should be used:

Incorrect:
Dr. Robert Coffey, Ph.D.
Dr. Frank Olsen, M.D.

Correct:
Dr. Martin Kelly
or
Martin Kelly, M.D.

Dr. Tamara Gotz
or
Tamara Gotz, Ph.D.

See Appendix 1 for suggestions on using numbers in written communications.

On the whole, abbreviations should not be used unless they also appear in the letterhead of the message being answered. Building or house numbers should be written in numerals except for *one*. Street names which are numbered should be written out from First to Tenth streets. Numerals should be used for street names past Tenth. And of course, zip codes should always be included.

The Salutation

Because most of us react much more favorably to our name than we do to an impersonal designation such as *Dear Friend, Dear Occupant, Dear Teacher, Dear Accountant,* names should be used whenever possible. Many organizations have found it advisable to type in, on hundreds or thousands of form letters, individual names and addresses. Marketing research indicates that most people respond favorably to that approach even if they are aware the letter itself is a form.

But what salutation should you use when you don't know the individual's name or you are writing to a company? A recent bulletin on business communication had this to say about salutations:

> *Whatever else women's rights groups have done, they most certainly have complicated letter salutation choices. . . . We did away with man—laws were passed that desexed job titles—and a* janitorial foreman *became a* janitorial supervisor; . . . chairmen, chairpersons; *even the schools found themselves with freshpersons. . . . But no one seems to have a good substitute for* Gentlemen. Gentlepersons? Gentlepeople? Dear People? Ladies and Gentlemen? To Whom It May Concern? . . .
>
> *The American Management Society has long promoted its Simplified Letter Style, eliminating both salutations and complimentary closes . . . many have long agreed that AMS has a point: Dear Mr. Block is not so dear when he doesn't pay his bills, and the writer of a letter making extravagant claims for a product might not seem so* Sincerely yours.[1]

At the present time, there are no easy answers. However, this seems to be the trend today:

1. If you know the addressee's name, use it: *Dear Mr. French; Dear Ms. Kelly; Dear Dr. Lyons.*

2. If the letter is going to an organization, use: *Ladies and Gentlemen.*

3. If the individual has a title and the name is not known or he or she is a high-level dignitary, use the appropriate saluation: *Dear Director;*

[1]D. H. Whalen, "Dear To Whom It May Concern," *News,* Vol. 1, No. 3, College Department, Harcourt Brace Jovanovich.

Dear Editor; Dear Mr. (or Madam) President; Your Eminence; Dear General.

There also is a trend toward putting more life into the salutation with such openings as "Thank you, Mr. Britt," "I was delighted, Ahmed," or "Your Check, Ms. Bailey." The first line of the body of the letter then begins with a capital letter and completes the sentence begun in the salutation.

What is the difference in meaning between *analysis* and *synthesis*? (See Appendix 1.)

In the final analysis, the salutations that are used usually will be selected according to the firm's policy and/or the writer's common sense and sense of courtesy and good taste.

In business letters, the salutation is almost always followed with a colon. In personal letters *(Dear Marty, Dear Betty,)*, the mark of punctuation following the salutation is a comma.

The Body

Chapters 5 through 10 of the text are largely concerned with different types of letters (sales, credit, inquiry and others) which make up the body. However, it is important to note that the format of the letter's body should always be visually attractive: carefully centered, adequate white space, and paragraphs which are relatively short.

The Complimentary Close

Like several other parts of the business letter, the complimentary close has changed slowly. Thomas Jefferson in 1789 closed his letter to George Washington with "Your most obedient and humble servant." Even when Aaron Burr challenged Alexander Hamilton to the fatal duel, he closed with "I have the honor to be Yours respt."

Various styles in the complimentary close are acceptable.

Today the more common close is *Yours truly, Sincerely, Sincerely yours, Yours sincerely.* To a lesser degree, *Cordially* or *Cordially yours* are used. But the logic of these certainly can be questioned: Is he or she "truly yours"? or even "sincerely yours"? Perhaps that is why many individuals are following the recommendation of dropping the complimentary close or are turning to such phrases as *Best regards, Warm regards* or even *See Your Ford Dealer, Ford for the Best* or *Ford Is Yours Truly.*

The Signature Section

The signature portion of the business letter is made up of three or four parts.

In most instances, the signature section is made up of three or four parts. The four-part signature includes the name of the company (usually typed in capital letters) and the writer's signature, typed name, and title. The name of the company (which appears in the letterhead) is usually omitted in a three-part signature.

When the writer is not available to sign the letter, a substitute (such as a secretary) may sign and add initials. However, this practice should be discouraged as much as possible. Most readers are offended by the initials and assume that the writer did not have fifteen seconds available to sign the letter and had a subordinate do it. Also the use of *per* or *by*, placed in front of the signature, is obsolete and should be avoided.

Miscellaneous Items

Aside from the basic format and parts of business letters, a good letter writer must be familiar with a variety of conventions of business letters. These include the use of attention lines, subject lines, identifying initials, enclosure lines, and carbon copies.

The Attention Line

Quite often an *attention line* is used in business letters. This is done when the writer desires the letter to go to a specific individual in a firm because that person either is familiar with the writer's needs or is handling the project with which the letter is concerned.

An attention line often will speed the processing of a letter.

If the letter is *addressed* to a particular person and that individual is no longer with the company, the letter may be returned to the sender. However, if the letter is sent to *the attention of* a person and that individual is no longer with the organization, the letter will be opened and processed by the individual's successor. Figure A2–5 shows an example of an attention line.

The Subject Line

The *subject line* also is used to improve efficiency and speed in handling correspondence. When carefully worded, it can replace the first paragraph usually used to introduce the transaction about which the letter is concerned. Figure A2–6 shows an example of a subject line.

The subject line can shorten a letter because it may contain reference information often placed in the first paragraph.

Identifying Initials

The usual custom is to place the dictator's and typist's initials in the lower left corner of the letter, as in Figure A2–1. However, there is a growing trend toward dropping this custom. The signature makes it unnecessary to use the writer's initials. And if the letter was typed in a word-processing center or in a typing pool, the typist's initials seem somewhat meaningless.

```
                        Bailey Brick Company
                        1212 West Detroit Street
                        Detroit, Michigan 48224

                        Attention: Ms. K. Korm, Treasurer

                        Ladies and Gentlemen:
```

```
                        Conway Corn Company
                        150 East Central Avenue
                        San Francisco, California 94117

                        Subject: Your invoice #24381

                        Ladies and Gentlemen:
```

Initials placed after the signature may prove useful when identification of the writer or typist is desired.

However, there are frequent instances in which a department or division head signs *all* the letters emanating from his department, even though six different people may be writing them. This is usually done so that he or she may know something about all areas' activities. In addition, it may be politically wise to have most of "this department's" letters signed by a vice-president rather than an assistant sales manager.

In such cases, the actual writer's initials appear in the left corner (with the typist's), but not the signer's initials. Some companies will use all three sets of initials. And in some instances, a firm will only use the typist's initials.

Enclosure Line

An *enclosure* notation may prove very useful to the reader in checking the completeness of the envelope's content.

The notation, *Enclosure,* is usually placed just below the identifying initials. It tells the reader that items in addition to the letter may be found in the envelope. This could be an article, check, invoice, or sample of a product.

The abbreviation *Encl.* is used or *Enclosure.* If more than one item is enclosed, the number is usually stated. Government agencies often identify each enclosure so that if one is withdrawn, it can be easily identified. Figure A2–1 shows a sample enclosure line.

Carbon Copies

When a copy of a letter sent to Mr. Hillman is also sent to another party, Mr. Hillman should be told that fact. Quite obviously, he would be offended if a copy were sent and he was not told. The notation *cc:*, at the bottom of the letter, informs the reader of carbons sent (see Figure A2–2).

In the event a copy of the letter is sent to Ms. Adjani without Mr. Hillman's being informed, the initials *bc* (blind carbon) or *bcc* (blind carbon copy) are used. Of course, that designation is only placed on the carbon and not on the original letter.

The notation *cc* is helpful in informing the letter's reader of the names of other recipients of the same letter.

Concluding Comments

It should again be emphasized, in this discussion on the mechanics of business letters, that there is no one correct method. Every organization develops a style it prefers which is consistent with its image. It may agree in whole or in part with the suggestions above. But for that company, the method makes sense.

A Sample Long Report

The primary purpose of this sample report is to give the reader an overall view of the format, design, and content of a long report. In order to conserve space in this book, segments of this report have been deleted.

May 9, 19___

Mr. Calvin Curtis
Executive Director
Los Angeles Marketing Association
12056 South Hope Street
Los Angeles, California 90007

Dear Mr. Curtis:

As authorized by you in our discussion on March 14, 19___, we have completed research on the topic of "The Status of Women in the Marketing Profession." Our findings and recommendations are presented in the attached report.

The purpose of our research was to determine the attitudes toward women and the opportunities for women in the marketing fields. Constraints, time, manpower and finances limited the scope and depth of our study.

The primary research source used was a mail questionnaire which was sent to men and women employed in various fields of marketing. Secondary information was gathered from periodicals, books, pamphlets, and newspapers.

Special credit for assistance in designing the questionnaire and gathering primary data is extended to Mr. Roger Seamans, Director of Marketing, Carter, Bruce, and Baker Corporation.

The completion of this project proved to be interesting and valuable. We feel that the information presented will be beneficial to the field of marketing as well as those women who are considering a career in that area.

It was a pleasure working on this challenging project. We stand ready to add information or answer questions which you may have.

Sincerely yours,

Angele Forthmann

Kimmie Jue

Angele Forthmann

Kimmie Jue

THE STATUS OF WOMEN

IN

THE MARKETING PROFESSION

Prepared for

Mr. Calvin Curtis
Executive Director
Los Angeles Marketing Association

Prepared by

Angele Forthman

Kimmie Jue

May 9, 19_

TABLE OF CONTENTS

ii

INTRODUCTION

Today women constitute an increasing percentage of the corporate labor force. The changing attitudes toward careers for women outside the home, and legislation prohibiting employment discrimination based on sex, have enabled women to make significant gains in their admission to traditionally male dominated positions in the business world.

The purpose of this report is to examine the current status of women in the marketing field.

Our primary research was gathered from the results of a mail questionnaire which was sent to a selective sample of 50 men and 50 women currently employed in various marketing positions throughout the Southern California area. Secondary information was secured from periodicals, books, and newspapers. A sample of our cover letter and questionnaire may be found in the appendix.

PURPOSE OF WOMEN IN MARKETING SURVEY

The survey was conducted in order to gather information concerning 1) attitudes toward women and 2) opportunities for women in the marketing field.

CONCLUSIONS

1. A Master's Degree in Business and broad work experience are necessary prerequisites for women for advancement into executive positions in the marketing field.

2. Tradition continues to impede women's progress in the corporate environment, as men are frequently reluctant to see women as career oriented.

3. Marriage and children are no longer viewed by women as deterrents to their careers. In fact, an increasing number of women are taking on a "Homemaker-plus" role.

4. Sex discrimination continues despite legislation designed to prevent it.

1

5. Increasing opportunities are available to women in the marketing fields of Advertising, Brand-Product Management, Marketing Research and Sales.

6. Women have a more difficult time than men in obtaining high ranking positions in the marketing field. In time, as women prove their qualifications, greater numbers will, however, secure positions in upper management.

RECOMMENDATIONS

1. Those women who are interested in rising to executive positions in the field of marketing should secure:

   a) an advanced degree in Business Administration: an MBA and/or Ph.D.
   b) broad work experience.

2. Women should attempt to understand the concept of team orientation as used in the corporate structure. They should learn to play the political games using support and competition in their proper context.

3. Women should continue their demands to be treated as "equals" by their male associates.

4. Women need to formulate goals and long-range plans for advancement in the corporate structure.

5. Women should use their "female" traits to the best working advantage.

6. Women should develop maturity, competence, aggressiveness, and confidence in themselves to be as effective as their male counterparts.

7. Women need to increase their commitment to their job.

8. Women should be able to adapt to lifestyle changes associated with corporate careers:

   a) travel
   b) relocation

2

SAMPLING METHOD

A selective sample was taken of 50 men and 50 women employed in various areas of the marketing profession. The list of potential respondents was developed using the American Marketing Association's Membership Roster for the years 19_ to 19_. Each individual was sent a 3-page questionnaire aimed at gathering reliable opinions concerning attitudes toward women and their opportunities in the field of marketing.

Response Rate

	Question-naires Sent	Question-naires Returned	% of Responses
Male	50	33	66%
Female	50	27	54%
	100	60	

As is indicated in the table above, there was a 60 percent return rate on the total number of questionnaires that were sent. It is interesting to note that we received a greater number of responses from men than women. This is a surprising result as the questionnaire was designed specifically to gather information on women in marketing, and we had assumed that it would be of greater interest to the female sector of the sample.

The universe was divided into an equal number of males and females to discover the differences in opinion of the sexes regarding women's status in the marketing field. Men and women respondents were chosen from the various areas of Marketing including Advertising, Education, Research, and Sales.

Depth of Survey Analysis

The assumption was made that women have a difficult time rising into traditionally male-dominated positions. The following variables were tested to discover the reasons why women have problems attaining upper management positions in marketing:

3

1) Education
2) Work experience
3) Acceptance by male superiors and subordinates
4) Career in addition to traditional female roles:
    a) Marriage
    b) Children

HYPOTHESIS

Women have a more difficult time than men in obtaining high ranking positions in the marketing field.

ANALYSIS OF SURVEY RESULTS

Survey results demonstrate that there are certain factors in the field of marketing that make it difficult for a woman to advance to positions traditionally held by men.

Education

A comparison of the responses showed that a greater percentage of male respondents had earned Master's Degrees in Business than had women, suggesting that these males were better qualified educationally to enter the business world. The majority of women indicated that they had earned Bachelor's Degrees. However, only 37% of the females sampled had majored in business, while 72% of the males had done so.

The majority of both male and female respondents agreed that their educational background was important to the securing of their present position. However, the males tended to place greater importance on their educational background than did the females.

Recent trends show that there has been an increase in the number of young college women pursuing Bachelor's and Master's Degrees in business. Women are realizing that advanced education is necessary for career advancement.

Work Experience

Experience is another prerequisite to women's success in the marketing profession. Many male respondents believed that a woman's lack of experience is a major deterrent to women obtaining executive

4

positions. Perhaps women will be able to fulfill this requirement of broad business experience as more opportunities become available to them. It is significant to note that the majority of respondents in the survey believed that their previous work experience was more important than their educational background in attaining their current employment position.

Acceptance by Male Superiors

Because working experience is so important to the success of women in marketing, it is essential that women be accepted by both male superiors and subordinates with whom they work.

Both male and female respondents expressed beliefs that some chauvinistic practices and policies prevail in the marketing field today. For example:

1) "There is continued resistance by males in upper management to accept women as equals."
2) "The 'old boy' attitude is still prevalent among certain male executives who feel that women are not completely career oriented, not qualified enough to handle an upper management position."

Tradition

Tradition continues to impede women's progress in the corporate environment. Respondents commented:

1) "The very fact that high-ranking marketing positions have been traditionally held by men is reason enough to explain the difficulties women encounter in their efforts to advance."
2) "The factors which influence success or failure have been established by men's traditions.

Acceptance by Male Subordinates

In an attempt to estimate how well women are accepted when they are placed into supervisory roles, respondents were asked to rate the following statement based upon a semantic differential: "Employees are more reluctant to accept supervision from women than from men."

5

1) An equal number of females agreed and disagreed with the statement cited above.
2) In contrast to the females, the majority of males disagreed with the statement and thus believed that employees are not more reluctant to accept supervision from women than from men.

The majority of both men and women felt that they did not receive positive support from members of the opposite sex with whom they work. When questioned as to whether they preferred having a staff composed primarily of males or females, the majority of respondents answered that they had no preference. Most felt that a staff composed of an equal balance of the two sexes is beneficial.

Career in Addition to Traditional Female Roles—Marriage and Children

"Marriage and children are no longer viewed by women as deterrents to their careers. More and more, they want to combine both—with the accent on better employment opportunities, child care service and maternity leave."[1]

The majority of male and female respondents believed that the traditional female roles associated with marriage and children could be compatible with career goals.

Outlook on Marketing Careers for Women

The majority of respondents agreed that opportunities available to women in the field of marketing have increased in the last five years. Both men and women felt that the Equal Pay legislation and prohibition against sex discrimination in Civil Rights legislation have improved women's chances in obtaining marketing positions.

As promotion is the means to career advancement, it is important to note that survey respondents indicated that 19 percent of the women had been denied promotion because of their sex—as opposed to zero percent of the men. This statistic suggests that some sex discrimination continues to exist despite legislative efforts to prevent it.

---

[1] Barbara Hackman Franklin, "Guest Editorial," *The Journal of Marketing*, (July 1977), pp. 10-11.

6

	Denied Promotion	
	Yes	No
Men	0−0%	33−100%
Women	5−19%	22−81%

Opportunities for Women in the Field of Marketing

No significant differences were noted between men's and women's opinions on the marketing fields which offer the best job opportunities for women. The four marketing fields most commonly mentioned in the respondents' answers were Advertising, Brand-Product Management, Marketing Research, and Sales.

The following section includes selective answers as to why respondents felt that these fields offered women the greatest opportunities.

Advertising

1) Women can use their creativity in this field.
2) Women have a better understanding and appreciation for what the public wants.
3) Women have the awareness and knowledge needed in the marketing of consumer products.

Brand-Product Management

1) Women have good analytical abilities. They understand the psychological aspects of marketing to females.
2) Women, through experience, know what products should and should not be on the market.

Marketing Research

1) Research has always been an opportunity path for women and subsequently they have made their biggest inroads here.
2) Women have greater acceptance in this field.
3) Women are viewed as being better qualitative researchers because of their sensitivity.

Sales

1) Retailing is traditionally more female dominated.
2) It's open to anyone who can show performance in dollars.

7

Advantages of Women as Related to the Marketing Field

There was no significant difference between the male and female responses concerning the advantages that women have over men that make them successful in the marketing field.

Many respondents believed that the qualities inherent to their sex can be advantages to women in their marketing career:

1) The favorable qualities which women possess include the following: intuition, emotionality, attention to detail and subtle control.
2) A woman's sex itself can be an advantage as respondents expressed in the following comments:

   a) Uniqueness of their sex in the boardroom.
   b) Sex—unfortunate but true, if you know how to use it.

However, 24 percent of the women and 30 percent of the men felt that women have no advantages over men that would make them successful in a marketing career.

8

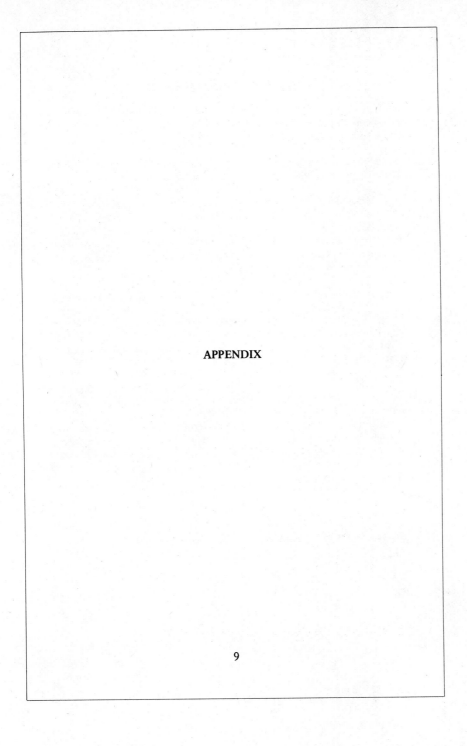

APPENDIX

9

913 North Roxbury Drive
Beverly Hills, CA   90210
April 10, 19___

Mr. John Aspery
Marketing Director
Coca Cola Corp.
3426 Wilshire Blvd.
Los Angeles, CA   90010

Dear Mr. Aspery:

Your knowledge and experience as a professional in the field of marketing can be of great benefit to us. We are conducting a survey to gather qualified opinions concerning attitudes toward women, and opportunities for women in a marketing career.

We are business students majoring in marketing at the University of Southern California, and are sending you this questionnaire in order to gather primary research material. When completed, this will provide important data to individuals in a wide variety of marketing positions and assist them in evaluating the status of women in the marketing field.

We would greatly appreciate it if you would take a few moments to answer our questionnaire. You may be sure that all responses will remain confidential. Because our information is being gathered under some time constraints, we ask that you return the completed form in the enclosed, stamped envelope before April 24, 19___. If you would like a copy of the results of this survey, please write to the address given above after May 9, 19___.

Many thanks for your cooperation.

Sincerely,

Angele Forthmann
Angele Forthmann

Kimmie Jue
Kimmie Jue

Enclosures

10

Questionnaire
WOMEN IN MARKETING SURVEY
(Responses recorded below by
number and percentage)

M=Male
F=Female

1. Sex
    ( ) Male   ( ) Female
    M−33=66%   *F−27=54%*

2. Age
    ( ) Under 25 yrs.   ( ) 35-44 yrs.   ( ) 55-64 yrs.
      M−0=0%   *M−13=39%*   *M−1=3%*
      F−2=7%   *F−5=19%*   *F−2=7%*

    ( ) 25-34 yrs.   ( ) 45-54 yrs.   ( ) 65 yrs. & over
      M−12=36%   *M−6=18%*   *M−1=3%*
      F−15=56%   *F−3=11%*   *F−0=0%*

3. Department and present position in company

    _____

4. Brief job description

    _____

    _____

5. Years with company
    ( ) Under 1 year   ( ) 3-5 years   ( ) 11-20 years
      M−5=15%   *M−7=21%*   *M−4=12%*
      F−6=22%   *F−4=15%*   *F−2=7%*

    ( ) 1-2 years   ( ) 6-10 years   ( ) Over 20 years
      M−4=12%   *M−6=18%*   *M−0=0%*
      F−9=33%   *F−3=11%*   *F−0=0%*

6. Years in present position with company
    ( ) Under 1 year   ( ) 3-5 years   ( ) 11-20 years
      M−9=27%   *M−8=24%*   *M−2=6%*
      F−8=30%   *F−4=15%*   *F−1=4%*

    ( ) 1-2 years   ( ) 6-10 years   ( ) Over 20 years
      M−8=24%   *M−6=18%*   *M−0=0%*
      F−11=41%   *F−3=11%*   *F−0=0%*

11

7. What is your educational background?
( ) High School Diploma
M−2=6%
F−3=11%

( ) Associate of Arts
M−0=0%
F−3=11%

( ) Bachelor's Degree
M−10=30%
F−14=52%

( ) Master's
M−20=61%
F−7=22%

( ) Ph.D.
M−1=3%
F−1=4%

8. How important was your educational background to the securing of your present position?
( ) Very important
M−14=42%
F−6=22%

( ) Fairly important
M−15=46%
F−12=44%

( ) Not important
M−4=12%
F−9=33%

9. How important was your previous work experience to the securing of your present position?
( ) Very important
M−27=82%
F−18=67%

( ) Fairly important
M−4=12%
F−5=19%

( ) Not important
M−2=6%
F−4=15%

10. Have you ever been denied promotion because of your sex?
( ) Yes
M−0=0%
F−5=19%

( ) No
M−33=100%
F−22=81%

11. Employees are more reluctant to accept supervision from women than from men.
( ) Strongly Agree
M−0=0%
F−1=4%

( ) Agree
M−10=30%
F−12=44%

( ) Disagree
M−16=49%
F−10=37%

( ) Strongly Disagree
M−2=6%
F−3=11%

( ) No opinion
M−5=15%
F−1=4%

12. Do you receive positive support from members of the opposite sex with whom you work?
( ) Always
M−15=45%
F−10=37%

( ) Usually
M−17=52%
F−11=41%

( ) Sometimes
M−1=3%
F−6=22%

( ) Not very often
M−0=0%
F−0=0%

( ) Never
M−0=0%
F−0=0%

12

13. Would you prefer having a staff composed primarily of
        ( ) Males   ( ) Females   ( ) No preference
        M—1=3%   M—1=3%   M—31=94%
        F—0=0%   F—2=7%   F—25=93%

    Why?_____
    _____

14. An attractive appearance is more important for a woman than
    for a man when being considered for a promotion.
        ( ) Strongly Agree   ( ) Agree   ( ) Disagree
            M—1=3%   M—6=18%   M—17=52%
            F—1=4%   F—10=37%   F—10=37%

                ( ) Strongly Disagree   ( ) No opinion
                    M—9=27%   M—0=0%
                    F—4=15%   F—2=7%

15. Marriage can be a hindrance to a woman who is attempting to
    further her marketing career.
        ( ) Strongly Agree   ( ) Agree   ( ) Disagree
            M—0=0%   M—10=30%   M—16=49%
            F—0=0%   F—5=19%   F—11=41%

                ( ) Strongly Disagree   ( ) No opinion
                    M—6=18%   M—1=3%
                    F—5=19%   F—6=22%

16. The raising of children can prevent a woman from achieving
    her full potential in a marketing career.
        ( ) Strongly Agree   ( ) Agree   ( ) Disagree
            M—1=3%   M—10=30%   M—16=49%
            F—3=11%   F—8=30%   F—12=44%

                ( ) Strongly Disagree   ( ) No opinion
                    M—4=12%   M—2=6%
                    F—2=7%   F—2=7%

17. Women are more reluctant to accept travel assignments than
    men.
        ( ) Strongly Agree   ( ) Agree   ( ) Disagree
            M—0=0%   M—6=18%   M—18=55%
            F—0=0%   F—6=22%   F—12=44%

                ( ) Strongly Disagree   ( ) No opinion
                    M—3=9%   M—6=18%
                    F—7=26%   F—2=7%

13

18. The opportunities available to women in the field of marketing have increased in the last five years.

( ) Yes   ( ) No   ( ) No opinion
M—31=94%   M—0=0%   M—2=6%
F—22=81%   F—1=4%   F—4=15%

19. The Equal-Pay Law and prohibition against sex discrimination in the Civil Rights Law have improved women's chances in obtaining marketing positions.

( ) Strongly Agree   ( ) Agree   ( ) Disagree
M—7=21%   M—15=46%   M—7=21%
F—1=4%   F—11=41%   F—6=22%

( ) Strongly Disagree   ( ) No opinion   ( ) No response
M—4=12%   M—0=0%   M—0=0%
F—2=7%   F—5=19%   F—2=7%

20. What marketing fields do you feel women have the best opportunities in? Why?*

21. What factors in your specific field make it difficult for a woman to advance to positions traditionally held by men?*

22. What advantages do women have over men that make them successful in your particular marketing field?*

23. What advantages do men have over women that make them successful in your particular marketing field?*

24. What areas do women need to improve upon in order to increase their overall effectiveness and contribution to the marketing profession?*

*In an effort to conserve pages in this book, the 75 comments which were selected from the respondents' replies to questions 20-24 (which appeared in the original paper), have been deleted.

14

BIBLIOGRAPHY

Crain, Sharie with Philip T. Drotning, *Taking Stock,* Chicago: Henry Regnery Co., 1977.

Franklin, Barbara Hackman, G, Commissioner, U.S. Consumer Product Safety Commission, "Guest Editorial," *Journal of Marketing,* July, 1977, pp. 10-11.

Harrigan, Betty Lehan, *Games Mother Never Taught You,* New York: Rawson Associates Publishers, Inc., 1977.

Higginson, Margaret V., Thomas L. Quick, *The Ambitious Woman's Guide to a Successful Career,* New York: Amacom, 1975.

Howard, N., "Sales Jobs Open Up for Women," *Dun's Review,* Vol. III, March, 1978, pp. 86-88.

Kanter, Rosabeth Moss, *Men and Women of the Corporation,* New York: Basic Books, Inc., 1977.

Kanuk, Leslie, "Women in Industrial Selling," *Journal of Marketing,* January, 1978, pp. 87-91.

Killian, Ray A., *The Working Woman,* New York: American Management Association, 1971.

Marketing News, Vol. 10, No. 16, February, 1977, "Emerging Male-Female Equality to Alter Some Marketing Patterns," pp. 2-4.

_____ , Vol. 10, No. 16, February, 1977, "Cliche' Thinking Still Bars Gains by Women, " p. 3.

_____ , Vol. 10, No. 16, February, 1977, "To Succees in Business Women Need to Work Well With Others," p. 4.

_____ , Vol. 10, No. 16, February, 1977, "To Succeed in Business Women Must and Can Learn to Lead, Build Ambition, Market Themselves," p. 6.

McCall, Suzanne H., "Meet the Workwife," *Journal of Marketing,* July, 1977, pp. 55-56.

Reynolds, Fred D., Melvin R. Crask and William D. Well, "The Modern Feminine Life Style," *Journal of Marketing,* July, 1977, pp. 38-45.

Robertson, Dan H., Donald W. Hackett, "Saleswomen, Perceptions, Problems, and Prospects," *Journal of Marketing,* July, 1977, pp. 65-71.

Scanlon, Sally, "Manage Sales? Yes, She Can," *Sales and Marketing Management,* Vol. 118, June, 1977, pp. 33-39.

Shaeffer, Ruth Gilbert, Edith F. Lynton, *Corporate Experiences in Improving Women's Job Opportunities,* New York: The Conference Board, 1977.

15

Index

Occupational Outlook for College Graduates, 405
Occupational Outlook Handbook, 403, 405
On Your Own (Matthews), 401
Open-ended questions, use of, in questionnaire, 239
Oral communications; *see* Speeches
Oral reports, advantages of using, 345
Orders
    refusal letters for, 125, 130, 133, 134, 135
    response letters for, 116–19
Organization
    editing for, 53, 64–65
    importance of, in communication planning, 17, 18, 29
    pattern of, for a no letter, 125, 126
Orwell, George, 37
Outline(s)
    advantages of making, 17, 27, 29
    preparation of, 23–25
    review of, 25–27
    use of, for written report, 232
    use of headings as, 251
Overhead projectors, use of, as visuals aids in speech presentations, 363–64

P

Passive voice, avoidance of, in effective writing, 37
Perceptions, differences in, as communication barrier, 2, 11
Periodicals, as secondary sources, 233–34
Periodic reports, as type of short reports, 249, 257–61, 263
Personal names, use of, in communication, 77
Personnel, role of, in word-processing triangle, 204
Persuasion, as purpose of speech presentation, 343, 346
Persuasive interview, 372
Photocopying machines, and reduction of original copy, 284, 415, 416–18
Photographs,
    use of, in resumé, 423–24
    use of, as visuals, 284, 302
Pie charts, use of, as visuals, 296, 298
Placement, use of, for emphasis in effective writing 42
Planning
    advantages of, 27, 29
    basic steps in, 17, 18–27
    importance of, 17, 18
Positive approach, use of, 75
Positive tone, as key to effective writing, 35, 46–47
Positive reinforcement, 74–75
Posture, importance of, in speech presentation, 335
Praise, role of, in communication, 76

Precision, as key to effective writing, 35, 37, 47–48
Presentations; *see* Speeches
Primary sources, use of, in gathering information for a report, 227, 235–42
Problem
    defining of, in planning communication, 18–20
    defining of, in written report, 229
Procedures, establishment of, in written report, 230–31
Product
    description of, in sales letter, 147
    knowledge of, as basic sales principle, 142
Progress reports, as type of short reports, 249, 254, 256, 257
Promotability, as vital in communication, 7
Promotional material, use of cover letter with, 150
Promotional material, use of, in sales letters, 141, 149–50
Promptness, importance of, in letter saying no, 129
Proofreading, importance of, 69
Proportion, editing for, 53, 64, 66
Proportional stratified sample, 236
Proposals, as type of short reports, 249, 254, 255
Public mailing lists, 150
Public speaking, courses in, 312
Purchased mailing lists, 152
Purpose
    importance of defining in planning communication, 18–20, 77
    stating specific in written report, 229–30

Q

Questionnaires
    deciding who to question, 236
    designing your own, 237–39
    introduction to, 239
    as primary source, 227, 235–36
    use of visuals in, 297, 299
    what kind of, 236–37
Questions, keys to handling in long presentations, 343, 357–58

R

Randall, Tony, 77
Random sample, 236
Readability, assessment of, 35, 40–42
Reader
    getting interest of, 144–47
    identification of, in written report, 229
    need to convince to act, 148–49, 221
Readers' Guide to Periodical Literature, 234

Reading and analyzing, as step in revision process, 53, 54, 69
Recognition, guidelines for making, 327–28
Reliability, as feature in good mailing list, 152
Repetition, use of, for emphasis in effective writing, 42
Reports
    basic rules in formatting, 249, 252, 253
    basic steps in planning, 227, 228–32
    basic strategies for, 271 272–74
    body of, 271, 280–83
    concluding comments in, 242–43
    different kinds of short, 249, 252–66
    front matter in, 271, 274–80
    gathering secondary information for, 227, 233–36
    headings in, 249, 251–52
    identification of reader of, 229
    logical arrangement of, 249, 250–51
    oral, 345
    orientation of, 228
    role of, in modern organization, 227–28
    as secondary source, 234
    supplements in, 271. 283–84
    use of primary sources for, 227, 235–42
    use of, as visual aids in speech presentations, 359–60
    use of visuals in, 284, 289–304
    writing effective, 227–44
Requests
    differences between inquiry and, 83, 88, 93
    refusal of, 125, 126, 128–29
Research
    primary sources for, 235–42
    secondary sources for, 233–35
Response letters, three-step process for completeness, 99, 100
Resumé
    format and length of, 413–14
    and inclusion of photographs, 423–24
    mention of salary requirements in, 423
    purpose of, 411, 413
    sections of, 411, 415, 418–23
    techniques for shortening. 411. 415, 416–18
    and use of data sheet to organize, 412–13
Retailer
    approach of, in seeking credit customer, 159, 160, 161
    procedures used by, to obtain credit information, 162, 165, 166
    response of, to credit application, 159, 162, 163
Revising
    basic steps of, 53, 54
    importance of, 53
Revolving credit, 158